DATE DUE

APR 1 2 1992	JUN 1 8 1999
AUG 1 2 1992	July 06
DEC 1 2 1992	OCT 1 2 1999
FEB 1 5 1993	FEB 2 4 2000
MAR 1 1993	MAY - 4 2000
MAR 1 8 1993	APR - 9 2003
APR 2 0 1993	APR - 2 2004
NOV - 6 1994	904381
DEC - 5 1994	
OCT 2 6 1995	
NOV 1 8 1995	
MAR 1 6 1996	
NOV 2 1 1996	
OCT 3 0 1997	
DEC - 1 1997	
DEC 1 1 1997	
APR - 3 1999	

BRODART, INC.   Cat. No. 23-221

The

CARL
ROGERS
READER

The
CARL
ROGERS
READER

Edited by

HOWARD KIRSCHENBAUM *and*

VALERIE LAND HENDERSON

Houghton Mifflin Company

Boston 1989

For information about permission to reproduce selections from
this book, write to Permissions, Houghton Mifflin Company,
2 Park Street, Boston, Massachusetts 02108.

Library of Congress Cataloging-in-Publication Data

Rogers, Carl R. (Carl Ransom), 1902–1987.
The Carl Rogers reader.

Bibliography: p.
Includes index.
1. Client-centered psychotherapy.   2. Humanistic
psychology.   I. Kirschenbaum, Howard.   II. Henderson,
Valerie Land.   III. Title.
RC481.R587   1989   616.89′14   88-32876
ISBN 0-395-51090-2
ISBN 0-395-48357-3 (pbk.)

Printed in the United States of America

D 10 9 8 7 6 5 4 3 2 1

Acknowledgments and copyright notices for
individual articles begin on page 507.

To

CARL RANSOM ROGERS (1902–1987)

Our colleague, teacher, and friend

CONTENTS

The Person in Process

Theory and Research

A Human Science

Education

The Helping Professions

A Philosophy of Persons

A More Human World

Introduction

Carl Ransom Rogers (1902–1987) was the most influential psychologist in American history.

He pioneered a major new approach to psychotherapy, known successively as the "nondirective," "client-centered," and "person-centered" approach.

He was the first person in history to record and publish complete cases of psychotherapy.

He carried out and encouraged more scientific research on counseling and psychotherapy than had ever been undertaken anywhere.

More than any individual, he was responsible for the spread of professional counseling and psychotherapy beyond psychiatry and psychoanalysis to all the helping professions — psychology, social work, education, ministry, lay therapy, and others.

He was a leader in the development and dissemination of the intensive therapeutic group experience sometimes called the "encounter group."

He was a leader in the humanistic psychology movement of the 1960s through the 1980s, which continues to exert a profound influence on society and the professions.

He was a pioneer in applying the principles of effective interpersonal communication to resolving intergroup and international conflict.

He was one of the helping professions' most prolific writers, authoring sixteen books and more than two hundred professional articles and research studies. Millions of copies of his books have been printed, including more than sixty foreign-language editions of his works.

In this volume we present the scope of that life's work—its breadth across so many areas of professional and human interest, and its depth in exploring a few central themes basic to all human relationships. Whatever the section—on therapy, personal growth, education, science, philosophy, social issues, or Rogers's own life—the personal, the professional, and the political are always present. Whatever the time of publication—with selections from 1942 to 1987, as well as previously unpublished writings—Rogers's unique, personal style of communication is evident.

Carl Rogers's influence, however, was due to much more than his writings. He also pioneered in using innovative nonprint media to popularize his ideas. The American Academy of Psychotherapists' tape library distributed thousands of copies of his therapeutic interviews to professionals around the world. He was often filmed conducting therapy or intensive group sessions. In the famous *Gloria* film series (Rogers et al., 1962), a single client was interviewed successively by Rogers, by gestalt therapist Fritz Perls, and by rational-emotive therapist Albert Ellis. The film *Journey into Self* (Farson, 1970), showing Rogers leading an encounter group, won an Academy Award for Best Feature-Length Documentary and received major national distribution.

Rogers's long career as an educator brought him into contact with thousands of students who were deeply affected by his courses and went on to spread his ideas and methods. Many of his classes at the University of Chicago (1945–1957), for example, regularly attracted hundreds of students who came from across the world to study with him. An active speaker at educational conventions, conferences, and meetings, he addressed and conducted demonstration therapy and encounter-group sessions before hundreds of thousands of participants throughout his career.

Beyond his personal impact as author, educator, and model, Rogers also was active in the politics of the helping professions. Among many offices and editorships held, he was New York State chairman and national Executive Committee member of the American Association of Social Workers, vice-president of the American Orthopsychiatric Association, the first president of the American Academy of Psychotherapists, and president of the American Psychology Association, which he helped reorganize in 1945. In 1963 he helped found the Association for Humanistic Psychology, while declining the offer to serve as its first president.

Recognition of his contributions in turn helped spread Rogers's work and testified to its importance. He received the American Psychology Association's Distinguished Scientific Contribution Award the first year it was given and in 1972 became the only person ever to receive both that award and the association's Distinguished Professional Contribution Award. His honorary degrees from universities around the world, guest professorships, and other awards are far too numerous to cite here.

Beyond the scope of his activities, equally important in contributing to Rogers's influence were his longevity and stamina. For fifty-nine years, from the time he began practicing psychology in 1928 to his death in 1987, he was an active professional. His first article (Rogers and Carson) appeared in 1930. Mentally and physically alert even in his eighties, he kept up an impressive schedule of lectures, workshops, writing, and travel.

Nevertheless, while a vast number of professionals in the fields of psychology, psychotherapy, education, counseling, social work, ministry, medicine, and other professions credit Carl Rogers as one of the most influential teachers and models in their careers and in many cases their lives, an equally impressive number would minimize or even criticize Rogers's contribution. Although his work is not held in high esteem in most academic settings, it continues to have a significant impact in the real world. This is evident in separate articles reported in the *Journal of Counseling Psychology* (Heesacker et al., 1982) and the *American Psychologist* (Smith, 1982). In the former journal, an investigation of "authors and specific articles and books . . . that have stood the test of time and are still influencing the field" ranked Rogers first in a group of major contributors. In the latter periodical, a questionnaire was sent to a random sample selected from Division 12 (Clinical Psychology) and Division 17 (Counseling Psychology) of the American Psychology Association. The survey results list the "Ten Most Influential Psychotherapists," and again Rogers is ranked first.

Ironically, although Rogers influenced and continues to influence the lives of millions of individuals treated in professional settings around the world, the public, by and large, would not even recognize his name. Rogers never sought wide publicity or fame. As much as he enjoyed his growing impact, he never consciously wrote for the "pop psychology" market. When one of his books, *On Encounter Groups*, did exhibit mass-market potential, he was invited to discuss it on a major television interview show. He declined. His publisher responded incredulously, "But one show will lead to another!" "That's what I'm afraid of," the shy and skeptical Rogers replied. (Nevertheless, the book sold a quarter of a million copies.)

Rogers's contribution was more subtle and profound than that of best-selling authors whose works briefly capture the national attention and are soon forgotten. He has been described as "a quiet revolutionary." His message was deceptively simple, yet profound in its implications: *All individuals have within themselves the ability to guide their own lives in a manner that is both personally satisfying and socially constructive. In a particular type of helping relationship, we free the individuals to find their inner wisdom and confidence, and they will make increasingly healthier and more constructive choices.*

Rogers taught, tested, and lived this "hypothesis," as he called it, for fifty-seven years. Over decades, he painstakingly clarified the characteristics of this helping relationship, and he and his colleagues and students applied it to every helping profession and to many areas of daily living. He demonstrated that the principles of human relationships that work in the therapist's office, the school, or the hospital also work for parents and youth leaders and friends. And as the years have passed, this hypothesis and the various approaches for implementing it have steadily changed the helping professions beyond recognition.

Not all professionals have been pleased with Rogers's influence. Many find his theory and methods oversimplified. Others argue that trusting the individual's resources for self-help will not work and might even do harm. Still others have minimized the significance of his contribution, saying there is little new in it or "We're already doing that." Sometimes critics have said all these things, expressing considerable ambivalence about the person-centered approach to helping relationships.

In effect, many critics have said, "We, too, trust the individual. We, too, use methods that help the patient, client, or student work out his or her own solutions. That's what helping is all about—not solving problems for people, but helping them solve their own problems; not directing others' lives, but facilitating their growth. However, that is not sufficient. We must also use our own experience and expertise to wisely question, interpret, inform, reinforce, or otherwise help lead our charges in positive, growthful directions."

The half century of controversy around Carl Rogers's work simply highlights a basic philosophical and methodological question that is still plaguing the helping professions: To what extent do we rely on the individual's ability to guide his own growth and development, and to what extent do we introduce outside motivation, strategies, guidance, direction, or even coercion?

That is why Rogers's work has been so controversial, maligned, and misunderstood as well as accepted and embraced. By taking an extreme position on the person-centered end of the helping continuum, and by exerting a half century's effectiveness as writer, teacher, and scientist in support of his position, Rogers became one of the pivotal figures in the much larger debate—the debate over the prediction and control of human behavior.

As teachers, parents, and therapists the world over know, we often have mixed feelings about giving freedom to our students, children, and clients. Beyond our own ambivalence, it is one thing to sincerely want to support an individual's growth and independence and quite another thing to know how to do it effectively. Many studies have shown that even those who believe they are mostly being facilitative in their behavior are often more directive than they realize. For example, therapists and teachers who assert that their clients and students speak for the majority of time in the counseling session or class often discover, when observed, that they themselves are doing most of the talking. Similarly, on a larger scale, as the example of totalitarian and even democratic states often demonstrates, it is one thing to say we believe in freedom and individual self-determination and quite another to practice it consistently.

Rogers spent his whole life not only asserting the importance of the democratic and libertarian ideal in all human relationships, but seeking ways to accomplish that ideal. He innovated, he described, he tested, he modified, he modeled, he even proselytized. For that he won hundreds of thousands of appreciative students whose work touches millions of lives each year. At the same time, however, he also won thousands of influential critics who have prevented Carl Rogers and the person-centered approach from becoming the mainstay of professional training in the academic institutions of the United States.

It is not only academia that has resisted Rogers's work. In a sense, the concern for creative human development competes for attention with an extremely strong current in modern society. For our technological age is increasingly impressed by new wonders of telecommunication, new drugs and cures, new hardware and software, new gadgets for work and leisure—the latest advances modern science and capitalism have to offer. Rogers's message points us in a different direction, at first glance much less exciting and more difficult: The answer to most of our problems lies not in technology but in relationships. What really matters is trust in ourselves and others, in communication, in how we handle our feelings and conflicts, in how we find meaning in our lives. In the twentieth century we have learned an enormous amount about how to get along with ourselves and with others. Put that knowledge to work and we may yet save the planet. Disregard it, as we focus our lives and fortunes on the next technological quick fix, and we may not survive.

That Carl Rogers has dramatically and permanently influenced the major helping professions of our society is beyond question. That his work has influenced millions in how they perceive the quality of life is also clear. For years to come, that work will undoubtedly continue to spread, as Rogers's colleagues and students and others working in similar directions continue to develop and promote the person-centered philosophy throughout the world.

Whether the person-centered approach to human relationships ultimately has a profound and lasting influence on American society and the world is much less certain. At this point, how the world decides to handle its human problems—crime, drugs, intergroup and international conflict, to name a few— will determine whether there will be societies or even a world in which person-centered approaches can survive. How large a part the work of Carl Rogers will play in influencing those decisions remains to be seen.

SPEAKING PERSONALLY

In both his professional and popular writings, Carl Rogers introduced a personal manner of expression that was hitherto rare or unknown in American professional and scientific communication. This personal expression involved both the style and content of his communication and took many years to develop.

Initially, like all good academic writers of his day, Rogers rarely spoke in the first person. A third-person self-reference in the introduction was about as personal as he got in his first four books. For example, in *The Clinical Treatment of the Problem Child* (1939), he wrote, "While the author has inevitably drawn upon the experience of the clinic with which he is associated, he has tried to include the experience and practice of others."

In 1951 he began testing the waters of personal expression in his introduction to *Client-Centered Therapy*, when in two consecutive sentences he went from "The author is deeply indebted to . . . for their contributions" to "In writing this book I have often . . ." The personal pronoun was then used in the rest of the introduction (but never in the body of the book), which included this passage, unusual for a professional volume:

> This book is about the highly personal experiences of each one of us. It is about a client in my office who sits there by the corner of the desk, struggling to be himself, yet deathly afraid of being himself—striving to see his experience as it is, wanting to *be* that experience, and yet deeply fearful of the prospect. This book is about me, as I sit there with that client, facing him, participating in that struggle as deeply and sensitively as I am able. It is about

me as I try to perceive his experience, and the meaning and the feeling and the taste and the flavor that it has for him. It is about me as I bemoan my very human fallibility in understanding that client, and the occasional failures to see life as it appears to him, failures which fall like heavy objects across the intricate, delicate web of growth which is taking place. It is about me as I rejoice at the privilege of being a midwife to a new personality—as I stand by with awe at the emergence of a self, a person, as I see a birth process in which I have had an important and facilitating part. It is about both the client and me as we regard with wonder the potent and orderly forces which are evident in this whole experience, forces which seem deeply rooted in the universe as a whole.

As Rogers began to emphasize the importance of the congruent therapist, teacher, or professional in all helping relationships, this led naturally to his wanting to be as personal and authentic as possible in his own professional communication. Meanwhile, he was developing the confidence to risk personal expression in academic settings, for by the late 1950s he had achieved the highest levels of prominence in his profession and had earned impeccable scientific credentials. If anyone could dare speak personally and not be dismissed as "soft" and unscientific, Rogers could; and so he did, often inserting his own voice when he felt it was appropriate. Thus, in one 1957 article, "A Note on 'The Nature of Man'" (Chapter 26), the journal editor included the following footnote:

> The editor raised a question with the author regarding the frequent use of the personal pronoun in the manuscript and received a reply which deserves quoting. "The fact that it is in quite personal form is not accidental nor intended to make it a letter. In recent years I have been experimenting with a more personal form of writing, for I believe that putting an article in more personal form makes it communicate more directly and, even more important, keeps us from sounding like oracles. Instead of saying 'This is so,' one is much more inclined to say 'I believe this is so.' I just wanted you to know the reason why it is expressed in a more personal way than is considered to be good scientific writing." This argument appeared particularly to fit the nature of the article in question and the original flavor of the writing is retained. — Ed.

Eventually this direct manner of addressing the reader or listener became a Carl Rogers hallmark, a subtle yet significant factor in his widespread impact. "I felt as though he were addressing me personally" was a sentiment often expressed by readers and listeners over the years, even when Rogers was speaking to hundreds or even thousands of people.

As significant as his personal style of communicating was the personal content he began including in his writings and speeches. In his earliest professional writings in the 1930s, Rogers often used case studies to illustrate his concepts. These real-life examples added interest, meaning, and credibility to his books and articles. Eventually he also began to use his own life as a case study, enriching his communication with personal anecdotes to speak directly to his audience in a meaningful way. Over the years, he also wrote a number of autobiographical essays exploring his own development as a professional or some particular theme in life, such as marriage or aging. In his last twenty years, he almost always began his books, essays, or speeches in a personal vein.

Given this pattern, we think it particularly appropriate to begin a collection of Carl Rogers's work on a personal note. We have no doubt he would have chosen the same course had he undertaken this volume. The first three selections are those we believe to be Rogers's most important personal essays. "This Is Me," his very first autobiographical essay, comes from his most popular book, *On Becoming a Person* (1961). In it he describes how his family background and three critical experiences with clients influenced his philosophy and methods as a therapist. In "My Own Marriage," Rogers speaks frankly about communication, sexuality, and support in his forty-six-year marriage with Helen (ultimately fifty-five years). "Growing Old: Or Older and Growing" conveys Rogers's perspective at seventy-five and, in an update, at seventy-eight. In it he explores his current activities and physical condition, the issues of serenity and intimacy, his attitude toward death, and Helen's dying. A lesser-known short essay, "On Reaching 85," published posthumously, rounds out this autobiographical section.

I
This Is Me

I have been informed that what I am expected to do in speaking to this group is to assume that my topic is "This Is Me." I feel various reactions to such an invitation, but one that I would like to mention is that I feel honored and flattered that any group wants, in a personal sense, to know who I am. I can assure you it is a unique and challenging sort of invitation, and I shall try to give to this honest question as honest an answer as I can.

So, who am I? I am a psychologist whose primary interest, for many years, has been in psychotherapy. What does that mean? I don't intend to bore you with a long account of my work, but I would like to take a few paragraphs from the preface to my book, *Client-Centered Therapy*, to indicate in a subjective way what it means to me. I was trying to give the reader some feeling for the subject matter of the volume, and I wrote as follows.

> What is this book about? Let me try to give an answer which may, to some degree, convey the living experience that this book is intended to be.
>
> This book is about the suffering and the hope, the anxiety and the satisfaction, with which each therapist's counseling room is filled. It is about the uniqueness of the relationship each therapist forms with each client, and equally about the common elements which we discover in all these relationships. This book is about the highly personal experiences of each one of us. It is about a client in my office who sits there by the corner of the desk, struggling to be himself, yet deathly afraid of being himself — striving to see his experience as it is, wanting to *be* that experience, and yet deeply fearful of the prospect. This book is about me, as I sit there with that client, facing him, participating in that struggle as deeply and sensitively as I am able. It is about me as I try to perceive his experience, and the meaning and the feeling and the taste and the flavor that it has for him. It is about me as I bemoan my very human fallibility in understanding that client, and the occasional failures to see life as it appears to him, failures which

On Becoming a Person. Boston: Houghton Mifflin, 1961, 4–27.

fall like heavy objects across the intricate, delicate web of growth which is taking place. It is about me as I rejoice at the privilege of being a midwife to a new personality—as I stand by with awe at the emergence of a self, a person, as I see a birth process in which I have had an important and facilitating part. It is about both the client and me as we regard with wonder the potent and orderly forces which are evident in this whole experience, forces which seem deeply rooted in the universe as a whole. The book is, I believe, about life, as life vividly reveals itself in the therapeutic process—with its blind power and its tremendous capacity for destruction, but with its overbalancing thrust toward growth, if the opportunity for growth is provided.

Perhaps that will give you some picture of what I do and the way I feel about it. I presume you may also wonder how I came to engage in that occupation, and some of the decisions and choices, conscious and unconscious, which were made along the way. Let me see if I can give you some of the psychological highlights of my autobiography, particularly as it seems to relate to my professional life.

My Early Years

I was brought up in a home marked by close family ties, a very strict and uncompromising religious and ethical atmosphere, and what amounted to a worship of the virtue of hard work. I came along as the fourth of six children. My parents cared a great deal for us, and had our welfare almost constantly in mind. They were also, in many subtle and affectionate ways, very controlling of our behavior. It was assumed by them and accepted by me that we were different from other people—no alcoholic beverages, no dancing, cards, or theater, very little social life, and *much* work. I have a hard time convincing my children that even carbonated beverages had a faintly sinful aroma, and I remember my slight feeling of wickedness when I had my first bottle of "pop." We had good times together within the family, but we did not mix. So I was a pretty solitary boy, who read incessantly, and went all through high school with only two dates.

When I was twelve my parents bought a farm and we made our home there. The reasons were twofold. My father, having become a prosperous businessman, wanted it for a hobby. More important, I believe, was the fact that it seemed to my parents that a growing adolescent family should be removed from the "temptations" of suburban life.

Here I developed two interests which have probably had some real bearing on my later work. I became fascinated by the great night-flying moths (Gene Stratton-Porter's books were then in vogue) and I became an authority on the gorgeous Luna, Polyphemus, Cecropia, and other moths which inhabited our woods. I laboriously bred the moths in captivity, reared the caterpillars, kept the cocoons over the long winter months, and in general realized some of the joys and frustrations of the scientist as he tries to observe nature.

My father was determined to operate his new farm on a scientific basis, so he bought many books on scientific agriculture. He encouraged his boys to have independent and profitable ventures of our own, so my brothers and I had a flock of chickens, and at one time or other reared from infancy lambs, pigs, and calves. In doing this I became a student of scientific agriculture, and have only realized in recent years what a fundamental feeling for science I gained in that way. There was no one to tell me that Morison's *Feeds and Feeding* was not a book for a fourteen-year-old, so I ploughed through its hundreds of pages, learning how experiments were conducted—how control groups were matched with experimental groups, how conditions were held constant by randomizing procedures, so that the influence of a given food on meat production or milk production could be established. I learned how difficult it is to test a hypothesis. I acquired a knowledge of and a respect for the methods of science in a field of practical endeavor.

College and Graduate Education

I started in college at Wisconsin in the field of agriculture. One of the things I remember best was the vehement statement of an agronomy professor in regard to the learning and use of facts. He stressed the futility of an encyclopedic knowledge for its own sake, and wound up with the injunction, "Don't be a damned ammunition wagon; be a rifle!"

During my first two college years my professional goal changed, as the result of some emotionally charged student religious conferences, from that of a scientific agriculturist to that of the ministry — a slight shift! I changed from agriculture to history, believing this would be a better preparation.

In my junior year I was selected as one of a dozen students from this country to go to China for an international World Student Christian Federation Conference. This was a most important experience for me. It was 1922, four years after the close of World War I. I saw how bitterly the French and Germans still hated each other, even though as individuals they seemed very likable. I was forced to stretch my thinking, to realize that sincere and honest people could believe in very divergent religious doctrines. In major ways I for the first time emancipated myself from the religious thinking of my parents, and realized that I could not go along with them. This independence of thought caused great pain and stress in our relationship, but looking back on it I believe that here, more than at any other time, I became an independent person. Of course there was much revolt and rebellion in my attitude during that period, but the essential split was achieved during the six months I was on this trip to the Orient, and hence was thought through away from the influence of home.

Although this is an account of elements which influenced my professional development rather than my personal growth, I wish to mention very briefly one profoundly important factor in my personal life. It was at about the time of my trip to China that I fell in love with a lovely girl whom I had known for many years, even in childhood, and we were married, with the very reluctant consent of our parents, as soon as I finished college, in order that we could go to graduate school together. I cannot be very objective about this, but her steady and sustaining love and companionship during all the years since has been a most important and enriching factor in my life.

I chose to go to Union Theological Seminary, the most liberal in the country at that time (1924), to prepare for religious work. I have never regretted the two years there. I came in contact with some great scholars and teachers, notably Dr. A. C. McGiffert, who believed devoutly in freedom of inquiry, and in following the truth no matter where it led.

Knowing universities and graduate schools as I do now — knowing their rules and their rigidities — I am truly astonished

at one very significant experience at Union. A group of us felt
that ideas were being fed to us, whereas we wished primarily to
explore our own questions and doubts, and find out where they
led. We petitioned the administration that we be allowed to set
up a seminar for credit, a seminar with no instructor, where the
curriculum would be composed of our own questions. The seminary was understandably perplexed by this, but they granted
our petition! The only restriction was that in the interests of the
institution a young instructor was to sit in on the seminar, but
would take no part in it unless we wished him to be active.

I suppose it is unnecessary to add that this seminar was deeply
satisfying and clarifying. I feel that it moved me a long way
toward a philosophy of life which was my own. The majority of
the members of that group, in thinking their way through the
questions they had raised, thought themselves right out of religious work. I was one. I felt that questions as to the meaning
of life, and the possibility of the constructive improvement of
life for individuals, would probably always interest me, but I
could not work in a field where I would be required to believe
in some specified religious doctrine. My beliefs had already
changed tremendously, and might continue to change. It seemed
to me it would be a horrible thing to *have* to profess a set of
beliefs, in order to remain in one's profession. I wanted to find
a field in which I could be sure my freedom of thought would
not be limited.

Becoming a Psychologist

But what field? I had been attracted, at Union, by the courses
and lectures on psychological and psychiatric work, which were
then beginning to develop. Goodwin Watson, Harrison Elliott,
Marian Kenworthy all contributed to this interest. I began to
take more courses at Teachers College, Columbia University,
across the street from Union Seminary. I took work in philosophy of education with William H. Kilpatrick, and found him a
great teacher. I began practical clinical work with children under
Leta Hollingworth, a sensitive and practical person. I found
myself drawn to child guidance work, so that gradually, with
very little painful readjustment, I shifted over into the field of
child guidance, and began to think of myself as a clinical psychologist. It was a step I eased into, with relatively little clear-

cut conscious choice, rather just following the activities which interested me.

While I was at Teachers College I applied for, and was granted, a fellowship or internship at the then new Institute for Child Guidance, sponsored by the Commonwealth Fund. I have often been grateful that I was there during the first year. The organization was in a chaotic beginning state, but this meant that one could do what he wanted to do. I soaked up the dynamic Freudian views of the staff, which included David Levy and Lawson Lowrey, and found them in great conflict with the rigorous, scientific, coldly objective, statistical point of view then prevalent at Teachers College. Looking back, I believe the necessity of resolving that conflict in me was a most valuable learning experience. At the time I felt I was functioning in two completely different worlds, "and never the twain shall meet."

By the end of this internship it was highly important to me that I obtain a job to support my growing family, even though my doctorate was not completed. Positions were not plentiful, and I remember the relief and exhilaration I felt when I found one. I was employed as psychologist in the Child Study Department of the Society for the Prevention of Cruelty to Children, in Rochester, New York. There were three psychologists in this department, and my salary was $2,900 per year.

I look back at the acceptance of that position with amusement and some amazement. The reason I was so pleased was that it was a chance to do the work I wanted to do. That by any reasonable criterion it was a dead-end street professionally, that I would be isolated from professional contacts, that the salary was not good even by the standards of that day, seems not to have occurred to me, as nearly as I can recall. I think I have always had a feeling that if I was given some opportunity to do the thing I was most interested in doing, everything else would somehow take care of itself.

The Rochester Years

The next twelve years in Rochester were exceedingly valuable ones. For at least the first eight of these years, I was completely immersed in carrying on practical psychological service, diagnosing and planning for the delinquent and underprivileged children who were sent to us by the courts and agencies, and in many instances carrying on "treatment interviews." It was a period of relative professional isolation, where my only concern was in trying to be more effective with our clients. We had to live with our failures as well as our successes, so that we were forced to learn. There was only one criterion in regard to any method of dealing with these children and their parents, and that was, "Does it work? Is it effective?" I found I began increasingly to formulate my own views out of my everyday working experience.

Three significant illustrations come to mind, all small, but important to me at the time. It strikes me that they are all instances of disillusionment—with an authority, with materials, with myself.

In my training I had been fascinated by Dr. William Healy's writings, indicating that delinquency was often based upon sexual conflict, and that if this conflict was uncovered, the delinquency ceased. In my first or second year at Rochester I worked very hard with a youthful pyromaniac who had an unaccountable impulse to set fires. Interviewing him day after day in the detention home, I gradually traced back his desire to a sexual impulse regarding masturbation. Eureka! The case was solved. However, when placed on probation, he again got into the same difficulty.

I remember the jolt I felt. Healy might be wrong. Perhaps I was learning something Healy didn't know. Somehow this incident impressed me with the possibility that there were mistakes in authoritative teachings, and that there was still new knowledge to discover.

The second naive discovery was of a different sort. Soon after coming to Rochester I led a discussion group on interviewing. I discovered a published account of an interview with a parent, approximately verbatim, in which the caseworker was shrewd, insightful, clever, and led the interview quite quickly to the heart of the difficulty. I was happy to use it as an illustration of good interviewing technique.

Several years later, I had a similar assignment and remembered this excellent material. I hunted it up again and reread it. I was appalled. Now it seemed to me to be a clever legalistic type of questioning by the interviewer which convicted this parent of her unconscious motives, and wrung from her an admission of her guilt. I now knew from my experience that such an interview would not be of any lasting help to the parent or the child. It made me realize that I was moving away from any approach which was coercive or pushing in clinical relationships, not for philosophical reasons, but because such approaches were never more than superficially effective.

The third incident occurred several years later. I had learned to be more subtle and patient in interpreting a client's behavior to him, attempting to time it in a gentle fashion which would gain acceptance. I had been working with a highly intelligent mother whose boy was something of a hellion. The problem was clearly her early rejection of the boy, but over many interviews I could not help her to this insight. I drew her out, I gently pulled together the evidence she had given, trying to help her see the pattern. But we got nowhere. Finally I gave up. I told her that it seemed we had both tried, but we had failed, and that we might as well give up our contacts. She agreed. So we concluded the interview, shook hands, and she walked to the door of the office. Then she turned and asked, "Do you ever take adults for counseling here?" When I replied in the affirmative, she said, "Well then, I would like some help." She came to the chair she had left, and began to pour out her despair about her marriage, her troubled relationship with her husband, her sense of failure and confusion, all very different from the sterile "case history" she had given before. Real therapy began then, and ultimately it was very successful.

This incident was one of a number which helped me to experience the fact — only fully realized later — that it is the *client* who knows what hurts, what directions to go, what problems are crucial, what experiences have been deeply buried. It began to occur to me that unless I had a need to demonstrate my own cleverness and learning, I would do better to rely upon the client for the direction of movement in the process.

Psychologist or ?

During this period I began to doubt that I was a psychologist. The University of Rochester made it clear that the work I was doing was not psychology, and they had no interest in my teaching in the Psychology Department. I went to meetings of the American Psychological Association and found them full of papers on the learning processes of rats and laboratory experiments which seemed to me to have no relation to what I was doing. The psychiatric social workers, however, seemed to be talking my language, so I became active in the social work profession, moving up to local and even national offices. Only when the American Association for Applied Psychology was formed did I become really active as a psychologist.

I began to teach courses at the university on how to understand and deal with problem children, under the Department of Sociology. Soon the Department of Education wanted to classify these as education courses, also. (Before I left Rochester, the Department of Psychology, too, finally requested permission to list them, thus at last accepting me as a psychologist.) Simply describing these experiences makes me realize how stubbornly I have followed my own course, being relatively unconcerned with the question of whether I was going with my group or not.

Time does not permit to tell of the work of establishing a separate Guidance Center in Rochester, nor the battle with some of the psychiatric profession which was included. These were largely administrative struggles which did not have too much to do with the development of my ideas.

My Children

It was during these Rochester years that my son and daughter grew through infancy and childhood, teaching me far more about individuals, their development, and their relationships than I could ever have learned professionally. I don't feel I was a very good parent in their early years, but fortunately my wife was, and as time went on I believe *I* gradually became a better and more understanding parent. Certainly the privilege during these years and later, of being in relationship with two fine, sensitive youngsters through all their childhood pleasure and pain, their adolescent assertiveness and difficulties, and on into their adult years and the beginning of their own families, has been a priceless one. I think my wife and I regard as one of the most satisfying achievements in which we have had a part the fact that we can really communicate in a deep way with our grown-up children and their spouses, and they with us.

Ohio State Years

In 1940 I accepted a position at Ohio State University. I am sure the only reason I was considered was my book on the *Clinical Treatment of the Problem Child*, which I had squeezed out of vacations and brief leaves of absence. To my surprise, and contrary to my expectation, they offered me a full professorship. I heartily recommend starting in the academic world at this level. I have often been grateful that I have never had to live through the frequently degrading competitive process of step-by-step promotion in university faculties, where individuals so frequently learn only one lesson — not to stick their necks out.

It was in trying to teach what I had learned about treatment and counseling to graduate students at Ohio State University that I first began to realize that I had perhaps developed a distinctive point of view of my own, out of my experience. When I tried to crystallize some of these ideas and present them in a paper at the University of Minnesota in December 1940, I found the reactions were very strong. It was my first experience of the fact that a new idea of mine, which to me can seem all shiny and glowing with potentiality, can to another person be a great threat. And to find myself the center of criticism, of arguments pro and con, was disconcerting and made me doubt and question. Nevertheless I felt I had something to contribute, and wrote the manuscript of *Counseling and Psychotherapy*, setting forth what I felt to be a somewhat more effective orientation to therapy.

Here again I realize with some amusement how little I have cared about being "realistic." When I submitted the manuscript, the publisher thought it was interesting and new, but wondered what classes would use it. I replied that I knew of only two — a course I was teaching and one in another university. The publisher felt I had made a grave mistake in not writing a text which would fit courses already being given. He was very dubious that he could sell 2,000 copies, which would be necessary to break even. It was only when I said I would take it to another publisher that he decided to make the gamble. I don't know which of us has been more surprised at its sales — 70,000 copies to date and still continuing.

Recent Years

I believe that from this point to the present time my professional life — five years at Ohio State, twelve years at the University of Chicago, and four years at the University of Wisconsin — is quite well documented by what I have written. I will very briefly stress two or three points which have some significance for me.

I have learned to live in increasingly deep therapeutic relationships with an ever-widening range of clients. This can be and has been extremely rewarding. It can be and has been at times very frightening, when a deeply disturbed person seems to demand that I must be more than I am, in order to meet his need. Certainly the carrying on of therapy is something which demands continuing personal growth on the part of the therapist, and this is sometimes painful, even though in the long run rewarding.

I would also mention the steadily increasing importance which research has come to have for me. Therapy is the experience in which I can let myself go subjectively. Research is the experience in which I can stand off and try to view this rich subjective experience with objectivity, applying all the elegant methods of science to determine whether I have been deceiving myself. The conviction grows in me that we shall discover laws of personality and behavior which are as significant for human progress or human understanding as the law of gravity or the laws of thermodynamics.

In the last two decades I have become somewhat more accustomed to being fought over, but the reactions to my ideas continue to surprise me. From my point of view I have felt that I have always put forth my thoughts in a tentative manner, to be accepted or rejected by the reader or the student. But at different times and places psychologists, counselors, and educators have been moved to great wrath, scorn, and criticism by my views. As this furor has tended to die down in these fields it has in recent years been renewed among psychiatrists, some of whom sense, in my way of working, a deep threat to many of their most cherished and unquestioned principles. And perhaps the storms of criticism are more than matched by the damage done by uncritical and unquestioning "disciples" — individuals who have acquired something of a new point of view for themselves and have gone forth to do battle with all and sundry, using as weapons both inaccurate and accurate understandings of me and my work. I have found it difficult to know, at times, whether I have been hurt more by my "friends" or my enemies.

Perhaps partly because of the troubling business of being struggled over, I have come to value highly the privilege of getting away, of being alone. It has seemed to me that my most fruitful periods of work are the times when I have been able to get completely away from what others think, from professional expectations and daily demands, and gain perspective on what I am doing. My wife and I have found isolated hideaways in Mexico and in the Caribbean where no one knows I am a psychologist; where painting, swimming, snorkeling, and capturing some of the scenery in color photography are my major activities. Yet in these spots, where no more than two to four hours a day goes for professional work, I have made most of whatever advances I have made in the last few years. I prize the privilege of being alone.

SOME SIGNIFICANT LEARNINGS

There, in very brief outline, are some of the externals of my professional life. But I would like to take you inside, to tell you some of the things I have learned from the thousands of hours I have spent working intimately with individuals in personal distress.

I would like to make it very plain that these are learnings which have significance for *me*. I do not know whether they would hold true for you. I have no desire to present them as a guide for anyone else. Yet I have found that when another person has been willing to tell me something of his inner directions this has been of value to me, if only in sharpening my realization that my directions are different. So it is in that spirit that I offer the learnings which follow. In each case I believe they became a part of my actions and inner convictions long before I realized them consciously. They are certainly scattered learnings, and incomplete. I can only say that they are and have been very important to me. I continually learn and relearn them.

I frequently fail to act in terms of them, but later I wish that I had. Frequently I fail to see a new situation as one in which some of these learnings might apply.

They are not fixed. They keep changing. Some seem to be acquiring a stronger emphasis, others are perhaps less important to me than at one time, but they are all, to me, significant.

I will introduce each learning with a phrase or sentence which gives something of its personal meaning. Then I will elaborate on it a bit. There is not much organization to what follows except that the first learnings have to do mostly with relationships to others. There follow some that fall in the realm of personal values and convictions.

I might start off these several statements of significant learnings with a negative item. *In my relationships with persons I have found that it does not help, in the long run, to act as though I were something that I am not.* It does not help to act calm and pleasant when actually I am angry and critical. It does not help to act as though I know the answers when I do not. It does not help to act as though I were a loving person if actually, at the moment, I am hostile. It does not help for me to act as though I were full of assurance if actually I am frightened and unsure. Even on a very simple level I have found that this statement seems to hold. It does not help for me to act as though I were well when I feel ill.

What I am saying here, put in another way, is that I have not found it to be helpful or effective in my relationships with other people to try to maintain a façade; to act in one way on the surface when I am experiencing something quite different underneath. It does not, I believe, make me helpful in my attempts to build up constructive relationships with other individuals. I would want to make it clear that while I feel I have learned this to be true, I have by no means adequately profited from it. In fact, it seems to me that most of the mistakes I make in personal relationships, most of the times in which I fail to be of help to other individuals, can be accounted for in terms of the fact that I have, for some defensive reason, behaved in one way at a surface level, while in reality my feelings run in a contrary direction.

A second learning might be stated as follows — *I find I am more effective when I can listen acceptantly to myself, and can be myself.* I feel that over the years I have learned to become more adequate in listening to *myself*; so that I know, somewhat more adequately than I used to, what I am feeling at any given moment — to be able to realize I *am* angry, or that I *do* feel rejecting toward this person; or that I feel very full of warmth and affection for this individual; or that I am bored and uninterested in what is going on; or that I am eager to understand this individual or that I am anxious and fearful in my relationship to this person. All of these diverse attitudes are feelings which I think I can listen to in myself. One way of putting this is that I feel I have become more adequate in letting myself *be* what I *am*. It becomes easier for me to accept myself as a decidedly imperfect person, who by no means functions at all times in the way in which I would like to function.

This must seem to some like a very strange direction in which to move. It seems to me to have value because the curious paradox is that when I accept myself as I am, then I change. I believe that I have learned this from my clients as well as within my own experience — that we cannot change, we cannot move away from what we are, until we thoroughly *accept* what we are. Then change seems to come about almost unnoticed.

Another result which seems to grow out of being myself is that relationships then become real. Real relationships have an exciting way of being vital and meaningful. If I can accept the fact that I am annoyed at or bored by this client or this student, then I am also much more likely to be able to accept his feelings in response. I can also accept the changed experience and the changed feelings which are then likely to occur in me and in him. Real relationships tend to change rather than to remain static.

So I find it effective to let myself be what I am in my attitudes; to know when I have reached my limit of endurance or of tolerance, and to accept that as a fact; to know when I desire to mold or manipulate people, and to accept that as a fact in myself. I would like to be as acceptant of these feelings as of feelings of warmth, interest, permissiveness, kindness, understanding, which are also a very real part of me. It is when I do accept all these attitudes as a fact, as a part of me, that my relationship with the other person then becomes what it is, and is able to grow and change most readily.

I come now to a central learning which has had a great deal of significance for me. I can state this learning as follows: *I have found it of enormous value when I can permit myself to understand another person.* The way in which I have worded this statement may seem strange to you. Is it necessary to *permit* oneself to understand another? I think that it is. Our first reaction to most of the statements which we hear from other people is an immediate evaluation, or judgment, rather than an understanding of it. When someone expresses some feeling or attitude or belief, our tendency is, almost immediately, to feel "That's right"; or "That's stupid"; "That's abnormal"; "That's unreasonable"; "That's incorrect"; "That's not nice." Very rarely do we permit ourselves to *understand* precisely what the meaning of his statement is to him. I believe this is because understanding is risky. If I let myself really understand another person, I might be changed by that understanding. And we all fear change. So as I say, it is not an easy thing to permit oneself to understand an individual, to enter thoroughly and completely and empathically into his frame of reference. It is also a rare thing.

To understand is enriching in a double way. I find when I am working with clients in distress, that to understand the bizarre world of a psychotic individual, or to understand and sense the attitudes of a person who feels that life is too tragic to bear, or to understand a man who feels that he is a worthless and inferior individual—each of these understandings somehow enriches me. I learn from these experiences in ways that change me, that make me a different and, I think, a more responsive person. Even more important, perhaps, is the fact that my understanding of these individuals permits them to change. It permits them to accept their own fears and bizarre thoughts and tragic feelings and discouragements, as well as their moments of courage and kindness and love and sensitivity. And it is their experience as well as mine that when someone fully understands those feelings, this enables them to accept those feelings in themselves. Then they find both the feelings and themselves changing. Whether it is understanding a woman who feels that very literally she has a hook in her head by which others lead her about, or understanding a man who feels that no one is as lonely, no one is as separated from others as he, I find these understandings to be of value to me. But also, and even more importantly, to be understood has a very positive value to these individuals.

Here is another learning which has had importance for me. *I have found it enriching to open channels whereby others can communicate their feelings, their private perceptual worlds, to me.* Because understanding is rewarding, I would like to reduce the barriers between others and me, so that they can, if they wish, reveal themselves more fully.

In the therapeutic relationship there are a number of ways by which I can make it easier for the client to communicate himself. I can by my own attitudes create a safety in the relationship which makes such communication more possible. A sensitiveness of understanding which sees him as he is to himself, and accepts him as having those perceptions and feelings, helps too.

But as a teacher also I have found that I am enriched when I can open channels through which others can share themselves with me. So I try, often not too successfully, to create a climate in the classroom where feelings can be expressed, where people can differ — with each other and with the instructor. I have also frequently asked for "reaction sheets" from students — in which they can express themselves individually and personally regarding the course. They can tell of the way it is or is not meeting their needs, they can express their feelings regarding the instructor, or can tell of the personal difficulties they are having in relation to the course. These reaction sheets have no relation whatsoever to their grade. Sometimes the same sessions of a course are experienced in diametrically opposite ways. One student says, "My feeling is one of indefinable revulsion with the tone of this class." Another, a foreign student, speaking of the same week of the same course, says, "Our class follows the best, fruitful and scientific way of learning. But for people who have been taught for a long, long time, as we have, by the lecture type, authoritative method, this new procedure is ununderstandable. People like us are conditioned to hear the instructor, to keep passively our notes and memorize his reading assignments for the exams. There is no need to say that it takes long time for people to get rid of their habits regardless of whether or not their habits are sterile, infertile and barren." To open myself to these sharply different feelings has been a deeply rewarding thing.

I have found the same thing true in groups where I am the administrator, or perceived as the leader. I wish to reduce the need for fear or defensiveness, so that people can communicate their feelings freely. This has been most exciting, and has led me to a whole new view of what administration can be. But I cannot expand on that here.

There is another very important learning which has come to me in my counseling work. I can voice this learning very briefly. *I have found it highly rewarding when I can accept another person.*

I have found that truly to accept another person and his feelings is by no means an easy thing, any more than is understanding. Can I really permit another person to feel hostile toward me? Can I accept his anger as a real and legitimate part of himself? Can I accept him when he views life and its problems in a way quite different from mine? Can I accept him when he feels very positively toward me, admiring me and wanting to model himself after me? All this is involved in acceptance, and it does not come easy. I believe that it is an increasingly common pattern in our culture for each one of us to believe, "Every other person must feel and think and believe the same as I do." We find it very hard to permit our children or our parents or our spouses to feel differently than we do about particular issues or problems. We cannot permit our clients or our students to differ from us or to utilize their experience in their own individual ways. On a national scale, we cannot permit another nation to think or feel differently than we do. Yet it has come to seem to me that this separateness of individuals, the right of each individual to utilize his experience in his own way and to discover his own meanings in it—this is one of the most priceless potentialities of life. Each person is an island unto himself, in a very real sense; and he can only build bridges to other islands if he is first of all willing to be himself and permitted to be himself. So I find that when I can accept another person, which means specifically accepting the feelings and attitudes and beliefs that he has as a real and vital part of him, then I am assisting him to become a person: and there seems to me great value in this.

The next learning I want to state may be difficult to communicate. It is this. *The more I am open to the realities in me and in the other person, the less do I find myself wishing to rush in to "fix things."* As I try to listen to myself and the experiencing going on in me, and the more I try to extend that same listening attitude to another person, the more respect I feel for the complex processes of life. So I become less and less inclined to hurry in to fix things, to set goals, to mold people, to manipulate and push them in the way that I would like them to go. I am much more content simply to be myself and to let another person be himself. I know very well that this must seem like a strange, almost an Oriental point of view. What is life for if we are not going to do things to people? What is life for if we are not going to mold them to our purposes? What is life for if we are not going to teach them the things that *we* think they should learn? What is life for if we are not going to make them think and feel as we do? How can anyone hold such an inactive point of view as the one I am expressing? I am sure that attitudes such as these must be a part of the reaction of many of you.

Yet the paradoxical aspect of my experience is that the more I am simply willing to be myself, in all this complexity of life, and the more I am willing to understand and accept the realities in myself and in the other person, the more change seems to be stirred up. It is a very paradoxical thing—that to the degree that each one of us is willing to be himself, then he finds not only himself changing, but he finds that other people to whom he relates are also changing. At least this is a very vivid part of my experience, and one of the deepest things I think I have learned in my personal and professional life.

Let me turn now to some other learnings which are less concerned with relationships, and have more to do with my own actions and values. The first of these is very brief. *I can trust my experience.*

One of the basic things which I was a long time in realizing, and which I am still learning, is that when an activity *feels* as though it is valuable or worth doing, it *is* worth doing. Put another way, I have learned that my total organismic sensing of a situation is more trustworthy than my intellect.

All of my professional life I have been going in directions

which others thought were foolish, and about which I have had many doubts myself. But I have never regretted moving in directions which "felt right," even though I have often felt lonely or foolish at the time.

I have found that when I have trusted some inner nonintellectual sensing, I have discovered wisdom in the move. In fact I have found that when I have followed one of these unconventional paths because it felt right or true, then in five or ten years many of my colleagues have joined me, and I no longer need to feel alone in it.

As I gradually come to trust my total reactions more deeply, I find that I can use them to guide my thinking. I have come to have more respect for those vague thoughts which occur in me from time to time which *feel* as though they were significant. I am inclined to think that these unclear thoughts or hunches will lead me to important areas. I think of it as trusting the totality of my experience, which I have learned to suspect is wiser than my intellect. It is fallible, I am sure, but I believe it to be less fallible than my conscious mind alone. My attitude is very well expressed by Max Weber, the artist, when he says, "In carrying on my own humble creative effort, I depend greatly upon that which I do not yet know, and upon that which I have not yet done."

Very closely related to this learning is a corollary that *evaluation by others is not a guide for me.* The judgments of others, while they are to be listened to, and taken into account for what they are, can never be a guide for me. This has been a hard thing to learn. I remember how shaken I was, in the early days, when a scholarly, thoughtful man who seemed to me a much more competent and knowledgeable psychologist than I, told me what a mistake I was making by getting interested in psychotherapy. It could never lead anywhere, and as a psychologist I would not even have the opportunity to practice it.

In later years it has sometimes jolted me a bit to learn that I am, in the eyes of some others, a fraud, a person practicing medicine without a license, the author of a very superficial and damaging sort of therapy, a power seeker, a mystic, etc. And I have been equally disturbed by equally extreme praise. But I have not been too much concerned, because I have come to feel that only one person (at least in my lifetime, and perhaps ever) can know whether what I am doing is honest, thorough, open, and sound, or false and defensive and unsound, and I am that person. I am happy to get all sorts of evidence regarding what I am doing, and criticism (both friendly and hostile) and praise (both sincere and fawning) are a part of such evidence. But to weigh this evidence and to determine its meaning and usefulness is a task I cannot relinquish to anyone else.

In view of what I have been saying, the next learning will probably not surprise you. *Experience is, for me, the highest authority.* The touchstone of validity is my own experience. No other person's ideas, and none of my own ideas, are as authoritative as my experience. It is to experience that I must return again and again, to discover a closer approximation to truth as it is in the process of becoming in me.

Neither the Bible nor the prophets—neither Freud nor research—neither the revelations of God nor man—can take precedence over my own direct experience.

My experience is the more authoritative as it becomes more primary, to use the semanticist's term. Thus the hierarchy of experience would be most authoritative at its lowest level. If I read a theory of psychotherapy, and if I formulate a theory of psychotherapy based on my work with clients, and if I also have a direct experience of psychotherapy with a client, then the degree of authority increases in the order in which I have listed these experiences.

My experience is not authoritative because it is infallible. It is the basis of authority because it can always be checked in new primary ways. In this way its frequent error or fallibility is always open to correction.

Now another personal learning. *I enjoy the discovering of order in experience.* It seems inevitable that I seek for the meaning or the orderliness or lawfulness in any large body of experience. It is this kind of curiosity, which I find it very satisfying to pursue, which has led me to each of the major formulations I have made. It led me to search for the orderliness in all the conglomeration of things clinicians did for children, and out of that came my book on *The Clinical Treatment of the Problem Child.* It led me to formulate the general principles which seemed to be operative in psychotherapy, and that has led to several books and many articles. It has led me into research to test the various types of lawfulness which I feel I have encountered in my experience. It has enticed me to construct theories to bring together the orderliness of that which has already been experienced and to project this order forward into new and unexplored realms where it may be further tested.

Thus I have come to see both scientific research and the process of theory construction as being aimed toward the inward ordering of significant experience. Research is the persistent, disciplined effort to make sense and order out of the phenomena of subjective experience. It is justified because it is satisfying to perceive the world as having order, and because rewarding results often ensue when one understands the orderly relationships which appear in nature.

So I have come to recognize that the reason I devote myself to research, and to the building of theory, is to satisfy a need for perceiving order and meaning, a subjective need which exists in me. I have, at times, carried on research for other reasons — to satisfy others, to convince opponents and skeptics, to get ahead professionally, to gain prestige, and for other unsavory reasons. These errors in judgment and activity have only served to convince me more deeply that there is only one sound reason for pursuing scientific activities, and that is to satisfy a need for meaning which is in me.

Another learning which cost me much to recognize can be stated in four words. *The facts are friendly.*

It has interested me a great deal that most psychotherapists, especially the psychoanalysts, have steadily refused to make any scientific investigation of their therapy, or to permit others to do this. I can understand this reaction because I have felt it. Especially in our early investigations I can well remember the anxiety of waiting to see how the findings came out. Suppose our hypotheses were *dis*proved! Suppose we were mistaken in our views! Suppose our opinions were not justified! At such times, as I look back, it seems to me that I regarded the facts as potential enemies, as possible bearers of disaster. I have perhaps been slow in coming to realize that the facts are *always* friendly. Every bit of evidence one can acquire, in any area, leads one that much closer to what is true. And being closer to the truth can never be a harmful or dangerous or unsatisfying thing. So while I still hate to readjust my thinking, still hate to give up old ways of perceiving and conceptualizing, yet at some deeper level I have, to a considerable degree, come to realize that these painful reorganizations are what is known as *learning*, and that though painful, they always lead to a more satisfying because somewhat more accurate way of seeing life. Thus at the present time one of the most enticing areas for thought and speculation is an area where several of my pet ideas have *not* been upheld by the evidence. I feel if I can only puzzle my way through this problem that I will find a much more satisfying approximation to the truth. I feel sure the facts will be my friends.

Somewhere here I want to bring in a learning which has been most rewarding, because it makes me feel so deeply akin to others. I can word it this way. *What is most personal is most general.* There have been times when in talking with students or staff, or in my writing, I have expressed myself in ways so personal that I have felt I was expressing an attitude which it was probable no one else could understand, because it was so uniquely my own. Two written examples of this are the preface to *Client-Centered Therapy* (regarded as most unsuitable by the publishers) and an article on "Persons or Science." In these instances I have almost invariably found that the very feeling which has seemed to me most private, most personal, and hence most incomprehensible by others, has turned out to be an expression for which there is a resonance in many other people. It has led me to believe that what is most personal and unique in each one of us is probably the very element which would, if it were shared or expressed, speak most deeply to others. This has helped me to understand artists and poets as people who have dared to express the unique in themselves.

There is one deep learning which is perhaps basic to all of the things I have said thus far. It has been forced upon me by more than twenty-five years of trying to be helpful to individuals in personal distress. It is simply this. *It has been my experience that persons have a basically positive direction.* In my deepest contacts with individuals in therapy, even those whose troubles are most disturbing, whose behavior has been most antisocial, whose feelings seem most abnormal, I find this to be true. When I can sensitively understand the feelings which they are expressing, when I am able to accept them as separate persons in their own right, then I find that they tend to move in certain directions. And what are these directions in which they tend to move? The words which I believe are most truly descriptive are words such as positive, constructive, moving toward self-actualization, growing toward maturity, growing toward socialization. I have come to feel that the more fully the individual is understood and accepted, the more he tends to drop the false fronts with which he has been meeting life, and the more he tends to move in a direction which is forward.

I would not want to be misunderstood on this. I do not have a Pollyanna view of human nature. I am quite aware that out of defensiveness and inner fear individuals can and do behave in ways which are incredibly cruel, horribly destructive, immature, regressive, antisocial, hurtful. Yet one of the most refreshing and invigorating parts of my experience is to work with such individuals and to discover the strongly positive directional tendencies which exist in them, as in all of us, at the deepest levels.

Let me bring this long list to a close with one final learning which can be stated very briefly. *Life, at its best, is a flowing, changing process in which nothing is fixed.* In my clients and in myself I find that when life is richest and most rewarding, it is a flowing process. To experience this is both fascinating and a little frightening. I find I am at my best when I can let the flow of my experience carry me, in a direction which appears to be forward, toward goals of which I am but dimly aware. In thus floating with the complex stream of my experiencing, and in trying to understand its ever-changing complexity, it should be evident that there are no fixed points. When I am thus able to be in process, it is clear that there can be no closed system of beliefs, no unchanging set of principles which I hold. Life is guided by a changing understanding of and interpretation of my experience. It is always in process of becoming.

I trust it is clear now why there is no philosophy or belief or set of principles which I could encourage or persuade others to have or hold. I can only try to live by *my* interpretation of the current meaning of *my* experience, and try to give others the permission and freedom to develop their own inward freedom and thus their own meaningful interpretation of their own experience.

If there is such a thing as truth, this free individual process of search should, I believe, converge toward it. And in a limited way, this is also what I seem to have experienced.

2

My Own Marriage

I would like to tell you something of the marriage in which I have, as of this writing, been involved for over forty-seven years! To some of you it may seem unbelievably square, but I cannot agree. Helen and I often marvel, however, at how enriching our life together still is and we wonder how and why we have been so fortunate. I can't answer those questions, but I would like to give you something of the history of our marriage, as objectively as I can. Perhaps you can gain something from the account.

We lived within a block of each other in a Chicago suburb during most of our grammar school days. There were others who were often part of the group too, though she had more friends than I did. I moved away when I was thirteen, and I do not remember any special pangs at being away from her, nor did we communicate.

When I went to college, I was surprised to find that she had chosen the same university, though her interests were entirely different. She was my first date in college, largely because I was too shy to date a stranger. But as I dated other girls, I came to appreciate her many qualities which appealed to me — her gentleness, her straightforwardness, her thoughtfulness — not a brilliant academic glow, but the willingness to think openly about real issues, while I was more caught up in the desire to appear scholarly. I can remember being ashamed of her sometimes in

Becoming Partners: Marriage and Its Alternatives. New York: Delacorte Press, 1972, 21–29.

social groups because she seemed lacking in general and academic information.

Our friendship deepened. We went on hikes and picnics on which I was able to introduce her to the world of nature, which I loved. She taught me to dance and even sometimes to enjoy social events. I became more and more serious in my feelings for her. She liked me, but was not at all sure she wanted to marry me. Then, due to several circumstances, I was out of college for a year but kept writing her more and more passionate letters. When I returned, she had left college to take a job as a commercial artist in Chicago, so we were still separated most of the time. But at last she said yes. The night she told me she was now sure that she loved me and would marry me, I had to spend the rest of the night riding on a dirty, bumpy train to get back to my college classes, but I couldn't have cared less. I was in seventh heaven, walking on clouds. "She *loves* me! She loves *me*!" It was a peak experience I can never forget.

There were still twenty-two months of separation before we were married, and the correspondence was heavy. (Today it would have been phone calls.) I was fortunate in developing a business during my last two years of college which brought in a surprising amount of money, enough to get married on before starting graduate school.

Our parents approved the match, but not the marriage. To marry before completing one's education! How would I support her? Unheard of! Nevertheless, we were married (at age twenty-two) and went off to graduate school together. As we look back on it, we realize it was one of the wisest decisions we ever made.

We were both sexually inexperienced, extremely naive (though we thought ourselves very sophisticated); yet for months we lived in a joyous romantic haze, having moved a thousand miles from our families (a great idea!), finding the world's smallest apartment in New York, furnishing it to suit us, and loving each other mightily.

Because we had chosen to go to New York together, we could *grow* together. Helen took some of the courses I was taking. I learned from her art work. We discussed the books and shows we indulged in on next to no money. We both changed incredibly in our attitudes toward religion, politics, and all the issues of the day. She worked part-time jobs, I had a regular weekend job, but still we were together a great deal of the time, learning to share ideas, interests, feelings — in all but one area.

I became very dimly aware that though our sexual relationship was great for me, it was not that great for her. I realize, though, how little I understood the deeper meaning of her phrases: "Oh, not tonight"; "I'm too tired"; "Let's wait till some other time." There is no doubt the situation could have led to a crisis.

At this point sheer luck gave us a break, though like most good luck, it needed to be used. In my graduate school I learned that a psychiatrist, Dr. G. V. Hamilton, needed a few more young married men to complete a research study he was engaged in. Probably there was some pay involved, which would account for my snatching the opportunity so promptly. (Actually the study was a more personalized forerunner of the Kinsey researches, and very well done, though never widely known.) I went to Dr. Hamilton's office for two or three lengthy interviews. He questioned so calmly and easily about every aspect of my sexual development and life that I gradually found myself talking with almost equal ease. One thing I came to realize was that I just didn't *know* whether my wife had ever had an orgasm. She often seemed to enjoy our relationship, so I *assumed* I knew the answer. But the most important thing I learned was that the things in one's private life which cannot *possibly* be talked about *can* be talked about, easily and freely.

So then came the question, Could I translate this into my personal life? I began the frightening process of talking — *really* talking — with Helen about our sexual relationship. It was frightening because every question and every answer made one or the other of us so vulnerable — to attack, to criticism, to ridicule, to rejection. But we weathered it! Each learned to understand much more deeply the other's desires, taboos, satisfactions, and dissatisfactions in our sexual life. And while at first it led only to greater tenderness, and understanding, and improvement, gradually it led not only to orgasms for her, but to a full, continuing, satisfying, and enriching sexual relationship — in which we could talk out new difficulties as they arose.

That was terribly important to us and undoubtedly saved us from deep estrangements which might have split us asunder.

But the even more important thing was that we seem to have realized that the thing which cannot *possibly* be revealed to the other *can* be revealed, the problem which you *must keep* to yourself can be shared. While many times we have temporarily lost this learning, it has always returned in periods of crisis.

I certainly will not try to recount all of our marriage experience. There have been periods of greater remoteness from each other, and periods of great closeness. There have been periods of real stress, squabbles, annoyance, and suffering—though we are not the kind who fight—and periods of enormous love and supportiveness. And we have always continued to share. Neither has become so involved in his own life and activity that he has had no time for sharing with the other.

There is one annoying behavior which we have both exhibited at times, though I much more than Helen. When one spouse, in a social or public situation, ridicules or humiliates or puts down the other, almost always as a "joke," trouble is brewing. It must be a mark of my defensiveness that I can't think of a simple specific example of my own behavior, so I will use one from another couple recently in our home. We were speaking of drinking when he said, "facetiously," "Of course, my wife drinks too much." She flared up because she felt it was untrue and she resented being criticized in public. His reply was, "Oh, I was just joking." This is the kind of behavior in which I too have indulged, but Helen definitely calls me on it when we get home. I have come to see it for what it is—a cowardly cop-out. If I have some negative feeling about something she has done, I would much prefer to take the more courageous step of voicing it to her when we are alone, rather than "jokingly" needling her in a social situation. In similar fashion I learned, early in our marriage, that the sarcasm which was so much a part of my family life, where we were continually throwing verbal barbs at one another, was something which hurt her deeply and which she would not tolerate. I have learned much from her (and she from me).

One point on which we have never fully agreed is whether there is an element of possessiveness in a good marriage. I say no. She says yes. I formed a real attachment to another woman, an attachment which to my mind did not exclude Helen, but was *in addition* to my love for her. She did not see it the same way *at all* and was very upset. It was not so much jealousy as it was a deep anger at me, which she turned inward, feeling that she was "on the shelf" and inadequate. Here I am grateful that our grown-up daughter helped Helen to recognize her true feelings and reestablish communication between us. When we were able to share our real feelings, a resolution became possible, and Helen and I both remain good friends of the woman who was such a threat to her. Incidentally, each of us, on a number of important occasions, has been deeply helped by our son or daughter, and this is a priceless experience.

I think each of us has stood by the other very well in periods of individual pain or torment. I would like to give two examples of the way she has stood by me, and one in which I know she feels that I stood by her.

The first I will mention is that during my forties there was a period of nearly a year when I felt absolutely no sexual desire — for anyone. No medical cause was found. Helen was confident that my normal urges would return and simply stood with me in my predicament. It is easy to think up possible psychological causes, but none of them clicks as far as I'm concerned. It remains a mystery to me. But her quiet, continuing love meant a great deal to me and probably was the best therapy I could have had. At any rate, I gradually became sexually normal once more.

A more serious crisis built around an incredibly lengthy, poorly handled therapeutic relationship which I had with a severely schizophrenic girl. The story is a long one, but suffice it to say that partly because I was so determined to help her, I got to the point where I could not separate my "self" from hers. I literally lost my self, lost the boundaries of myself. The efforts of colleagues to help me were of no avail and I became convinced (and I think with some reason) that I was going insane.

One morning after an hour or so at the office I simply panicked. I walked home and told Helen, "I've *got* to get out of here! Far away!" She of course knew something of what I had been going through, but her reply was balm to my soul. She said, "Okay, let's go right now." After a few phone calls to staff members to ask them to take over my responsibilities, and some hasty packing, we were on the road inside of two hours and didn't return for more than six weeks. I had my ups and downs, and when I returned I went into therapy with one of my colleagues, gaining great help. But my point here is that throughout this whole period Helen was certain this state of mind would pass away, that I was not insane, and showed in every way how much she cared. Wow! That's the only way I can express my gratitude. That's what I mean when I say she has stood by me in critical periods. I have tried to do the same when she has been suffering one or another kind of torment.

Helen's mother suffered several strokes as she grew older. This had the unfortunate (but not rare) effect of markedly changing her personality. Where she had been a warm and kindly person with strong intellectual interests, she became a carping, suspicious, sometimes viciously hurtful person. This was terribly hard on her daughters, but particularly on Helen, who would feel terribly crushed and hurt by the psychological jabs which came from a mother with whom she had been very close. Her mother became impossible to live with and could not live alone. Then came hard decisions—to take her from her apartment; to place her in a nursing home (the best of which are forlorn places); to face the fact that she was no longer the person she had been. Helen felt terribly guilty about what she was doing to her mother, and her mother retained enough shrewdness to know how to intensify that guilt. Through six long and very trying years I believe I stood by Helen. She could not help but feel hurt, guilty, and upset by her twice-weekly visits to her mother. I could let her have those feelings, but also let her know that I thought the accusations false and the decisions sound, and that I believed she was doing the best anyone could in a most distressing and complex situation. I know that she was strengthened and helped by my standing by. Our physician son also greatly helped her to understand the physical and psychological deterioration which had taken place, and that her mother's complaints were not to be taken at face value.

As I look back over the many years of our life together, there are certain elements which appear important to me, though naturally I cannot be objective.

We came from the same community, with similar backgrounds and values.

We complemented each other. Someone has suggested that

of the many types of marriage, two exist at opposite ends of a continuum. One is the "geared" marriage in which each partner supplements the deficiencies of the other and they mesh comfortably, sometimes too placidly. The other is the conflictual marriage, in which the success of the marriage depends on the fact that the couple is continually endeavoring to work out constructively the many conflicts which would otherwise destroy the marriage. Ours is somewhere in the middle of this continuum, but slightly closer to the "geared" marriage. I tend to be a shy loner; Helen is more naturally and comfortably social. I tend to persevere at what I'm doing; she is the one to say, "Why don't we do this or that?" "Why don't we take a trip?" I grudgingly agree, but once under way I'm the more adventurous and childish and she is more steady. I've been a therapist, with an interest in research; she has been an artist and a lifelong worker in the planned-parenthood movement. Each of us has had the opportunity to learn much from the other's fields of interest. We have also been able to deal constructively with most of our conflicts and differences.

Consequently, each of us has always had a *separate* life and interest, as well as our life together. So we have never competed directly. When we have come close to it, it has been uncomfortable. When I took up painting for a time and did one or two passably good paintings, it made her uneasy. When I see her being far more helpful to a person than I could be, I confess my reaction is, "Oh my God! She's better than I am!" But these envies and this competitiveness have rarely been important.

In another area we are astonishingly noncompetitive, and this is in our taste. From the early years of our marriage we have found that if we are selecting a piece of furniture, a car, a gift, or even an item of clothing, we tend to choose the same thing. Sometimes I will say, "Okay, I've made up my mind; let me know when you've made your choice." When she does, it is, with astonishing frequency, the same selection I have made. I don't account for this. I just state it.

She was an excellent parent when the children were young. I would rate myself only fair as a father then—curiously enough, in those days I was more concerned with whether they were disturbing me than with whether what they were doing was in the direction of promoting their own growth. As our two children became older I could communicate with them fully as well as and sometimes better than she.

Perhaps that's enough to indicate some of the many ways we supplement each other. But these balances shift: where I always used to be the better read of us, in recent years, as more and more demands have been made on my time, she is better read and I rely on her to keep me informed of much that is going on.

We have been through periods of sickness and operations, but never at the same time, so each has been able to see the other through the difficult period. In general, though the troubles of older years occasionally assail us, we have retained fundamentally good health.

David Frost gave a definition of love on TV which went something like this: "Love is when each person is more concerned for the other than he is for himself." I think this description fits all the best moments of our marriage. I realize that this can also be a disastrous definition of love, when it means that one or the other gives up his self out of consideration for the other. This has not been true in our case.

I suppose the most profound statement I could make about our marriage—and I can't explain it adequately—is that each has always been willing and eager for the other to *grow*. We have *grown* as individuals and in the process we have grown together.

One final paragraph about our present state, as we have reached the biblical "threescore and ten." We have so much of shared living and suffering and struggle and joy that we also fulfill Truman Capote's definition of love: "Love is when you don't have to finish the sentence." In the middle of some event or scene Helen may say to me, "Do you remember when we . . . ?" and I say, "Of course," and we both laugh together because we know we are both thinking of the same experience. And while our sex life is not quite the same as in our twenties or thirties, our physical closeness, our "snuggling," and our sex relationships are somewhat like a chord which is beautiful not only in itself, but also for its many, many overtones which enrich it far beyond the simple chord. In short, we are incredibly fortunate though at times we have had to work very hard to preserve that good fortune.

Lest you think that this makes everything rosy, I should add that our two children have had their full share of marital difficulties. So our growth together into a satisfying relationship for ourselves has constituted no guarantee for our children.

3
Growing Old: Or Older and Growing

What is it like to be seventy-five years old? It is not the same as being fifty-five years old, or thirty-five, and yet, for me, the differences are not so great as you might imagine. I'm not sure whether my story will be of any use or significance to anyone else, because I have been so uniquely fortunate. It is mostly for myself that I am going to set down a few perceptions and reactions. I have chosen to limit myself to the decade from age sixty-five to seventy-five, because sixty-five marks, for many people, the end of a productive life and the beginning of "retirement," whatever that means!

THE PHYSICAL SIDE

I do feel physical deterioration. I notice it in many ways. Ten years ago I greatly enjoyed throwing a Frisbee. Now my right shoulder is so painfully arthritic that this kind of activity is out of the question. In my garden I realize that a task which would have been easy five years ago, but difficult last year, now seems like too much, and I had better leave it for my once-a-week gardener. This slow deterioration, with various minor disorders of vision, heartbeat, and the like, informs me that the physical portion of what I call "me" is not going to last forever.

Yet I still enjoy a four-mile walk on the beach. I can lift heavy objects, do all the shopping, cooking, and dishwashing when my wife is ill, carry my own luggage without puffing. The female form still seems to me one of the loveliest creations of the universe, and I appreciate it greatly. I feel as sexual in my *interests*

A Way of Being. Boston: Houghton Mifflin, 1980, 70–95.

as I was at thirty-five, though I can't say the same about my ability to perform. I am delighted that I am still sexually alive, even though I can sympathize with the remark of Supreme Court Justice Oliver Wendell Holmes upon leaving a burlesque house at age eighty: "Oh to be seventy again!" Yes, or sixty-five, or sixty!

So, I am well aware that I am obviously old. Yet from the inside I'm still the same person in many ways, neither old nor young. It is that person of whom I will speak.

ACTIVITIES

New Enterprises

In the past decade I have embarked on many new ventures involving psychological or even physical risk. It puzzles me that in most instances my engagement in these enterprises was triggered by a suggestion or a remark made by someone else. This makes me realize that frequently there must be a readiness in me, of which I am not aware, which springs into action only when someone presses the appropriate button. Let me illustrate.

My colleague Bill Coulson, along with a few others, said to me in 1968, "Our group should form a new and separate organization." Out of that suggestion came the Center for Studies of the Person — the zaniest, most improbable, and most influential nonorganization imaginable. Once the idea of the center had been suggested, I was very active in the group that brought it into being; I helped nurture it — and ourselves — during the first difficult years.

A niece of mine, Ruth Cornell, an elementary schoolteacher, asked, "Why is there no book of yours on our reading lists in Education?" This sparked the initial thinking that led to my book *Freedom to Learn.*

I never would have considered trying to influence the status-conscious medical profession had it not been for my colleague Orienne Strode's dream of having a humanizing impact on physicians through intensive group experiences. Skeptical but hopeful, I devoted energy to helping start the program. We ran a great risk of failure. Instead, the program has become widely influential. Nine hundred medical educators have participated in the encounter groups, along with many spouses and some physicians-in-training, who bring in the "worm's-eye view" of medical education. It has been an exciting and rewarding development, now completely independent of any but the most minor assistance from me.

This summer we held our fifth sixteen-day intensive Workshop in the Person-Centered Approach. These workshops have taught me more than any other one venture in the past decade. I have learned and put into practice new ways of being myself. I have learned cognitively and intuitively about the group process and about group-initiated ways of forming a community. These have been tremendous experiences, involving a strong staff which has become a close professional family. We have done more and more risking as we try out new ways of being with a group. And how did I become involved in this large and time-consuming enterprise? Four years ago my daughter, Natalie, said to me, "Why don't we do a workshop together, perhaps around a client-centered approach?" Neither of us could have possibly guessed all that would grow out of that conversation.

My book *Carl Rogers on Personal Power* (1977) likewise found its initial spark in a conversation. Alan Nelson, a graduate student at the time, challenged me on my statement that there was no "politics" in client-centered therapy. This led me into a line of thought that I must have been very ready to pursue, because portions of the book simply wrote themselves.

Foolhardy or Wise?

The most recent and perhaps most risky venture was the trip that I and four other CSP members took to Brazil. In this case, the organizing efforts, the vision, and the persuasiveness of Eduardo Bandeira were the factors that caused me to agree to go. Some people believed the trip would be too long and hard for me at my age, and I had a few of these qualms myself about fifteen-hour plane flights and the like. And some felt it was arrogant to think that our efforts could in any way influence a vast country. But the opportunity to train Brazilian facilitators, most of whom had attended our workshops in the United States, in order that they could put on their own intensive workshops, was very attractive.

Then there was another opportunity. We were to meet audiences of six hundred to eight hundred people in three of Brazil's largest cities. These were two-day institutes, in which we would be together for a total of about twelve hours. Before we left the United States, we agreed that with meetings of such a large size and such a short duration, we would necessarily have to rely on giving talks. Yet, as the time approached, we felt more and more strongly that to talk *about* a person-centered approach, without sharing the control and direction of the sessions, without giving the participants a chance to express themselves and experience their own power, was inconsistent with our principles.

So we took some extremely far-out gambles. In addition to very short talks, we tried leaderless small groups, special-interest groups, a demonstration encounter group, dialogue between staff and audience. But the most daring thing was to form a large circle of eight hundred people (ten to twelve deep) and permit feelings and attitudes to be expressed. Microphones were handed about to those who wished to speak. Participants and staff took part as equals. There was no one person or group exercising leadership. It became a mammoth encounter group. There was much initial chaos, but then people began to listen to one another. There were criticisms — sometimes violent — of the staff and of the process. There were persons who felt they had never learned so much in such a short time. There were the sharpest of differences. After one person blasted the staff for not answering questions, not taking control and giving evidence, the next person said, "But when, if ever, have we all felt so free to criticize, to express ourselves, to say *anything*?" Finally, there was a constructive discussion of what participants would do with their learnings in their back-home situations.

After the first evening in São Paulo, when the session had been extremely chaotic and I was keenly aware that we had but six hours more with the group, I remember refusing to talk with anyone about that meeting. I was experiencing enormous confusion. Either I had helped launch an incredibly stupid experiment doomed to failure, or I had helped to innovate a whole new way of permitting eight hundred people to sense their own potentialities and to participate in forming their own learning experience. There was no way to predict which it would prove to be.

Perhaps the greater the risk, the greater the satisfaction. In São Paulo, the second evening, there was a real sense of community, and persons were experiencing significant changes in themselves. Informal follow-up in the weeks and months since then bear out the worthwhileness of the experience for hundreds of people in each of the three cities.

Never have I felt an extended trip to have been so valuable. I learned a great deal, and there is no doubt that we managed to create a facilitative climate in which all kinds of creative things — at personal, interpersonal, and group levels — happened. I believe we left a mark on Brazil, and certainly Brazil changed all of us. Certainly we have extended our vision of what can be done in very large groups.

So those are some of the activities — all extremely profitable to me — into which I have been drawn during this period.

Risk Taking

In these activities there has been, in each case, an element of risk. Indeed it seems to me that the experiences I value most in my recent life all entail considerable risk. So I should like to pause for a moment and speculate as to the reasons behind my taking of chances.

Why does it appeal to me to try the unknown, to gamble on something new, when I could easily settle for ways of doing things that I know from past experience would work very satisfactorily? I am not sure I undersand fully, but I can see several factors that have made a difference.

The first factor concerns what I think of as my support group, the loose cluster of friends and close associates, most of whom have worked with me in one or another of these endeavors. In the interactions of this group, there is no doubt that we actually or implicitly encourage one another to do the new or daring thing. For example, I am certain that, acting singly, no member of our Brazil group would have gone so far in experimentation as did the five of us working together. We could gamble because if we failed, we had colleagues who believed in us, who could help put the pieces back together. We gave each other courage.

A second element is my affinity for youth, and for the emerging lifestyle that younger people are helping to bring about. I cannot say why I have this affinity, but I know it exists. I have written about "the emerging person" of tomorrow, and I myself am drawn toward this newer way of being and living. I have wondered if I might simply be engaging in wishful thinking in describing such a person. But now I feel confirmed, for I have discovered that the Stanford Research Institute (1973) has completed a study in which it estimates that forty-five million Americans are committed to "a way of living that reflects these inner convictions: first that it is better to have things on a human scale; second that it is better to live frugally, to conserve, recycle, not waste; and third that *the inner life*, rather than externals, is central" (Mitchell, 1977). I belong to that group, and trying to live in this new way is necessarily risky and uncertain.

Another factor: I am bored by safety and sureness. I know that sometimes when I prepare a talk or paper, it is very well received by an audience. This tells me that I could give the talk twenty times to twenty different audiences and I would be assured of a good reception. I simply cannot do this. If I give the same talk three or four times, I become bored with myself. I cannot bear to do it again. I could earn money, I could obtain a positive reaction, but I can't do it. I'm bored by knowing how it will turn out. I'm bored to hear myself saying the same things. It is necessary to my life to try something new.

But perhaps the major reason I am willing to take chances is that I have found that in doing so, whether I succeed or fail, I *learn*. Learning, especially learning from experience, has been a prime element in making my life worthwhile. Such learning helps me to expand. So I continue to risk.

WRITINGS

In thinking about this talk I asked myself, "What have I produced during this past decade? I was utterly astonished at what I found. The list of my publications, which my secretary keeps up to date, tells me that I have turned out four books, some forty shorter pieces, and several films since I turned sixty-five! This is, I believe, more than I have published or produced during any previous decade. I simply cannot believe it!

Furthermore, each of the books is on a distinctively different subject, though they are all tied together by a common philosophy. *Freedom to Learn*, in 1969, concerns my unconventional approach to education. My book on encounter groups, published in 1970, expresses my accumulating learnings on this exciting development. In 1972, *Becoming Partners* was published; this book pictures many of the new patterns in relationships between men and women. And now, *Carl Rogers on Personal Power* explores the emerging politics of a person-centered approach, as applied to many fields.

Of the two-score papers, four stand out in my mind — two of them looking forward, two backward. An article on empathy ("Empathic — An Unappreciated Way of Being") consolidates what I have learned about that extremely important way of being, and I think well of this paper. I also like the freshness of my statement on "Do We Need 'A' Reality?" Then, two other papers reflect upon the development of my philosophy of interpersonal relationships ("My Philosophy of Interpersonal Relationships and How It Grew") and my career as a psychologist ("In Retrospect: Forty-Six Years").

I look on this surge of writing with wonder. What is the explanation? Different persons in their later years have had very individual reasons for their writing. At age eighty, Arnold Toynbee asks himself the question, "What has made me work?" He responds, "*Conscience.* In my attitude toward work I am American-minded, not Australian-minded. To be always working and still at full stretch, has been laid upon me by my conscience as a duty. This enslavement to work for work's sake is, I suppose, irrational, but thinking so would not liberate me. If I slacked, or even just slackened, I should be conscience-stricken and therefore uneasy and unhappy, so this spur seems likely to continue to drive me as long as I have any working power left in me" (Toynbee, 1969). To live such a driven life seems very sad to me. It certainly bears little resemblance to my motivation.

I know that Abraham Maslow, in the years before his death, had a different urge. He experienced a great deal of internal pressure because he felt there was so much he had to say that was still unsaid. This urge to get it all down kept him writing to the end.

My view is quite different. My psychoanalyst friend Paul Bergman wrote that no person has more than one seminal idea in his or her lifetime; all writings by that person are simply further explications of that one theme. I agree. I think this describes my products.

Certainly, one reason for writing is that I have a curious mind. I like to see and explore the implications of ideas — mine and others'. I like to be logical, to pursue the ramifications of a thought. I am deeply involved in the world of feeling, intuition, nonverbal as well as verbal communication, but I also enjoy thinking and writing about that world. Conceptualizing the world clarifies its meaning for me.

Yet there is, I believe, a much more important reason for my writing. It seems to me that I am still — inside — the shy boy who found communication very difficult in interpersonal situations; who wrote love letters which were more eloquent than his direct expressions of love; who expressed himself freely in high school themes, but felt himself too "odd" to say the same things in class. That boy is still very much a part of me. Writing is my way of communicating with a world to which, in a very real sense, I feel I do not quite belong. I wish very much to be understood, but I don't expect to be. Writing is the message I seal in the bottle and cast into the sea. My astonishment is that people on an enormous number of beaches — psychological and geographical — have found the bottles and discovered that the messages speak to them. So I continue to write.

LEARNINGS

Taking Care of Myself

I have always been better at caring for and looking after others than I have in caring for myself. But in these later years I have made progress.

I have always been a very *responsible* person. If someone else is not looking after the details of an enterprise or the persons in a workshop, I must. But I have changed. In our 1976 Workshop on the Person-Centered Approach in Ashland, Oregon, when I was not feeling well, and at the 1977 workshop in Arcozelo, Brazil, I shed all responsibility for the conduct of these complex undertakings and left it completely in the hands of others. I needed to take care of myself. So I let go of all responsibility except the responsibility—and the satisfaction—of being myself. For me it was a most unusual feeling: to be comfortably irresponsible with no feelings of guilt. And, to my surprise, I found I was more effective that way.

I have taken better care of myself physically, in a variety of ways. I have also learned to respect my psychological needs. Three years ago a workshop group helped me to realize how harried and driven I felt by outside demands—"nibbled to death by ducks" was the way one person put it, and the expression captured my feelings exactly. So I did what I have never done before: I spent ten days absolutely alone in a beach cottage which had been offered me, and I refreshed myself immensely. I found I thoroughly enjoyed being with me. I *like* me.

I have been more able to ask for help. I ask others to carry things for me, to do things for me, instead of proving that I can do it myself. I can also ask for personal help. When Helen, my wife, was very ill, and I was close to the breaking point from being on call as a twenty-four-hour nurse, a housekeeper, a professional person in much demand, and a writer, I asked for help—and got it—from a therapist friend. I explored and tried to meet my own needs. I explored the strain that this period was putting on our marriage. I realized that it was necessary for my survival to live *my* life, and that this must come first, even though Helen was so ill. I am not quick to turn to others, but I am much more aware of the fact that I can't handle everything by myself. In these varied ways, I do a better job of prizing and looking after the person that is me.

Serenity?

It is often said or assumed that the older years are years of calm and serenity. I have found this attitude misleading. I believe I do have a longer perspective on events outside of myself, and hence I am often more of an objective observer than I once was. Yet, in contrast to this, events that touch me personally often evoke a stronger reaction than they would have years ago. When I am excited, I get very high. When I am concerned, I am more deeply disturbed. Hurts seem sharper, pain is more intense, tears come more easily, joy reaches higher peaks, even anger—with which I have always had trouble—is felt more keenly. Emotionally, I am more volatile than I used to be. The range from feeling depressed to feeling elated seems greater, and either state is more easily triggered.

Perhaps this volatility is due to my risk-taking style of living. Perhaps it comes from the greater sensitivity acquired in encounter groups. Perhaps it is a characteristic of the older years that has been overlooked. I do not know. I simply know that my feelings are more easily stirred, are sharper. I am more intimately acquainted with them all.

Opening Up to New Ideas

During these years I have been, I think, more open to new ideas. The ones of most importance to me have to do with inner space—the realm of the psychological powers and the psychic capabilities of the human person. In my estimation, this area constitutes the new frontier of knowledge, the cutting edge of discovery. Ten years ago I would not have made such a statement. But reading, experience, and conversation with some who are working in these fields have changed my view. Human beings have potentially available a tremendous range of intuitive powers. We are indeed wiser than our intellects. There is much evidence. We are learning how sadly we have neglected the capacities of the nonrational, creative "metaphoric mind"—the right half of our brain. Biofeedback has shown us that if we let ourselves function in a less conscious, more relaxed way, we can learn at some level to control temperature, heart rate, and all kinds of organic functions. We find that terminal cancer patients, when given an intensive program of meditation and fantasy training focused on overcoming the malignancy, experience a surprising number of remissions.

I am open to even more mysterious phenomena—precognition, thought transference, clairvoyance, human auras, Kirlian photography, even out-of-the-body experiences. These phenomena may not fit with known scientific laws, but perhaps we are on the verge of discovering new types of lawful order. I feel I am learning a great deal in a new area, and I find the experience enjoyable and exciting.

Intimacy

In the past few years, I have found myself opening up to much greater intimacy in relationships. I see this development as definitely the result of workshop experiences. I am more ready to touch and be touched, physically. I do more hugging and kissing of both men and women. I am more aware of the sensuous side of my life. I also realize how much I desire close psychological contact with others. I recognize how much I need to care deeply for another and to receive that kind of caring in return. I can say openly what I have always recognized dimly: that my deep involvement in psychotherapy was a cautious way of meeting this need for intimacy without risking too much of my person. Now I am more willing to be close in other relationships and to risk giving more of myself. I feel as though a whole new depth of capacity for intimacy has been discovered in me. This capacity has brought me much hurt, but an even greater share of joy.

How have these changes affected my behavior? I have developed deeper and more intimate relationships with men; I have been able to share without holding back, trusting the security of the friendship. Only during my college days—never before or after—did I have a group of really trusted, intimate men friends. So this is a new, tentative, adventurous development which seems very rewarding. I also have much more intimate communication with women. There are now a number of women with whom I have platonic but psychologically intimate relationships which have tremendous meaning for me.

With these close friends, men and women, I can share any aspect of my self—the painful, joyful, frightening, crazy, insecure, egotistical, self-deprecating feelings I have. I can share fantasies and dreams. Similarly, my friends share deeply with me. These experiences I find very enriching.

In my marriage of so many years, and in these friendships, I am continuing to learn more in the realm of intimacy. I am becoming more sharply aware of the times when I experience pain, anger, frustration, and rejection, as well as the closeness born of shared meanings or the satisfaction of being understood and accepted. I have learned how hard it is to confront with negative feelings a person about whom I care deeply. I have learned how expectations in a relationship turn very easily into demands made on the relationship. In my experience, I have found that one of the hardest things for me is to care for a person for whatever he or she *is*, at that time, in the relationship. It is so much easier to care for others for what I *think* they are, or *wish* they would be, or feel they *should* be. To care for this person for what he or she is, dropping my own expectations of what I want him or her to be for me, dropping my desire to change this person to suit my needs, is a most difficult but enriching way to a satisfying intimate relationship.

All of this has been a changing part of my life during the past decade. I find myself more open to closeness and to love.

PERSONAL JOYS AND DIFFICULTIES

In this period, I have had some painful and many pleasant experiences. The greatest stress revolves around coping with Helen's illness, which during the past five years has been very serious. She has met her pain and her restricted life with the utmost of courage. Her disabilities have posed new problems for each of us, both physical and psychological — problems that we continue to work through. It has been a very difficult period of alternating despair and hope, with currently much more of the latter.

She is making remarkable progress in fighting her way back, often by sheer force of will, to a more normal life, built around her own purposes. But it has not been easy. She first had to choose whether she wanted to live, whether there was any purpose in living. Then I have baffled and hurt her by the fact of my own independent life. While she was so ill, I felt heavily burdened by our close togetherness, heightened by her need for care. So I determined, for my own survival, to live a life of my own. She is often deeply hurt by this, and by the changing of my values. On her side, she is giving up the old model of being the supportive wife. This change brings her in touch with her anger at me and at society for giving her that socially approved role. On my part, I am angered at any move that would put us back in the old complete togetherness; I stubbornly resist anything that seems like control. So there are more tensions and difficulties in our relationship than ever before, more feelings that we are trying to work through, but there is also more honesty, as we strive to build new ways of being together.

So this period has involved struggle and strain. But it has also contained a wealth of positive experiences. There was our golden wedding celebration three years ago — several days of fun in a resort setting with our two children, our daughter-in-law, and all six of our grandchildren. It is such a joy to us that our son and daughter are now not only our offspring, but two of our best and closest friends, with whom we share our inner lives. There have been numerous intimate visits with them individually, and similar visits with close friends from other parts of the country. There is the continuing and growing closeness with our circle of friends here — all of them younger.

For me there have been the pleasures of gardening and of long walks. There have been honors and awards, more than I believe I deserve. The most touching was the honorary degree I received from Leiden University on the occasion of its four hundredth anniversary, brought to me by a special emissary from this ancient Dutch seat of learning. There have been the dozens of highly personal letters from those whose lives have been touched or changed by my writings. These never cease to amaze me. That I could have had an important part in altering the life of a man in South Africa or a woman in the outback of Australia still seems a bit incredible — like magic, somehow.

THOUGHTS REGARDING DEATH

And then there is the ending of life. It may surprise you that at my age I think very little about death. The current popular interest in it surprises me.

Ten or fifteen years ago I felt quite certain that death was the total end of the person. I still regard that as the most likely prospect; however, it does not seem to me a tragic or awful prospect. I have been able to *live* my life — not to the full, certainly, but with a satisfying degree of fullness — and it seems natural that my life should come to an end. I already have a degree of immortality in other persons. I have sometimes said that, psychologically, I have strong sons and daughters all over the world. Also, I believe that the ideas and the ways of being that I and others have helped to develop will continue, for some time at least. So if I, as an individual, come to a complete and final end, aspects of me will still live on in a variety of growing ways, and that is a pleasant thought.

I think that no one can know whether he or she fears death

until it arrives. Certainly, death is the ultimate leap in the dark, and I think it is highly probable that the apprehension I feel when going under an anesthetic will be duplicated or increased when I face death. Yet I don't experience a really deep fear of this process. So far as I am aware, my fears concerning death relate to its circumstances. I have a dread of any long and painful illness leading to death. I dread the thought of senility or of partial brain damage due to a stroke. My preference would be to die quickly, before it is too late to die with dignity. I think of Winston Churchill. I didn't mourn his death. I mourned the fact that death had not come sooner, when he could have died with the dignity he deserved.

My belief that death is the end has, however, been modified by some of my learnings of the past decade. I am impressed with the accounts by Raymond Moody (1975) of the experience of persons who have been so near death as to be declared dead, but who have come back to life. I am impressed by some of the reports of reincarnation, although reincarnation seems a very dubious blessing indeed. I am interested in the work of Elisabeth Kübler-Ross and the conclusions she has reached about life after death. I find definitely appealing the views of Arthur Koestler that individual consciousness is but a fragment of a cosmic consciousness, the fragment being reabsorbed into the whole upon the death of the individual. I like his analogy of the individual river eventually flowing into the tidal waters of the ocean, dropping its muddy silt as it enters the boundless sea.

So I consider death with, I believe, an openness to the experience. It will be what it will be, and I trust I can accept it as either an end to, or a continuation of, life.

CONCLUSION

I recognize that I have been unusually fortunate in my health, in my marriage, in my family, in my stimulating younger friends, in the unexpectedly adequate income from my books. So I am in no way typical.

But for me, these past ten years have been fascinating — full of adventuresome undertakings. I have been able to open my self to new ideas, new feelings, new experiences, new risks. Increasingly I discover that being alive involves taking a chance, acting on less than certainty, engaging with life.

All of this brings change and for me the process of change *is* life. I realize that if I were stable and steady and static, I would be living death. So I accept confusion and uncertainty and fear and emotional highs and lows because they are the price I willingly pay for a flowing, perplexing, exciting life.

As I consider all the decades of my existence, there is only one other, the period at the Counseling Center at the University of Chicago, which can be compared to this one. It too involved risk, learning, personal growth, and enrichment. But it was also a period of deep personal insecurity and strenuous professional struggle, much more difficult than these past years. So I believe I am being honest when I say that, all in all, this has been the most satisfying decade in my life. I have been increasingly able to be myself and have enjoyed doing just that.

As a boy, I was rather sickly, and my parents have told me that it was predicted I would die young. This prediction has been proven completely wrong in one sense, but has come profoundly true in another sense. I think it is correct that I will never live to be old. So now I agree with the prediction: I believe that I will die *young*.

UPDATE — 1979

I choose to fill out this chapter by concentrating on one very full year — 1979 — in which pain, mourning, change, satisfaction, and risk were all markedly present.

Living the Process of Dying

In the eighteen months prior to my wife's death in March 1979, there were a series of experiences in which Helen and I and a number of friends were all involved, which decidedly changed my thoughts and feelings about dying and the continuation of the human spirit. The experiences were intensely personal, and some day I may write fully about them. For now, I can only hint. The following story is mostly about Helen, but I will concentrate on my portion of the experience.

Helen was a great skeptic about psychic phenomena and immortality. Yet, upon invitation, she and I visited a thoroughly honest medium, who would take no money. There, Helen experienced, and I observed, a "contact" with her deceased sister, involving facts that the medium could not possibly have known. The messages were extraordinarily convincing, and all came through the tipping of a sturdy table, tapping out letters. Later, when the medium came to our home and *my own table* tapped out messages in our living room, I could only be open to an incredible, and certainly nonfraudulent experience.

Helen also had visions and dreams of her family members, which made her increasingly certain that she would be welcomed "on the other side." As death came closer, she "saw" evil figures and the devil by her hospital bed. But when it was suggested by a friend that these might be creations of her own mind, she dismissed them, finally dismissing the devil by telling him he had made a mistake in coming, and she was not going with him. He never reappeared.

Also in these closing days, Helen had visions of an inspiring white light which came close, lifted her from the bed, and then deposited her back on the bed.

In this chapter, I mentioned that in these last years the distance between us had grown increasingly great. I wanted to care for her, but I was not at all sure that I loved her. One day, when she was very near death, I was in an internal frenzy which I could not understand at all. When I went to the hospital as usual to feed her her supper, I found myself pouring out to her how much I had loved her, how much she had meant in my life, how many positive initiatives she had contributed to our long partnership. I felt I had told her all these things before, but that night they had an intensity and sincerity they had not had before. I told her she should not feel obligated to live, that all was well with her family, and that she should feel free to live or die, as *she* wished. I also said I hoped the white light would come again that night.

Evidently I had released her from feeling that she had to live — for others. I later learned that when I left, she called together the nurses on the floor, thanked them for all they had done for her, and told them she was going to die.

By morning she was in a coma, and the following morning

she died very peacefully, with her daughter holding her hand, several friends and I present.

That evening, friends of mine who had a long-standing appointment with the medium previously mentioned held a session with this woman. They were very soon in contact with Helen, who answered many questions: she had heard everything that was said while she was in a coma; she had experienced the white light and spirits coming for her; she was in contact with her family; she had the form of a young woman; her dying had been very peaceful and without pain.

All these experiences, so briefly suggested rather than described, have made me much more open to the possibility of the continuation of the individual human spirit, something I had never before believed possible. These experiences have left me very much interested in all types of paranormal phenomena. They have quite changed my understanding of the process of dying. I now consider it possible that each of us is a continuing spiritual essence lasting over time, and occasionally incarnated in a human body.

That all of these thoughts contrast sharply with some of the closing portions of the chapter, written only two years earlier, is obvious.

Activity and Risk

Perhaps partly in spite of, and partly because of, Helen's death, I have recently accepted more invitations than usual to participate with other staff members in workshops at home and abroad. The list includes a workshop for educators in Venezuela; a large, turbulent workshop near Rome, with an international staff; a brief but deep experience with a Paris program for training group facilitators; a very rewarding regional person-centered workshop on Long Island (the second year with the same eastern staff); a person-centered workshop at Princeton, with many foreign participants; a fascinating workshop in Poland, held at a resort near Warsaw; and a beautifully flowing four-day workshop on "Life Transitions" in Pawling, New York.

I would like to comment on two of the programs mentioned above. The Princeton workshop, consisting of ninety persons, was probably the most difficult for me of any of the workshops in which I have participated. Yet, at least one of the staff feels it was the best such program we have ever conducted. For me, it was very painful, and the group only reached the edge, I felt, of becoming a community.

I perceive a number of factors as having made the workshop a painful experience. The staff had decided that this seventh annual person-centered workshop would be our last in this series; we felt very close to one another, but we were moving in different directions individually and we did not want these person-centered workshops to become a "routine" experience. The staff, from its long experience together, was probably more acceptant of negative, hostile, critical feelings than ever before — and they were expressed in abundance by participants, directed toward one another and toward the staff. There were a large number from foreign countries, and their scorn, contempt, and anger at the United States and at the American participants was freely voiced. There were two persons who knew exactly how the workshop should be conducted. (The two views were very different, but they both were strongly against our unstructured approach, and each attracted quite a following, though not enough to change the general direction of the workshop.) There were also several participants who showed evidence of deep personal disturbance.

When all these factors were added to the usual chaos of a large group trying to develop its own program and find its own way, the result was horrendous. Frustration and anger were very frequently expressed. When some members endeavored to move in creative and positive ways, they were blocked by others. It seemed genuinely uncertain whether the trust placed in these individuals to sense and use their own power constructively would be justified. We were all our own worst enemies. Only toward the end of the ten days did the faint beginnings of a unity in divergence, and a community built on diversity, show themselves. Yet, to my surprise, many participants wrote later to tell of their very positive learnings and changes, which emerged from the pain, the turbulence — and the closeness. I too learned, but it was difficult learning.

The Polish workshop was unusual for a number of reasons. I could hardly believe the degree of interest in my work, which drew together ninety people, both professional and nonprofessional. The Polish staff felt insecure, so the facilitation came largely from the four Americans who were present. This was a disappointment at the time, because I had hoped for more Polish leadership. In the middle of the week-long session, as individuals sensed their power and began to use it, many, especially the professionals, used it to hurt others. Hurtful labels and diagnoses, skillful put-downs, became quite prominent. To me, it resembled Princeton, and I thought, "Oh, no! Not again!" But largely due to a beautifully honest Polish woman, a staff member, people began to be aware of the consequences of such behavior, and it dropped away. By the end of the week, we were a close and loving community.

I was unaware of the full measure of what had occurred until I received a letter from a participant some months later, from which I quote: "People here talk of the 'historic event' that took place in Leskarzev — so many diverse people, so many professionals, psychiatrists and psychologists (each of them possessing the ultimate truth about the helping relationship), hating and putting each other down constantly on an everyday basis — all of them now integrated, and yes, without losing their own personality, without any imposing." I am happy that I did not know in advance of the professional rivalry and backbiting.

I found the group as a whole to be very sophisticated, intelligent, and often more scholarly than a similar American group. Although they lived in a Socialist country, their problems, feelings, ways of coping, and their desire for openness and integrity seemed very similar to what I have found in every land.

Personal Matters

As the year drew to a close, I was increasingly aware of my capacity for love, my sensuality, my sexuality. I have found myself fortunate in discovering and building relationships in which these needs can find expression. There has been pain and hurt, but also joy and depth.

The year was capped on January 8, 1980, when a large group of friends came to my home, bringing food, drink, songs, and surprises to celebrate my seventy-eighth birthday. It was a wild, wonderful, hilarious party — full of love, caring, fellowship, and happiness — which I will never forget.

So I still feel I fit the second part of the title of this chapter. I sense myself as older and growing.

REFERENCES

Mitchell, A. Quoted in *Los Angeles Times*, February 28, 1977.

Moody, R. A., Jr. *Life after life*. New York: Bantam Books, 1975.

Stanford Research Institute. *Changing images of man*. Policy Research Report No. 3. Menlo Park, California, 1973.

Toynbee, A. Why and how I work. *Saturday Review*, April 5, 1969, p. 22.

4
On Reaching 85

By the time this is in print, I will have passed my eighty-fifth birthday. Though I care very little for the external celebration of this occasion, I do have some personal thoughts about what it means to me to be eighty-five. For the most part I feel incredibly fortunate, so these notes will be in the nature of a private thanksgiving.

I am in good health and have plenty of energy. I feel truly blessed in this respect. My poor vision is my only major physical flaw. Reading, always a central part of my life, is now difficult and laborious. But to have only one serious deficiency, at this age, is something for which I am grateful.

I have a circle of close and supportive friends, and I am glad that included in that circle are my son and daughter. This psychological "home base" is very important to me.

I feel deeply privileged to have lived long enough to see the international influence of my work. Two documents arriving yesterday constitute a small sample. One mentions finding 165 published papers on the person-centered group approach between 1970 and 1986. The shocker is that these 165 articles are those written and published in *Japan*! The other letter tells of a large conference in Brazil devoted to the client-centered/person-

Person-Centered Review, Vol. 2, No. 2, May 1987, 150–152. Reprinted by permission of Sage Publications, Inc.

centered approach. And I could mention Italy and West Germany and Great Britain and Australia and Mexico and Switzerland and Austria and Hungary and Greece — and the list goes on and on, of countries where there is significant and ongoing work in the person-centered approach.

The most recent and perhaps the most exciting addition to that list is Russia. I have recently returned from two intensive workshops and a number of large public meetings in the Soviet Union. I could scarcely believe the extensive knowledge of my work that I found there. The impact we had on Soviet psychologists was profound. I say that with some assurance, because many members of the Moscow workshop spoke publicly of their experience, two days after the workshop, to a most prestigious Scientific Council. To hear them tell others of the personal and professional changes resulting from the workshop was for me a magnificent reward.

I have been fortunate beyond words to have been deeply and personally involved in three of the world's "hottest" areas of tension — Northern Ireland, Central America, and South Africa. It was years ago that I helped to facilitate a group from Belfast containing militant Protestants, militant Catholics, and English. We learned that even these ancient feuds could be greatly softened in a brief intensive group.

In 1985 I was the leading facilitator of a group of policymakers and shapers of public opinion from Central America. Participants came from Costa Rica, Honduras, Nicaragua, El Salvador, Colombia, Venezuela, Mexico, the United States, and nine other interested countries. It was a new, challenging, and difficult experience, dealing with government leaders, ambassadors, legislators, authors — many of whom came with little knowledge of or interest in the psychological aspects of tension reduction or mutual dialogue. We learned enormously.

In 1986 a colleague and I facilitated intensive groups — equal numbers of black and white participants — in South Africa. Never have I experienced such depths of rage, bitterness, and pain (on the part of the blacks), or such fear and guilt and prejudice (on the part of the whites). The best evidence of the outcome is the urgent invitation to return again in 1987.

I do not believe I deceive myself as to the significance of these efforts. Certainly we had no obvious influence on the total situation in any of these countries. But I derive much satisfaction from knowing that, on a small scale, we were able to demonstrate, in each of these tension-filled groups, that meaningful dialogue could be established, that conflicts could be reduced, that a more realistic mutual understanding could emerge. We worked only on a test-tube scale, but we showed what was possible. Now the question is whether there is the social will to multiply these efforts.

From a personal point of view, I look with surprised satisfaction on the fact that I have been able to participate in dealing with such crucial conflicts. I could never have dreamed of such events at age sixty-five! I also feel grateful to the multitude of persons who made these ventures possible. In each case I have been on the visible tip of the iceberg, while the unsung efforts of countless individuals have made the events possible.

I view another portion of my life with astonishment and a sense of awe. I am forced to realize that, through my writings, I am in personal touch with many hundreds of thousands of people! Translated into more than a dozen languages, my written words have touched the hearts and minds and lives of more persons than I can imagine. My surprise is deepened by the knowledge that almost all of my books and articles were written because there was something I wanted to say. The current method of writing "for the market" is foreign to me. So it is doubly surprising that my work has spread so far. To know that I have touched the life of a man in Egypt, a woman in the Australian outback, a student in the Soviet Republic of Georgia, is most rewarding.

I hope it is clear that my life at eighty-five is better than anything I could have planned, dreamed of, or expected. And I cannot close without at least mentioning the love relationships that nurture me, enrich my being, and invigorate my life. I do not know when I will die, but I do know that I will have lived a full and exciting eighty-five years!

THE THERAPEUTIC
RELATIONSHIP

No single volume did more to influence the practice of counseling and psychotherapy in the United States than Carl Rogers's *Counseling and Psychotherapy*, published in 1942. Because of the importance of this work, three chapters are included here.

Ironically, it was not a new method of therapy that this work introduced. Others had been advocating less directive, less interpretive approaches for the counseling field, and Rogers acknowledged their contribution. What he did do was, first, synthesize what a number of these practitioners were discovering and translate this synthesis into a clear description of the therapeutic process, which he called "A Newer Psychotherapy."

Then, in "The Directive Versus the Nondirective Approach," he drew the battle lines. (*Versus* is an unusually strong term for academic writing.) In this article Rogers contrasted the specific behavior of "directive" as opposed to "nondirective" counselors in a much more detailed fashion than had yet been attempted. Although it was only the beginning of his research on therapists' behavior, it served to call the attention of the entire profession to what counselors and therapists actually do when their office doors close. What therapists, reading that "the directive counselors used on the average almost six times as many words as the nondirective," would not be forced to question how much they actually talk in their own sessions?

Still, aside from the case Rogers was building for a more nondirective approach, *Counseling and Psychotherapy* would not have been nearly as important a work had it not included "The Case of Herbert Bryan," the first recorded, fully transcribed, and published psychotherapy case in history. The first interview of that eight-session case is included here, just as Rogers presented it, with every word spoken by the client (or "subject," abbreviated "S") and the counselor ("C," Rogers himself), along with Rogers's running commentary on the interview.

The book also popularized the use of the word *client* in lieu of *patient*, which previously was the typical term used to describe the adult recipient of counseling or therapy. The new term suggested a new way of regarding the person coming for help and, therefore, a new way of viewing the therapist-client relationship. Rogers was implicitly suggesting that counseling or the therapeutic process could be employed by helpers in many professions, not only medically trained psychiatrists or psychoanalysts. With this book, Rogers became the conscience of thousands of counselors and therapists across the country. By being so clear, so extreme, and so vivid in his presentation of the "newer counseling viewpoint," he forced the profession to examine itself more closely than ever before. Whether they agreed with Rogers or not, his colleagues found themselves weighing their behavior against his standards.

Yet it was not long before Rogers began to recognize some of the limitations of his own work. He came to believe that the nondirective approach overemphasized specific counselor *techniques*, and did not give enough attention to the counselor's *attitudes* toward the client and how the client perceived the relationship. Gradually, he came to believe that the quality of the relationship—specifically the therapist's congruence (genuineness), unconditional positive regard (prizing, acceptance, trust), and empathy (understanding from the client's viewpoint)—were more important factors in therapeutic change than the specific techniques the therapist employed. In one of his most famous articles, presented here, he catalogues "The Characteristics of a Helping Relationship."

For still another thirty years Rogers studied, subtly refined, and advocated the client-centered or person-centered approach to therapy and all human relationships. Finally, in "A Client-centered/Person-centered Approach to Therapy," a 1986 article, he not only summarizes the essential client-centered viewpoint, but suggests some new elements in the relationship—an intuitive, even spiritual dimension—which he had begun to explore more fully at the time of his death. The article shows Rogers conducting a counseling session with a woman in South Africa. While the depth of his empathy increased over the years and is powerfully present in this interview, the similarities between his approach here and that of a half century earlier with Herbert Bryan are unmistakable. For him, a relatively nondirective approach to therapy remained the most genuine and effective way he knew to communicate the realness, prizing, and understanding essential to therapeutic growth.

We have combined and included two short, later pieces that illustrate his lifelong interest in elucidating the therapeutic relationship. Not only do "Reflection of Feelings" and "Transference" shed further light on important aspects of therapy; they also show Carl Rogers in his last years still keenly engaged intellectually with advancing the subtle nuances of client-centered theory and practice.

5
A Newer Psychotherapy

CHARACTERISTIC STEPS IN THE THERAPEUTIC PROCESS

There is nothing so difficult to put into words as a point of view. Let us turn to the process of therapy. What happens? What goes on during a period of contacts? What does the counselor do? The client? The sections which follow attempt to state, briefly and in somewhat oversimplified form, the different steps in the process, as the writer has seen them occur many times, and to illustrate them with excerpts from clinical records. Although these different aspects of therapy are described separately and placed in a specific order, it should be emphasized that they are not discrete events. The processes mingle and shade into one another. They occur only approximately in the order given here.

Counseling and Psychotherapy. Boston: Houghton Mifflin, 1942, 30–45.

1. The individual comes for help. Rightly recognized, this is one of the most significant steps in therapy. The individual has, as it were, taken himself in hand, and taken a responsible action of the first importance. He may wish to deny that this is an independent action. But if it is nurtured, it can lead directly toward therapy. It may as well be mentioned here that events insignificant in themselves often provide in therapy just as satisfactory a ground for self-understanding, for responsible action, as more important occasions. This may be made clear by an example from the record of Arthur, a boy who had been sent into a remedial course (Psychology 411) which automatically exposed him to counseling. Within the first three minutes of the first interview this exchange took place (phonographic recording):

C. I don't think that I know very much how you happened to come in — I mean, I don't know whether someone suggested you come to see me or whether you had some things on your mind that you were disturbed about and wanted some help with.

S. I talked with Miss G. at the Arts office and she suggested that I take the course. Then my instructor told me I would see you, so I came.

C. That's how you came to take the course, because it was suggested to you.

S. Mm-hm.

C. So I suppose that's why you came in to see me, too. I mean that—

S. Yeah.

C. Well, now, one thing that I think I'd like to have straight at the outset is this; if there is anything that I can do to help you work through some of the things that may be bothering you, I'll be very glad to do so. And on the other hand, I don't want you to think that you have to come to see me, or that it is part of what you must do for the course, or anything of that kind. Sometimes a person has difficulty with their school work or sometimes with other things. They can work it through better if they talk it over with someone else and try to get at the bottom of it, but I think that should be up to them, and I just want to make it plain at the very start that if you wish to see me, perhaps I can save this time once a week and you can come in and talk things over—but you don't have to. Now, I don't know—you might tell me a little bit more about how you happened to take 411—I believe because Miss G. suggested it to you.

S. Yes, Miss G. suggested it to me. She didn't think my study habits were good. If they were good, they didn't seem to be very beneficial on my grades and everything. So she thought that maybe if I'd get in this, I'd learn better study habits and make better use of time and concentration, and so forth.

C. So that—your purpose in taking it is to satisfy Miss G.

S. That's right. No, it isn't that. It's for my own improvement.

C. I see.

S. Dust off my study methods and habits and better use of time and how to concentrate.

C. Mm-hm.

S. I'm just taking—She suggested it to me and I'm taking it for my own benefit.

C. I see. So that you got into it partly because she suggested it, but part of it was your own desire to get into something like that, is that it?

S. I thought I needed it, so I signed up. (*Laughs.*)

C. Well, now, I'm more interested in why you thought you needed it than why Miss G. thought you needed it. Why did *you* think you needed it?

Note in this opening of the first interview the complete dependence of the student in his initial statements. He takes no responsibility for taking the course or for coming to the counselor. When this attitude is recognized and clarified, he gradually veers over to a statement in which the responsibility is shared ("She suggested it to me and I'm taking it for my own benefit"), and finally takes full responsibility for his actions ("I thought I needed it, so I signed up"). It is difficult to overemphasize the difference this makes in counseling. If it is implicit that the counselor or some third person is responsible for the student's being present in the counseling situation, then suggestion or advice are almost the only avenues of approach open. If the client himself accepts responsibility for bringing himself, he also accepts the responsibility for working upon his problems.

2. The helping situation is usually defined. From the first the client is made aware of the fact that the counselor does not have the answers, but that the counseling situation does provide a place where the client can, with assistance, work out his own solutions to his problems. Sometimes this is done in rather general terms, while in other instances the situation is most plainly defined in terms of concrete issues, such as responsibility for appointments, or responsibility for steps to be taken and decisions to be made.

In the interview with Arthur, quoted above, we find an example of one way in which the situation is defined by the counselor, when it is explained that Arthur is under no compulsion, but may make use of the situation if he wishes. Obviously this type of intellectual explanation is not enough. The whole conduct of the interviews must reinforce this idea until the client feels that it is a situation in which he is free to work out the solutions that he needs.

Another example may be given from a first interview with a mother, Mrs. L. (from whose record there will be further quotations later on). This mother and her ten-year-old son had come to the clinic because of the mother's vehement complaints about the son. After two diagnostic contacts the situation was put up to the mother as a difficulty in their relationships, and she was asked whether she and her boy would like to work through this problem. She had tentatively and somewhat fearfully agreed, and she came in for the first contact with the psychologist who was to act as therapist. Here is the counselor's account (not phonographic) of a portion of this first treatment interview.

> As it was nearing the end of the hour, and I wanted to get something toward the settling up of the hour, I said, "How does your husband feel about your coming up here to work the problem through with us?" And she laughed slightly and said, "Well, he's sort of indifferent about it. But he did say something to the effect that he didn't want to be experimented on, or something —didn't want to be treated like white rats."
>
> And I said, "And you feel, too, perhaps, that is what will happen." "Well, I just don't know what will be done." And I assured her that she needn't feel that we were going to do anything at all strange or peculiar; that it would be a matter of her talking things

through with me, and Jim with Mr. A., to see if we could think things through together to see how they both felt about the situation and to think out some of the relationships between them and other members of the family, and get a view of the interrelationships within the family.

At that she said, "Well, perhaps Marjorie, too—maybe there is something a little funny about her. Maybe she is mixed up in it too."

Note that the counselor makes it plain that it is her task to provide a place and an atmosphere in which problems can be thought through and relationships recognized more clearly. She does not imply in any way that it is her responsibility to give the answers. The fact that this is understood by the mother is indicated by the fact that she then feels free to bring in a new aspect of the problem—the sister—and to suggest that she will wish to work on that, too.

Still another example may be given to illustrate how the situation is often defined in terms of actual responsibilities, no matter how minor they may be. In a first counseling interview with a student, some verbal explanations of the situation were given early in the contact, but toward the end of the interview this exchange took place (phonographic recording):

S. I think maybe the next time I come in to see you, it will be something different. Maybe I'll have a little bit better idea what to talk about by then.

C. Would you like to come in next Friday at this time?

S. Yes, it's all right with me.

C. It's up to you.

S. It's up to me?

C. I'm here. I'd be glad to do anything I can do for you.

S. All right, sir, I think I'll be there.

C. All right.

In this brief excerpt, much has happened. The student makes a somewhat independent statement, showing that he plans at least to share the responsibility for the use of the next hour. The counselor encourages this by putting the decision about the appointment up to the student. The student, feeling this is the usual meaningless gesture, leaves the responsibility with the counselor by saying, "Yes, it's all right with me." When the counselor shows that the counseling situation really belongs to the client, the student's surprise is clearly indicated in the phonographic record as he says, "It's up to *me*?" His whole tone changes as he then responds in a firm and decisive manner, "All right, sir, I think I'll be there" — genuinely accepting the responsibility for the first time.

Thus, through words, actions, or both, the client is helped to feel that the counseling hour is his — to use, to take responsibility for, an opportunity freely to be himself. With children words are of less use, and the situation must be defined almost entirely in terms of freedoms and responsibilities, but the underlying dynamics seem much the same.

3. The counselor encourages free expression of feelings in regard to the problem. To some extent this is brought about by the counselor's friendly, interested, receptive attitude. To some extent it is due to improved skill in treatment interviewing. Little by little we have learned to keep from blocking the flow of hostility and anxiety, the feelings of concern and the feelings of guilt, the ambivalences and the indecisions which come out freely if we have succeeded in making the client feel that the hour is truly his, to use as he wishes. I suppose that it is here that counselors have exercised the most imagination and have most rapidly improved their techniques of catharsis. This can be illustrated by brief excerpts from two contacts, one with the mother, Mrs. L., and one with her ten-year-old son, Jim. These are both from the first therapeutic contacts with mother and child.

During this first hour the mother spends a full half-hour telling with feeling example after example of Jim's bad behavior. She tells of his quarrels with his sister, of his refusal to dress, of his annoying manner of humming at the table, of his bad behavior in school, of his failure to help at home, and the like. Each of her comments has been highly critical of the boy. A brief segment toward the end of this tirade is given below (not phonographic).

> I said, "What things have you tried in helping him to do more as you would like?" "Well, last year," she said, "we put him in a special school, and I've tried rewarding him for things, and I've

tried knocking off his allowance for things that he does that he shouldn't do, but by the time the day is over his allowance is practically all used up. I've put him in a room alone and I've ignored him until I've just felt frantic, nearly ready to scream." And I said, "Perhaps sometimes you do actually —" And she said (very quickly), "Yes, sometimes I do actually scream about it. I used to think I had a lot of patience with him, but I don't any more. The other day my sister-in-law came over for a meal and Jim was whistling during dinner. I told him not to, but he kept right on. Finally he did quit. Later my sister-in-law said she would have knocked him right off the chair if he had done that when she told him to quit. But I've found it just doesn't do any good to get after him that way." I said, "You feel that it wouldn't do any good to use as strong measures as she said."

She replied, "No. And his table manners, that's another thing that's terrible. He eats most of the time with his fingers, even though he has a nice sterling silver knife, fork, and spoon of his own. And maybe he will pick up a piece of bread and eat a piece, eat a hole right out of the middle of it, or stick his finger clear down through the whole stack of slices of bread. And wouldn't you think a boy of his age would know better than to do that?" And I said, "That makes you both feel pretty terrible, you and your husband, too."

She replied, "Yes, of course. And sometimes he can be just as good as gold. For instance, yesterday he was good all day, and in the evening he told his daddy that he had been a good boy."

Note the fact that the counselor's sole aim is not to impede this flow of hostile and critical feeling. There is no attempt to persuade the mother that her boy is bright, essentially normal, pathetically eager for affection, though all of that is true. The counselor's whole function at this stage is to encourage free expression.

What this means in terms of a child is best shown by listening in on a portion of Jim's contact with a second psychologist during that same hour. This is Jim's first play-therapy contact. He indulges in some preliminary play and then makes a clay image which he identifies as his father. A great deal of dramatic play with this figure goes on, most of it centered around the struggle of Jim in getting his father out of bed and the father's resistance to this (the reverse of the home situation, as might be guessed).

Jim played both parts in different voices and the following is from the phonographic recording, with *F.* and *J.* inserted to indicate which voice is being used.

> *F.* "I want you to stay and help me." *J.* "I ain't goin' to. I want to make somethin' of it." *F.* "Oh, ya do, do you?" *J.* "Yeah, I want to make somethin' of it!" *F.* "O.K., come on, make somethin' of it!" *J.* "All right you! (*Striking him and knocking head off.*) He won't get back on in a hurry. Huh, I'll take a piece of ya off, that'll fix him. There. I'll make you weak, that'll fix him. Now don't you go to sleep on me again! (*Very short pause.*) Oh, say, what did you do, go to sleep? Hah, hah!" *F.* "I didn't go to sleep." *J.* "Well, you must have done *somethin'*! I'm gettin' tired of your impudence. Get up, get up, get up (*shouting*), come on, dad, get up."

A few moments later he pretends that someone is holding his father up in the air to torture him. His play follows:

> *J.* "Let's git that guy for making his kid hold him all day. (*Short pause.*) They got 'im." *F.* "Hey, let me down." *J.* "Not till you promise to let your boy go for all day." *F.* "No, I won't." *J.* "All right, then, you're going to have to balance up high, see, and you are going to like it, and you'll do it." *F.* "Help, you guys, I'm fallin'. Help!!" (*Short pause as he drops clay and crushes it.*) *J.* "That's all, folks. (*Pause.*) He ain't there. He fell off a cliff in a car."

These two excerpts may make plain how deep and how violent are the feelings spontaneously expressed if the counselor does not block them. The counselor has more than a negative function in this process, perhaps best described as a separate aspect of therapy.

4. The counselor accepts, recognizes, and clarifies these negative feelings. Here is a subtle point which seems to be very difficult for students to grasp. If the counselor is to accept these feelings, he must be prepared to respond, not to the intellectual content of what the person is saying, but to the feeling which underlies it. Sometimes the feelings are deep ambivalences, sometimes they are feelings of hostility, sometimes they are feelings of inadequacy. Whatever they are, the counselor endeavors, by what he says and by what he does, to create an atmosphere in which the client can come to recognize that he has these negative feelings and can accept them as a part of himself, in-

stead of projecting them on others or hiding them behind defense mechanisms. Frequently the counselor verbally clarifies these feelings, not trying to interpret their cause or argue in regard to their utility—simply recognizing that they exist, and that he accepts them. Thus, such phrases as "You feel pretty bitter about this," "You want to correct this fault, but still you don't want to," "What you are saying sounds as though you feel pretty guilty," seem to crop out rather frequently in this type of therapy, and nearly always, if they are accurate portrayals of feeling, allow the individual to go forward in a freer fashion.

Sufficient examples of this type of help have already been given. In the excerpt from the case of Arthur (pages 64–65), almost every statement of the counselor, with the exception of the long explanation, is an attempt to verbalize and clarify the feeling the student has been expressing about coming in. In the first fragment from the case of Mrs. L. (page 66), the counselor makes no attempt to combat the mother's implied fear of being treated "like white rats"; she merely recognizes and accepts that fear. In the second excerpt from this case (pages 68–69), there are further examples of this aspect of therapy. The counselor accepts the mother's frantic feeling, her hopelessness, her annoyance, and her despair without criticism, without argument, without undue sympathy, accepting those feelings merely as a fact, and verbalizing them in somewhat clearer form than the mother has put them. The counselor is, it will be noted, alert to the feeling, not the content, of the mother's complaints. Thus, when the mother wails about Jim's table manners, there is no attempt to respond in terms of table etiquette, but in terms of the mother's obvious feeling about it. Note, however, that the counselor does not go beyond what the mother has already expressed. This is highly important, since real damage can be done by going too far and too fast, and verbalizing attitudes of which the client is not yet conscious. The aim is to accept completely and to recognize those feelings which the client has been able to express.

5. When the individual's negative feelings have been quite fully expressed, they are followed by the faint and tentative expressions of the positive impulses which make for growth. There is nothing which gives more surprise to the student who

is learning this type of therapy for the first time than to find that this positive expression is one of the most certain and predictable aspects of the whole process. The more violent and deep the negative expressions (provided they are accepted and recognized), the more certain are the positive expressions of love, of social impulses, of fundamental self-respect, of desire to be mature.

This is plainly shown in the interview with Mrs. L. (page 69) to which reference has just been made. After all her antagonistic feeling has been fully accepted, it is inevitable that she should slowly work through to the positive feeling which comes out so suddenly in her statement, "And sometimes he can be just as good as gold."

With Jim, her son, it is a longer time before the positive feelings break through. For three contacts (spaced a week apart) he keeps up his aggressive play, torturing, beating, and killing father images and Satan images (sometimes called "dad"). During the latter part of the third hour his dramatic play continues and becomes a dream, then not a dream.

> "No, it wasn't any dream. I meant it. Now that will be a warning to you (*beating the clay image*). Now that will teach you not to be funny with your kids! Then the guy wakes up and finds it is all a dream, and he says, 'It's about time I got out of these dreams.' "
> Then Jim ceased playing with the clay, and wandered about the room a bit. He took a newspaper clipping out of his pocket, showing a picture to the psychologist and saying, "Chamberlain looked like such a nice man, so I cut out his picture and carried it with me."

This was his first statement of positive feeling toward anyone. Following it there was never more than a mild expression of hostility, and the change in the therapeutic situation was roughly paralleled by the change in the home.

6. The counselor accepts and recognizes the positive feelings which are expressed, in the same manner in which he has accepted and recognized the negative feelings. These positive feelings are not accepted with approbation or praise. Moralistic values do not enter into this type of therapy. The positive feelings are accepted as no more and no less a part of the personality than the negative feelings. It is this acceptance of both the mature

and the immature impulses, of the aggressive and the social attitudes, of the guilt feelings and the positive expressions, which gives the individual an opportunity for the first time in his life to understand himself as he is. He has no need to be defensive about his negative feelings. He is given no opportunity to over-value his positive feelings. And in this type of situation, insight and self-understanding come bubbling through spontaneously. Unless one has thus watched insight develop, it is difficult to believe that individuals can recognize themselves and their patterns so effectively.

7. This insight, this understanding of the self and acceptance of the self, is the next important aspect of the whole process. It provides the basis on which the individual can go ahead to new levels of integration. One graduate student says with genuine feeling: "I'm really just a spoiled brat, but I do want to be normal. I wouldn't let anyone else say that of me, but it's true." A husband says: "I know now why I feel mean toward my wife when she's sick, even though I don't want to feel that way. It's because my mother predicted when I married her that I'd always be saddled with a sick wife." A student says, "I see now why I hated that prof — he criticized me just like my dad did." Mrs. L., the mother whose remarks have already been quoted, makes this surprising statement about her relationship with her boy, after she has worked through most of her hostile feelings and some positive feelings during a number of therapeutic contacts. This is the counselor's account:

> One of the things that she brought up was that he seems to want attention, but that the methods he uses get negative attention. After we had talked a little bit about that she said, "Perhaps what would do him most good would be for him to have some affection and love and consideration entirely apart from any correcting. Now, I guess that we've been so busy correcting him that we haven't had time to do anything else." Her expression of that indicated that she really felt that a change of program might do some good. And I said, "That is a very good observation on your part and nobody needs to tell you that that is what you feel really has happened." She said, "No, I know that's what has happened."

8. Intermingled with this process of insight — and it should again be emphasized that the steps outlined are not mutually

exclusive, nor do they proceed in a rigid order—is a process of clarification of possible decisions, possible courses of action. Often this is infused with a somewhat hopeless attitude. Essentially the individual seems to be saying: "This is what I am, and I see that much more clearly. But how can I reorganize myself in any different fashion?" The counselor's function here is to help clarify the different choices which might be made, and to recognize the feeling of fear and the lack of courage to go ahead which the individual is experiencing. It is not his function to urge a certain course of action or to give advice.

9. Then comes one of the fascinating aspects of such therapy, the initiation of minute, but highly significant, positive actions. An extremely withdrawn high-school boy, who has expressed his fear and hatred of others and has also come to recognize his deeply buried desire to have friends, spends a whole hour giving all the reasons why he would be too terrified to accept a social invitation he has had. He even leaves the office saying he will probably not go. He is not urged. It is sympathetically recognized that such action would take a great deal of courage, and that while he wishes he had such fortitude, he may not be able to take such a step. He goes to the party, and is enormously helped in his self-confidence.

To give still another illustration from the record of Mrs. L., the following positive forward step followed immediately the outstanding statement of insight quoted above. Again this is the psychologist's account:

> I said, "Then giving him attention and affection when he is not demanding it in any way would perhaps do him a lot of good." Then she said, "Now you may not believe this, but as old as he is he still believes in Santa Claus, at least he did last year. Of course he may be trying to pull the wool over my eyes, but I don't think so. Last year he was away taller than any of the other kids who went up to talk to Santa in the stores. Now this year I've just *got* to tell him the truth. But I'm so afraid he will tell Marjorie. I was wondering if maybe I could tell him about it and it would be our secret between us. I would let him know that he is a big boy now and mustn't tell Marjorie. That it's *our* secret and he's a big boy and he can help me keep things. And also, if I can get her to go to bed early enough—she's such a little wiggle worm, but

if I can get her to go to bed — perhaps he can help me with some of the Christmas things. And then on Christmas Eve — that's when we have our Christmas — I'll send the other children over to grandmother's house while we get ready and Jim can stay at the house and help me to get the things ready." The way she spoke it seemed that she felt it would be quite a pleasure to have Jim help. (She seemed really more enthuasiastic about it than about anything so far.) So I said, "It will be quite a bit of pleasure, won't it, to think that you have a ten-year-old boy who can help with the Christmas work." With a sparkle in her eyes she replied that it would be fun for him to be able to help her, and that she felt it would do him a lot of good. I replied that I thought so too and that it would certainly be something to try.

One can only comment here that once insight is achieved the actions that are taken are likely to be admirably suited to the new insight. Thus, having achieved better emotional under-standing of the relationship between herself and her boy, Mrs. L. translates that insight into action which shows how much she has gained. Her plan gives Jim her special affection in a very adroit way, helps him to be more mature, avoids making the younger sister jealous — in short, it shows that she can now carry out with genuine motivation the type of behavior which will solve her problem. If such behavior had been suggested to her after the diagnosis of the case, she would almost certainly have rejected the suggestion or carried it out in such a way as to cause it to be a failure. When it grows out of her own insightful drive to be a better, more mature mother, it will be successful.

10. The remaining steps need not hold us long. Once the individual has achieved considerable insight and has fearfully and tentatively attempted some positive actions, the remaining aspects are elements of further growth. There is, first of all, a development of further insight — more complete and accurate self-understanding as the individual gains courage to see more deeply into his own actions.

11. There is increasingly integrated positive action on the part of the client. There is less fear about making choices, and more confidence in self-directed action. The counselor and client are now working together in a new sense. The personal relationship between them is at its strongest. Very often the client wants for

the first time to know something of the clinician as a person and expresses a friendly and genuine interest which is very distinctive. Actions are brought into the discussion for consideration, but there is no longer the dependence and fear which were noticeable earlier. As an example, this excerpt is taken from the record of one of the closing interviews with a mother who has successfully gained insight:

> Mrs. J. says, "I don't know what you have done to us, to Patty and me, but everything's all right. I couldn't have wanted a nicer little girl, I should say for the past three weeks. Oh, yesterday she had sort of an off day. She didn't want to come when I'd call her, that is, not right away. She was a little bit down, but she wasn't ugly. I don't know if I can make you see what I mean, but there's a difference in her naughtiness. It's not as if she, well, is ugly, especially to me." C. responded, "I know what you mean, I think. It is that she doesn't refuse just to hurt you." Mrs. J. nodded and said, "That's it. It's a more natural sort of thing."

As is often true in this type of therapy, certain of the behavior symptoms remain, but the mother has a totally different feeling about them and about her ability to handle them.

12. There is a feeling of decreasing need for help, and a recognition on the part of the client that the relationship must end. Often there are apologies for having taken so much of the counselor's time. The counselor helps to clarify this feeling as he has done before, by accepting and recognizing the fact that the client is now handling his situation with increased assurance and that he will not wish to continue the contacts much longer. As at the first, there is neither compulsion on the client to leave, nor attempt on the part of the counselor to hold the client.

During this aspect of therapy there are likely to be expressions of personal feeling. Often the client makes some such statement as "I shall miss coming; I have enjoyed these contacts so much." The counselor can reciprocate these feelings. There is no doubt that we do become emotionally involved, to a certain healthy extent, when personal growth takes place under our very eyes. A time limit is set for the contacts, and they are brought to a reluctant but healthy close. Sometimes, in the last contact, the client brings up a number of old problems or new ones, as though in a gesture to retain the relationship, but the atmosphere is very different from that in the first contacts, when those problems were real.

These seem to be the essential elements of the therapeutic process as it is being carried on in a variety of organizations and with a variety of problems — with parents and their children, even very young children; in situations demanding marital counseling; in situations of maladjustment and neurotic behavior among students; in situations of difficult vocational choice; in short, in most instances where the individual finds himself facing a serious problem of adjustment.

It will be readily recognized that the analysis given above might be differently organized. In a process with so many subtleties, any attempt to break it down into steps or elements contains much that is subjective and approximate, rather than objective and exact. Yet as a whole the therapy that has been described is an orderly, consistent process — even a predictable process in its major outlines. It is very different from an approach which is diffuse, opportunistic, stressing the notion that "every case is different." It is a process which has sufficient unity to provide suitable hypotheses for experimental tests.

6
The Directive Versus the Nondirective Approach

CHARACTERISTICS OF DIRECTIVE AND NONDIRECTIVE VIEWPOINTS

The difference between these viewpoints in counseling is by no means a theoretical one. In his unpublished thesis, "The Development and Evaluation of a Measure of Counseling Interview Procedures," E. H. Porter[1] had some suggestive data regarding counselors that hold directive and nondirective views. The number of interviews concerned in his various comparisons are small, but the consistency of the results is impressive. Porter asked a group of expert judges to classify all the counselor responses

Counseling and Psychotherapy. Boston: Houghton Mifflin, 1942, 118–128.

and conversations in nineteen phonographically recorded interviews into various categories which will be described later. In addition, he asked the judges to rate each interview according to its directiveness. The instructions to the judges ran: "The value of 11 on the scale represents an interview in which the direction has been furnished entirely by the counselor. The value of 1 represents an interview in which the counselor has refused directly or indirectly to take the responsibility for directing and consequently has forced the client to accept the responsibility for directing the interview. You are not to judge whether the counselor did a good job of directing or of not directing. Rate the interview only on the relative degree of directiveness or nondirectiveness."

When this rating had been completed and the more directive interviews were compared with the less directive, certain differences in pattern were strikingly suggested. By taking Porter's data and regrouping certain of his facts, these differences may be shown in modified tabular form. Of Porter's nineteen interviews, nine were rated rather low in directiveness, with ratings of from 1.5 to 5.6 on an 11-point scale, with an average directiveness score of 3.3. The remaining ten were quite definitely directive, with ratings of 9.3 to 10.8, with an average of 10.2.* Five counselors were represented in the group which was low in directiveness, and six counselors were represented in the high-directiveness group, so that the results were not particularly influenced by the specific practices of any one counselor. In each group there were interviews conducted by both experienced and inexperienced counselors, and interviews from the first, middle, and closing phases of a series, the two groups being roughly equivalent in these respects. If we now examine the data to see whether certain types of counselor response or conversation are characteristic of either group, we find sharp differences. There are eleven categories of response which are much more heavily used by the directive group. There are three categories much

---

*It is probable that this clear dichotomy is atypical of counseling as a whole, though further studies would be necessary to discover how directiveness would distribute itself on a continuum.

more heavily used by the nondirective group, and four categories which are used about equally by both groups.

This material is shown below (Tables 1–3). It should be kept in mind that the whole study was confined to the counselor's part in the interview. There is no classification of client responses. In the tables there appear the descriptive categories as defined by Porter and used by the judges. One of the brief illustrative examples which was used by the judges is given with

(text continues on p. 82)

TABLE 1. COUNSELOR TECHNIQUES CHARACTERISTIC OF THE DIRECTIVE GROUP

	Average No. per Interview	
Item	Directive Group	Nondirective Group
1a.* Counselor defines the interview situation in terms of diagnostic or remedial procedures. *Example.* "I don't know what your trouble is, but we can get at it in part through the tests you take and in part through what we do here in the interview."	1.7	.5
2b. Counselor indicates topic but leaves development to client. *Ex.* "Would you care to tell me a little more about that?"	13.3	6.3
2c. Counselor indicates topic and delimits development to confirmation, negation, or the supplying of specific items of information. *Ex.* "How long ago was it that you took it?" "Here or at home?" "What course was that in?"	34.1	4.6

*The number preceding each item is that used by Porter and shows the order in which they occurred in his sheet for rating interviews. In general, category 1 refers to those techniques related to defining the interview situation; category 2 to those techniques which bring out and develop the problem situation; category 3 to techniques for developing the client's insight and understanding; 4 to techniques of giving information or explanation; 5 to those techniques which sponsor client activity or foster the making of decisions.

Table 1. Counselor Techniques Characteristic of the Directive Group, Continued

| | | Average No. per Interview | |
	Item	*Directive Group*	*Nondirective Group*
3*d*.	Counselor identifies a problem, source of difficulty, condition needing correction, etc., through test interpretations, evaluative remarks, etc. *Ex.* "One of your difficulties is that you haven't had a chance to compare yourself with others."	3.7	.3
3*e*.	Interprets test results, but not as indicating a problem, source of difficulty, etc. *Ex.* "This indicates that 32 percent of college freshmen read the test material more rapidly than you did."	1.2	.1
3*f*.	Expresses approval, disapproval, shock, or other personal reaction in regard to the client. *Ex.* "Good! Grand! That's a nice start."	2.6	.6
4.	Counselor explains, discusses, or gives information related to the problem or treatment. *Ex.* "Well, I don't think that's the only reason. Some people who know a great deal about it get just as nervous as the ones who don't."	20.3	3.9
5*a, b*.	Counselor proposes client activity, directly, or through questioning technique, or in response to question of what to do. *Ex.* "I think that you ought to quit that job and put as much time in on your schoolwork as possible."	10.0	1.3
5*c*.	Counselor influences the making of a decision by marshaling and evaluating evidence, expressing personal opinion, persuading pro or con. *Ex.* "Well, it's up to you, but I'd at least give it a try."	5.2	.3
5*f*.	Counselor reassures the client. *Ex.* "Now you may run across a lot of difficulty, but don't let it discourage you. You'll come out all right."	.9	.2

Table 2. Counselor Techniques Characteristic of the Nondirective Group

	Average No. per Interview	
Item	*Directive Group*	*Nondirective Group*
1*b*. Defines the interview situation in terms of client responsibility for directing the interview, reaching decisions, etc.	.5	1.9
Ex. "And sometimes people find that by talking over their problems with someone else they get a much better picture."		
3*b*. Counselor responds in such a way as to indicate recognition of expression of feeling or attitude in immediately preceding verbal response.	1.2	10.3
Ex. "And that makes you feel pretty low."		
3*c*. Counselor responds in such a way as to interpret or recognize feeling or attitude expressed in some way other than in the immediately preceding response.	.7	9.3
Ex. "Maybe you didn't want to come this morning."		

Table 3. Techniques Common to Both Groups

	Average No. per Interview	
Item	*Directive Group*	*Nondirective Group*
2*a*. Counselor uses lead which forces the choosing and developing of topic upon client.	.6	.6
Ex. "What's on your mind this morning?"		
3*a*. Counselor responds in such a way as to indicate recognition of subject content.	6.1	6.0
Ex. "And that test comes up Tuesday." "Humph! So neither method worked."		
5*d*. Counselor indicates decision is up to client.	.4	.6
Ex. "That's up to you."		
5*e*. Counselor indicates acceptance or approval of decision.	.8	.6
Ex. "I think you're on the right track there."		

each item in order to put more concrete meaning into the definition. The number of each type of counselor remarks per interview for the directive and the nondirective groups is shown in the right-hand columns.

SOME SIGNIFICANT CONTRASTS

Examination of these three tables will bring to light several significant differences between the two therapeutic approaches. In the first place, the more directive counselors are more active in the counseling situation—they do much more of the talking. There are on the average one hundred and seven classifiable items of counselor response per interview in the directive interviews, and only forty-nine in the nondirective interviews. Conversely, of course, the client does much less talking. In an analysis of word count in these interviews, Porter found that the ratio of counselor words to counselee words ranged from .15 to 4.02. In other words, at one extreme the client talked nearly seven times as much as the counselor. At the other extreme the counselor talked four times as much as the client—a statistical example of what it means to try to "get a word in edgeways." If we compare these two extreme counselors, the second talked more than twenty-five times as much as the first.

There was a striking relationship between the ratio of words spoken by counselor and counselee and the degree of directiveness. In the ten directive interviews, the average ratio was 2.77, the counselor talking nearly three times as much as the client. In the nine nondirective interviews the average ratio was .47, the counselor talking less than half as much as the client. It will be noted from these two ratios that the directive counselors used on the average almost six times as many words as the nondirective—one of the sharpest differences found in the whole study. This makes graphic the fact that in nondirective counseling the client comes "to talk out his problems." In a directive contact the counselor talks to the client.

We find in these tables that differences in method center around such techniques as persuading the client, pointing out problems needing correction, interpreting test results, and asking specific questions, all of which are much more characteristic of the directive approach than the nondirective; or around such a technique as recognizing and interpreting the client's verbally expressed feelings or his feelings as expressed in actions, a technique characteristic of the nondirective group. Here again we note the fundamental contrast in emphasis, the directive group stressing those techniques which control the interview and move the client toward a counselor-chosen goal, the nondirective group stressing those means which cause the client to be more conscious of his own attitudes and feelings, with a consequent increase in insight and self-understanding.

Since the comparison in Tables 1, 2, and 3 is somewhat clouded by the fact that the directive counselors are so much more active in the interview, another comparison of the same material will be made by listing in parallel columns in Table 4 the counseling

TABLE 4. TECHNIQUES MOST FREQUENTLY EMPLOYED

(in order of frequency)

Directive Counselor Group	*Nondirective Counselor Group*
1. Asks highly specific questions, delimiting answers to yes, no, or specific information. (34.1)	1. Recognizes in some way the feeling or attitude which the client has just expressed. (10.3)
2. Explains, discusses, or gives information related to the problem or treatment. (20.3)	2. Interprets or recognizes feelings or attitudes expressed by general demeanor, specific behavior, or earlier statements. (9.3)
3. Indicates topic of conversation but leaves development to client. (13.3)	3. Indicates topic of conversation but leaves development to client. (6.3)
4. Proposes client activity. (9.4)	4. Recognizes the subject content of what the client has just said. (6.0)
5. Recognizes the subject content of what the client has just said. (6.1)	5. Asks highly specific questions, delimiting answer to yes, no, or specific information. (4.6)
6. Marshals the evidence and persuades the client to undertake the proposed action. (5.3)	6. Explains, discusses, or gives information related to the problem or treatment. (3.9)
7. Points out a problem or condition needing correction. (3.7)	7. Defines the interview situation in terms of the client's responsibility for using it. (1.9)

techniques most frequently employed by each group, listed in order of frequency. Only the seven techniques most frequently used are listed for each group, as the others are used very little. In this table the techniques are rephrased from the more formal definitions used in the previous tables. The number in parentheses following each item indicates its average frequency per interview.

From Table 4 we might draw certain tentative conclusions based, it must be remembered, on study of a very small number of interviews, whose value, however, is enhanced by the fact that they are completely recorded through electrical recording devices. It might be said that counseling of the directive sort is characterized by many highly specific questions to which specific answers are expected, and by information and explanation given by the counselor. These two techniques account for more than half of the counselor's part in this type of treatment interviewing. The counselor further gives the client opportunity to express his attitudes on specified topics, and points out to the client problems and conditions which he, the counselor, has observed to be in need of correction. He clarifies or restates or recognizes the subject content of what the client has told him. He endeavors to bring about change by proposing the action the client should take, and by bringing to bear both evidence and personal influence to insure that such action will be taken.

On the other hand, counseling of the nondirective sort is characterized by a preponderance of client activity, the client doing most of the talking about his problems. The counselor's primary techniques are those which help the client more clearly to recognize and understand his feelings, attitudes, and reaction patterns, and which encourage the client to talk about them. One half of the counselor items fall into these categories. The counselor may further achieve this aim by restating or clarifying the subject content of the client's conversation. Not infrequently he gives the client opportunity to express his feelings on specified topics. Less frequently he asks specific questions of an information-getting sort. Occasionally he gives information or explanations related to the client's situation. Although not the type of technique which could be used frequently, there is considerable redefinition of the interviewing situation as being primarily the client's situation, to use for his own growth.

Some Practical Implications. It may seem to some that the writer has gone to unnecessary lengths to indicate that there is a real and fundamental difference in the directiveness of different counselors and therapists. The reason for endeavoring to make these differences as plain as possible is that there is a definite tendency for all counselors to consider themselves as being non-coercive and nondirective. Most of the counselors who received high directiveness ratings did not believe that they took the lead in the interviewing, selected the goal, suggested what the client should do, and persuaded him to do it. Consequently, there is a tendency to assume that all counseling is basically alike and that differences in techniques are minor. Porter's study is significant in illustrating that this is certainly not the case, and that progress in our understanding of psychotherapy will be advanced by recognizing the sharp contrasts which exist in therapeutic viewpoints, rather than by assuming a harmony of ideas for which there is no basis in fact.

If the reader wishes to test out some of the facts which have been given above, he may apply a crude device to any interview which is recorded verbatim. If he reads alternate items only, one of the following will be found to be true: (1) He may find that reading the counselor conversations alone is enough to give the gist, the general trend, of the interview. If this is the case, the interview is definitely directive. (2) He may find that reading the client items only will give a reasonably adequate picture of the interview as a whole. If so, the counseling is definitely nondirective. (3) He may find that reading alternate items gives nothing but confusion, and that either counselor or counselee items by themselves give little picture of the gist of the interview. If this is true, the interview would represent some midpoint between directiveness and nondirectiveness.

UNDERLYING PURPOSES

Back of these differences between the directive and nondirective approaches lie deeper differences in the philosophy of counseling and the values which are assumed to be important. In the field of applied science, value judgments have a part, and often an important part, in determining the choice of techniques. Hence we shall do well to understand the implicit purposes of both directive and nondirective counseling.

The first basic difference in purpose centers around the question of who is to choose the client's goals. The directive group assumes that the counselor selects the desirable and the socially approved goal which the client is to attain, and then directs his efforts toward helping the subject to attain it. An unstated implication is that the counselor is superior to the client, since the latter is assumed to be incapable of accepting full responsibility for choosing his own goal. Nondirective counseling is based on the assumption that the client has the right to select his own life goals, even though these may be at variance with the goals that the counselor might choose for him. There is also the belief that if the individual has a modicum of insight into himself and his problems, he will be likely to make this choice wisely. This viewpoint is unusually well phrased by Robert Waelder, who, because of his background, clothes his ideas in Freudian terminology. "The basic idea of Freud's psychoanalysis . . . is impartiality toward the patient's inner conflicts. . . . Without taking any part in these never-ceasing struggles, psychoanalysis aims exclusively at letting light and air into the battlefield by making conscious the unconscious elements of the conflicts. The idea is that if the mature ego of an adult has full access to all the forces involved, it should be capable of finding an adequate and tolerable, at least nonpathological, solution to these conflicts, and capable of finding a workable proportion between satisfying desires and keeping them under effective control."*

The nondirective viewpoint places a high value on the right

---

*Waelder, Robert, in "Areas of Agreement in Psychotherapy," *American Journal of Orthopsychiatry*, vol. 10, no. 4 (October 1940), p. 705. It is of interest that this statement of Dr. Waelder's was made in order to emphasize a viewpoint which he felt was distinctive of Freudian psychoanalysis. The representatives of other viewpoints in the symposium made it plain, however, that this was one of the basic principles of all effective psychotherapies, and Dr. Goodwin Watson, the chairman, in summing up the discussion observed that "we seem to have reached the conclusion that psychoanalysis did give much of the initial impetus toward a relationship in which the therapist tries not to let his own values influence the patient, and that the past twenty years have seen all other psychotherapies move toward much the same ideal." Ibid., p. 708.

of every individual to be psychologically independent and to maintain his psychological integrity. The directive viewpoint places a high value upon social conformity and the right of the more able to direct the less able. These viewpoints have a significant relationship to social and political philosophy as well as to techniques of therapy.

As a consequence of this difference in value judgments, we find that the directive group tends to focus its efforts upon the problem which the client presents. If the problem is solved in a manner which can be approved by the counselor, if the symptoms are removed, the counseling is considered successful. The nondirective group places its emphasis upon the client himself, not upon the problem. If the client achieves through the counseling experience sufficient insight to understand his relation to the reality situation, he can choose the method of adapting to reality which has the highest value for him. He will also be much more capable of coping with future problems that arise, because of his increased insight and his increased experience in independent solution of his problems.

It will be evident that the approach of the nondirective group applies to the overwhelming majority of clients who have the capacity to achieve reasonably adequate solutions for their problems. Counseling, from this viewpoint, cannot be the only method for dealing with that small group—the psychotic, the defective, and perhaps some others—who have not the capacity to solve their own difficulties, even with help. Neither does it apply to children or adults who are faced with impossible demands from their environments. For the great bulk of maladjusted individuals, however—children, young people, or adults—some reasonable adjustment between the individual and his social environment is possible. For this group a therapeutic approach which encourages growth and responsible maturity has much to offer.

REFERENCE

1. Porter, E. H. The development and evaluation of a measure of counseling interview procedures. Unpublished Ph.D. dissertation, Ohio State University, Columbus, Ohio, 1941.

7
The Case of Herbert Bryan

FIRST INTERVIEW

Saturday the First

C_1.* Well, now, we were so concerned yesterday about these various aspects of whether or not we were to go ahead with it, that I don't know that I have as clear a picture as I'd like to have of what's on your mind, so go ahead and tell me.

S_1. Well, as accurately as I can convey the idea, I would term it a blocking which has manifestations in several fields.

C_2. M-hm.

S_2. The—in my earlier childhood the symptom of blocking which was emphasized on my consciousness most was in speech. I developed a speech impediment along about the sixth grade. Then, as I matured, I noticed a blocking in sexual situations. However, not—not in the voyeuristic situation, only in an intercourse situation; oftentimes I had difficulty there. Also an unpleasant tight feeling in the lower abdomen, as if, to use an analogy, there were some sort of a cold, hard axe or some

C_1. The counselor by this very broad kind of opening question makes it easy for the client to discuss his problem in any way he wishes. Note that S_1, 2, and 3 are all in response to this one question.

S_1, 2, 3, 4, 5, 6. This sequence of client statements is a classical example of a neurotic's description of his problems. The bizarre physical symptoms, the feelings of tension, are typical. As the case progresses, the reader will wish to compare the problems as at first presented with the real problems which cause the basic difficulty. Note that this sophisticated individual gives a very sophisticated picture of his problems. The naive individual will give a naive picture of his problems. In either case, it is unlikely that the problem as initially stated is the fundamental formulation.

---

*Throughout these interviews the responses of the counselor (C) and the subject (S) are numbered for easy reference. The footnotes which accompany the interview material are numbered correspondingly.

Counseling and Psychotherapy. Boston: Houghton Mifflin, 1942, 265–287.

other such thing pressing against the libido in such a way as to block it.

C3. M-hm.

S3. Now, another interesting angle there, this negative feeling was at first referred to my chest. There was sort of a dull, cold ache there. I'd get cold hands and have an increase in heartbeat at certain times, in certain situations where I was blocked. And then that feeling began to go down, as it were. That's the best way I can describe it. I mean, I guess actually—I mean, that's the way that I referred the feeling, as traveling downward.

C4. M-hm. And does it cause you more distress than it used to, or is that no different?

S4. I hardly know what to say there. I used to be very distressed about my speech, although that's not as bad as it was. I used to, uh—I used to be a very bad—a very bad stutterer, uh—then I sort of—sort of—sort of got my mind off of it and more or less forced myself to ignore it and to go ahead anyway, even though it was a terrific tension for me to go into certain situations.

C5. M-hm.

S5. But—uh, in later years, the actual feeling itself seems to have—that is, the feeling seems to have been—seems to have been, shall we say, compressed, as well as moved. That is, I feel that it has been intensified and in moving downward has become more compressed. I mean, that's the sensation I get.

C6. M-hm. M-hm.

S6. It's only a vague sort of cold and dull feeling in the chest, then it becomes more and more intensified as it moved down lower. And sometimes it gets very excruciating. I just seem to be held down, as it were, blocked in all realms of life.

C7. A feeling of real pain, is that what you mean?

C4. Here is a moderately directive question, limiting the client to a specified area for discussion. However, the question is distinctly a response to the feeling of distress Mr. Bryan has been expressing, rather than to the intellectual content. It might have been better for the counselor simply to recognize the material expressed, in some such statement as, "You've noticed a real change in these symptoms?"

S4. As soon as he mentions his previous problem of stuttering, Mr. Bryan begins to stutter, and this continues in *S5.*

C7. This counselor response is definitely helpful in bringing progress. It must

*S*7. Oh, yes.

*C*8. M-hm.

*S*8. And then sometimes for short periods it mysteriously goes. I mean, there's no particular ideology with its going. I get release, and then I'm very active and very happy during these short periods — I'd say they occur — oh, I have one or two good days a month when I'm practically free of it, but I never know when they're going to come on, or when my bad periods —

*C*9. And you say that you feel this does block you in a good many areas of life?

*S*9. In practically all areas of life — anything which you could mention. I hesitate to meet people — I hesitate to canvass for my photographic business. I feel a terrific aversion to any kind of activity, even dancing. I normally enjoy dancing very well. But when my inhibition, or whatever you wish to call it, is on me powerfully, it is an ordeal for me to dance. I notice a difference in my musical ability. On my good days I can harmonize with other people singing.

*C*10. M-hm.

*S*10. I have a good ear for harmony then. But when I'm blocked, I seem to lose that, as well as my dancing ability. I feel very awkward and stiff.

already be evident to the counselor that these are psychological, not organic, sufferings. The usual reaction is to question, in some way, their validity. Any such implication would have thrown the client on the defensive and made him intent on proving that his pain was real. The counselor's recognition that he is describing real pain helps Mr. Bryan to feel that he is genuinely understood, and makes it possible for him to go ahead and tell of times when he is not suffering (*S*8).

*C*9. Here it seems evident that the counselor has just assimilated the second half of the client's statement *S*6, and is now responding to it. Our phonographic records indicate that this occurs quite frequently and that responses are often made, not to the preceding speech, but to an earlier one. This is not necessarily a criticism. The feeling that is thus verbally recognized is a real one, and the recognition of it leads Mr. Bryan to expand it more fully, bringing it more completely into the open. This is the usual result of recognition of feeling.

*S*9. Here we gain the first diagnostic inkling as to what purposes Mr. Bryan's symptoms may serve. They may help to keep him from work activities and from social contacts.

C_{11}. M-hm. So that both in your work and in your recreation you feel blocked.

S_{11}. I don't want to do anything. I just lie around. I get no gusto for any activity at all.

C_{12}. You just feel rather unable to do things, is that it?

S_{12}. Well, I actually feel pressure on me just like that (*pointing to abdomen*), as near as I can refer it, uh—pressing down right on my dynamo, as you might say.

C_{13}. M-hm. And you— In spite of the difficulty that it causes you, you feel pretty sure that it isn't physical?

S_{13}. Oh, I know that it isn't physical. Well, for several reasons—I've had thorough check-ups for one thing. For another, the fact that it leaves me, and leaves me very, very suddenly. Within a half a minute, I can have a complete change.

C_{14}. Is that so? (*Pause.*) Can you tell me about any of those times?

S_{14}. Well, it's just the painful weighty feeling leaves me. And it never leaves me with the same ideological counterpart. I mean, I might be thinking about something else or I might be working on a self-psychoanalytic technique which I thought would be helpful. And sometimes certain thoughts help my release. Other times those exact same thoughts—the exact same self-technique doesn't work at all.

C_{15}. M-hm. So that you feel that it goes and comes absolutely beyond your control.

C_{11}, C_{12}. Good instances of entirely nondirective responses which simply recognize the feeling being expressed, make conversation easy, and enable the client to continue to explore his attitudes.

C_{13}. This question and its answer seem to be the one unit of a strictly diagnostic nature in the whole series of contacts. Here is a client who seems obviously suitable for counseling help. He is adult and sufficiently in control of his environment to be carrying on a business. He is under psychological stress, as indicated by his conversation. His intelligence is clearly above average, as indicated by his vocabulary. This one question is settled at this point. Whether consciously planned for this purpose or not, the counselor has shrewdly put his finger on the one point on which diagnostic knowledge was necessary.

C_{14}. The one directive diagnostic question, C_{13}, puts the client in the question-answering frame of mind, and hence there comes a pause which the counselor has to break, this time with a less directive question.

C_{15}. This is the type of response which shows that the counselor has been

S15. Yes. My impression is that the whole thing is — has nothing to do with my conscious thought or it is not under my conscious control. So that except under the voyeuristic situation I mentioned — If I were to be feeling bad, and then would look out and see a woman undressed, then I'd feel happy.

C16. At those times you wouldn't have any of this feeling of pressure or distress.

S16. No. Oddly enough, that's the one touchstone that always seems to —

C17. You feel that's some kind of a clue to it.

S17. Well, yes, I think so. Now, sometimes I can have an enjoyable intercourse — other times, it isn't enjoyable — it's almost a mechanical process — I don't get very much sensation.

C18. So that in that situation, you're not at all sure that you'll be free of this feeling, or free of difficulty.

S18. Well, I know beforehand that if I have a bad day, why it isn't going to do me much good. Although I have had the difficulty leave me, and leave me rather suddenly, so that I was able to carry on O.K.

C19. But, I mean, that may or may not happen, where as I understand it, in what you described as a voyeuristic situation, you're pretty sure there that —

S19. I always have the euphoria there, yes.

thinking deeply about the emotionalized attitude which the client is expressing. He responds very definitely to that feeling and not at all to the content.

C18, C19. Evidently a clumsy attempt on the counselor's part to respond to Mr. Bryan's statement that it is only in "the voyeuristic situation" that he feels satisfied.

C1 to S19, inclusive. Note how necessary it is to follow the pattern of the client's feeling if the counselor is to discover with any accuracy what the real issues are. Up to this point, the counselor might, with the best of intentions, have seized upon any of these problems as being the one upon which to focus attention — the abdominal physical symptoms, the voyeuristic satisfactions, which sound vaguely compulsive, the sexual maladjustment, the difficulties in adjusting to social situations. To investigate each of these areas by questioning might indicate which of these problems is most significant, but might never discover some deeper problem underlying all. This would be a most time-consuming process, with no guarantee of success. Obviously the swifter and more realistic method is to encourage expression, in full confidence that the client will gradually take the counselor to the heart of his problems.

*C*20. Well, you've thought of that yourself as a clue. Do you have any notion as to what that ties up with, or what the origin —

*S*20. Well, I can trace the origin. When I was very young, back in the first grade, we had a couple of girl student roomers with us, and they used to exhibit to me; that is, I think they actually did it deliberately, and I got quite a sex kick.

*C*21. When was this, you say? What grade? You said something about the grade you were in.

*S*21. First grade.

*C*22. I see.

*S*22. I was about five then. That's my earliest form of sexual pleasure, and it was associated with that sort of a fantasy. And I think I've analyzed it further — the actual feeling is one of vicarious exhibitionism; that is, it's more intense when I know that the girl is actually exhibiting to me, rather than just being accidental.

*C*23. M-hm. You've analyzed this thing quite a bit as to various aspects of it. Can you tell me any more of your thinking about it? You say that you feel this is perhaps the origin of it —

*S*23. Well, of course that would account for the positive feelings. Now to account for the negative feelings. I was raised in a very Victorian and puritan manner. My mother even whipped me one time for talking with a friend of mine. She thought it was terrible. We had noticed, well, different animals and so forth, and she was very horrified. I remember she worked up to quite a dramatic climax. She said, "Well, did you talk about locusts?" and "Did you mention animals?" and then "Did you mention human beings?" Worked up to a climax, and then she whipped

*C*20. Evidently the counselor again feels the need of using a moderately directive question in order to keep the conversation going. While the question follows the lead given by the client in *S*16, a simple recognition of feeling, "That's the one situation in which you're sure of satisfaction," would probably have been more helpful.

*C*23. A very broad, nondirective type of lead, which, as usual, is productive.

*S*20, *S*22, *S*23. Note how Mr. Bryan, in these items, places all the responsibility for his problems upon others. The counselor catches this underlying feeling and responds to it at least partially in *C*24.

me for, well, for even mentioning the facts. I suppose I assumed that if it were horrible to talk about, it would even be more horrible to do. Then my father had very definite ascetic notions—it's a medieval concept—"mortification of the flesh"—that sort of thing. When he was a young man he went on a fast and all that sort of thing to make himself more spiritual. He's outgrown that sort of thing, but he was very intense that way as a young man. I think that comes from his mother. She was very much of a Calvinist—very much opposed to card playing, dancing, things like that. He had quite an attachment to his mother. I'm sure she dominated his life.

*C*24. So that you feel your folks are somewhat the basis of some of your difficulty?

*S*24. Well, psychologically and of course philosophically you can carry it back there, I'm sure. But, yes, I'd say this is entirely a matter of conditioning. But I don't know whether realizing one's conditioning should effect a therapy or whether there must be something more. I used to have the idea that if I would recall all the childhood events consciously and bring them up to my consciousness from the subconscious, there would be release there, but either I haven't thought of something, either there is something there that hasn't been thought of, or realizing it hasn't done any good.

*C*25. Whatever you've done hasn't worked enough to free you from the problem, is that it?

*S*25. No, when I do think of unpleasant childhood episodes, it seems to intensify rather than do it any good. So I—

*C*26. Then you've simply lived with this for quite a number

---

*S*24. Intellectually, this client "knows all the answers." Unless counseling has more to offer him than intellectual content, it is obviously doomed to failure.

*C*25. This is a point where it would have been very easy for the counselor to become involved in an intellectual discussion of therapy. It is to his credit that he responds only to the feeling.

*C*26. Why did the counselor interrupt here? This seems to be a quite unnecessary directive question breaking into the flow of feeling. It leads to brief client responses ending in a pause (*S*28), which the counselor has to break with another rather directive question. This in turn leads to a repetition of the symptoms originally described (*S*29), and it is only following this that a fresh start in recognition of feeling is made. This is a minor example of the way in which clumsy handling by the counselor can delay progress.

of years. Why is it any worse now, or why are you trying definitely to do something about it?

S26. Well, it's just reached the point where it becomes unbearable. I'd rather be dead than live as I am now.

C27. You'd rather be dead than live as you are now? Can you tell me a little bit more about that?

S27. Well, I hope. Of course we always live on hope.

C28. Yes.

S28. But—No, I don't have any conscious suicidal urge or anything like that. It's just that—looking at it rationally, I feel that I'm—that I'm in the red now and I wouldn't want to keep on living in the red. (*Pause.*)

C29. Well, can you tell me in any more detailed way what—in what way it blocks you so much that you really feel sometimes that you'd be better off dead?

S29. Well, I don't know if I can any more accurately describe the sensation. It's just a—a very impressive and painful weight as if an axe were pressing on the whole abdomen, pressing down, I can almost—I can almost sense the position and I feel that it's oppressing me very radically, that is, that it goes right down to the roots of my dynamic energy, so that no matter in what field I essay any sort of effort, I find the blocking.

C30. It really just cripples you as far as anything else is concerned.

S30. Yes. M-hm. And that even has a physical counterpart. When I walk, that is, when I'm feeling badly, I walk hunched over and sort of like I had a bellyache, which I actually do have, psychologically.

C31. M-hm. It just makes you more or less half a man, is that it? And only half able to do your work—

S31. Yes. It's just as if I had an axe in me literally, you might say. I feel it in my very core of energy—it's blocked and oppressed in that painful way. It's a deep-seated thing, because conversely when I get the release I feel a deep-seated flowing of energy.

C32. When you feel all right—you feel very much all right.

C30, C31, C32, C33. These responses constitute a productive following of the client's pattern of emotionalized attitudes.

*S*32. Oh, yes, yes. Very dynamic—my mind works much more rapidly and everything's all right. Anything I try I do successfully.

*C*33. And what you want is to find ways of increasing the amount of time that you have that dynamic self, is that it?

*S*33. Oh, yes. Be that way all the time. I don't see any reason why I couldn't be. The whole thing is psychological, and I want to get at it.

*C*34. Well, I think possibly one way of doing that might be to talk somewhat more about the ways in which it does block you, I mean, what—in your work, for instance, and some other things.

*S*34. Well, the blocking is so universal, almost anything I could mention, it would hold true. Now, do you want me to go ahead and mention the ways?

*C*35. Well, possibly not. But you feel that it really prevents you from doing anything that you might wish to do?

*S*35. On my bad days I just can't do anything, and it isn't what you would call lethargy, although that is what it would seem to the observer. It's actually a tying up; that is, I feel the conflict going on within me. I have an intense inward feeling that the impulses and the inhibitions are so accurately blocked and counterbalanced that it leads to inertia.

*C*36. Plenty of energy there, but it's just lost in the balance.

*S*36. Yes. I'm quite aware of that.

*C*37. You say those feelings mean a good deal of conflict. Can you tell any more about those?

*S*37. Well, I referred there to the tone, which is one of energy, with the inhibition cracking down on the energy, no matter in what realm I wish to be energetic. That is, if—well, if I'm feeling that way and somebody wants to give a party or there's work to

---

*C*34. This is the first attempt on the part of the counselor to define verbally the counseling relationship, and it is only a minor gesture in that direction. However, every counselor response tends in one way or another to structure the relationship, and the client must have, even at this point, some recognition of the unusual freedom of the relationship and its lack of any strongly directive aspects. Following this brief explanation, there is the usual slight amount of difficulty in getting the client to take the lead again in the conversation and to talk freely and without restriction (*S*34 and *C*35). From this point, however, the client goes on, picturing his difficulty for the first time as a conflict.

be done or there's something I want to read or some intellectual problem I want to think about, why, I'm not able to do it. But when I have my good days, I do achieve so much, you see, that it's very disheartening to me to have bad days, because I know what I can achieve when I have my release.

C38. You feel that if you were at your best, your abilities and achievements and all would really be topnotch.

S38. I've done some writing which the professors at M—— University have liked. Now I find that that's blocked—that was one of the last things to be blocked, by the way. I could write up until I was a junior and that became blocked.

C39. M-hm. And then there was a time when you couldn't even do that?

S39. Yes. I haven't been able to write since, except in a very sporadic manner. But I like to write, and that is perhaps my main ambition—to write novels. I had a course at M—— in novel writing and liked it very much—did A work in that.

C40. And tell me, what sort of thing stopped you from writing—I mean, if you could do it up to a point.

S40. It was a feeling that stopped me. That is, my impression of my ailment is that it is a feeling—there is never any constant ideological pattern. It's simply blind feeling.

C41. And gradually this feeling grew to a point where you couldn't write?

S41. I don't know whether it grew up to that point, or whether writing came under its influence independent of its quantitative growth.

C42. I see. Well, then, perhaps it became focused more on writing.

S42. Well, writing came into the fold and it blocked that too.

C43. So that gradually that circle has grown until everything you might want to do is within that circle of blocked activities.

C40. This direct question is in line with the client's feeling, and in the rapid give and take of the interview we cannot expect perfection. Nevertheless, it is plain that a better response on the part of the counselor would have been, "You like to write, but this blocking keeps you from it." It often seems difficult to catch and bring into the open the ambivalent impulses.

C43, S43, C44. Adequate recognition of attitudes brings the flow of feeling around again to the same point which was poorly recognized at C18, C19. The

*S*43. Except voyeurism.

*C*44. So that the satisfaction you get from voyeurism is almost the only thing from which you're sure at the present time that you can gain satisfaction?

*S*44. Well, yes, that and food.

*C*45. Appetite is still good. M-hm.

*S*45. M-hm, although when I'm in awfully bad condition, I lose my appetite to a very considerable extent. That doesn't happen very often.

*C*46. Well, I think that the sort of thing that perhaps we can do in our discussions together is to explore this thing pretty fully—uh, find out what it means to you and why it has blocked you in different situations and gradually see if we can find ways of dealing with it. I think that's the—

*S*46. As I analyze myself, I'm sure that there is some impulse for me to cling to it—that it's—

*C*47. That there is some what?

*S*47. An impulse for me to retain my inhibition—it's paradoxical. I get some sort of inner satisfaction out of it evidently.

*C*48. There is a feeling you have a certain tendency to cling to this, even though you don't like it.

*S*48. And, of course, that's invariably borne out—I feel this way about psychological changes—if a person wholeheartedly

phonographic recordings indicate that this frequently occurs. If the client expresses some attitude which has significance for him, and this is misunderstood or inadequately recognized by the counselor, the same attitude is likely to be expressed again later. Adequate recognition, on the other hand, tends to lead to further and deeper expression.

*C*46. Here the counselor makes a more complete and satisfactory attempt to define the type of help which the client can expect from counseling.

*S*46, *S*47. Is it because the counselor's remarks sound almost as though he were bringing the interview to a close that Mr. Bryan is able to reveal this highly significant feeling? Or is it merely that having revealed his superficial symptoms, he is now ready to recognize that they are to some extent symptoms that he wants? At any rate, in this one interview, he has gone through three levels of expression of his problems. At first they are described as pain, suffering, maladjustment. Then (*S*35) they are described as conflicting forces within himself. Now they are recognized as symptoms to which he clings, in spite of his desire to change. This is actually the beginning of insight, a clearer degree of self-understanding.

*C*48. Fortunately the counselor recognizes and states clearly the ambivalent wants to change, the change automatically occurs. Of course, perhaps that's a little bit tautological. I don't know. My own impression of these things, or my intuition about them, I should say much more accurately, is that if the person really wants to change, why the change occurs, so there must be some reason, or must be some—and I do sense that I have an emotional something that's clinging to my neurosis—not willing to give it up.

C49. You feel that conceivably if you wanted wholeheartedly to get rid of it, possibly you could get rid of it.

S49. Why, I know that I could get rid of it then. But, of course, that's defining wholeheartedness in terms of getting rid of it, so it becomes tautological.

C50. Yes. M-hm. But you say that at times you do sense a certain amount of tendency to cling to it. Can you say any more about that, or times when you felt that?

S50. I wrestle with it, but I know that I'm not wrestling powerfully enough. I know that the other aspect of my personality wants to preserve the status quo. Well, after all, the whole thing is occurring within me, and it's what might be termed a war within my own house.

C51. Part of your problem is to discover who and what are the enemy in your own home.

S51. Yes. I feel that there's some sort of a hidden touchstone that provides the driving force for the oppression, and that there is—I feel that it is a blind impulse, rather immune to logic, but of course not necessarily immune to change, that is, I mean, there are other ways besides logic, of course—

C52. In other words, you haven't been able to reason yourself out of it—nor has anyone else, is that it?

S52. Yes. In other words, I even get the impression that I have a full cognitive appreciation of the difficulty and that even if I

feeling which is being expressed. This enables the client further to express his feeling in what are the most significant items of this first interview. They show clear progress in exploration at more than a superficial level.

C51. Here the counselor takes the opportunity to define again what counseling can mean, putting it in terms of the client's symbols, which is always a sound device.

S52. This intelligent and sophisticated client can put into words what most were — even if there were no more new ideas to come out, that that would have nothing to do with the change. That is, of course, I have a theory of persuasion anyway. Of course that's in the philosophic realm. I don't believe that anybody is ever persuaded by logic or reasoning — it's emotional undercurrents which undergo the change, and logic, that's just a rationalization — sort of a rack to hang your coat on.

$C53$. In other words, you feel that nobody could persuade you out of this situation.

$S53$. No. I feel that I already know the logic of it, but that doesn't effect a cure. Now, I feel that in the last analysis — I think that psychoanalysis is probably a matter of prestige — prestige persuasion. I feel that if I get a confidence in you, that you know more about it than I do — that regardless of the logic — that is, I feel I am your equal in logic, but that you are my superior in certain emotion-changing techniques.

$C54$. In other words, if you felt that gradually you had enough confidence, and so on, in me, I might be able to bring about some change in you, but you couldn't very well do that by yourself.

$S54$. Well, let's put it this way. Right now, the part of my

---

clients feel — that they cannot be talked out of, or argued out of, or persuaded out of, their problems.

$C53$. Here, again, the counselor must have been tempted to agree or disagree. He wisely does neither, but merely clarifies the attitude that is being expressed.

$S53$. Here the client refers to the process as psychoanalysis. In $S48$ he refers to his neurosis. It is the client, not the counselor, who is using the technical terminology. Whether the counselor should endeavor to correct him, to explain the difference between this counseling process and a classical analysis, is doubtful. It would almost certainly become an intellectual detour, delaying real progress.

$C54$. This is an interesting point. The counselor might have used this opportunity to define his role in this type of therapy. Instead, he merely recognizes the client's dependent feeling. Probably this was the better choice. If he had failed to recognize it, undoubtedly it would have cropped out again.

$S54, C55, S55, C56$. In this interchange the client is clearly asking the counselor to supply the motivation which he needs. The counselor neither agrees nor refuses. He further defines the relationship as a situation in which a clear choice can be made. At the conclusion of $C56$, in the statement "whether you want to vote the same way," he implies a unity in the client which has by no means been expressed. This is really a very subtle beginning of interpretation, which could easily be overdone.

personality that wants to change is outvoted. We're going to have to change the balance of power. Now, how to change that — how to get a majority in the house — I don't know. I've tried several techniques on myself and had some talks with a man at M—— University; and I feel this way — now it sort of comes down to a sort of philosophic — what shall we say? — sort of a get-no-where thing, that is, when you're in such a position where the negatives outweigh, how are you going to get the motivation to change the situation?

C55. You feel that you've got this thing fairly well analyzed; you realize it is a balance of power within yourself —

S55. But I can't lift myself up by the bootstraps, as it were.

C56. Yes. I think you do have a remarkably good intellectual analysis of the situation, and you feel quite rightly that you can't lift yourself by your bootstraps. It's possible, though, that as we explore this thing you can at least decide clearly whether you want to vote the same way you're voting now, or whether there may be other ways of —

S56. Well, to draw another analogy, I feel that I have so much energy, so much reservoir of energy — now, what I want to do is to get the negatives to desert to the positive side. Which will be a double-barreled gain, you see, and will probably occur very rapidly once the ball gets rolling. But when the negatives are in power, why, of course how can the ball begin to roll?

C57. Can you, uh — not today, but one question that you may

C57. Here is the second blunder of the hour. The counselor departs from sound recognition of feeling. Instead of some such response as "You feel that someone else must start the ball rolling," he asks a direct question which goes deep into the client's situation. If Mr. Bryan were fully aware of why his "neg-ative" side was in power, he would have little need of help. The counselor draws nothing but a confused and somewhat defensive answer (S57), and follows it with another direct question which endeavors to tie the client down to a specific situation, that of dancing (C58). The client makes a partial response, and then definitely retreats into a long philosophical statement (S59) which has no direct relation to his problems and is as far as possible from being specific. The counselor only brings him out of this by a recognition of the pleasure he is getting in being philosophical (C60). However, this whole section of the interview, from C57 to C67, is much less profitable because of two directive questions. This indicates how easily the course of constructive therapy can be diverted by errors which may not be recognized as errors at the time.

want to be thinking over is, what are these negative votes?

*S*57. Well, as I have it analyzed now, it seems to be just a blanket feeling operative in all these realms. You mean, can I refer the feeling — you mean would there be any ideological aspects to it?

*C*58. I think we might get further if we talked about it in specific terms. You say you like to dance, for example. And still this thing crops up there, too, and blocks you from enjoying dancing. Well, can you tell me more about that — I mean what your feelings are while you're dancing, or what it is that seems to —

*S*58. M-hm. Well, I enjoy music very much and especially creative music, that is, improvised music — that is, where the musicians are not reading — where they close their eyes and play as they feel. I like the creativeness of that sort of thing, and I like powerful rhythm, and I feel that when I'm dancing, that's a form of expression which gives me satisfaction when I'm not blocked. I don't —

*C*59. M-hm. You like the rhythmic expression, you like the musical aspect of it.

*S*59. I don't marshal the universe to favor dancing — it's not necessarily a superior form of activity — that is, I don't — well, I don't have any notion that it is superior. Our values are our private absolutes. There are no cosmic yardsticks whereby to measure our values — that is, we either like a thing or we don't. There's no use moralizing about our likes and dislikes. One form of enjoyment is not superior or inferior to any other form of enjoyment. In other words, I don't evaluate values philosophically. Of course, we all do it psychologically. I think that's what the Latins meant years ago when they said "De gustibus nondisputandum." Concerning feelings — one should not rationalize — one should not evaluate. One can evaluate means, but I don't see how they can evaluate —

*C*60. You like to consider the philosophical implications of most of your ideas, don't you?

*S*60. Yes. I get an intense enjoyment out of philosophizing. I have several friends — we sit for hours and philosophize.

*C*61. You really do like that?

*S*61. Yes. Especially (*he names a certain school of thought*). I'm very much interested in that.

*C*62. M-hm. And when you're discussing philosophical issues, what about this problem of blocking—free from it, or not?

*S*62. No. That's the thing that saddens me quite a bit. When I wax enthusiastic philosophically, I oftentimes have quite a blocking in my speech—maybe you notice how I hesitate. Now, my hesitation is not a groping for words, although that's a sort of a—well, I want to make it seem so, for sort of what you might call protective coloration.

*C*63. Defend yourself a little bit that way?

*S*63. Yeah. I like to make people think that I'm groping for just the exact word—that I'm a careful thinker, but actually I know right off what I want to say, and when I am fluent, I get very exact and nice diction without having to grope for a word.

*C*64. So that in that particular situation your blocking keeps you from being your best and fluent self. And in that situation, it's speech blocking that is primarily—

*S*64. Well, yes. I mean it seems like—well, there wouldn't be any other blocking. No other form of activity than speech is going on, and that's the thing, of course, which I notice—that is, of course the thought—my thought is also to a certain extent blocked—that is, they sort of go hand in hand. When I'm able to speak more fluently, I'm able to think more fluently.

*C*65. M-hm.

*S*65. But even when I can think clearly, my speech is sometimes blocked. It is the blocking that would be the last to go. When I'm in a philosophic discussion, I feel very angry that I'm not as fluent as the others, because I know that I'm just as intelligent as they are. Be able to hold up my end just as well only I'm not able to have the actual oral expression.

*C*66. If you could express yourself as well as the others, you would be as good or better than they are in the discussion. (*Pause.*) Well, what other aspects of this whole thing comes to your mind?

*S*66. Let's see, we've mentioned—music, work, and sex. I feel, to reiterate, that it's just sort of a pan-operative thing.

*C*67. And, I gather, feel very much discouraged about it.

*S*67. I feel this—that it is keeping me so far under my ceiling that I think that's an essential part of it. If—well, of course, if I were unimaginative and unintelligent, perhaps—well, I don't know, it's hard to say; maybe everyone thinks they have a ceiling that's a lot higher than they are, but regardless of comparisons,

I don't — I'm not interested primarily in comparing myself with other people. I just want to fulfill my own personality as much as I can.

C68. And you feel quite confident within yourself that —

S68. Not a bit of doubt of it. I know that I have far greater potentialities than I have achieved yet. In the artistic realm and in the intellectual realm —

C69. So that up to date your whole life situation is simply that you would be really outstanding except that this blocking keeps you from it. And then, too, as you say, you feel that to some extent you keep that blocking there in some way.

S69. There's some impulse — there's some reason why the negatives are in power and why, even when I wrestle with the negative feeling, I know that the wrestler is in the minority and the negative feeling outweighs.

C70. You know you're licked before you start to fight?

S70. Yet I always have a hope that I will come upon some sort of touchstone that will set the inhibition free. No, I'm a hopeful person — sometimes I wonder — I think I've been very unhappy, comparatively speaking, and yet I sometimes wonder why I am so cheerful, in a way — that is, I have a hopeful, cheerful disposition and all of my friends regard me as a very happy person, yet I know that I have undergone years and years — and sometimes the awful monotony of my miseries is appalling — day after day to have the same feeling and then also at night. I have nightmares lots of times, and my sleep doesn't at all rest me, such times.

C71. M-hm. M-hm.

S71. So I feel that I have an incubus, as it were, year in and year out. Sometimes it gets rather appalling.

C72. M-hm. A steady grind. And yet in spite of that steady

C69. The counselor summarizes two of the important attitudes which have been expressed. This statement might also serve as a description of the typical neurotic pattern. "My life would be noteworthy," says the neurotic, "were it not for the fact that my neurosis prevents me and excuses me from attempting to live it."

S70. The client, having made real progress, now returns temporarily to a restatement of his original symptoms. Acceptance of this attitude (C72) leads to more positive views.

grind, you feel that you — you still feel you may find your way, or fight your way out.

*S*72. In my fantasies I always imagine myself as being cured and achieving certain goals. I never have pessimistic fantasies. The alter ego that I set up is one of me cured, so that my potentialities may fulfill themselves.

*C*73. Yes. What sort of achievements do you fantasy about?

*S*73. Well, I want to write — I want to be musical and dance, and I want to be a connoisseur of beautiful women, and I want to have a reasonably luxurious standard of living — say about twenty-five, fifty thousand a year.

*C*74. So that you have a generally high —

*S*74. I know that I can do it. I know damn well I could do it, because I've had flashes of what I can be when I'm without this, and although they are short flashes, the achievements that I make within those short flashes could be very accurately reduced to an arithmetical projection which would show me what I would do if I were completely released all the time.

*C*75. So that you, minus this blocking, would really go places.

*S*75. That sounds a bit Rotarian. Perhaps I should clarify my position. I don't have a bourgeois ambition in that I want fame alone. I'm the sort of fellow that, if I got what I wanted, I would not mind whether the world applauded or booed — I'm my own supreme court.

*C*76. M-hm.

*S*76. But — well, perhaps that's not significant — I don't know.

*C*77. Well, it is significant — you have your own — you say you have your own standards and it's by those standards you gauge what you do —

*S*77. If I wrote a novel, I would like it to make money, but if it didn't make money, it would be all right if I were satisfied with it. The money angle wouldn't be too important.

*C*78. Well, you've given me quite a good all-round picture of

*C*78. The counselor begins to bring the interview to a close. He lapses temporarily into a doctor-patient description of the relationship, but there is no evidence that this does any damage. He could just as easily have said, "You have explored many aspects of your problems, and that is probably all we can do for today."

your situation. I think probably that's as much as we can do in one session.

*S*78. I think perhaps, to sum it up, that the origin is sexual, but that a sexual blocking, that is, is such a fundamental blocking that it blocks all. I don't know whether that's too Freudian for you, but I feel that sex is sort of a dynamo and is the source of energy for other activities too.

*C*79. Well, now, I'd put it this way, as to the way we can go at that. I think that the best way to work through some of this is for you, when you come in next time, to take up those aspects of it about which you feel the most concern or which are disturbing you most at the moment. Maybe it will be the sexual aspect; maybe it'll be something very different from that. Whatever the thing is that is of greatest concern at the moment, let's work that through and explore it. Perhaps we can find out what some of these negative votes are. I mean, if you can get a little clearer feeling as to what this balance of power consists of — why it is that in some ways you wish to keep this painful problem — then we'll be further along.

*S*79. Well, I think I know why I want to keep it. I want to keep it for the voyeuristic pleasure, because I know that when I don't have it I get no enjoyment from voyeurism at all. On the other hand, I get pleasure from intercourse when I'm without it, but when it returns, the remembered intercourse wouldn't be pleasurable, you see.

*C*80. M-hm.

*S*80. In other words, we remember, not in the past, but in the present, so that when I'm neurotic I can't pleasurably remember an experience that was pleasurable to me at the time when I happened to be released.

*C*79. The first portion of this conversation is helpful in that it defines the client's responsibility for the direction of the counseling interviews. In the last portion the counselor returns to the same direct question which delayed therapy before (*C*57) and unwisely tried to give this problem as a "homework assignment." This would seem to be the third blunder in the interview.

*S*79, *S*80, *S*81, *S*82. The client is determined to answer the counselor's questions at once. To some extent this represents further insight. To some extent it is almost certainly an attempt to prolong the interview. The counselor has definitely to call a halt (*C*85).

*C*81. M-hm. All right, that is helpful. That's one value that it has to you — that it enables you to — while you have your problem, bad as it is, it does give you one certain type of satisfaction that you can't get —

*S*81. M-hm. And I think another angle on that would be that that would always be available, whereas intercourse wouldn't be. Perhaps that's one reason why I cling to the neurosis, because I can always get a voyeuristic fantasy.

*C*82. M-hm.

*S*82. I'm sure that this — that the inhibition is a fear. And I admit that I do have these Victorian fears of sexual activity, and probably in the Victorian concept, probably voyeurism would be less terrible than actual intercourse.

*C*83. That's why you feel perhaps less guilty about that —

*S*83. M-hm. Well, it's more powerful —

*C*84. — and less fear of punishment —

*S*84. — and a feeling of guilt. Here's the way I can perhaps illustrate it diagrammatically. Here (*pointing to head*) and here (*pointing to chest*) I am pretty balanced. I know exactly what I want and how to get it. But down here (*pointing to lower abdomen*) there's blocking. Now it used to be that the disturbance here (*chest*) rather confused me up here (*head*), but since the negative feeling has gone down to here (*abdomen*), what it amounts to is — that I'm a pagan intellectually and in my heart, but in my guts I'm a perfect puritan.

*C*85. Yes. That's an excellent statement. Well, let's consider various angles of that next time you come in. Now, we should — I was looking over my calendar just before you came. I could see you next Tuesday at four o'clock; would that be a convenient time for you? I thought perhaps we might try to work in a couple of contacts next week — I'm not sure that I can make them as frequent as that later on.

*S*85. Well, I imagine at the outset it's probably better to have more frequency, isn't it?

*C*86. If it can be arranged, m-hm.

*S*86. Well, now my time can be adjusted to suit yours. I mean, this thing's so important to me, that you just name the date and I'll adjust myself accordingly.

*C*87. Well, let's say Tuesday at four and Friday at four.

S87. Tuesday and Friday at four.

C88. Is that feasible, or not?

S88. I see my dentist at 1.45 Tuesday, and yes—he'll be through with me before four.

C89. Well, then I'll put those on my calendar.

S89. Tuesday and Friday, both at four?

C90. Both at four.

S90. All right, sir.

C91. O.K. We'll see what we can do on it.

S91. All right.

8

The Characteristics of a Helping Relationship

My interest in psychotherapy has brought about in me an interest in every kind of helping relationship. By this term I mean a relationship in which at least one of the parties has the intent of promoting the growth, development, maturity, improved functioning, improved coping with life of the other. The other, in this sense, may be one individual or a group. To put it in another way, a helping relationship might be defined as one in which one of the participants intends that there should come about, in one or both parties, more appreciation of, more expression of, more functional use of the latent inner resources of the individual.

Now it is obvious that such a definition covers a wide range of relationships which usually are intended to facilitate growth. It would certainly include the relationship between mother and child, father and child. It would include the relationship between the physician and his patient. The relationship between teacher and pupil would often come under this definition, though some teachers would not have the promotion of growth as their intent. It includes almost all counselor-client relationships, whether we are speaking of educational counseling, vocational counseling,

Personnel and Guidance Journal, Vol. 37, 1958, 6–16.

or personal counseling. In this last-mentioned area it would include the wide range of relationships between the psychotherapist and the hospitalized psychotic, the therapist and the troubled or neurotic individual, and the relationship between the therapist and the increasing number of so-called normal individuals who enter therapy to improve their own functioning or accelerate their personal growth.

These are largely one-to-one relationships. But we should also think of the large number of individual-group interactions which are intended as helping relationships. Some administrators intend that their relationship to their staff groups shall be of the sort which promotes growth, though other administrators would not have this purpose. The interaction between the group therapy leader and his group belongs here. So does the relationship of the community consultant to a community group. Increasingly the interaction between the industrial consultant and a management group is intended as a helping relationship. Perhaps this listing will point up the fact that a great many of the relationships in which we and others are involved fall within this category of interactions in which there is the purpose of promoting development and more mature and adequate functioning.

The Question

But what are the characteristics of those relationships which *do* help, which do facilitate growth? And at the other end of the scale is it possible to discern those characteristics which make a relationship unhelpful, even though it was the sincere intent to promote growth and development? It is to these questions, particularly the first, that I would like to take you with me over some of the paths I have explored, and to tell you where I am, as of now, in my thinking on these issues.

THE ANSWERS GIVEN BY RESEARCH

It is natural to ask first of all whether there is any empirical research which would give us an objective answer to these questions. There has not been a large amount of research in this area as yet, but what there is is stimulating and suggestive. I cannot report all of it but I would like to make a somewhat extensive sampling of the studies which have been done and state very briefly some of the findings. In so doing, oversimplification is necessary, and I am quite aware that I am not doing full justice to the researches I am mentioning, but it may give you the feeling that factual advances are being made and pique your curiosity enough to examine the studies themselves, if you have not already done so.

Studies of Attitudes

Most of the studies throw light on the attitudes on the part of the helping person which make a relationship growth-promoting or growth-inhibiting. Let us look at some of these.

A careful study of parent-child relationships made some years ago by Baldwin and others (1) at the Fels Institute contains interesting evidence. Of the various clusters of parental attitudes toward children, the "acceptant-democratic" seemed most growth-facilitating. Children of these parents with their warm and equalitarian attitudes showed an accelerated intellectual development (an increasing I.Q.), more originality, more emotional security and control, less excitability than children from other types of homes. Though somewhat slow initially in social development, they were, by the time they reached school age, popular, friendly, nonaggressive leaders.

Where parents' attitudes are classed as "actively rejectant" the children show a slightly decelerated intellectual development, relatively poor use of the abilities they do possess, and some lack of originality. They are emotionally unstable, rebellious, aggressive, and quarrelsome. The children of parents with other attitude syndromes tend in various respects to fall in between these extremes.

I am sure that these findings do not surprise us as related to child development. I would like to suggest that they probably apply to other relationships as well, and that the counselor or physician or administrator who is warmly emotional and expressive, respectful of the individuality of himself and of the other, and who exhibits a nonpossessive caring, probably facilitates self-realization much as does a parent with these attitudes.

Let me turn to another careful study in a very different area. Whitehorn and Betz (2, 18) investigated the degree of success

achieved by young resident physicians in working with schizophrenic patients on a psychiatric ward. They chose for special
study the seven who had been outstandingly helpful, and seven
whose patients had shown the least degree of improvement. Each
group had treated about fifty patients. The investigators examined all the available evidence to discover in what ways the
A group (the successful group) differed from the B group. Several significant differences were found. The physicians in the A
group tended to see the schizophrenic in terms of the personal
meaning which various behaviors had to the patient, rather than
seeing him as a case history or a descriptive diagnosis. They also
tended to work toward goals which were oriented to the personality of the patient, rather than such goals as reducing the
symptoms or curing the disease. It was found that the helpful
physicians, in their day-by-day interaction, primarily made use
of active personal participation — a person-to-person relationship. They made less use of procedures which could be classed
as "passive permissive." They were even less likely to use such
procedures as interpretation, instruction or advice, or emphasis
upon the practical care of the patient. Finally, they were much
more likely than the B group to develop a relationship in which
the patient felt trust and confidence in the physician.

Although the authors cautiously emphasize that these findings
relate only to the treatment of schizophrenics, I am inclined to
disagree. I suspect that similar facts would be found in a research
study of almost any class of helping relationship.

Another interesting study focuses upon the way in which the
person being helped perceives the relationship. Heine (11) studied individuals who had gone for psychotherapeutic help to psychoanalytic, client-centered, and Adlerian therapists. Regardless
of the type of therapy, these clients report similar changes in
themselves. But it is their perception of the relationship which
is of particular interest to us here. When asked what accounted
for the changes which had occurred, they expressed some differing explanations, depending on the orientation of the therapist. But their agreement on the major elements they had found
helpful was even more significant. They indicated that these
attitudinal elements in the relationship accounted for the changes
which had taken place in themselves: the trust they had felt in

the therapist; being understood by the therapist; the feeling of independence they had had in making choices and decisions. The therapist procedure which they had found most helpful was that the therapist clarified and openly stated feelings which the client had been approaching hazily and hesitantly.

There was also a high degree of agreement among these clients, regardless of the orientation of their therapists, as to what elements had been unhelpful in the relationship. Such therapist attitudes as lack of interest, remoteness or distance, and an over-degree of sympathy, were perceived as unhelpful. As to procedures, they had found it unhelpful when therapists had given direct specific advice regarding decisions or had emphasized past history rather than present problems. Guiding suggestions mildly given were perceived in an intermediate range — neither clearly helpful nor unhelpful.

Fiedler, in a much quoted study (7), found that expert therapists of differing orientations formed similar relationships with their clients. Less well known are the elements which characterized these relationships, differentiating them from the relationships formed by less expert therapists. These elements are an ability to understand the client's meanings and feelings; a sensitivity to the client's attitudes; a warm interest without any emotional overinvolvement.

A study by Quinn (14) throws light on what is involved in understanding the client's meanings and feelings. His study is surprising in that it shows that "understanding" of the client's meanings is essentially an attitude of *desiring* to understand. Quinn presented his judges only with recorded therapist statements taken from interviews. The raters had no knowledge of what the therapist was responding to or how the client reacted to his response. Yet it was found that the degree of understanding could be judged about as well from this material as from listening to the response in context. This seems rather conclusive evidence that it is an attitude of wanting to understand which is communicated.

As to the emotional quality of the relationship, Seeman (16) found that success in psychotherapy is closely associated with a strong and growing mutual liking and respect between client and therapist.

An interesting study by Dittes (4) indicates how delicate this relationship is. Using a physiological measure, the psychogalvanic reflex, to measure the anxious or threatened or alerted reactions of the client, Dittes correlated the deviations on this measure with judges' ratings of the degree of warm acceptance and permissiveness on the part of the therapist. It was found that whenever the therapist's attitudes changed even slightly in the direction of a lesser degree of acceptance, the number of abrupt GSR deviations significantly increased. Evidently when the relationship is experienced as less acceptant the organism organizes against threat, even at the physiological level.

Without trying fully to integrate the findings from these various studies, it can at least be noted that a few things stand out. One is the fact that it is the attitudes and feelings of the therapist, rather than his theoretical orientation, which is important. His procedures and techniques are less important than his attitudes. It is also worth noting that it is the way in which his attitudes and procedures are *perceived* which makes a difference to the client, and that it is this perception which is crucial.

"Manufactured" Relationships

Let me turn to research of a very different sort, some of which you may find rather abhorrent, but which nevertheless has a bearing upon the nature of a facilitating relationship. These studies have to do with what we might think of as manufactured relationships.

Verplanck (17), Greenspoon (8), and others have shown that operant conditioning of verbal behavior is possible in a relationship. Very briefly, if the experimenter says "Mhm," or "Good," or nods his head after certain types of words or statements, those classes of words tend to increase because of being reinforced. It has been shown that using such procedures one can bring about increases in such diverse verbal categories as plural nouns, hostile words, statements of opinion. The person is completely unaware that he is being influenced in any way by these reinforcers. The implication is that by such selective reinforcement we could bring it about that the other person in the relationship would be using whatever kinds of words and making whatever kinds of statements we had decided to reinforce.

Following still further the principles of operant conditioning as developed by Skinner and his group, Lindsley (12) has shown that a chronic schizophrenic can be placed in a "helping relationship" with a machine. The machine, somewhat like a vending machine, can be set to reward a variety of types of behaviors. Initially it simply rewards—with candy, a cigarette, or the display of a picture—the lever-pressing behavior of the patient. But it is possible to set it so that many pulls on the lever may supply a hungry kitten—visible in a separate enclosure—with a drop of milk. In this case the satisfaction is an altruistic one. Plans are being developed to reward similar social or altruistic behavior directed toward another patient, placed in the next room. The only limit to the kinds of behavior which might be rewarded lies in the degree of mechanical ingenuity of the experimenter.

Lindsley reports that in some patients there has been marked clinical improvement. Personally I cannot help but be impressed by the description of one patient who had gone from a deteriorated chronic state to being given free grounds privileges, this change being quite clearly associated with his interaction with the machine. Then the experimenter decided to study experimental extinction, which, put in more personal terms, means that no matter how many thousands of times the lever was pressed, no reward of any kind was forthcoming. The patient gradually regressed, grew untidy, uncommunicative, and his grounds privilege had to be revoked. This (to me) pathetic incident would seem to indicate that even in a relationship to a machine, trustworthiness is important if the relationship is to be helpful.

Still another interesting study of a manufactured relationship is being carried on by Harlow and his associates (10), this time with monkeys. Infant monkeys, removed from their mothers almost immediately after birth, are, in one phase of the experiment, presented with two objects. One might be termed the "hard mother," a sloping cylinder of wire netting with a nipple from which the baby may feed. The other is a "soft mother," a similar cylinder made of foam rubber and terry cloth. Even when an infant gets all his food from the "hard mother" he clearly and increasingly prefers the "soft mother." Motion pictures show that he definitely "relates" to this object, playing with it, enjoying it, finding security in clinging to it when strange objects are near, and using that security as a home base for venturing into the frightening world. Of the many interesting and challenging implications of this study, one seems reasonably clear. It is that no amount of direct food reward can take the place of certain perceived qualities which the infant appears to need and desire.

Two Recent Studies

Let me close this wide-ranging—and perhaps perplexing— sampling of research studies with an account of two very recent investigations. The first is an experiment conducted by Ends and Page (5). Working with hardened chronic hospitalized alcoholics who had been committed to a state hospital for sixty days, they tried three different methods of group psychotherapy. The method which they believed would be most effective was therapy based on a two-factor theory of learning; a client-centered approach was expected to be second; a psychoanalytically oriented approach was expected to be least efficient. Their results showed that the therapy based upon a learning theory approach was not only not helpful, but was somewhat deleterious. The outcomes were worse than those in the control group which had no therapy. The analytically oriented therapy produced some positive gain, and the client-centered group therapy was associated with the greatest amount of positive change. Follow-up data, extending over one and one-half years, confirmed the in-hospital findings, with the lasting improvement being greatest in the client-centered approach, next in the analytic, next the control group, and least in those handled by a learning theory approach.

As I have puzzled over this study, unusual in that the approach to which the authors were committed proved *least* effective, I find a clue, I believe, in the description of the therapy based on learning theory (13). Essentially it consisted (*a*) of pointing out and labeling the behaviors which had proved unsatisfying, (*b*) of exploring objectively with the client the reasons behind these behaviors, and (*c*) of establishing through reeducation more effective problem-solving habits. But in all of this interaction the aim, as they formulated it, was to be impersonal. The therapist "permits as little of his own personality to intrude as humanly possible." The "therapist stresses personal anonymity in his activities, i.e., he must studiously avoid impressing the patient with his own (therapist's) individual personality characteristics." To me this seems the most likely clue to the failure of this approach, as I try to interpret the facts in the light of the other research studies. To withhold one's self as a person and to deal with the other person as an object does not have a high probability of being helpful.

The final study I wish to report is one just being completed by Halkides (9). She started from a theoretical formulation of mine regarding the necessary and sufficient conditions for therapeutic change (15). She hypothesized that there would be a significant relationship between the extent of constructive personality change in the client and four counselor variables: (*a*) the degree of empathic understanding of the client manifested by the counselor; (*b*) the degree of positive affective attitude (unconditional positive regard) manifested by the counselor toward the client; (*c*) the extent to which the counselor is genuine, his words matching his own internal feeling; and (*d*) the extent to which the counselor's response matches the client's expression in the intensity of affective expression.

To investigate these hypotheses she first selected, by multiple objective criteria, a group of ten cases which could be classed as "most successful" and a group of ten "least successful" cases. She then took an early and late recorded interview from each of these cases. On a random basis she picked nine client-counselor interaction units—a client statement and a counselor response —from each of these interviews. She thus had nine early interactions and nine later interactions from each case. This gave her several hundred units which were now placed in random order. The units from an early interview of an unsuccessful case might be followed by the units from a late interview of a successful case, etc.

Three judges, who did not know the cases or their degree of success, or the source of any given unit, now listened to this material four different times. They rated each unit on a seven-point scale, first as to the degree of empathy, second as to the counselor's positive attitude toward the client, third as to the counselor's congruence, or genuineness, and fourth as to the degree to which the counselor's response matched the emotional intensity of the client's expression.

I think all of us who knew of the study regarded it as a very bold venture. Could judges listening to single units of interaction possibly make any reliable rating of such subtle qualities as I have mentioned? And even if suitable reliability could be obtained, could eighteen counselor-client interchanges from each case — a minute sampling of the hundreds or thousands of such interchanges which occurred in each case — possibly bear any relationship to the therapeutic outcome? The chance seemed slim.

The findings are surprising. It proved possible to achieve high reliability between the judges, most of the interjudge correlations being in the 0.80's or 0.90's, except on the last variable. It was found that a high degree of empathic understanding was significantly associated, at a .001 level, with the more successful cases. A high degree of unconditional positive regard was likewise associated with the more successful cases, at the .001 level. Even the rating of the counselor's genuineness, or congruence — the extent to which his words matched his feelings — was associated with the successful outcome of the case, and again at the .001 level of significance. Only in the investigation of the matching intensity of affective expression were the results equivocal.

It is of interest too that high ratings of these variables were not associated more significantly with units from later interviews than with units from early interviews. This means that the counselor's attitudes were quite constant throughout the interviews. If he was highly empathic, he tended to be so from first to last. If he was lacking in genuineness, this tended to be true of both early and late interviews.

As with any study, this investigation has its limitations. It is concerned with a certain type of helping relationship, psychotherapy. It investigated only four variables thought to be significant. Perhaps there are many others. Nevertheless it represents a significant advance in the study of helping relationships. Let me try to state the findings in the simplest possible fashion. It seems to indicate that the quality of the counselor's interaction with a client can be satisfactorily judged on the basis of a very small sampling of his behavior. It also means that if the counselor is congruent, or transparent, so that his words are in line with his feelings rather than the two being discrepant; if the counselor

likes the client, unconditionally; and if the counselor understands the essential feelings of the client as they seem to the
client—then there is a strong probability that this will be an
effective helping relationship.

Some Comments

These then are some of the studies which throw at least a
measure of light on the nature of the helping relationship. They
have investigated different facets of the problem. They have
approached it from very different theoretical contexts. They
have used different methods. They are not directly comparable.
Yet they seem to me to point to several statements which may
be made with some assurance. It seems clear that relationships
which are helpful have different characteristics from relationships which are unhelpful. These differential characteristics have
to do primarily with the attitudes of the helping person on the
one hand and with the perception of the relationship by the
"helpee" on the other. It is equally clear that the studies thus
far do not give us any final answers as to what is a helping relationship, nor how it is to be formed.

HOW CAN I CREATE A HELPING RELATIONSHIP?

I believe each of us working in the field of human relationships
has a similar problem in knowing how to use such research
knowledge. We cannot slavishly follow such findings in a mechanical way or we destroy the personal qualities which these
very studies show to be valuable. It seems to me that we have to
use these studies, testing them against our own experience and
forming new and further personal hypotheses to use and test in
our own further personal relationships.

So rather than try to tell you how you should use the findings
I have presented, I should like to tell you the kind of questions
which these studies and my own clinical experience raise for me,
and some of the tentative and changing hypotheses which guide
my behavior as I enter into what I hope may be helping relationships, whether with students, staff, family, or clients. Let me
list a number of these questions and considerations.

1. Can I *be* in some way which will be perceived by the other person as trustworthy, as dependable or consistent in some deep sense? Both research and experience indicate that this is very important, and over the years I have found what I believe are deeper and better ways of answering this question. I used to feel that if I fulfilled all the outer conditions of trustworthiness — keeping appointments, respecting the confidential nature of the interviews, etc. — and if I acted consistently the same during the interviews, then this condition would be fulfilled. But experience drove home the fact that to act consistently acceptant, for example, if in fact I was feeling annoyed or skeptical or some other nonacceptant feeling, was certain in the long run to be perceived as inconsistent or untrustworthy. I have come to recognize that being trustworthy does not demand that I be rigidly consistent but that I be dependably real. The term "congruent" is one I have used to describe the way I would like to be. By this I mean that whatever feeling or attitude I am experiencing would be matched by my awareness of that attitude. When this is true, then I am a unified or integrated person in that moment, and hence I can *be* whatever I deeply *am*. This is a reality which I find others experience as dependable.

2. A very closely related question is this: Can I be expressive enough as a person that what I am will be communicated unambiguously? I believe that most of my failures to achieve a helping relationship can be traced to unsatisfactory answers to these two questions. When I am experiencing an attitude of annoyance toward another person but am unaware of it, then my communication contains contradictory messages. My words are giving one message, but I am also in subtle ways communicating the annoyance I feel, and this confuses the other person and makes him distrustful, though he too may be unaware of what is causing the difficulty. When as a parent or a therapist or a teacher or an administrator I fail to listen to what is going on in me, fail because of my own defensiveness to sense my own feelings, then this kind of failure seems to result. It has made it seem to me that the most basic learning for anyone who hopes to establish any kind of helping relationship is that it is safe to be transparently real. If in a given relationship I am reasonably congruent, if no feelings relevant to the relationship are hidden

either to me or the other person, then I can be almost sure that the relationship will be a helpful one.

One way of putting this which may seem strange to you is that if I can form a helping relationship to myself—if I can be sensitively aware of and acceptant toward my own feelings—then the likelihood is great that I can form a helping relationship toward another.

Now, acceptantly to be what I am, in this sense, and to permit this to show through to the other person, is the most difficult task I know and one I never fully achieve. But to realize that this *is* my task has been most rewarding because it has helped me to find what has gone wrong with interpersonal relationships which have become snarled and to put them on a constructive track again. It has meant that if I am to facilitate the personal growth of others in relation to me, then I must grow, and while this is often painful it is also enriching.

3. A third question is: Can I let myself experience positive attitudes toward this other person—attitudes of warmth, caring, liking, interest, respect? It is not easy. I find in myself, and feel that I often see in others, a certain amount of fear of these feelings. We are afraid that if we let ourselves freely experience these positive feelings toward another we may be trapped by them. They may lead to demands on us or we may be disappointed in our trust, and these outcomes we fear. So as a reaction we tend to build up distance between ourselves and others— aloofness, a "professional" attitude, an impersonal relationship.

I feel quite strongly that one of the important reasons for the professionalization of every field is that it helps to keep this distance. In the clinical areas we develop elaborate diagnostic formulations, seeing the person as an object. In teaching and in administration we develop all kinds of evaluative procedures, so that again the person is perceived as an object. In these ways, I believe, we can keep ourselves from experiencing the caring which would exist if we recognized the relationship as one between two persons. It is a real achievement when we can learn, even in certain relationships or at certain times in those relationships, that it is safe to care, that it is safe to relate to the other as a person for whom we have positive feelings.

4. Another question the importance of which I have learned

in my own experience is: Can I be strong enough as a person to be separate from the other? Can I be a sturdy respecter of my own feelings, my own needs, as well as his? Can I own and, if need be, express my own feelings as something belonging to me and separate from his feelings? Am I strong enough in my own separateness that I will not be downcast by his depression, frightened by his fear, nor engulfed by his dependency? Is my inner self hardy enough to realize that I am not destroyed by his anger, taken over by his need for dependence, nor enslaved by his love, but that I exist separate from him with feelings and rights of my own? When I can freely feel this strength of being a separate person, then I find that I can let myself go much more deeply in understanding and accepting him because I am not fearful of losing myself.

5. The next question is closely related. Am I secure enough within myself to permit him his separateness? Can I permit him to be what he is — honest or deceitful, infantile or adult, despairing or overconfident? Can I give him the freedom to be? Or do I feel that he should follow my advice, or remain somewhat dependent on me, or mold himself after me? In this connection I think of the interesting small study by Farson (6) which found that the less well adjusted and less competent counselor tends to induce conformity to himself, to have clients who model themselves after him. On the other hand, the better adjusted and more competent counselor can interact with a client through many interviews without interfering with the freedom of the client to develop a personality quite separate from that of his therapist. I should prefer to be in this latter class, whether as parent or supervisor or counselor.

6. Another question I ask myself is: Can I let myself enter fully into the world of his feelings and personal meanings and see these as he does? Can I step into his private world so completely that I lose all desire to evaluate or judge it? Can I enter it so sensitively that I can move about in it freely, without trampling on meanings which are precious to him? Can I sense it so accurately that I can catch not only the meanings of his experience which are obvious to him, but those meanings which are only implicit, which he sees only dimly or as confusion? Can I extend this understanding without limit? I think of the client

who said, "Whenever I find someone who understands a *part* of me at the time, then it never fails that a point is reached where I know they're *not* understanding me again. . . . What I've looked for so hard is for someone to understand."

For myself I find it easier to feel this kind of understanding, and to communicate it, to individual clients than to students in a class or staff members in a group in which I am involved. There is a strong temptation to set students "straight," or to point out to a staff member the errors in his thinking. Yet when I can permit myself to understand in these situations, it is mutually rewarding. And with clients in therapy, I am often impressed with the fact that even a minimal amount of empathic understanding—a bumbling and faulty attempt to catch the confused complexity of the client's meaning—is helpful, though there is no doubt that it is most helpful when I can see and formulate clearly the meanings in his experiencing which for him have been unclear and tangled.

7. Still another issue is whether I can be acceptant of each facet of this other person which he presents to me. Can I receive him as he is? Can I communicate this attitude? Or can I only receive him conditionally, acceptant of some aspects of his feelings and silently or openly disapproving of other aspects? It has been my experience that when my attitude is conditional, then he cannot change or grow in those respects in which I cannot fully receive him. And when—afterward and sometimes too late—I try to discover why I have been unable to accept him in every respect, I usually discover that it is because I have been frightened or threatened in myself by some aspect of his feelings. If I am to be more helpful, then I must myself grow and accept myself in these respects.

8. A very practical issue is raised by the question: Can I act with sufficient sensitivity in the relationship that my behavior will not be perceived as a threat? The work we are beginning to do in studying the physiological concomitants of psychotherapy confirms the research by Dittes in indicating how easily individuals are threatened at a physiological level. The psychogalvanic reflex—the measure of skin conductance—takes a sharp dip when the therapist responds with some word which is just a little stronger than the client's feelings. And to a phrase such as, "My

you *do* look upset," the needle swings almost off the paper. My desire to avoid even such minor threats is not due to a hypersensitivity about my client. It is simply due to the conviction based on experience that if I can free him as completely as possible from external threat, then he can begin to experience and to deal with the internal feelings and conflicts which he finds threatening within himself.

9. A specific aspect of the preceding question but an important one is: Can I free him from the threat of external evaluation? In almost every phase of our lives — at home, at school, at work — we find ourselves under the rewards and punishments of external judgments: "That's good"; "that's naughty." "That's worth an A"; "that's a failure." "That's good counseling"; "that's poor counseling." Such judgments are a part of our lives from infancy to old age. I believe they have a certain social usefulness to institutions and organizations such as schools and professions. Like everyone else I find myself all too often making such evaluations. But, in my experience, they do not make for personal growth and hence I do not believe that they are a part of a helping relationship. Curiously enough a positive evaluation is as threatening in the long run as a negative one, since to inform someone that he is good implies that you also have the right to tell him he is bad. So I have come to feel that the more I can keep a relationship free of judgment and evaluation, the more this will permit the other person to reach the point where he recognizes that the locus of evaluation, the center of responsibility, lies within himself. The meaning and value of his experience is in the last analysis something which is up to him, and no amount of external judgment can alter this. So I should like to work toward a relationship in which I am not, even in my own feelings, evaluating him. This I believe can set him free to be a self-responsible person.

10. One last question: Can I meet this other individual as a person who is in process of *becoming*, or will I be bound by his past and by my past? If, in my encounter with him, I am dealing with him as an immature child, an ignorant student, a neurotic personality, or a psychopath, each of these concepts of mine limits what he can be in the relationship. Martin Buber, the existentialist philosopher of the University of Jerusalem, has a

phrase, "confirming the other," which has had meaning for me. He says, "Confirming means . . . accepting the whole potentiality of the other. . . . I can recognize in him, know in him, the person he has been . . . *created* to become . . . I confirm him in myself, and then in him, in relation to this potentiality that . . . can now be developed, can evolve" (3). If I accept the other person as something fixed, already diagnosed and classified, already shaped by his past, then I am doing my part to confirm this limited hypothesis. If I accept him as a process of becoming, then I am doing what I can to confirm or make real his potentialities.

It is at this point that I see Verplanck, Lindsley, and Skinner, working in operant conditioning, coming together with Buber, the philosopher or mystic. At least they come together in principle, in an odd way. If I see a relationship as only an opportunity to reinforce certain types of words or opinions in the other, then I tend to confirm him as an object—a basically mechanical, manipulable object. And if I see this as his potentiality, he tends to act in ways which support this hypothesis. If, on the other hand, I see a relationship as an opportunity to "reinforce" *all* that he is, the person that he is with all his existent potentialities, then he tends to act in ways which support *this* hypothesis. I have then—to use Buber's term—confirmed him as a living person, capable of creative inner development. Personally I prefer this second type of hypothesis.

Conclusion

In the early portion of this paper I reviewed some of the contributions which research is making to our knowledge *about* relationships. Endeavoring to keep that knowledge in mind I then took up the kind of questions which arise from an inner and subjective point of view as I enter, as a person, into relationships. If I could, in myself, answer all the questions I have raised in the affirmative, then I believe that any relationships in which I was involved would be helping relationships, would involve growth. But I cannot give a positive answer to most of these questions. I can only work in the direction of the positive answer.

This has raised in my mind the strong suspicion that the optimal helping relationship is the kind of relationship created by a person who is psychologically mature. Or to put it in another way, the degree to which I can create relationships which facilitate the growth of others as separate persons is a measure of the growth I have achieved in myself. In some respects this is a disturbing thought, but it is also a promising or challenging one. It would indicate that if I am interested in creating helping relationships I have a fascinating lifetime job ahead of me, stretching and developing my potentialities in the direction of growth.

I am left with the uncomfortable thought that what I have been working out for myself in this paper may have little relationship to your interests and your work. If so, I regret it. But I am at least partially comforted by the fact that all of us who are working in the field of human relationships and trying to understand the basic orderliness of that field are engaged in the most crucial enterprise in today's world. If we are thoughtfully trying to understand our tasks as administrators, teachers, educational counselors, vocational counselors, therapists, then we are working on the problem which will determine the future of this planet. For it is not upon the physical sciences that the future will depend. It is upon us who are trying to understand and deal with the interactions between human beings — who are trying to create helping relationships. So I hope that the questions I ask of myself will be of some use to you in gaining understanding and perspective as you endeavor, in your way, to facilitate growth in your relationships.

REFERENCES

1. Baldwin, A. L., J. Kalhorn, and F. H. Breese. Patterns of parent behavior. *Psychol. Monogr.*, 1945, *58*, No. 268, 1–75.
2. Betz, B. J., and J. C. Whitehorn. The relationship of the therapist to the outcome of therapy in schizophrenia. *Psychiat. Research Reports #5. Research techniques in schizophrenia.* Washington, D.C., American Psychiatric Association, 1956, 89–117.
3. Buber, M., and C. Rogers. Transcription of dialogue held April 18, 1957, Ann Arbor, Mich. Unpublished manuscript.
4. Dittes, J. E. Galvanic skin response as a measure of patient's reaction to therapist's permissiveness. *J. Abnorm. & Soc. Psychol.*, 1957, *55*, 295–303.
5. Ends, E. J., and C. W. Page. A study of three types of group psy-

chotherapy with hospitalized male inebriates. *Quar. J. Stud. Alcohol,* 1957, *18,* 263–277.

6. Farson, R. E. Introjection in the psychotherapeutic relationship. Unpublished doctoral dissertation, University of Chicago, 1955.

7. Fiedler, F. E. Quantitative studies on the role of therapists' feelings toward their patients. In Mowrer, O. H. (Ed.), *Psychotherapy: theory and research.* New York: Ronald Press, 1953, Chap. 12.

8. Greenspoon, J. The reinforcing effect of two spoken sounds on the frequency of two responses. *Amer. J. Psychol.,* 1955, *68,* 409–416.

9. Halkides, G. An experimental study of four conditions necessary for therapeutic change. Unpublished doctoral dissertation, University of Chicago, 1958.

10. Harlow, H. F. The nature of love. *Amer. Psychol.,* 1958, *13,* 673–685.

11. Heine, R. W. A comparison of patients' reports on psychotherapeutic experience with psychoanalytic, nondirective, and Adlerian therapists. Unpublished doctoral dissertation, University of Chicago, 1950.

12. Lindsley, O. R. Operant conditioning methods applied to research in chronic schizophrenia. *Psychiat. Research Reports #5. Research techniques in schizophrenia.* Washington, D.C.: American Psychiatric Association, 1956, 118–153.

13. Page, C. W., and E. J. Ends. A review and synthesis of the literature suggesting a psychotherapeutic technique based on two-factor learning theory. Unpublished manuscript, loaned to the writer.

14. Quinn, R. D. Psychotherapists' expressions as an index to the quality of early therapeutic relationships. Unpublished doctoral dissertation, University of Chicago, 1950.

15. Rogers, C. R. The necessary and sufficient conditions of psychotherapeutic personality change. *J. Consult. Psychol.,* 1957, *21,* 95–103.

16. Seeman, J. Counselor judgments of therapeutic process and outcome. In Rogers, C. R., and R. F. Dymond, (Eds.). *Psychotherapy and personality change.* University of Chicago Press, 1954, Chap. 7.

17. Verplanck, W. S. The control of the content of conversation: reinforcement of statements of opinion. *J. Abnorm. & Soc. Psychol.,* 1955, *51,* 668–676.

18. Whitehorn, J. C., and B. J. Betz. A study of psychotherapeutic relationships between physicians and schizophrenic patients. *Amer. J. Psychiat.,* 1954, *111,* 321–331.

9
Reflection of Feelings and Transference

REFLECTION OF FEELINGS

Although I am partially responsible for the use of this term to describe a certain type of therapist response, I have, over the years, become very unhappy with it. A major reason is that "reflection of feelings" has not been infrequently taught as a technique, and sometimes a very wooden technique at that. On the basis of written client expressions, the learner is expected to concoct a "correct" reflection of feeling—or even worse, to select the "correct" response from a multiple-choice list. Such training has very little to do with an effective therapeutic relationship. So I have become more and more allergic to the use of the term.

At the same time I know that many of my responses in an interview—as is evident from published examples—would seem to be "reflections of feeling." Inwardly I object. I am definitely *not* trying to "reflect feelings."

Then I receive a letter from my friend and former colleague, Dr. John Shlien of Harvard, which still further complicates my dilemma. He writes:

> "Reflection" is unfairly damned. It was rightly criticized when you described the wooden mockery it could become in the hands of insensitive people, and you wrote beautifully on that point. But you neglected the other side. It is an instrument of artistic virtuosity in the hands of a sincere, intelligent, empathic listener. It made possible the development of client-centered therapy, when the philosophy alone could not have. Undeserved denigration of the technique leads to fatuous alternatives in the name of "congruence."

Puzzling over this matter, I have come to a double insight. From my point of view as therapist, I am *not* trying to "reflect feelings." I am trying to determine whether my understanding

Person-Centered Review, Vol. 1, No. 4, November 1986, 375–377, and Vol. 2, No. 2, May 1987, 182–188. Reprinted by permission of Sage Publications, Inc.

of the client's inner world is correct — whether I am seeing it as he or she is experiencing it at this moment. Each response of mine contains the unspoken question, "Is this the way it is in you? Am I catching just the color and texture and flavor of the personal meaning you are experiencing right now? If not, I wish to bring my perception in line with yours."

On the other hand, I know that from the client's point of view we are holding up a mirror of his or her current experiencing. The feelings and personal meanings seem sharper when seen through the eyes of another, when they are reflected.

So I suggest that these therapist responses be labeled not "Reflections of Feeling," but "Testing Understandings," or "Checking Perceptions." Such terms would, I believe, be more accurate. They would be helpful in the training of therapists. They would supply a sound motivation in responding, a questioning desire rather than an intent to "reflect."

But in understanding the client's experience, we can realize that such responses do serve as a mirror. This is beautifully expressed by Sylvia Slack (1985, pp. 41–42) as she tells of her reactions in a therapy interview held in front of a large audience, and videotaped.

> Watching the tapes helped me to visualize the counseling process more clearly. It was like Dr. Rogers was a magical mirror. The process involved my sending rays toward that mirror. I looked into the mirror to get a glimpse of the reality that I am. If I had sensed the mirror was affected by the rays being received, the reflection would have seemed distorted and not to be trusted. Although I was aware of sending rays, their nature was not truly discernible until they were reflected and clarified by the mirror. There was a curiosity about the rays and what they revealed about me. This experience allowed me an opportunity to get a view of myself that was untainted by the perceptions of outside viewers. This inner knowledge of myself enabled me to make choices more suited to the person who lives within me.

As she hints here, and goes on to elaborate, it is important that the therapist's understanding be so sensitively correct that the mirror image is clear and undistorted. This means laying aside our own judgments and values in order to grasp, with delicate accuracy, the exact meaning the client is experiencing.

Thinking these thoughts and writing them out has been clarifying for me. I can continue, from the therapist's point of view, to test my understanding of my client by making tentative attempts to describe or portray his or her inner world. I can recognize that for my client these responses are, at their best, a clear mirror image of the meanings and perceptions that make up his or her world of the moment—an image that is clarifying and insight producing.

TRANSFERENCE

Feelings and emotions directed toward the therapist fall primarily into two groups. First are those feelings that are an understandable response to some of the attitudes and behaviors of the therapist. There may be resentment originating in an attitude of superiority of expertness in the therapist. The client feels looked down upon, and responds negatively. Such resentment may also be caused by incorrect or premature interpretations by the therapist, resulting in the client's feeling pushed or misunderstood. There may be anger at therapist prescriptions for client behavior. One client cooperated very well with Fritz Perls during an interview. Later, seeing a film of the interview, she was indignant at him and at herself. "*Why* did I *do* all those things he told me to do?!" In such instances as these, therapists may or may not be aware of the fact that negative client attitudes are simply a natural response to their statements or actions.

Positive feelings may also result from therapist behavior. Warm and loving feelings may arise in the client from an unexpected and very welcome depth of understanding on the part of the therapist; from small actions showing concern for the client's comfort; from such behavior as laying a hand on the client's arm during a moment of painful struggle; from such behavior as Heinz Kohut offering "two fingers" to a desperate analysand; from such things as helping a client put on a heavy coat, or casually offering transportation during a heavy rainstorm. It is entirely reasonable that the client should, in these circumstances, come to like or love the therapist, and want a loving response in return. Again, the therapist may or may not be aware of the fact that it is his or her statements or actions that are at the base of the client's feelings.

The second category of client reactions are the emotions that have little or no relationship to the therapist's behavior. These are truly "transferred" from their real origin to the therapist. They are projections. They may be triggered by something in the therapist—"You look like my father," or "You resemble a man I despise"—but the intensity of the feeling comes from within the client, and is not due to the behavior of the therapist.

These projected feelings may be positive feelings of love, sexual desire, adoration, and the like. They may be negative—hatred, contempt, fear, mistrust. Their true object may be a parent or other significant person in the client's life. Or, and this is less often recognized, they may be negative attitudes toward the self, which the client cannot bear to face.

From a client-centered point of view, it is not necessary, in responding to and dealing with these feelings, to determine whether they are therapist caused or are projections. The distinction is of theoretical interest, but is not a practical problem. In the therapeutic interaction, all of these attitudes—positive or negative, "transference" feelings, or therapist-caused reactions—are best dealt with in the same way. If the therapist is sensitively understanding and genuinely acceptant and nonjudgmental, therapy will move forward *through* these feelings. There is absolutely no need to make a special case of attitudes that are transferred to the therapist, and no need for the therapist to permit the dependence that is so often a part of other forms of therapy, particularly psychoanalysis. It is entirely possible to accept dependent feelings, without permitting the client to change the therapist's role.

All of this is well illustrated in a case example previously published, but still worthy of careful examination.

The client was an unmarried woman in her thirties, a decidedly disturbed individual. In her early interviews she struggled with painful feelings of guilt arising out of possible incestuous relations with her father. She could not be certain whether the events she described really occurred, or whether they were products of her imagination. She was slow in her speech, enabling the therapist to keep unusually complete notes, so what follows is nearly verbatim. Several excerpts from three interviews will indicate the depth of her "transference" feelings, and the way in which the therapist responded to them. They illuminate the way in which "transference" disappears when the feelings are expressed in a client-centered climate.

From Ninth Interview

S: This morning I hung my coat out there instead of here in your office. I've told you I like you, and I was afraid if you helped me on with the coat, I might turn around and kiss you.

C: You thought those feelings of affection might *make* you kiss me unless you protected yourself from them.

S: Well, another reason I left the coat out there is that I want to be dependent—but I want to show you I don't have to be dependent.

C: You both want to be, and to prove you don't have to be.

Toward end of interview

S: I've never told anyone they were the most wonderful person I've ever known, but I've told you that. It's not just sex. It's more than that.

C: You really feel very deeply attached to me.

From Tenth Interview—Toward Close of Interview

S: I think emotionally I'm dying for sexual intercourse but I don't do anything about it. . . . The thing I want is to have sexual intercourse with you. I don't dare ask you, 'cause I'm afraid you'd be nondirective.

C: You have this awful tension, and want so much to have relations with me.

S: (Goes on in this vein. Finally.) Can't we do something about it? This tension is awful! Will you relieve the tension. . . . Can you give me a direct answer? I think it might help both of us.

C: (Gently.) The answer would be no. I can understand how *desperately* you feel, but I would not be willing to do that.

S: (Pause. Sigh of relief.) I think that helps me. It's only when I'm upset that I'm like this. You have strength, and it gives me strength.

Twelfth Interview

S: (Silent for two minutes. Then begins to talk in hard flat voice, quite unlike her usual tone. Does not look at therapist. There was much repetition, but the following excerpts give the major thoughts.) You feel

I want to come, but I *don't*! I'm not coming anymore. It doesn't do any good. I don't like you. (*Her voice becomes venomous.*) I *hate* you! I wish you never were born.

C: (*His tone matching the depth of her feeling.*) You just *hate* me —*very* bitterly!

S: I think I'll throw you in the lake. I'll cut you up! You think people like you, but they don't. . . . You think you can attract women, but you *can't*. . . . I wish you were *dead*.

C: You *detest* me and you'd really like to get rid of me!

S: You think my father did bad things with me, but he didn't! You think he wasn't a good man but he *was*. You think I want intercourse, but I *don't*!

C: You feel I *absolutely misrepresent* all your thoughts.

S: You think you can get people to come in and tell you everything, and they'll think they're being helped but they're *not*! You just like to make 'em suffer. You think you can hypnotize them, but you *can't*! You think you're good, but you ain't. I hate you, I hate you, I *hate* you!

C: You feel I really like to make 'em suffer, but that I *don't* help them.

S: You think I haven't been straight, but I have. I *hate* you. All I've had is pain, pain, pain. You think I can't direct my own life, but I can. You think I can't get well, but I can. You think I had hallucinations, but I didn't. I hate you. (*Long pause. Leans on desk in strained, exhausted pose.*) You think I'm crazy, but I'm not.

C: You're sure I think you're crazy.

S: (*Pause.*) I'm tied, and I just can't get loose! (*Despairing tone of voice, and tears. Pause.*) I had a hallucination and I've *got* to get it out! . . . (*Goes on about her own deep conflicts, and tells of the hallucination she has experienced, with terrific tension in her voice, but with an attitude very different from that at beginning of interview.*)

Later in Interview

S: I knew at the office I had to get rid of this somewhere. I felt I could come down and tell you. I knew you'd understand. I couldn't say I hated myself. That's true but I couldn't say it. So I just thought of all the ugly things I could say to you instead.

C: The things you felt about yourself you couldn't say but you could say them about me.

S: I know we're getting to rock bottom . . . (Rogers, 1951, pp. 211–213)

Here are several comments about these excerpts. They show —again—that when the therapeutic conditions are present, the process of therapy moves forward. They show that this hypothesis holds for the exploration of so-called transference feelings, just as it does for the exploration of all other feelings.

This case shows that when the therapist's understanding is accurate and his acceptance is genuine, when there are no interpretations given and no evaluations made, "transference" attitudes tend to dissolve, and the feelings are directed toward their true object. In a climate of such safety, there is less need to deny feelings of awareness, and as a consequence the client becomes more accurately aware of the meaning of her experience, and develops new insight.

It is noteworthy that when the therapist responds to her question and states his unwillingness (on ethical grounds) to engage in sex, he speaks solely for himself, and of himself. There is no interpretation of her behavior, no judgment of her request.

In my opinion, interpretations tend to delay—not hasten— the process. If the therapist had said, "I think perhaps you are asking to re-create the incestuous relationship with your father"—an interpretation that might well be true—it would almost certainly have met strong resistance.

Psychoanalysts speak often of resistance and the difficulties in dealing with it. It is well to recognize that there are two types of resistance. There is the pain of revealing—to oneself and another—the feelings that have hitherto been denied to awareness. There is also the resistance to the therapist, created *by* the therapist. Offering interpretations, making diagnoses and other judgments—these are the usual way by which resistance is brought about—the resistance with which the therapist then must deal.

Here is the special virtue of the client-centered approach. By creating a relationship that is *safe*, the client has no need to resist the therapist, and hence is more free, as in this case, to deal with the resistance she finds in herself. She finds the situation safe enough to realize that all the thoughts and feelings she has projected onto the therapist are in fact thoughts and feelings she has about herself.

To me it seems clear that the most effective way of dealing with *all* feelings directed toward the therapist is through the creation of a therapeutic relationship that fulfills the conditions set forth in client-centered theory. To deal with transference feelings as a very special part of therapy, making their handling the very core of therapy, is to my mind a grave mistake. Such an approach fosters dependency and lengthens therapy. It creates a whole new problem, the only purpose of which appears to be the intellectual satisfaction of the therapist — showing the elaborateness of his or her expertise. I deplore it.

There is one additional point I would make. If dealing with the "transference neurosis" is so important to therapy, and brings about a greater depth of change in personality and behavior, why are there no data to back this up? Where are the recorded interviews that would demonstrate that the psychoanalytic view is more effective, more far-reaching in its results? Why the reluctance to make known what actually happens in the therapist's dealings with this core of the analytic process?

Having, years ago, read a transcript of a complete psychoanalysis, and having had the opportunity to listen to brief segments of psychoanalytic therapy, I believe I can understand the reluctance to make such data public. So the questions about transference will be debated and argued, but always one step removed from the data. The questions cannot be finally answered until psychoanalysts are willing to open their work to professional scrutiny.

REFERENCES

Rogers, C. R. (1951). *Client-centered therapy*. Boston: Houghton Mifflin.
Shlien, J. (1986, April 2). Personal correspondence.
Slack, S. (1985, Spring). Reflections on a workshop with Carl Rogers. *Journal of Humanistic Psychology, 25,* 35–42.

10
A Client-centered/Person-centered Approach to Therapy

What do I mean by a client-centered, or person-centered, approach? For me it expresses the primary theme of my whole professional life, as that theme has become clarified through experience, interaction with others, and research. This theme has been used and found effective in many areas, until the broad label "a person-centered approach" seems the most descriptive.

The central hypothesis of this approach can be briefly stated. It is that the individual has within himself or herself vast resources for self-understanding, for altering his or her self-concept, attitudes, and self-directed behavior—and that these resources can be tapped if only a definable climate of facilitative psychological attitudes can be provided.

There are three conditions that constitute this growth-promoting climate, whether we are speaking of the relationship between therapist and client, parent and child, leader and group, teacher and student, or administrator and staff. The conditions apply, in fact, in any situation in which the development of the person is a goal. I have described these conditions at length in previous writings (Rogers, 1959, 1961). I present here a brief summary from the point of view of psychotherapy, but the description applies to all the foregoing relationships.

The first element is genuineness, realness, or congruence. The more the therapist is himself or herself in the relationship, putting up no professional front or personal façade, the greater is the likelihood that the client will change and grow in a constructive manner. Genuineness means that the therapist is openly being the feelings and attitudes that are flowing within at the moment. There is a close matching, or congruence, between what is being experienced at the gut level, what is present in awareness, and what is expressed to the client.

The second attitude of importance in creating a climate for

In Kutash, I. and Wolf, A. (Eds.), *Psychotherapist's Casebook.* Jossey-Bass, 1986, 197–208.

change is acceptance, or caring, or prizing — unconditional positive regard. When the therapist is experiencing a positive, nonjudgmental, accepting attitude toward whatever the client *is* at that moment, therapeutic movement or change is more likely. Acceptance involves the therapist's willingness for the client to be whatever immediate feeling is going on — confusion, resentment, fear, anger, courage, love, or pride. It is a nonpossessive caring. When the therapist prizes the client in a total rather than a conditional way, forward movement is likely.

The third facilitative aspect of the relationship is empathic understanding. This means that the therapist senses accurately the feelings and personal meanings that the client is experiencing and communicates this acceptant understanding to the client. When functioning best, the therapist is so much inside the private world of the other that he or she can clarify not only the meanings of which the client is aware but even those just below the level of awareness. Listening, of this very special, active kind, is one of the most potent forces for change that I know.

There is a body of steadily mounting research evidence that, by and large, supports the view that when these facilitative conditions are present, changes in personality and behavior do indeed occur. Such research has been carried on in this and other countries from 1949 to the present. Studies have been made of changes in attitude and behavior in psychotherapy, in degree of learning in school, and in the behavior of schizophrenics. In general, they are confirming. (See Rogers, 1980, for a summary of the research.)

Trust

Practice, theory, and research make it clear that the person-centered approach is built on a basic trust in the person. This is perhaps its sharpest point of difference from most of the institutions in our culture. Almost all of education, government, business, much of religion, much of family life, much of psychotherapy, is based on a distrust of the person. Goals must be set, because the person is seen as incapable of choosing suitable aims. The individual must be guided toward these goals, since otherwise he or she might stray from the selected path. Teachers, parents, supervisors must develop procedures to make sure the individual is progressing toward the goal—examinations, inspections, interrogations. The individual is seen as innately sinful, destructive, lazy, or all three—as someone who must be constantly watched over.

The person-centered approach, in contrast, depends on the actualizing tendency present in every living organism—the tendency to grow, to develop, to realize its full potential. This way of being trusts the constructive directional flow of the human being toward a more complex and complete development. It is this directional flow that we aim to release.

One More Characteristic

I described above the characteristics of a growth-promoting relationship that have been investigated and supported by research. But recently my view has broadened into a new area that cannot as yet be studied empirically.

When I am at my best, as a group facilitator or a therapist, I discover another characteristic. I find that when I am closest to my inner, intuitive self, when I am somehow in touch with the unknown in me, when perhaps I am in a slightly altered state of consciousness in the relationship, then whatever I do seems to be full of healing. Then simply my *presence* is releasing and helpful. There is nothing I can do to force this experience, but when I can relax and be close to the transcendental core of me, then I may behave in strange and impulsive ways in the relationship, ways which I cannot justify rationally, which have nothing to do with my thought processes. But these strange behaviors turn out to be *right*, in some odd way. At those moments it seems that my inner spirit has reached out and touched the inner spirit of the other. Our relationship transcends itself and becomes a part of something larger. Profound growth and healing and energy are present.

This kind of transcendent phenomenon is certainly experienced at times in groups in which I have worked, changing the lives of some of those involved. One participant in a workshop put it eloquently: "I found it to be a profound spiritual experience. I felt the oneness of spirit in the community. We breathed together, felt together, even spoke for one another. I felt the power of the 'life force' that infuses each of us—whatever that is. I felt its presence without the usual barricades of 'me-ness' or 'you-ness'—it was like a meditative experience when I feel myself as a center of consciousness. And yet with that extraordinary sense of oneness, the separateness of each person present has never been more clearly preserved."

I realize that this account partakes of the mystical. Our experiences, it is clear, involve the transcendent, the indescribable, the spiritual. I am compelled to believe that I, like many others, have underestimated the importance of this mystical, spiritual dimension.

In this I am not unlike some of the more advanced thinkers in physics and chemistry. (For example, see Capra, 1982.) As they push their theories further, picturing a "reality" which has no solidity, which is no more than oscillations of energy, they too begin to talk in terms of the transcendent, the indescribable, the unexpected—the sort of phenomena that we have observed and experienced in the person-centered approach.

The person-centered approach, then, is primarily a way of being that finds its expression in attitudes and behaviors that create a growth-promoting climate. It is a basic philosophy rather than simply a technique or a method. When this philosophy is lived, it helps the person expand the development of his or her own capacities. When it is lived, it also stimulates constructive change in others. It empowers the individual, and when this personal power is sensed, experience shows that it tends to be used for personal and social transformation.

When this person-centered way of being is lived in psychotherapy, it leads to a process of self-exploration and self-discovery in the client and eventually to constructive changes in personality and behavior. As the therapist lives these conditions in the relationship, he or she becomes a companion to the client in this journey toward the core of self. This process is, I believe, illuminated in the case material that follows.

JAN — AND THE PROCESS OF CHANGE

Occasionally one interview will illustrate several aspects of the therapeutic process as it occurs in the changing relationship between therapist and client. Such an interview was the one I held with Jan. It was a half-hour demonstration therapy session, held onstage before a workshop of six hundred participants in Johannesburg, South Africa.

Several individuals had volunteered, and the next morning, shortly before the interview, my colleague Ruth Sanford told Jan that she had selected her as the client.

Jan and I took chairs facing each other, so that the audience had a side view of our interaction. We adjusted and tried out our microphones. Then I said that I wished a few moments of quiet to collect myself and get centered. I added that she might also like that time to become quiet, and a nod of her head indicated that she would. I used the time to forget the technicalities and to focus my mind on being present to Jan and open to anything she might express.

From this point on, the material is taken from the recorded interview. The excerpts given contain the main themes and significant points. The material omitted consists of further explication of some theme or the pursuit of some issue that was dropped.

The reader will find it profitable, I believe, to first read the interview as a whole, looking only at what Jan and I said, and skipping over the comments on the process that are interspersed from time to time. A second reading can then be done by segments, stopping to consider the comments on each segment.

CARL: Now I feel more ready. I don't know what you want to talk with me about, because we haven't done more than say hello to each other. But whatever you would like to bring up, I'd be very ready to hear. (*Pause.*)

JAN: I have two problems. The first one is the fear of marriage and children. And the other one is the age process, aging. It's very difficult to look into the future, and I find it very frightening.

CARL: Those are two main problems for you. I don't know which you'd rather pick up first.

JAN: I think the immediate problem is the age problem. I would rather start on it. If you can help on that, I would be very grateful.

CARL: Can you tell me a little bit more about the fear that you have of aging? As you get older, what?

JAN: I feel that I am in a panic situation. I am thirty-five years of age, and I've only got another five years till forty. It's very difficult to explain. I keep turning around and I want to run away from it.

CARL: It's enough of a fear that you really — it really sets off a panic in you.

JAN: Yes, and it's affecting my confidence as a person. (CARL: Mm-hm.) It's only started happening in the last eighteen months, two years, that I've suddenly realized: Hell's teeth, everything's catching up on me. Why do I feel like that?

CARL: And you didn't have those feelings very much until perhaps a year and a half ago. (*Pause.*) Was there anything special at that time that seemed to set it off?

My initial responses have two purposes. I want to make it completely safe for her to express herself, and so I recognize her feelings and ask nonspecific, nonthreatening questions. It is also part of my purpose to refrain from anything that would point in a particular direction or would imply any judgment. The direction the interview will take is completely up to her.

Jan has moved from *stating* her problems to beginning to *experience* the panic she is feeling. Her attitude is clearly that the help, if any, will come from me.

JAN: Not that I can recall, really. Well, my mother died at fifty-three (CARL: Mm-hm.), and she was a very young and very bright woman in many ways. But I think maybe that has something to do with it. I don't know.

CARL: You sort of felt that if your mother died at that early age, that was a possibility for you, too. (*Pause.*) And time began to seem a lot shorter.

JAN: Right!

Already Jan is using the safety of the relationship to explore her experience. Without being aware of its significance, her nonconscious intellect moves her into a consideration of her mother's death.

My response shows that I am beginning to feel at home in her inner world, and I go a bit beyond her description. My sense of her world is confirmed by her "Right!" If she had said, "No, that's not it," I would immediately have dropped my picture and tried to discover the meaning her statement did have for her. I have no investment in the correctness of my responses as I try to understand.

JAN: When I look at my mother's life—and she had many talents—she unfortunately, towards the end, became a bitter woman. The world owed her a living. Now I don't want ever to be in that situation. And at this point in time, I'm not. I've had a very full life—both very exciting and very sad at times. I've learned a lot and I've a lot to learn. But—I *do* feel that what happened to my mother is happening to me.

CARL: So that remains sort of a specter. Part of your fear is: "Look what happened to my mother, and am I following in the same path, (JAN: Right.) and will I feel that same fruitlessness, perhaps?

JAN: (*Long pause.*) Do you want to ask me some more questions, because I think that will help you to draw information out of me? I just can't—everything is a whirlwind, (CARL: Mm-hmm.) going around in circles.

CARL: Things are just going around so fast inside of you, you don't quite know where to (JAN: Where to begin.) take hold. I don't know whether you want to talk anymore about your relationship to your mother's life, your fear of that, or what?

A long pause on the part of the client is frequently fruitful. I wait with interest to see what follows.

First comes a clear indication that in her mind I am the authority, I am the doctor. She will fit into my wishes.

For my part, I don't refuse verbally to follow the medical model, to be the all-wise doctor. I simply do not *behave* as an authority figure. Instead, I show that I understand her confusion and leave her with a nonspecific lead.

It is interesting that she interjects to finish my sentence for me. It is an indication that in her *experience* she is recognizing that we are together in this search—on the same side of the table, as it were, rather than the doctor on one side, the "patient" on the other.

JAN: The older I get, though, the stronger I feel about the marriage situation. Now whether the two are related, I don't know. But the fear of getting married, and being committed, and children—I find very, very frightening. And it's getting stronger as I get older—

CARL: It's a fear of commitment, and a fear of having children? And all that seems to be a growing fear, all those fears seem to be increasing.

JAN: Yes. I'm not afraid of commitment. For instance, when it comes to my work, to friendship, to doing certain things. But to me marriage is very—

CARL: So you're not a person who's irresponsible or anything like that— (JAN: No, not at all.) You're committed to your work, you're committed to friends. It's just that the notion of being tied into marriage—that's scary as hell.

The long pause leads Jan to open up and explore her fear of marriage.

The client "increasingly differentiates and discriminates the objects of his feelings and perceptions, including . . . his self, his experiences, and the interrelationships between them" (Rogers, 1959, p. 216). Jan certainly illustrates this statement in my theory as she recognizes her fear—not of commitment but only of a special commitment.

We now are definitely companions in the search to know her self, her deeper, inner self. We are free to take part in each other's statements.

JAN: (*After long silence.*) Do you want me to speak?

CARL: I wish I could help you get a handle on some of those things that are going around in your head.

JAN: Um, (*Pause.*) I really didn't think I'd be called up here today. Otherwise I'd have made a list! (*Pause.*) Would my problem be—My love is for the arts, right? I'm very much involved with music and dancing. I'd like to be able to just throw everything up and devote my life to music and dancing. But unfortunately the society that we live in today forces one to work and live up to a certain social standard. It's not something I regret. It's something I miss, something I really want to do. But how do I do it? Has that got something to do with—as I say, I'm getting older, and I keep turning around and running back.

CARL: So what you're telling me is, you *do* have a purpose in life, you *do* have something you really want to do — (JAN: Oh, yes.) To commit yourself to music, to the arts, but you feel society prevents you from doing that. But what you would like to do is to throw up everything else and just concentrate on your love of music.

JAN: Right.

When Jan is struggling to know in which direction to move in her exploration, she endeavors to give the responsibility to me. I simply express my very real feeling.

Her next statement is striking evidence that there is great advantage in letting the client take the lead in the interview. The first long silence led to her exploration of the marriage issue. This one leads to a surprisingly positive aspect of her self-image. For someone who has seemed unsure, her love of the arts seems sure and certain.

My response has the advantage of bringing fully into awareness her positive aims and goals. There is value in holding up a mirror to the client.

From the point of view of therapeutic process, Jan "experiences fully, in awareness, feelings which have in the past been denied to awareness, or distorted in awareness" (Rogers, 1959, p. 216).

JAN: In the last eighteen months everything — it's quite strange, but — the situation is becoming *vital*. I was led to believe that when one grows older, one became more patient, more tolerant. I've really not had a care in the world. It's only now that I have a real *problem*, and I don't know how to cope with it.

CARL: It seems to me that in the last eighteen months, everything seems very, very important — every moment, every aspect of life (JAN: Yes.) seems more vital and more significant. And the question seems deeper: "What am I going to do?"

JAN: (*Pause.*) Can you answer a question for me, Dr. Carl? Can you see the two related: the marriage issue, the aging process, or not?

CARL: Yes, it seems to me that they're related in your talking about them, and that you're saying the fears grow stronger, as time goes by, both of marriage and of children and of commitment, as well as a fear of aging — that it seems a package of fears. And alongside that, you've been saying that "I know what I want to commit myself to — I just can't."

Jan *experiences* the urgency of the issues in her life and her help-lessness in dealing with them. Following a familiar pattern, she turns to the authority for an answer.

She has already related these two issues in her conversation, and I simply feed back to her the essence of her own feelings and their meanings. It is not obstinacy on my part that refuses to give any answer from me. It is a profound belief that the best answer can come only from within the client and that Jan is, in fact, answering her question by what she has been saying.

JAN: Mmm. And it's not — it's got absolutely nothing to do with giving. Just the fear of being trapped. As I am trapped in my age right now.

CARL: You get this feeling of being *trapped*, trapped by the year you're in, trapped by the age you are, and the fear of being trapped by marriage as well. (*Pause.*) So life has become a fright-ening prospect.

It is interesting to follow her search for the right word — the right metaphor — to match her feelings. She has tried out *fear*, *panic*, *feelings being vital*, and now *trapped*. Finding a word, a phrase, a metaphor that exactly matches the inner felt meaning of the moment helps the client to experience the feeling more fully.

I am now quite comfortably moving about in her inner world, sensing the way she feels, even when she has not put it fully into words.

JAN: Yes. (*Pause.*) I still carry on, (CARL: Mm-hmmm.) you know, and I try to keep this deep down inside of me. (*Pause.*) I don't walk into the office and say, "Help, please, I'm thirty-five. What am I going to do?" It's not that at all. I can still, if I want to put my shorts on and wear my pigtails, but that's not it. It's — it's fear of being trapped.

CARL: And those fears that you have, they don't prevent you from functioning in the world. That goes on O.K., but never-theless they are fears deep inside, and the biggest fear of all is the fear of being trapped, in so many different ways.

I failed here to respond to her growing awareness of the incongruence between what she is experiencing and the façade with which she faces the world. I also missed the casual reference to shorts and pigtails, clearly another positive facet of her self-concept. Usually the therapist is given another chance if he misses significant meanings, and that opportunity is given to me in the next interchange.

JAN: And yet people say to me, "Jan, you're in your prime. You've got everything going for you!" And little do they know inside what I feel.

CARL: That's right. So that outside and to an observer, you are in your prime and you have everything going for you. But that's not Jan inside. Jan inside is quite different from that.

JAN: (*Long pause—whispers.*) Do you want me to say something else? (*Laughter from Carl and audience.*) I'm just nervous as hell up here!

CARL: You can take all the time you want, because I feel I'm getting acquainted with that frightened little Jan that is inside.

JAN: So the more I talk, the more I'm helping you to get through to me, is that right?

CARL: The more you're getting through to *me*.

JAN: This may be related, and it may be able to help you: whether it's something to do with the amateur dramatics that I used to be involved with, I don't know, but I love playing the naughty little girl. And whenever I want to get away with something or I want something, I would play that naughty little girl.

CARL: That's a part that you know very well. (JAN *laughs.*) You've acted it in many plays. (JAN: And it works!) It *works—* the naughty little girl can get away with things. And one other thing that you said: that you're trying to help *me*. I guess I hope that what we're doing here will help *you*. (JAN: Thank you.) (*Pause.*) Because—I feel that when you're telling me things, it's not for my benefit. I hope that you can get better acquainted with yourself by telling us some of those things.

Here is Jan's clearest statement of her view of the relationship: that she, if told to do so, will give me information so that I, the expert, can then be the external agent of help for her. The successfulness of my attempt to shift the locus of responsibility to her is uncertain. I do not believe she understands what I am saying, and her "Thank you" makes it clear to her I am still the active helping agent.

What has play-acting a naughty little girl to do with her problems? I do not know, but I deeply trust that her nonconscious mind is taking a path that will lead us to the areas most relevant to her fears.

JAN: I have discussed this problem with one other person, who has been through this experience. She knows the traumatic effects that it has on a person. She herself went through similar feelings. And she said, "You know, it's very strange, but I have been able to overcome that, over a period of time—with the help of one or two people." I think the important thing is (*Pause.*) to be able to relate to somebody that you can trust and have confidence in, who can spend the time with you. But it's very difficult to find.

CARL: But what you would like is someone you really could trust to help you go through and grow through this difficult period.

JAN: Mmm, of being trapped. (*Laughs.*) So, I just don't know how to cope with it. I really don't.

CARL: Feel that it's a little too much for you.

JAN: Well, it's a part of my everyday life, you know, from the moment I wake up to the moment I go to bed. Obviously I don't discuss it with many people. For fear of the reaction, really, I think. It's important to try and find somebody who's been in the same boat—who knows what you're going through.

CARL: So you really are seeking—somebody, the somebody you need, the somebody you want, the somebody you could trust.

She describes very well the kind of nonjudgmental, understanding, caring, trustworthy relationship that everyone desires. It is a good description of a truly therapeutic relationship, another evidence of the fact that, fundamentally, "the client knows best."

JAN: Yes. I am trying to do it on my own, but I find it's not easy. (CARL: That's right.) To have somebody pushing me, saying, you know, "I *know* you can do it, you *can* do it, you *will* do it, you *are* going to do it," and that would—

CARL: That would really help.

JAN: Just one person who can believe in me.

CARL: One person who believes in you enough to say, "Sure you can do it — you're O.K. You're going to get through it!" But you can't tell that to yourself.

JAN: No — and I try to be positive, and joke about it. But I, I'm just very scared. I'm going backwards. I'm not going forwards — (*Long pause.*) I have tried to — push it to one side. I have tried to — wash it by the wayside, erase it. I've tried stopping myself when I think about it. But even that doesn't work anymore. (*Pause.*) It's almost, metaphorically speaking only, as if I am walking into darkness. I'm coming out of the light and into the darkness. (CARL: Ahh.) Do you understand what I mean. (CARL: Yes, I surely do.) Because I fear again now —

CARL: And it's so risky, coming from a lighted spot into the darkness, into the unknown. (JAN: Right.) Such a chance, and so frightening.

JAN: (*Pause.*) I can't think of anything else to say, other than — how do I overcome it? (*Pause.*) I do feel at the moment it's a very lonely problem — I'm sure other people have been through it. Other people haven't. And they probably think, "Hell, what's the *problem?*" I even joke about it sometimes, to myself, and say, "I think I'll put an ad in the paper — you never (*laughing*) know what response you'll get!" (*Pause.*) It's the laughing and, you know, I tend to try and laugh it off.

CARL: But you wish so much that there was this other person, this person from outside, who would give you confidence, who could help you through this tough time.

JAN: Yes, because although I do pray — I have my own feelings about religion — I believe in spiritual development. And maybe for me this is a karmic conditioning, I don't know. That's another thing, of course, that's going on in my mind: it's a part of my development, as it were. But I feel that it's not enough; I must have physical contact. (*Pause.*) Somebody I can relate to —

Throughout this segment she experiences the full depth of her hopelessness, her inability to deal with her fears, her desire for a helping relationship with another, her conviction that help must come from the outside, the laughing face with which she hides her pain.

I walk with her, psychologically, along this path of discouragement. I do light up at her use of the light-into-darkness metaphor. The reason is evident in my next response.

CARL: Somebody you can relate to. And I guess that—this may seem like a silly idea, but—I wish that one of those friends could be that naughty little girl. I don't know whether that makes any sense to you or not, but if that kind of sprightly, naughty little girl that lives inside could accompany you from the light into the dark—as I say, that may not make any sense to you at all.

JAN: (*In a puzzled voice.*) Can you elaborate on that a little more for me?

CARL: Simply that maybe one of your best friends is the you that you hide inside, the fearful little girl, the naughty little girl, the real you that doesn't come out very much in the open.

JAN: (*Pause.*) And I must admit—what you have just said, and looking at it in retrospect—I've lost a lot of that naughty little girl. In fact, over the last eighteen months, that naughty little girl has disappeared.

This was the kind of intuitive response that I have learned to trust. The expression just formed itself within me and wanted to be said. I advanced it very tentatively, and from her initial blank and puzzled look, I thought that perhaps it was completely irrelevant and unhelpful, but her next response shows that it touched something deep in her.

I have come to value highly these intuitive responses. They occur infrequently (this is the first one I have captured in a recording), but they are almost always helpful in advancing therapy. In these moments I am perhaps in a slightly altered state of consciousness, indwelling in the client's world, completely in tune with that world. My nonconscious intellect takes over. I know much more than my conscious mind is aware of. I do not form my responses consciously, they simply arise in me, from my nonconscious sensing of the world of the other.

CARL: Has disappeared. Uh-huh, uh-huh. (*Laughs.*) Then I wasn't so far wrong. Maybe you ought to look her up! (*Laughter.*)

JAN: Would you like her number? (*Laughter.*)

CARL: I would! (*Laughter.*) I think she would be fun, and I don't think she would be so frightened. She sounds pretty sassy! (*Laughter.*)

JAN: (*Dubiously.*) So even though I'm getting older, I can still be a naughty little girl?

CARL: Well, I don't know — I'm only eighty, but I can still be a naughty little boy. (*Much laughter and applause.*)

JAN: (*Laughing.*) I won't make any comments! (*Pause.*) Would that change my feelings about marriage?

CARL: I think that's a very significant question you're asking yourself. If you were a better friend of the little girl inside of you, would that make you less fearful of the risk of marriage? I feel badly that she's been missing for the last eighteen months, I really do.

JAN: (*Pause.*) You're so right. You've really hit the nail on the head. And —

It is clear that our relationship has become a comfortable, companionable joint search. We can be humorous about serious things. It is an open, trusting relationship.

For Jan the realization sinks in that she has been denying a significant part of her experience, of herself, and that this is a deeply important fact.

I like my responses. They are spontaneous and funny but entirely serious in their intent.

CARL: I'm sorry, but we're going to have to stop in a few minutes.

JAN: O.K. — I'm fifteen minutes fast, because I'm always late. (*Laughs.*)

CARL: Fifteen minutes older? (*Much laughter.*)

JAN: (*Laughing*) Let's see, it's ten to —

CARL: Yes, then I think we'll stop. Is that all right?

JAN: Yes. You've been a great help, and I'd like to thank you very much indeed.

The ending seems abrupt, but time was up, and her willingness to joke about the situation seemed to indicate that she could close without feeling deprived. In addition, this was a point of real closure in the interview itself.

Significant Elements in the Interview

This interview contains many elements that are characteristic of a person-centered approach to psychotherapy or to any helping relationship. I will mention some of them.

1. A nonjudgmental acceptance of every feeling, every thought, every change of direction, every meaning that she finds in her experience. I believe this acceptance is complete, with one exception, which it is useful to note. I show real acceptance of her desire to be dependent, to rely on me as the authority who will give the answers. Notice that I accept her *wish* to be dependent. This does *not* mean that I will behave in such a way as to meet her expectations. I can more easily accept her dependent feelings, because I know where I stand, and I know that I will not *be* her authority figure, even though I am perceived as such.

But at one point my acceptance is not complete. She says, in effect, "I'll talk more to help you in your task," and instead of completely accepting her perception of the relationship, I make two futile attempts to change her perception. I respond, in effect, "What we are doing is to help you, not me." She disregards this, and no damage is done to the process.

2. A deep understanding of her feelings and of the personal meanings she finds in her experience, bringing to bear all the sensitivity of which I am capable. I am sufficiently successful in entering her private world that she feels increasingly safe in the relationship and able to express whatever comes to mind.

This sensitive empathy is so deep that my intuition takes over at one point and, in a way that seems mysterious, is in touch with a very important part of her with which she has lost contact. At this point we are perhaps in a mutual and reciprocal altered state of consciousness.

3. A companionship in her search for herself. As a therapist, I do not want to lead the client, since she knows, better than I, the pathway to the sources of her pain. (Of course, this is a nonconscious knowing, but it is there nevertheless.) I do not wish to fall behind in my understanding, because then the exploration would become too frightening for her. What I wish is to be at her side, occasionally falling a step behind, occasionally a step ahead when I can see more clearly the path we are on, and taking a leap ahead only when guided by my intuition.

4. A trust in the "wisdom of the organism" to lead us to the core of her problems. In the interview I have a complete trust that she will move into the areas that are relevant to her distress. No matter how shrewd I might be as a clinician, I could never have guessed that her mother's death or her love of the arts or the role she played on the stage years ago would have any relevance to resolving her fears. But when trusted, her organism, her nonconscious mind—call it what you will—can follow the path that leads to the crucial issues.

So, as a therapist, I want to make it possible for my client to move in her own way, and at her own pace, to the heart of her conflicts.

5. Helping the client to experience her feelings *fully*. The best example is when she lets herself experience, quite completely, the *hopelessness* of being *trapped*. Once such a troubling feeling has been felt to its full depth and breadth, one can move on. It is an important part of movement in the process of change.

It is worth noting that when she says, with great conviction, "You've really hit the nail on the head," it is clear that she is *experiencing* something definitely helpful to her, and yet she does not verbalize what this is. No matter. It is the experiencing that is important, and the therapist doesn't need to know precisely what it is (although in this case she informed him the next day).

Perhaps pointing out these elements will have made it clear that a person-centered approach in therapy leads to a very subtle, often intricate process, a process that has an organic flow of its own. For the therapist to be fully present as an understanding, caring person is highly important in making this process possible, although the most crucial events take place in the feelings and experiencings of the client.

The Outcome for Jan

Immediately after the interview, in describing her experience to the participants, Jan said, "For me, strangely enough, though I'm very nervous, I found it very exciting. I needed help, and I think I've found an answer, thanks to Dr. Carl." This might be taken simply as politeness were it not for a subsequent conversation.

The next morning Jan told me that the interchange about the

"naughty little girl" had initiated a self-searching. She realized that not only was the naughty little girl missing, but several other parts of her self had also disappeared during the past eighteen months. "I realize that to face life as a whole person, I need to find those missing parts of me." She said that for her the interview had proved to be a "soul-shaking experience." The process that started in the interview appears to be continuing in her.

REFERENCES

Capra, F. *Turning Point: Science, Society and the Rising Culture.* New York: Bantam Books, 1982.

Rogers, C. R. A theory of therapy, personality and interpersonal relationships, as developed in the client-centered framework. In Koch, S. (Ed.), *Psychology: A Study of a Science*, Vol. 3. *Formulations of the Person and the Social Context.* New York: McGraw-Hill, 1959, 184–256.

Rogers, C. R. *On Becoming a Person.* Boston: Houghton Mifflin, 1961.

Rogers, C. R. Client-centered psychotherapy. In Kaplan, H. I., Sadock, B. J. and Freedman, A. M. (Eds.), *Textbook of Psychiatry*, 3. Baltimore: William and Wilkins Co., 1980, 2153–2186.

THE PERSON IN PROCESS

As humans grow from infancy to adulthood, an internal rift gradually develops, a rift that separates our immediate awareness from our own deeper "experiencing." In order to receive approval and love, we learn to suppress those feelings and expressions of ourselves that are deemed unacceptable to the important caretakers in our lives. Our need to be loved and accepted can impair our ability to be "congruent," to be whole and genuine. As infants the "locus of evaluation" is firmly embedded within us, but as we grow physically, emotionally, and intellectually, we learn to "introject" the evaluations that come to us from the external world until, for many of us, it is no longer possible to recognize the difference between what is internal and what is external, to know who we really are.

These are some of the issues that Carl Rogers observed, researched, and wrote about throughout his career. Again and again, he described the process by which his clients in particular, and people in general, come to lose touch with important parts of themselves and to experience the loss of self-esteem and the psychological and social problems that inevitably result from this incongruence.

Nowhere is this destructive process more graphically and tragically illustrated than in the case of Ellen West. In "Ellen West —and Loneliness," Rogers presents his own analysis of this famous psychotherapy case, eloquently describing Ellen's gradual estrangement from herself and from all those around her.

While Ellen West's experience demonstrates, in an individual case, how a troubled patient gradually loses touch with the "wisdom of her organism," the same basic phenomenon occurs, to some degree, in the average, well-adjusted person. Rogers's article "Toward a Modern Approach to Values: The Valuing Process in the Mature Person" presents a more thorough and generalized description of the internal transition that occurs as we slowly move from being self-determining, as in infancy, to a condition in which we have given over to the external world our ability to evaluate for ourselves. This loss of self reaches such a marked degree in some of us that we are no longer able to bring to awareness what it is our organism is undergoing—we no longer know what we think or what we feel.

Rarely one to dwell on the negative or tragic sides of the human dilemma, Rogers was always most interested in exploring the process of "becoming a person"—of discovering, accepting, and, when appropriate, of expressing and living the deeper, fuller levels of one's being. The second part of his essay on the valuing process describes how individuals can reclaim the locus of evaluation and accept responsibility for their own lives. He concludes by discussing how his experiences in therapy have led him to the conviction that a more mature valuing process leads the individual not only toward enhanced personal development but in the direction of constructive contribution to the whole species.

In "Shall We Get Married?," from his 1972 book *Becoming Partners: Marriage and Its Alternatives*, Rogers applies his interest in this developmental process to the specific experience of losing and finding oneself in marriage. He gives two illustrations of marital relationships, one that ultimately ended in divorce and one that was improved by the honest expression of some painful truths. In both situations, an observation Rogers often stated about all human relationships played an important part, that is, when strong and persistent feelings are unexpressed, the relationship will be affected adversely. As usual, Rogers stressed not the *outcomes* of the partnerships, though no one could question that this is of tremendous importance to the couples involved, but the healthy or unhealthy *communication process* within and between the partners.

In the end, whether viewing marriages, individuals in therapy, or the average person's struggles with identity, loneliness, and relationships, Rogers's interest always returned to the person in process. His insights and eloquence about the process of becoming a person were what drew so many professionals and laypersons alike to his work.

II
Ellen West — and Loneliness

I would like to give my view of the basic isolation felt by modern man. I will then indicate the way in which I see Ellen West as an illustration of the development of this loneliness to a tragic point.

There are many ways of looking at loneliness, but I wish to focus on two elements of the sense of aloneness which we so often see in our clients and in others. The first is the estrangement of man from himself, from his experiencing organism. In this fundamental rift, the experiencing organism senses one meaning in experience, but the conscious self clings rigidly to another, since that is the way it has found love and acceptance from others. Thus, we have a potentially fatal division, with most behavior being regulated in terms of meanings perceived in awareness, but with other meanings sensed by the physiological organism being denied and ignored because of an inability to communicate freely within oneself.

The other element in our loneliness is the lack of any relationship in which we communicate our real experiencing — and hence our real self — to another. When there is no relationship in which we are able to communicate both aspects of our divided self — our conscious façade and our deeper level of experiencing — then we feel the loneliness of not being in real touch with any other human being.

Is this loneliness contemporary only? Perhaps. In earlier times, the individual also distrusted or ignored his experiencing in

Review of Existential Psychology and Psychiatry, Vol. 1, No. 2, May 1961, 94–101. Also in expanded form in Rogers, C. R. and Rosenberg, R. L., *A Pessoa Como Centro* (São Paulo, Brazil: Editoria Pedagógica e Universitária Ltda., 1977) and *A Way of Being* (Boston: Houghton Mifflin, 1980), 165–180.

order to keep the regard of significant others. But the façade he adopted, the meaning he now felt he had found in his experiences, became a unified and strongly supportive set of beliefs and meanings. His whole social group tended to perceive life and experience in the same way, so that while he had unwittingly given up his deepest self, at least he had taken on a consistent, respected, approved self by which he could live. An early Puritan, for example, must have experienced much inward strain as he denied vast areas of his organismic experiencing. It is doubtful, however, if he experienced as much isolation and aloneness as our clients today.

Modern man, like the members of earlier and more homogeneous groups, deserts his own experiencing to take on the way of being that will bring love. But the façade he adopts is taken over only from parents or a few others, and he is continually exposed to the knowledge that although that façade is approved by some, others see life in very different fashions. There is no security in any single façade. Hence, to a degree probably unknown before, modern man *experiences* his loneliness, his cut-off-ness, his isolation both from his own deeper being and from others.

In the remainder of this paper I will discuss this very fundamental present-day type of isolation, using as an example the highly informative history of a young woman known as Ellen West.

I am pleased that this case was chosen as the basis of this symposium. First, Ellen West's diaries and letters add much personal richness to the account. There are also included observations and reports by physicians, therapists, and diagnosticians, further adding to the completeness. Second, the full account of the case is available in both German (Binswanger, 1944–1945) and English (Binswanger, 1958). Finally, the case illustrates the way in which some of the best-known persons in the psychiatric and psychotherapeutic field thought and worked as of a generation or more ago.

I cannot possibly give the whole tragic history of Ellen West —which in its published form covers more than thirty closely packed pages—but I shall choose and comment on a few of the crucial events of her life.

First, her youth. Up to the age of twenty I see her as being as whole, as integrated, as the average person. It is easy for clinicians to read pathology into a history, especially with the advantages of hindsight, but I do not see pathology here. Ellen is a girl who is lively, headstrong, sensitive, defiant, questioning, competitive, emotional, expressive, variable—in short, a living person. She is devoted to her father. She wants very much to be a boy—until she meets a boy she likes. She wonders what life is for. She has idealistic dreams of great achievement for herself. None of these characteristics necessarily portends a black future. On the contrary, she seems to be a richly variable and sensitive adolescent, with much promise.

"Her twentieth year is full of happiness, yearning and hopes."* She is eager to find a vital, serious, loving man. She takes pleasure in eating and drinking. But during this year there occurs a significant estrangement from herself. "She becomes engaged to a romantic foreigner, but at her father's wish breaks the engagement." Our facts are meager, but I suspect, from the lack of any protest on her part, that she adopts her father's feelings as if they were her own. If we put this episode in schematic form, her realization would be something like this: "I thought my feelings meant that I was in love. I felt I was doing the positive and meaningful thing to get engaged. But my experiencing cannot be trusted. I was not in love. My engagement was not a meaningful commitment. I cannot be guided by what I experience. To do so would be to act wrongly, and to lose my father's love."

Within a few weeks of this time she is eating too much and growing fat—the first appearance of what was to become her major symptom. It is perhaps indicative of the beginnings of her lack of trust in herself that she begins to diet only when teased by her companions. She feels an increasing need to live her life in terms of the expectations of others, since her own impulses are unreliable.

It is not difficult to see why she begins to despise herself shortly after this time, and even to perceive death as "a glorious woman." After all, she is an untrustworthy organism, a misleading cluster of experiencings, deserving to be despised. Her diary reports "shadows of doubt and of dread," which soon translate into a

---

*This quotation and those that follow are taken from the chapter in May et al. (1958).

dread of getting fat. Nor is it surprising that she is frightened at the "evil spirits" in her — the unaccepted and denied feelings that haunt her.

I am sure this was not the first real estrangement between her self and her underlying feelings, but there seems little doubt but that it was a deeply significant one. It went a long way in destroying her confidence in herself as a being capable of autonomy. Even though her good spirits return, and she has happy periods, she has given up a part of her self and introjected as her own the feelings of her father.

During this period she is full of fluctuations. She wants to do something great; she hopes for a social revolution; she works very hard as a student; she establishes reading rooms for children. But at times she is "a timid, earthly worm"; she longs for death and has her tutor reread the sentence "The good die young." Occasionally, "life has triumphed again." She has an "unpleasant affair with a riding teacher." She has a "breakdown." She is very overconcerned with her weight.

When she is twenty-four, there is another point at which she even more fully loses confidence in herself. Though she still is unsure enough of herself to need her old governess with her, she is nevertheless happy in her studies. "The diary breathes joy of life and sensuality." She falls in love with a student. This was evidently a deep commitment, judging by its lasting and pervasive qualities. She becomes engaged, but again her parents insist that her experiencing is erroneous. They demand a temporary separation. So to her it must seem that the relationship is not real, is not wise, is better given up. Once more, she distrusts and disregards her own experience and introjects her parents' feelings. She gives up the relationship and, with it, any trust in herself as capable of wise self-direction. Only the experience of others can be trusted. At this time, she turns to her doctor for help.

Had she rebelled at this point, had she possessed the strength to fight for her own experiencing of her own world, she would have been true to her deeper feelings and would, quite literally, have saved her potentially autonomous self. But instead of rebellion there is only a terrible depression and a hatred of her body, which is obviously a totally untrustworthy organism for dealing with life. The extent to which she has surrendered her self is indicated by her terrific dieting. As she says later, "Something in me rebels against becoming fat. Rebels against becoming healthy, having plump red cheeks, becoming a simple, robust woman, as corresponds to my true nature."

In other words, if she were to trust her own feelings, desires, experiences, she would become a robust, plump young woman and marry the student she loves. But her feelings have been proven completely unreliable, her desires and experiences totally untrustworthy guides. So she must not only deny her feelings for her loved one; she also must starve and coerce her body into a form approved by others but completely opposite from her own tendencies. She has lost, completely, her trust in her own experiencing as the basis for living.

I shall comment briefly on one other episode. She finds her cousin to be a possible mate, and this choice is approved by her family. They plan to marry. But for two more years, until age twenty-eight, she vacillates between her cousin and the student she has loved. She goes to see the student and breaks off with him, leaving, in her words, an "open wound." We know nothing of the content of this most crucial interaction, but I would speculate that her psychological life hung in the balance here. Should she trust her own experiencing and choose the person she loves, or should she choose her cousin? Her own feelings are cooler toward the cousin, but for him she *should* feel all the approved feelings she is supposed to feel. I suspect that she realized dimly that if she chose the student, she would be choosing the uncharted path of autonomous selfhood. If she chose her cousin, she would be living the life expected of her by others, but it would be a safe and approved pretense. She chose her cousin and married him, thus renouncing still further any trust in her self.*

---

*To show how differently the same episode can be viewed, here is Dr. Binswanger's comment, as he contrasts the struggle she feels between the "ideal" and the "real" parts of herself. He compares "the blonde beloved who is part of the ethereal (ideal) world and the other (the cousin) who stands with both feet firmly on the ground. . . . Life on the earth wins out again." I fear this indicates — both for Dr. Binswanger and for me — that our values show through even when we are trying to make "objective" observations!

By the age of thirty-two, she is totally obsessed with the idea that she *must* make herself thin. To this end she starves herself and takes sixty laxative pills a day! Not surprisingly, she has little strength. She tries psychoanalysis but feels she is not helped. She says, "I analyzed with my mind, but everything remained theory"; and, "The analyst can give me discernment, but not healing." However, when the analysis is broken off by circumstances, she becomes worse.

During this period she speaks of her ideal love, the student. She says to her husband in a letter, "At that time you were the life I was ready to accept and to give up my ideal for. But it was . . . a forced resolve." She appears to be trying desperately to have the feelings that others want her to have, but she has to force herself.

From here on, the estrangement within herself leads to more estrangement and to more and more feelings of isolation from others. It is not surprising that her first attempt at suicide comes at a point when her second analyst, working with her in the hospital to which she was sent, repeats the now familiar pattern. Her husband wants to be with her in the hospital—and she wants him to be with her. But the father-figure, the analyst, knows better, and he sends the husband away. He destroys still further any lingering confidence she might have in herself as a self-directing person.

From this point on, the isolation is ever greater, and the tragedy closes in. She goes to more doctors, to more psychiatrists, becoming increasingly an object in the eyes of those dealing with her. She is finally placed in Dr. Binswanger's sanitarium, where she remains for a number of months.

During this period there are continuing differences over her diagnosis. Emil Kraepelin, the noted psychiatrist, diagnoses her during one of her depressed periods as a victim of melancholia. Her second analyst diagnoses her as having a "severe obsessive neurosis combined with manic-depressive oscillations." A consulting psychiatrist says that her problem is a "psychopathic constitution progressively unfolding." He says she is not schizophrenic, because there is no intellectual defect. But Drs. Bleuler and Binswanger are in agreement that her situation is "progressive schizophrenic psychosis (schizophrenia simplex)." They see little hope for her and say, "It was clear that a release from the institution meant certain suicide."

Since Ellen was aware of a number of these discussions, she must have come to seem to herself not a person but some strange abnormal mechanism, completely out of her control, going its own way to destruction. One looks in vain through all these "diagnoses" for any trace of recognition that the doctors were dealing with a human person! It is not hard to understand Ellen's words: "I confront myself as a strange person. I am afraid of myself." Or, at another time: "On this one point I am insane — I am perishing in the struggle against my nature. Fate wanted to have me fat and strong, but I want to be thin and delicate." Indeed, she is perishing in the struggle with her nature. Her organism wants to be healthy and strong, but the introjected "I" — the false self she has taken on to please others — wants to be, as she says at one point, thin and "intellectual."

The wise doctors, in spite of the risk of suicide, come to the following conclusion: "No definitely reliable therapy is possible. We therefore resolved to give in to the patient's demand for discharge." She left the hospital. Three days later, she seemed well and happy, ate well for the first time in years, and then took a lethal dose of poison. She was thirty-three. Her epitaph might well be her own words: "I feel myself, quite passively, the stage on which two hostile forces are mangling each other."

What went so fatally wrong in the life of Ellen West? I hope I have indicated my belief that what went wrong is something that occurs to some degree in the life of every one of us, but that in her case was exaggerated. As infants, we live in our experience; we trust it. When the baby is hungry, he neither doubts his hunger nor questions whether he should make every effort to get food. Without being in any way conscious of it, he is a self-trusting organism. But at some point, parents or others say to him, in effect, "If you feel *that* way, I won't love you." And so he feels what he *should* feel, not what he *does* feel. To this degree, he builds up a self that feels what it should feel, only occasionally seeing frightening glimpses of what his organism, of which the self is a part, is actually experiencing. In Ellen's case, this process operated in an extreme fashion. In some of the most significant moments of life, she was made to feel that her own experiencing was invalid, erroneous, wrong, and unsound, and that what she *should* be feeling was something quite different. Unfortunately for her, her love for her parents, especially her father, was so strong that she surrendered her own capacity for trusting her experience and substituted theirs, or his. She gave up being her self. This observation, made by one of her doctors during her last year, is no surprise: "Though as a child she was wholly independent of the opinion of others, she is now completely dependent on what others think." She no longer has any way of knowing what she feels or what her opinion is. This is the loneliest state of all—an almost complete separation from one's autonomous organism.

What went wrong with her treatment? Here is an intelligent, sensitive young woman, seeking help. The prognosis, by modern standards, would seem very favorable. Why such complete failure? I am sure opinions differ, but I should like to state mine.

The greatest weakness in her treatment was that no one involved seems to have related to her as a *person*—a person worthy of respect, a person capable of autonomous choice, a person whose inner experiencing is a precious resource to be drawn upon and trusted.

Rather, she seems to have been dealt with as an object. Her first analyst helps her to *see* her feelings but not to experience them. This only makes her more of an object to herself and still further estranges her from living in and drawing upon her experience. Wisely, she says that the "analyst can give me discernment, but not healing." The analyst points out to her that she is an individual with such and such dynamics. She agrees with him, though surely not on the basis of experiencing these dynamic feelings. She is simply following the pattern which has already isolated her—distrusting her own experiencing and trying to believe and feel what she should feel, what the expert tells her she feels.

Then comes the comic-tragic argument over her diagnosis, of which she was evidently quite aware. The doctors disagree as to what type of object she is: She is manic-depressive. She is obsessive-compulsive. She is a case of melancholia. She is treatable. She is not. Then comes the final, incredible decision: She is suicidal, schizophrenic, and hopeless for treatment; therefore, we will discharge her and let her commit suicide. This at least was one prediction that was fulfilled.

"I scream but they do not hear me." Ellen's words ring in my ears. No one *did* hear her as a person. Beyond her childhood years—and perhaps not even then—neither her parents, nor her two analysts, nor her physicians ever seem to have respected her enough to hear her deeply. They did not deal with her as a person capable of meeting life, a person whose experiencing is trustworthy, whose inner feelings are worthy of acceptance. How, then, could she listen to herself or respect the experiencing going on within her?

"I am isolated. I sit in a glass ball, I see people through a glass wall. I scream, but they do not hear me." What a desperate cry for a relationship between two persons. She never experienced what Buber has called "healing through meeting." There was no one who could meet her, accept her, as she was.

Reading this tragic case angers me (as will have been evident), but it also encourages me. I feel angry at the tragic waste of a human being, encouraged because I feel that we have learned enough during the intervening years that if Ellen West came today to my office, or to the offices of many therapists I know, she would be helped. Let me try to sketch this possibility. To do it most vividly, I will assume that she came to my office at about the age of twenty-four. This is the time when she did seek medical help, so it is reasonable to assume that today she would have sought psychological help. It is just after she has separated, at the insistence of her parents, from the student whom she loves.

Even from just a reading of the case I feel sure I would find no barrier to feeling acceptant toward this depressed, unhappy, emaciated, self-starved young woman. I would sense both what she is and what her potentialities are, and I would be willing for her to be both, or either.

I feel sure that our contacts would start with themes such as the following: "I am very depressed, with no reason for my depression." "I can't bear to be alone, but I don't know why." "I hate myself when I'm fat, and I *have* to be thin, but again I don't know the reason for this." "I did love this student, but I don't believe it would have been a wise match. My father and mother felt he was not the man for me." As I understood each of these feelings and accepted her right to *be* these feelings, other attitudes would tentatively and fearfully appear: her disappointment at the separation from her fiancé; the strong feelings that she had, and still has for him; her resentment (a very frightening feeling) toward her father. Slowly, gradually, she would discover that she could experience and be both love and resentment toward her father, both love and resentment toward me, both fear of independent living and eagerness for independent living, both the desire to be a man and the desire to be a woman, both the desire to be a plump, robust, contented wife and the desire to be a slim, brilliant, competitive achiever of social reform. She could experience both her hunger and desire to eat and be plump and her fear of being fat, ugly, and disapproved of by friends. She could say, as she did say, "I am afraid of myself, of the feelings to which I am defenselessly delivered over every minute." Little by little, she could freely experience all of these feelings, all of these elements of herself.

She would discover that some of these feelings are very frightening indeed. To explore and to *experience* both the risk and the excitement of being an independent person is one of those fearful elements. Another person, a client of mine, expressed this realization in a statement which Ellen would be likely to make. She said:

> I have all the symptoms of fright. . . . It really seems like I'm cut loose and very vulnerable. . . . Still, I have a feeling of *strength*. . . . I'm feeling it internally now, a sort of surging up, or force . . . something really big and strong. And yet at first it was almost a physical feeling of just being out *alone*, and sort of cut off from a support I have been carrying around. . . . (*Pause.*) . . . I have the feeling that now I am going to begin to *do* more things.

This is an example of what I mean by experiencing a feeling fully and acceptantly, in a safe relationship. It represents, in my judgment, a moment of change — probably physiological, irreversible change. As Ellen experienced, in a similar way, these different hidden facets of herself, she would find herself changing. This time the changed self that emerged would be based on her organismic reactions, her inner experiencing, and not on the values and expectations of others.

She would find that she did not have to struggle against her nature, against her feelings. Rather, she would find that when she could be open to all her experiencing—both her inner experiencing, and her experiencing of the demands and attitudes of others—she would have a basis by which to live. She would discover that her experiencing, if she could be open to it and could listen sensitively for its meaning, would provide a constructive guide for her behavior and for her life.

This is not to say that the process would be smooth or comfortable. To be a person—sometimes opposing her parents, sometimes standing against social pressures, often choosing to act even though uncertain of the outcome—this would be painful, costly, sometimes even terrifying. But it would be *very* precious: to be oneself is worth a high price. It would also have many other valuable aspects.

In the therapeutic relationship, where all of herself was accepted, she could discover that it was safe to communicate her self more completely. She would discover that she did not need to be lonely and isolated, that another could understand and share the meaning of her experience. She would discover, too, that in this process she had made friends with herself—that her body, her feelings, and her desires were not enemy aliens but friendly and constructive parts of herself. It would be unnecessary for her to utter those desperate words, "I am perishing in the struggle against my nature." Her two essential estrangements would have been assuaged. She would be in a good and communicative relationship with herself. She would also have found it safe to *be* her full self in a relationship. As a consequence, she would find herself relating with more of herself to others, and again discovering that it is not dangerously unsafe, but rather far more satisfying, to be one's real self in relating to others.

It is by such a process, in my judgment, that the glass wall would have dissolved. She would have found life adventurous, often painful. It would be a never-ending puzzlement to discover the behavior that would best harmonize with her complex and contradictory feelings. But she would be vital and real and in relationship to herself and others. She would have resolved for herself the great loneliness of contemporary man.

I cannot apologize for having stated with confidence and optimism the probable outcome of therapeutic events for Ellen, had she had the opportunity to participate in person-centered therapy. My experience justifies no other conclusion. I am not sure she would move as far as I have indicated, but that she would move in this direction I have no doubt, providing I had been able to create a person-to-person therapeutic relationship.

For myself, I draw certain lessons from this case of Ellen West. The first is that in every respect in which we make an object of the person — whether by diagnosing him, analyzing him, or perceiving him impersonally in a case history — we stand in the way of our therapeutic goal. To make an object of a person has been helpful in treating physical ills; it has not been successful in treating psychological ills. We are deeply helpful only when we relate as persons, when we risk ourselves as persons in the relationship, when we experience the other as a person in his own right. Only then is there a meeting at a depth that dissolves the pain of aloneness in both client and therapist.

REFERENCES

Binswanger, L. Der Fall Ellen West, *Schweizer Archiv für Neurologie und Psychiatrie*, 1944, *53*, 255–277; *54*, 69–117, 330–360; 1945, *55*, 16–40.

Binswanger, L. The case of Ellen West. In May, R., Angel, E., & Ellenberger, H. F. (Eds.), *Existence: A new dimension in psychiatry and psychology.* New York: Basic Books, 1958.

May, R., Angel, E., & Ellenberger, H. F. (Eds.), *Existence: A new dimension in psychiatry and psychology.* New York: Basic Books, 1958.

12

Toward a Modern Approach to Values: The Valuing Process in the Mature Person

There is a great deal of concern today with the problem of values. Youth, in almost every country, is deeply uncertain of its value orientation; the values associated with various religions have lost

Journal of Abnormal and Social Psychology, Vol. 68, No. 2, 1964, 160–167. Copyright © 1964 by the American Psychological Association. Reprinted by permission of the publisher.

much of their influence; sophisticated individuals in every culture seem unsure and troubled as to the goals they hold in esteem. The reasons are not far to seek. The world culture, in all its aspects, seems increasingly scientific and relativistic, and the rigid, absolute views on values which come to us from the past appear anachronistic. Even more important, perhaps, is the fact that the modern individual is assailed from every angle by divergent and contradictory value claims. It is no longer possible, as it was in the not too distant historical past, to settle comfortably into the value system of one's forebears or one's community and live out one's life without ever examining the nature and the assumptions of that system.

In this situation it is not surprising that value orientations from the past appear to be in a state of disintegration or collapse. Men question whether there are, or can be, any universal values. It is often felt that we may have lost, in our modern world, all possibility of any general or cross-cultural basis for values. One natural result of this uncertainty and confusion is that there is an increasing concern about, interest in, and a searching for, a sound or meaningful value approach which can hold its own in today's world. I share this general concern. I have also experienced the more specific value issues which arise in my own field, psychotherapy. The client's feelings and convictions about values frequently change during therapy. How can he or we know whether they have changed in a sound direction? Or does he simply, as some claim, take over the value system of his therapist? Is psychotherapy simply a device whereby the unacknowledged and unexamined values of the therapist are unknowingly transmitted to an unsuspecting client? Or should this transmission of values be the therapist's openly held purpose? Should he become the modern priest, upholding and imparting a value system suitable for today? And what would such a value system be? There has been much discussion of such issues, ranging from thoughtful and empirically based presentations such as that of D. D. Glad (1959) to more polemic statements. As is so often true, the general problem faced by the culture is painfully and specifically evident in the cultural microcosm which is called the therapeutic relationship.

I should like to attempt a modest approach to this whole problem. I have observed changes in the approach to values as the individual grows from infancy to adulthood. I observe further changes when, if he is fortunate, he continues to grow toward true psychological maturity. Many of these observations grow out of my experience as a therapist, where I have had the rich opportunity of seeing the ways in which individuals move toward a richer life. From these observations I believe I see some directional threads emerging which might offer a new concept of the valuing process, more tenable in the modern world. I have made a beginning by presenting some of these ideas partially in previous writings (1951, 1959); I would like now to voice them more clearly and more fully.

I would stress that my vantage point for making these observations is not that of the scholar or philosopher: I am speaking from my experience of the functioning human being, as I have lived with him in the intimate experience of therapy, and in other situations of growth, change, and development.

Some Definitions

Before I present some of these observations, perhaps I should try to clarify what I mean by values. There are many definitions which have been used, but I have found helpful some distinctions made by Charles Morris (1956). He points out that *value* is a term we employ in different ways. We use it to refer to the tendency of any living beings to show preference, in their actions, for one kind of object or objective rather than another. This preferential behavior he calls *operative values*. It need not involve any cognitive or conceptual thinking. It is simply the value choice which is indicated behaviorally when the organism selects one object, rejects another. When the earthworm, placed in a simple Y maze, chooses the smooth arm of the Y instead of the path which is paved with sandpaper, he is indicating an operative value.

A second use of the term might be called *conceived values*. This is the preference of the individual for a symbolized object. Usually in such a preference there is anticipation or foresight of the outcome of behavior directed toward such a symbolized object. A choice such as "Honesty is the best policy" is such a conceived value.

A final use of the term might be called *objective value*. People use the word in this way when they wish to speak of what is objectively preferable, whether or not it is in fact sensed or conceived of as desirable. What I have to say involves this last definition scarcely at all. I will be concerned with operative values and conceptualized values.

The Infant's Way of Valuing

Let me first speak about the infant. The living human being has, at the outset, a clear approach to values. He prefers some things and experiences, and rejects others. We can infer from studying his behavior that he prefers those experiences which maintain, enhance, or actualize his organism, and rejects those which do not serve this end. Watch him for a bit:

Hunger is negatively valued. His expression of this often comes through loud and clear.

Food is positively valued. But when he is satisfied, food is negatively valued, and the same milk he responded to so eagerly is now spit out, or the breast which seemed so satisfying is now rejected as he turns his head away from the nipple with an amusing facial expression of disgust and revulsion.

He values security, and the holding and caressing which seem to communicate security.

He values new experience for its own sake, and we observe this in his obvious pleasure in discovering his toes, in his searching movements, in his endless curiosity.

He shows a clear negative valuing of pain, bitter tastes, sudden loud sounds.

All of this is commonplace, but let us look at these facts in terms of what they tell us about the infant's approach to values. It is first of all a flexible, changing, valuing *process*, not a fixed system. He likes food and dislikes the same food. He values security and rest, and rejects it for new experience. What is going on seems best described as an organismic valuing process, in which each element, each moment of what he is experiencing is somehow weighed, and selected or rejected, depending on whether, at this moment, it tends to actualize the organism or not. This complicated weighing of experience is clearly an organismic, not a conscious or symbolic function. These are operative, not conceived values. But this process can nonetheless deal with complex value problems. I would remind you of the experiment in which young infants had spread in front of them a score or more of dishes of natural (that is, unflavored) foods. Over a period of time they clearly tended to value the foods which enhanced their own survival, growth, and development. If for a time a child gorged himself on starches, this would soon be balanced by a protein "binge." If at times he chose a diet deficient in some vitamin, he would later seek out foods rich in this very vitamin. He was utilizing the wisdom of the body in his value choices, or perhaps more accurately, the physiological wisdom of his body guided his behavioral movements, resulting in what we might think of as objectively sound value choices.

Another aspect of the infant's approach to value is that the source or locus of the evaluating process is clearly within himself. Unlike many of us, he *knows* what he likes and dislikes, and the origin of these value choices lies strictly within himself. He is the center of the valuing process, the evidence for his choices being supplied by his own senses. He is not at this point influenced by what his parents think he should prefer, or by what the church says, or by the opinion of the latest "expert" in the field, or by the persuasive talents of an advertising firm. It is from within his own experiencing that his organism is saying in nonverbal terms, "This is good for me." "That is bad for me." "I like this." "I strongly dislike that." He would laugh at our concern over values, if he could understand it. How could anyone fail to know what he liked and disliked, what was good for him and what was not?

The Change in the Valuing Process

What happens to this highly efficient, soundly based valuing process? By what sequence of events do we exchange it for the more rigid, uncertain, inefficient approach to values which characterizes most of us adults? Let me try to state briefly one of the major ways in which I think this happens.

The infant needs love, wants it, tends to behave in ways which will bring a repetition of this wanted experience. But this brings complications. He pulls baby sister's hair, and finds it satisfying to hear her wails and protests. He then hears that he is "a naughty, bad boy," and this may be reinforced by a slap on the hand. He is cut off from affection. As this experience is repeated, and many, many others like it, he gradually learns that what "feels good" is often "bad" in the eyes of others. Then the next step occurs, in which he comes to take the same attitude toward himself which these others have taken. Now, as he pulls his sister's hair, he solemnly intones, "Bad, bad boy." He is introjecting the value judgment of another, taking it as his own. He has deserted the wisdom of his organism, giving up the locus of evaluation, and is trying to behave in terms of values set by another, in order to hold love.

Or take another example at an older level. A boy senses, though perhaps not consciously, that he is more loved and prized by his parents when he thinks of being a doctor than when he thinks of being an artist. Gradually he introjects the values attached to being a doctor. He comes to want, above all, to be a doctor. Then in college he is baffled by the fact that he repeatedly fails in chemistry, which is absolutely necessary to becoming a physician, in spite of the fact that the guidance counselor assures him he has the ability to pass the course. Only in counseling interviews does he begin to realize how completely he has lost touch with his organismic reactions, how out of touch he is with his own valuing process.

Let me give another instance from a class of mine, a group of prospective teachers. I asked them at the beginning of the course, "Please list for me the two or three values which you would most wish to pass on to the children with whom you will work." They turned in many value goals, but I was surprised by some of the items. Several listed such things as "to speak correctly," "to use good English, not to use words like ain't." Others mentioned neatness—"to do things according to instructions"; one explained her hope that "when I tell them to write their names in the upper right-hand corner with the date under it, I want them to do it *that way*, not in some other form."

I confess I was somewhat appalled that for some of these girls the most important values to be passed on to pupils were to avoid bad grammar, or meticulously to follow teacher's instructions. I felt baffled. Certainly these behaviors had not been *experienced* as the most satisfying and meaningful elements in their own lives. The listing of such values could only be accounted for by the fact that these behaviors had gained approval—and thus had been introjected as deeply important.

Perhaps these several illustrations will indicate that in an attempt to gain or hold love, approval, esteem, the individual relinquishes the locus of evaluation which was his in infancy, and places it in others. He learns to have a basic *dis*trust for his own experiencing as a guide to his behavior. He learns from others a large number of conceived values, and adopts them as his own, even though they may be widely discrepant from what he is experiencing. Because these concepts are not based on his own valuing, they tend to be fixed and rigid, rather than fluid and changing.

Some Introjected Patterns

It is in this fashion, I believe, that most of us accumulate the introjected value patterns by which we live. In this fantastically complex culture of today, the patterns we introject as desirable or undesirable come from a variety of sources and are often highly contradictory in their meanings. Let me list a few of the introjections which are commonly held.

Sexual desires and behaviors are mostly bad. The sources of this construct are many—parents, church, teachers.

Disobedience is bad. Here parents and teachers combine with the military to emphasize this concept. To obey is good. To obey without question is even better.

Making money is the highest good. The sources of this conceived value are too numerous to mention.

Learning an accumulation of scholarly facts is highly desirable.

Browsing and aimless exploratory reading for fun is undesirable. The source of these last two concepts is apt to be in school, the educational system.

Abstract art, or "pop" art, or "op" art is good. Here the people we regard as sophisticated are the originators of the value.

Communism is utterly bad. Here the government is a major source.

To love thy neighbor is the highest good. This concept comes from the church, perhaps from the parents.

Cooperation and teamwork are preferable to acting alone. Here companions are an important source.

Cheating is clever and desirable. The peer group again is the origin.

Coca-Cola, chewing gum, electric refrigerators, and automobiles are all utterly desirable. This conception comes not only from advertisements, but is reinforced by people all over the world. From Jamaica to Japan, from Copenhagen to Kowloon, the "Coca-Cola culture" has come to be regarded as the acme of desirability.

This is a small and diversified sample of the myriads of conceived values which individuals often introject, and hold as their own, without ever having considered their inner organismic reactions to these patterns and objects.

Common Characteristics of Adult Valuing

I believe it will be clear from the foregoing that the usual adult — I feel I am speaking for most of us — has an approach to values which has these characteristics:

The majority of his values are introjected from other individuals or groups significant to him, but are regarded by him as his own.

The source or locus of evaluation on most matters lies outside of himself.

The criterion by which his values are set is the degree to which they will cause him to be loved or accepted.

These conceived preferences are either not related at all, or not clearly related, to his own process of experiencing.

Often there is a wide and unrecognized discrepancy between the evidence supplied by his own experience and these conceived values.

Because these conceptions are not open to testing in experience, he must hold them in a rigid and unchanging fashion. The alternative would be a collapse of his values. Hence his values are "right" — like the law of the Medes and the Persians, which changeth not.

Because they are untestable, there is no ready way of solving contradictions. If he has taken in from the community the conception that money is the *summum bonum* and from the church the conception that love of one's neighbor is the highest value, he has no way of discovering which has more value for *him*. Hence a common aspect of modern life is living with absolutely contradictory values. We calmly discuss the possibility of dropping a hydrogen bomb on Russia, but then find tears in our eyes when we see headlines about the suffering of one small child.

Because he has relinquished the locus of evaluation to others and has lost touch with his own valuing process, he feels profoundly insecure and easily threatened in his values. If some of these conceptions were destroyed, what would take their place? This threatening possibility makes him hold his value conceptions more rigidly or more confusedly, or both.

The Fundamental Discrepancy

I believe that this picture of the individual, with values mostly introjected, held as fixed concepts, rarely examined or tested, is the picture of most of us. By taking over the conceptions of others as our own, we lose contact with the potential wisdom of our own functioning, and lose confidence in ourselves. Since these value constructs are often sharply at variance with what is going on in our own experiencing, we have in a very basic way divorced ourselves from ourselves, and this accounts for much of modern strain and insecurity. This fundamental discrepancy between the individual's concepts and what he is actually experiencing, between the intellectual structure of his values and the valuing process going on unrecognized within him — this is a part of the fundamental estrangement of modern man from himself. This is a major problem for the therapist.

Restoring Contact with Experience

Some individuals are fortunate in going beyond the picture I have just given, developing further in the direction of psychological maturity. We see this happen in psychotherapy where we endeavor to provide a climate favorable to the growth of the person. We also see it happen in life, whenever life provides a therapeutic climate for the individual. Let me concentrate on this further maturing of a value approach as I have seen it in therapy.

In the first place let me say somewhat parenthetically that the therapeutic relationship is *not* devoid of values. Quite the contrary. When it is most effective, it seems to me, it is marked by one primary value: namely, that this person, this client, has worth. He as a person is valued in his separateness and uniqueness. It is when he senses and realizes that he is prized as a person that he can slowly begin to value the different aspects of himself. Most importantly, he can begin, with much difficulty at first, to sense and to feel what is going on within him, what he is feeling, what he is experiencing, how he is reacting. He uses his experiencing as a direct referent to which he can turn in forming accurate conceptualizations and as a guide to his behavior. E. T. Gendlin (1961, 1962) has elaborated the way in which this occurs. As his experiencing becomes more and more open to him, as he is able to live more freely in the process of his feelings, then significant changes being to occur in his approach to values. It begins to assume many of the characteristics it had in infancy.

Introjected Values in Relation to Experiencing

Perhaps I can indicate this by reviewing a few of the brief examples of introjected values which I have given, and suggesting what happens to them as the individual comes closer to what is going on within him.

> The individual in therapy looks back and realizes, "But I *enjoyed* pulling my sister's hair — and that doesn't make me a bad person."
> The student failing chemistry realizes, as he gets close to his own experiencing — "I don't value being a doctor, even though my parents do; I don't like chemistry; I don't like taking steps toward being a doctor; and I am not a failure for having these feelings."
> The adult recognizes that sexual desires and behavior may be richly satisfying and permanently enriching in their consequences, or shallow and temporary and less than satisfying. He goes by his own experiencing, which does not always coincide with the social norms.
> He considers art from a new value approach. He says, "This picture moves me deeply, means a great deal to me. It also happens to be an abstraction, but that is not the basis for my valuing it."
> He recognizes freely that this Communist book or person has attitudes and goals which he shares as well as ideas and values which he does not share.
> He realizes that at times he experiences cooperation as meaningful and valuable to him, and that at other times he wishes to be alone and act alone.

Valuing in the Mature Person

The valuing process which seems to develop in this more mature person is in some ways very much like that in the infant, and in some ways quite different. It is fluid, flexible, based on this particular moment, and the degree to which this moment is experienced as enhancing and actualizing. Values are not held rigidly, but are continually changing. The painting which last year seemed meaningful now appears uninteresting, the way of working with individuals which was formerly experienced as good now seems inadequate, the belief which then seemed true is now experienced as only partly true, or perhaps false.

Another characteristic of the way this person values experience is that it is highly differentiated, or as the semanticists would say, extensional. As the members of my class of prospective teachers learned, general principles are not as useful as sensitively discriminating reactions. One says, "With this little boy, I just felt I should be very firm, and he seemed to welcome that, and I felt good that I had been. But I'm not that way at all with the other children most of the time." She was relying on her experiencing of the relationship with each child to guide her behavior. I have already indicated, in going through the examples, how much more differentiated are the individual's reactions to what were previously rather solid monolithic introjected values.

In another way the mature individual's approach is like that of the infant. The locus of evaluation is again established firmly within the person. It is his own experience which provides the value information or feedback. This does not mean that he is not open to all the evidence he can obtain from other sources. But it means that this is taken for what it is—outside evidence—and is not as significant as his own reactions. Thus he may be told by a friend that a new book is very disappointing. He reads two unfavorable reviews of the book. Thus his tentative hypothesis is that he will not value the book. Yet if he reads the book his valuing will be based upon the reactions it stirs in him, not on what he has been told by others.

There is also involved in this valuing process a letting oneself down into the immediacy of what one is experiencing, endeavoring to sense and to clarify all its complex meanings. I think of a client who, toward the close of therapy, when puzzled about an issue, would put his head in his hands and say, "Now what *is* it that I'm feeling? I want to get next to it. I want to learn what it is." Then he would wait, quietly and patiently, trying to listen to himself, until he could discern the exact flavor of the feelings he was experiencing. He, like others, was trying to get close to himself.

In getting close to what is going on within himself, the process is much more complex than it is in the infant. In the mature person, it has much more scope and sweep, for there is involved in the present moment of experiencing the memory traces of all the relevant learnings from the past. This moment has not only its immediate sensory impact, but it has meaning growing out of similar experiences in the past. It has both the new and the old in it. So when I experience a painting or a person, my experiencing contains within it the learnings I have accumulated from past meetings with paintings or persons, as well as the new impact of this particular encounter. Likewise the moment of experience contains, for the mature adult, hypotheses about consequences. "I feel now that I would enjoy a third drink, but past learnings indicate that I may regret it in the morning." "It is not pleasant to express forthrightly my negative feelings to this person, but past experience indicates that in a continuing relationship it will be helpful in the long run." Past and future are both in this moment and enter into the valuing.

I find that in the person I am speaking of (and here again we see a similarity to the infant) the criterion of the valuing process is the degree to which the object of the experience actualizes the individual himself. Does it make him a richer, more complete, more fully developed person? This may sound as though it were a selfish or unsocial criterion, but it does not prove to be so, since deep and helpful relationships with others are experienced as actualizing.

Like the infant, too, the psychologically mature adult trusts and uses the wisdom of his organism, with the difference that he is able to do so knowingly. He realizes that if he can trust all of himself, his feelings and his intuitions may be wiser than his mind, that as a total person he can be more sensitive and accurate than his thoughts alone. Hence he is not afraid to say — "I feel that this experience (or this thing, or this direction) is good. Later I will probably know *why* I feel it is good." He trusts the totality of himself.

It should be evident from what I have been saying that this valuing process in the mature individual is not an easy or simple thing. The process is complex, the choices often very perplexing and difficult, and there is no guarantee that the choice which is made will in fact prove to be self-actualizing. But because whatever evidence exists is available to the individual, and because he is open to his experiencing, errors are correctable. If a chosen course of action is not self-enhancing this will be sensed and he can make an adjustment or revision. He thrives on a maximum feedback interchange, and thus, like the gyroscopic compass on a ship, can continually correct his course toward becoming more of himself.

Some Propositions Regarding the Valuing Process

Let me sharpen the meaning of what I have been saying by stating three propositions which contain the essential elements of this viewpoint. While it may not be possible to devise empirical tests of each proposition in its entirety, yet each is to some degree capable of being tested through the methods of science. I would also state that though the following propositions are stated firmly in order to give them clarity, I am actually advancing them as decidedly tentative hypotheses.

1. *There is an organismic base for an organized valuing process within the human individual.*

It is hypothesized that this base is something the human being shares with the rest of the animate world. It is part of the functioning life process of any healthy organism. It is the capacity for receiving feedback information which enables the organism continually to adjust its behavior and reactions so as to achieve the maximum possible self-enhancement.

2. *This valuing process in the human being is effective in achieving self-enhancement to the degree that the individual is open to the experiencing which is going on within himself.*

I have tried to give two examples of individuals who are close to their own experiencing: the tiny infant who has not yet learned to deny in his awareness the processes going on within; and the psychologically mature person who has relearned the advantages of this open state.

3. *One way of assisting the individual to move toward openness to experience is through a relationship in which he is prized as a separate person, in which the experiencing going on within him is empathically under-*

stood and valued, and in which he is given the freedom to experience his own feelings and those of others without being threatened in doing so.

This proposition obviously grows out of therapeutic experience. It is a brief statement of the essential qualities in the therapeutic relationship. There are already some empirical studies, of which the one by Barrett-Lennard (1962) is a good example, which gives support to such a statement.

Propositions Regarding the Outcomes of the Valuing Process

I come now to the nub of any theory of values or valuing. What are its consequences? I should like to move into this new ground by stating bluntly two propositions as to the qualities of behavior which emerge from this valuing process. I shall then give some of the evidence from my own experience as a therapist in support of these propositions.

4. *In persons who are moving toward greater openness to their experiencing, there is an organismic commonality of value directions.*

5. *These common value directions are of such kinds as to enhance the development of the individual himself, of others in his community, and to make for the survival and evolution of his species.*

It has been a striking fact of my experience that in therapy, where individuals are valued, where there is greater freedom to feel and to be, certain value directions seem to emerge. These are not chaotic directions but instead have a surprising commonality. This commonality is not dependent on the personality of the therapist, for I have seen these trends emerge in the clients of therapists sharply different in personality. This commonality does not seem to be due to the influences of any one culture, for I have found evidence of these directions in cultures as divergent as those of the United States, Holland, France, and Japan. I like to think that this commonality of value directions is due to the fact that we all belong to the same species — that just as a human infant tends, individually, to select a diet similar to that selected by other human infants, so a client in therapy tends, individually, to choose value directions similar to those chosen by other clients. As a species there may be certain elements of experience which tend to make for inner development and which would be chosen by all individuals if they were genuinely free to choose.

Let me indicate a few of these value directions as I see them in my clients as they move in the direction of personal growth and maturity.

> They tend to move away from façades. Pretense, defensiveness, putting up a front, tend to be negatively valued.
>
> They tend to move away from "oughts." The compelling feeling of "I ought to do or be thus and so" is negatively valued. The client moves away from being what he "ought to be," no matter who has set that imperative.
>
> They tend to move away from meeting the expectations of others. Pleasing others, as a goal in itself, is negatively valued.
>
> Being real is positively valued. The client tends to move toward being himself, being his real feelings, being what he is. This seems to be a very deep preference.
>
> Self-direction is positively valued. The client discovers an increasing pride and confidence in making his own choices, guiding his own life.
>
> One's self, one's own feelings, come to be positively valued. From a point where he looks upon himself with contempt and despair, the client comes to value himself and his reactions as being of worth.
>
> Being a process is positively valued. From desiring some fixed goal, clients come to prefer the excitement of being a process of potentialities being born.
>
> Perhaps more than all else, the client comes to value an openness to all of his inner and outer experience. To be open to and sensitive to his own *inner* reactions and feelings, the reactions and feelings of others, and the realities of the objective world—this is a direction which he clearly prefers. This openness becomes the client's most valued resource.
>
> Sensitivity to others and acceptance of others is positively valued. The client comes to appreciate others for what they are, just as he has come to appreciate himself for what he is.
>
> Finally, deep relationships are positively valued. To achieve a close, intimate, real, fully communicative relationship with another person seems to meet a deep need in every individual, and is very highly valued.

These then are some of the preferred directions which I have observed in individuals moving toward personality maturity. Though I am sure that the list I have given is inadequate and perhaps to some degree inaccurate, it holds for me exciting possibilities. Let me try to explain why.

I find it significant that when individuals are prized as persons, the values they select do not run the full gamut of possibilities. I do not find, in such a climate of freedom, that one person comes to value fraud and murder and thievery, while another values a life of self-sacrifice, and another values only money. Instead there seems to be a deep and underlying thread of commonality. I dare to believe that when the human being is inwardly free to choose whatever he deeply values, he tends to value those objects, experiences, and goals which make for his own survival, growth, and development, and for the survival and development of others. I hypothesize that it is characteristic of the human organism to prefer such actualizing and socialized goals when he is exposed to a growth-promoting climate.

A corollary of what I have been saying is that in *any* culture, given a climate of respect and freedom in which he is valued as a person, the mature individual would tend to choose and prefer these same value directions. This is a highly significant hypothesis which could be tested. It means that though the individual of whom I am speaking would not have a consistent or even a stable system of conceived values, the valuing process within him would lead to emerging value directions which would be constant across cultures and across time.

Another implication I see is that individuals who exhibit the fluid valuing process I have tried to describe, whose value directions are generally those I have listed, would be highly effective in the ongoing process of human evolution. If the human species is to survive at all on this globe, the human being must become more readily adaptive to new problems and situations, must be able to select that which is valuable for development and survival out of new and complex situations, must be accurate in his appreciation of reality if he is to make such selections. The psychologically mature person as I have described him has, I believe, the qualities which would cause him to value those experiences which would make for the survival and enhancement of the human race. He would be a worthy participant and guide in the process of human evolution.

Finally, it appears that we have returned to the issue of universality of values, but by a different route. Instead of universal values "out there," or a universal value system imposed by some group — philosophers, rulers, or priests — we have the possibility of universal human value directions emerging from the experiencing of the human organism. Evidence from therapy indicates that both personal and social values emerge as natural, and experienced, when the individual is close to his own organismic valuing process. The suggestion is that though modern man no longer trusts religion or science or philosophy or any system of beliefs to *give* him his values, he may find an organismic valuing base within himself which, if he can learn again to be in touch with it, will prove to be an organized, adaptive, and social approach to the perplexing value issues which face all of us.

Summary

I have tried to present some observations, growing out of experience in psychotherapy, which are relevant to man's search for some satisfying basis for his approach to values.

I have described the human infant as he enters directly into an evaluating transaction with his world, appreciating or rejecting his experiences as they have meaning for his own actualization, utilizing all the wisdom of his tiny but complex organism.

I have said that we seem to lose this capacity for direct evaluation, and come to behave in those ways and to act in terms of those values which will bring us social approval, affection, esteem. To buy love we relinquish the valuing process. Because the center of our lives now lies in others, we are fearful and insecure, and must cling rigidly to the values we have introjected.

But if life or therapy gives us favorable conditions for continuing our psychological growth, we move on in something of a spiral, developing an approach to values which partakes of the infant's directness and fluidity but goes far beyond him in its richness. In our transactions with experience we are again the locus or source of valuing, we prefer those experiences which in the long run are enhancing, we utilize all the richness of our cognitive learning and functioning, but at the same time we trust the wisdom of our organism.

I have pointed out that these observations lead to certain basic statements. Man has within him an organismic basis for valuing.

To the extent that he can be freely in touch with this valuing process in himself, he will behave in ways which are self-enhancing. We even know some of the conditions which enable him to be in touch with his own experiencing process.

In therapy, such openness to experience leads to emerging value directions which appear to be common across individuals and perhaps even across cultures. Stated in older terms, individuals who are thus in touch with their experiencing come to value such directions as sincerity, independence, self-direction, self-knowledge, social responsibility, and loving interpersonal relationships.

I have concluded that a new kind of emergent universality of value directions becomes possible when individuals move in the direction of psychological maturity, or more accurately, move in the direction of becoming open to their experiencing. Such a value base appears to make for the enhancement of self and others, and to promote a positive evolutionary process.

REFERENCES

Barrett-Lennard, G. T. Dimensions of therapist response as causal factors in therapeutic change. *Psychological Monographs*, 1962, *76* (43, Whole No. 562).

Gendlin, E. T. Experiencing: A variable in the process of therapeutic change. *American Journal of Psychotherapy*, 1961, *15*, 233–245.

Gendlin, E. T. *Experiencing and the creation of meaning.* New York: The Free Press of Glencoe, Division of the Macmillan Co., 1962.

Glad, D. D. *Operational values in psychotherapy.* New York: Oxford University Press, 1959.

Morris, C. W. *Varieties of human value.* Chicago: University of Chicago Press, 1956.

Rogers, C. R. *Client-centered therapy.* Boston: Houghton Mifflin Co., 1951. Chapter XI, 522–524.

Rogers, C. R. A theory of therapy, personality and interpersonal relationships. In S. Koch (Ed.), *Psychology: A study of a science*, Vol. III. *Formulations of the person and the social context.* New York: McGraw-Hill, 1959, 185–256.

13
Shall We Get Married?

Let's look at a few facts. In California in 1970 there were 173,000 marriages and approximately 114,000 "dissolutions of marriage." In other words, for every 100 couples who married there were 66 who were permanently parting. This is admittedly a distorted picture because a new law became effective in 1970 permitting couples to "dissolve" their marriages without trying to blame the "guilty party," simply on the basis of an agreement. The dissolution becomes final in six months instead of a year, as previously. So let us look at 1969. In that year for every 100 couples marrying, 49 were getting divorced. Somewhat more would have been divorced, but they were waiting for the new law to come into effect. In Los Angeles County (essentially the city of Los Angeles) in 1969 divorces equaled 61 percent of the number of marriages. In 1970, under the new law, the number of dissolutions of marriage in the county was 74 percent of the number of marriages. Three couples were getting their marriages dissolved while four couples were getting married! And in 1971 in Los Angeles County there were 61,560 marriage licenses issued and 48,221 suits filed for dissolution of marriage, 79 percent of the number that were marrying. These are not final *actions*, because the final outcomes will not be known for some time, but they are steps indicating *intent*. Thus in 1971 for every five couples intending to marry, four were intending to dissolve their marriages! In the course of three years there was a *61 percent, 74 percent, 79 percent* rate of breakup of marriages in one of the country's largest cities. I believe those couples, and these figures, are trying to tell us something!

Some of you may say, "Yes, but that's *California*." I have purposely chosen that state because in social and cultural behaviors what Californians are doing today the rest of the nation — as has been shown in numerous ways — will be doing tomorrow. And

Becoming Partners: Marriage and Its Alternatives. New York: Delacorte Press, 1972, 9–21.

I have chosen Los Angeles County because what an urban center is doing today appears to become the norm for the country tomorrow. So as a very modest statement we may say that more than one out of every two marriages in California ends in dissolution of the partnership. And in urban areas — better educated and more in tune with everything modern — the ratio is three out of four or even four out of five.

In my contacts with young people it has become clear to me, beyond the shadow of a doubt, that the contemporary young person tends to have a distrust of marriage as an institution. He has seen too many flaws in it. He has often seen it fail in his own home. Instead, a relationship between a man and a woman is significant, and worth trying to preserve, only when it is an enhancing, growing experience for each person. There are very few reasons why marriage makes for economic well-being, as used to be true in early Colonial days in this country when husband and wife constituted a very necessary working team. The young person of today is not impressed by the fact that, religiously, a marriage should last "until death do us part." Rather he tends to regard the vows of complete permanence in marriage as clearly hypocritical. It is obvious from observing the behavior of married couples that if they were truthful, the persons involved would vow to live together "in sickness and in health" so long as the marriage was an enriching and satisfying experience for each one.

There are many who view with alarm the present state of marriage. To them it is proof that our culture has lost its moral standards, that we are in a period of decadence, and that it is only a question of time until we are penalized by an angry God for creating this sink of immorality in which we flounder. While I would agree that there are many signs that our culture is indeed in crisis and that it may be coming apart at the seams, I tend to see it in a different perspective. These are agonizing times for many, including many married couples. It is perhaps that we are living under the malediction contained in the ancient Chinese saying "I *curse* you; may you live in an important age."

To me it seems that we are living in an important and uncertain age, and the institution of marriage is most assuredly in an uncertain state. If 50 to 75 percent of Ford or General Motors cars completely fell apart within the early part of their lifetimes as automobiles, drastic steps would be taken. We have no such well-organized way of dealing with our social institutions, so people are groping, more or less blindly, to find alternatives to marriage (which is certainly *less* than 50 percent successful). Living together without marriage, living in communes, extensive child-care centers, serial monogamy (with one divorce after another), the women's liberation movement to establish the woman as a person in her own right, new divorce laws which do away with the concept of guilt—these are all gropings toward some new form of man-woman relationship for the future. It would take a bolder man than I to predict what will emerge.

Instead, I want in this chapter to present a number of vignettes of real marriages, each of which takes a different form, each of which raises profound questions—of morals, of practicality, of personal desirability. It is my hope that even if no answers are provided, there will be much data for thought and for personal decision-making.

Why Joan Married

Listen to Joan, a young woman, now divorced, as she shares with an encounter group some of the background components of her marriage. I find that her account has many significant meanings for me, and I will share some of those later. Here's Joan:

> I guess I got married for all the wrong reasons. At the time it was the thing to do. "Here are all my friends getting married, what am I gonna do? I'm a senior in college, that's pretty old. I better start thinking about marriage. I don't know what else I can do. I can teach but that's not enough."
> The person that I married was a very popular man and I was a very insecure person, *very* insecure; and I thought, well, golly, I'm going with this person and everybody likes *him*, so maybe if I marry him, everybody will like *me*! The man that I married, I didn't feel he really listened, but I did feel security. That, and not knowing what I'd do when I graduated—that's why I got married.

A bit later she goes into more detail as to the kind of thinking that preceded her marriage.

The reason why I got engaged was because a very good friend of mine had gotten engaged and she had a very pretty ring, and was making all these wedding plans. My friends were saying, "God, Joan, when are you and Max getting married? You've been going together for three years now. You better not let him get away. If you let *him* get away, you're stupid!" My mother said, "Oh, Joan, when are you going to find another person like Max? He's so outstanding and responsible and mature and secure." I felt, "This is the one I should marry because my close friends, my roommate, my mother all say it," and although I had these doubts going on inside me, I thought, "Well, you're so insecure and so stupid that you don't know your own feelings." I thought, "They know what's best for you and you don't so you had better follow their advice."

I had guts enough to tell Max why I was doing it and I said I was really kind of scared to get married and said, "I don't know if this is really right for me." And he said, "Don't worry. You'll learn to love me." I did learn to love him in a brotherly way, but it didn't go beyond that.

When the wedding gifts were unwrapped and all the newness wore off, and the newness of having a baby wore off, then I really started feeling, "Oh, you stupid idiot, you should have listened to *yourself*": because I had been saying those things to me, but I just wouldn't listen because I thought I was too screwed up to know what was best for me. So I was right after all.

There are several elements which, for me, stand out in Joan's experience. First of all, it shows how prone we all are to yield to social pressures. A female college senior should be planning to get married, and socially that's *that*.

The dangers of advice stand out so very clearly. Out of love and caring and concern her mother and her good friends all know what is best for her to do. How easy it is to direct the life of another and how very difficult it is to live your own!

The fear of squarely facing one's own problems. Joan knew she was insecure. She knew she was frightened of the future. She realized she couldn't get to her own feelings. But instead of facing those inner problems squarely and directly, she did what so many of us do; she built the illusion that she could find the solution outside herself—in another.

Finally, what impresses me is that Joan, as is true of so many others, experiences no trust in her own feelings, her own inner unique reactions. She is dimly aware of the doubts she has about the relationship, of the lack of a feeling of deep love, of her unreadiness really to commit herself to this man. But these are only feelings. *Only feelings!* It is not until after marriage, and after having a child, that she realizes what reliable guides her gut reactions were, if she had only *trusted* them enough to *listen* to them.

Losing One's Self—and Its Effect on a Marriage

Next I would like to present a picture of a good marriage which disintegrated. I think we can see some of the elements at work in causing it to fail. So here is the story of Jay, a promising young instructor in journalism, and Jennifer, a sociology major interested in international problems as well as art. I have known them for many years and their parents are friends of mine. They were both about twenty when they met, and their initial acquaintance grew up around the mutual interest they discovered in world issues. They are in their early forties now. They both came from educated backgrounds, though Jay's father, a highly cultivated person, was largely self-educated. They were of different religious faiths, but neither of them took any great stock in orthodoxy, and their beliefs could more adequately be described as humanistic. They were married, and the marriage seemed a very happy one indeed. In the course of several years a boy and a girl arrived. Here was the first point at which the possibility of a rift emerged. Jay came from a familial and cultural background in which a child was adored. He felt that nothing was too good for his children and that every whim of each child was to be obeyed. Jennifer went along with him to some extent, but this was not *her* way and she differed openly with Jay on this. Jay seemed an admirable father. Unlike many men, he loved nothing better than to spend a day with his children, and he had the capacity of becoming at those times very much of a child himself.

As Jay moved up in his profession he was called upon to spend periods of time abroad—in European, Latin American, and Asian countries. On any extended trip the whole family went along. They met interesting people, explored new cultures, and Jay and Jennifer even worked together on some of the foreign projects. It seemed to be an idyllic marriage and a very close-knit family. Yet there were subtle flaws in the personality and behavior of each—deficiencies which seemed to feed on the other's deficiencies, until little by little, since they were not openly faced and mutually talked out, they made this idyllic marriage intolerable. Let me give a very condensed account of this subtle downward spiral.

Jennifer, before her marriage, had been an extremely independent, creative, innovative person, always starting things and carrying out projects which others were not bold enough to do. Yet in her marriage she adopted the role of being her husband's support, of doing what he wanted done in the way he wished it done. She felt this was the way a wife should behave. She even wrote to him before their marriage, she tells me, that she was not too sure of herself and that she wanted to live her life through his.

Jay is a charming person with a high degree of charisma; a brilliant intellectual, an exciting conversationalist. Not surprisingly, his were the friends invited to their home. He was the central focus of the evening, while Jennifer did a splendid job of providing the food, the drinks, the aesthetic setting for the evening. She would try, but usually ineffectually, to enter the conversation or to introduce a topic of her own. At some level her resentment at this situation built up, though it never really surfaced until they had been married twelve or fourteen years. Up to that time she was really unaware of any of her resentments. Perhaps this was due to her life in her own family, where negative feelings were almost never expressed.

At any rate, without being conscious of what was happening, she turned her resentment inward. How could she be so inadequate, so worthless, so unappreciative that she could not enjoy her husband as others did? She simply gave up her own self in order to try to be the wife whom Jay wanted and needed. Søren Kierkegaard's statement comes to mind: "The greatest danger, that of losing one's own self, may pass off quietly as if it were nothing; every other loss, that of an arm, a leg, five dollars, etc., is sure to be noticed." Though this sentence was written more than a century ago, it was incredibly true of Jennifer, and it took her years to discover the loss.

Another important facet of their relationship was Jay's dependence on her, evident in many ways, but especially in the making of important decisions. Though outwardly a highly competent professional person, he seemed to have great difficulty arriving at decisions and frequently managed to get Jennifer to make a statement as to what decision *she* thought he should make. Then he would make that choice. If it didn't work out well, she was certainly partly to blame and in subtle ways he let her know it.

His dependence and his inability to be a strong and decisive father built up more and more suppressed anger in Jennifer, until she found, to her horror, that she hated to hear his car coming in after work. Her reaction was "Here comes my third child," and a deeply despondent feeling settled on her like a cloud.

This unconscious turning inward of all her negative feelings about the relationship caused her to be more and more depressed until thoughts of suicide were increasingly frequent. One day she found herself taking the steps that would lead to her own death. She was sure that she was worthless, that neither Jay nor her parents would miss her, that no one cared for her, and she might as well end it. Then *something* in her rebelled. There was at least a dawning feeling that she had a *right* to *live*. She immediately sat down and wrote to a psychiatrist whom she knew and in whom she had confidence, asking for an early appointment, which was given. She entered therapy and continued for a long time.

This was definitely the turning of the corner for her, but not for the marriage. As she became more open in the relationship, some of her long pent-up anger and resentment poured out on Jay, often to his bewilderment. He had given her everything she wanted. He had been a father who loved his home, his wife, and his children. Who was this angry new woman who called him dependent, who felt he was not enough of a man sexually for her, who resented the excitement he created in social conversations? Her parents felt some of the same puzzlement, for she heaped on them the accumulated resentments of long ago, which often had little to do with the present relationship.

Jay felt strongly that he was not to blame for the situation, that he had always acted as a proper husband should, and that obviously Jennifer was "sick." He had been generous, helpful, stimulating, and completely faithful. He was at a loss to understand the situation, and certainly felt that he was not the one who needed to change. Hence, though they made several attempts to work out some of their problems with a marriage counselor, these efforts were not successful, and in some respects they worsened the situation. Jay could always present himself in such an articulate and favorable way that even the counselor was to some extent won over, leaving Jennifer more angry than ever.

Jennifer began demanding that Jay be the husband whom she wanted and expected. Jay for his part simply wanted Jennifer to go back to being the helpmate whom he had known for almost fifteen years. He would continue to be the loving person he had been if she would return to being the loving wife she had been. The marriage became more and more acrimonious, the air between them full of hostility, until divorce remained the only sensible answer.

I would make only two comments about this marriage. Though Jay and Jennifer were not perfectly matched, there is every reason to believe that it could have been a satisfying marriage. It is easy enough with hindsight to see that if Jennifer had from the first insisted on being her true self, the marriage would have had much more strife *and* much more hope. Ideally, if when she first felt dominated in conversation she had expressed her resentment to him, as a feeling in herself, it is highly likely that some mutually satisfactory solution could have been found. The same is true of her unhappiness over being forced to be the one who guided the children, of her annoyance at his dependent weakness, of her disappointment in his lack of sexual aggressiveness. If she could have voiced these attitudes as they arose, before they had built up to a high pressure; if she could have voiced them as feelings existing in her, not as the accusations they later became, then the likelihood that they would be met by the expression of feelings from him, and the possibility of coming to a deeper mutual understanding and to a resolution of the difficulties, would have been greater. It seems tragic that a marriage with great and exciting potential should have become a failure. Out of it, has come a strong and creative Jennifer who will never again, I believe, sacrifice herself to meet the needs and demands of another.

And Jay — had he been faced with these feelings when they occurred — would of necessity have realized that he was not always the excellent father and husband he felt he was, that he was not always right, that he was not only contributing to the marriage love and caring (which he was) but was also arousing anger and resentment and feelings of inadequacy in his wife. He then could have become openly a more human, childish, fallible person. Instead, he feels confirmed in his view that he was an excellent husband and father, that there was no sense of strain in the marriage so far as he could see, until Jennifer for unknown reasons "went off the track." He sees the breakup of the marriage as unnecessary and wrong. For him, Jennifer's thinking about the relationship gradually became an ugly caricature of something that was truly beautiful, creative, and often joyful. He simply does not understand this at all, except that he is sure that it was not his doing. It is sad to see such a lack of insight in so brilliant a person.

The Rescue of a Marriage

I learned a great deal from counseling a young wife, Peg Moore. Although this took place a number of years ago, her concerns, and my learnings, are as "now" as the latest pop record. I had known Peg in one of my classes, a bouncy, spontaneous, good-humored young woman with the wholesome appearance of the All-American Girl. But a bit later she comes to me for counseling. Her complaint is that her husband, Bill, is very formal and reserved with her, that he doesn't talk to her or share his thinking with her, is inconsiderate, that they are sexually incompatible and rapidly growing apart. I found myself feeling, "How tragic it is that such a lively, exciting girl is married to a wooden image of a man." But as she continues to talk out her attitudes she becomes more open, a mask drops away, and the picture changes drastically. She expresses the deep guilt feeling which she has regarding her life before her marriage, when she had affairs with a number of men, mostly married men. She realizes that though with most people she is a gay and spontaneous person, with her husband she is stiff, controlled, lacking in spontaneity. She also sees herself as demanding that he be exactly what she wishes him to be.

At this point counseling is interrupted by my absence from the city. She continues to write to me, expressing her feelings and adding, "If I could only say these things to him [her husband] I could be myself at home. But what would that do to his trust in people? Would you find me repulsive if you were my husband and learned the truth? I wish I were a 'nice gal' instead of a 'Babe.' I've made such a mess of things."

This is followed by a letter from which a lengthy quotation seems justified. She tells how irritable she has been — how disagreeable she was when company dropped in one evening. After they left,

> I felt like a louse for behaving so badly. . . . I was still feeling sullen, guilty, angry at myself and Bill — and just about as blue as they come.
>
> So, I decided to do what I've been really wanting to do and putting off because I felt it was more than I could expect from any man — to tell Bill just what was making me act that terrible way. It was even harder than telling you — and that was hard enough. I couldn't tell it in such minute detail but I did manage to get out some of those sordid feelings about my parents and then even more about those "damn" men. The nicest thing I've ever heard him say was, "Well, maybe I can help you there" — when speaking of my parents. And he was very accepting of the things I had done. I told him how I felt so inadequate in so many situations — because I have never been allowed to do so many things — even to know how to play cards. We *talked, discussed,* and really got down deep into so many of both our feelings. I didn't tell him as completely about the men — their names, but I did give him an idea of about how many. Well, he was so understanding and things have cleared up so much that I TRUST HIM. I'm not afraid now to tell him those silly little illogical feelings that keep popping into my head. And if I'm not afraid then maybe soon those silly things will stop popping. The other evening when I wrote to you I was almost ready to pull out — I even thought of just leaving town. (Escaping the whole affair.) But I realized that I'd just keep running from it and not be happy until it was faced. We talked over children and though we've decided to wait until Bill is closer to finishing school, I'm happy with this ar-

rangement. Bill feels as I do about the things we want to do for
our children—and most important the things we *don't* want to
do to them. So if you don't get any more desperate sounding
letters, you know things are going along as okay as can be expected.

Now, I'm wondering—have you known all along that that was
the only thing I could do to bring Bill and me close? That was
the one thing I kept telling myself wouldn't be fair to Bill. I
thought it would ruin his faith in me and in everyone. I had a
barrier so big between Bill and me that I felt he was almost a
stranger. The only way I pushed myself to do it was to realize
that if I didn't at least try his response to the things that were
bothering me, it wouldn't be fair to him—to leave him without
giving him a chance to prove that he could be trusted. He proved
even more than that to me—he's been down in hell too with his
feelings—about his parents, and a good many people in general.
(Rogers, 1961, pp. 316–317)

It is interesting to ask how much psychological energy is con-
sumed by spouses who are trying to live behind a mask in their
marriages. Peg had clearly felt that she was acceptable only if
she maintained a façade of respectability. Unlike Jennifer, she
was somewhat *aware* of her feelings, but believed that if she
showed them, she would be utterly rejected.

For me the significance of the story does *not* lie in the fact that
she told her husband of her past sexual experiences. I do not
think that is the lesson to be learned from it. I have known happy
marriages in which one spouse has concealed certain experiences
from the other, but has been able to do so comfortably. In Peg's
case this concealment had built up an enormous barrier, so that
she could not be real in the relationship.

One rule of thumb which I have found helpful for myself is
that in any continuing relationship, any persistent feeling had
better be expressed. Suppressing it can only damage the relationship. The first sentence is not stated casually. Only if it is a
significant continuing relationship, and only if it is a recurring
or persistent feeling, is it necessary to bring the feeling into the
open in the relationship. If this is not done, what is unexpressed
gradually poisons the relationship, as it did in Peg's case. So
when she asks, "Have you known all along that that was the only
thing I could do to bring Bill and me close?" my answer would

depend on what she means. I certainly believe that it was the sharing of her real feelings which rescued the marriage, but whether it was necessary to tell Bill the details of her behavior is something only she could decide.

Incidentally, a birth announcement and a note several years later indicated that both the marriage and their child seemed healthy.

REFERENCE

Rogers, C. R. *On Becoming a Person.* Boston: Houghton Mifflin, 1961.

THEORY AND RESEARCH

Throughout his career, Carl Rogers was often criticized by academicians as being "soft," unscholarly, unrealistic, or "lightweight." As one reviewer put it, "Like another American philosopher, Huckleberry Finn, Carl Rogers can get in almost anywhere because the draft of his vessel is so terribly shallow." Another said, "He has treated the 'soft' side of psychology in a 'soft' manner when it needed tough-mindedness."

This was an ironic charge, because psychological theory and particularly research occupied a central focus for the first thirty-five years of Rogers's career. In fact, in 1956, along with two other prominent psychologists — Kenneth W. Spence and Wolfgang Kohler — he was selected to receive the first Distinguished Scientific Contribution Award ever presented by the American Psychological Association. Rogers's citation read:

> . . . for developing an original method to objectify the description and analysis of the psychotherapeutic process, for formulating a testable theory of psychotherapy and its effects on personality and behavior, and for extensive systematic research to exhibit the value of the method and explore and test the implications of the theory. His imagination, persistence, and flexible adaptation of scientific method in his attack on the formidable problems involved in the understanding and modification of the individual person have moved this area of psychological interest within the boundaries of scientific psychology.

Of many professional honors he received, this was the one he most prized throughout his life. Later, when he moved to California in 1963, research played a smaller part in his work; yet he always respected research and often cited his and other studies, not only in therapy, but in education, encounter groups, and other areas of his interest.

The first selection here, "What I Learned from Two Research Studies," describes a period in the thirties and forties when Rogers was becoming more deeply immersed in psychological research. It is a portion of a recorded interview with Rogers in April 1986, conducted as part of the Oral History Project of the Archives of Humanistic Psychology, based at the University of California, Santa Barbara. It captures some of the personal flavor of Rogers's early work and initial research orientation.

The next selection highlights an important development in the history of psychotherapy — the phonographic recording of psychotherapy and the use of these recordings in psychotherapeutic research and training. Unknown to Rogers and almost anyone else at the time, the Yale Institute of Human Relations had recorded and transcribed, but never published, the first complete psychoanalysis case in 1935. It was not until Rogers and his student Bernard Covner developed their own recording apparatus, recorded and transcribed one hundred or so interviews, and published the complete "Case of Herbert Bryan" in Rogers's *Counseling and Psychotherapy* (1942) that the profession became aware of this powerful new tool for the advancement of the field.

Today, when cassette recording and videotaping have become common, widely accessible tools for all practitioners, it is hard to imagine the difficulties involved in the pioneering days of recording therapeutic interviews. "The Use of Electrically Recorded Interviews in Improving Psychotherapeutic Techniques" conveys some of that early excitement, but does not convey the full complexity of the recording process. Actually, *two* phonographs were required, so while one record was being turned or removed, the other machine could begin recording without missing a word. This had to be done about every three minutes. Meanwhile it was necessary to continue cleaning off the shavings that the stylus cut into the recording discs. In a few months, Rogers and Covner had about eight hundred record faces in their collection. Most of Rogers's and much of the profession's subsequent research was made possible by the recording he developed and popularized.

The remaining selections in this section were two of Rogers's favorite essays. "The Necessary and Sufficient Conditions of Therapeutic Personality Change" is a brief but extreme statement of Rogers's theory of therapy, put in the "if-then" terminology of experimental research. It was one of his most heuristically important pieces, leading to many fruitful research studies by himself and others.

Pleased with this shorter theoretical statement, two years later Rogers went on to write a longer, seventy-page formulation of "A Theory of Therapy, Personality, and Interpersonal Relationships, As Developed in the Client-Centered Framework," published in Koch's multivolume work *Psychology: A Study of a Science* (1959). Rogers believed this was his most scholarly, complete, and well-developed theoretical formulation, was very proud of it, and was always puzzled that hardly anyone ever seemed to know or care about its existence.

Because we agree that the Koch essay is one of Rogers's most important and little-known writings, we have excerpted about one fourth of the entire work here, representing the scope and style of the entire piece. Not included are a seventeen-page glossary with definitions of terms, many additional references to research studies that support most of the theoretical assertions, and further discussion of each major hypothesis and its research context. While relatively dry in comparison to his typical, personal writing style, we believe there is an elegance and breadth in this formulation that will reward the careful reader.

14
What I Learned from Two Research Studies

I want to tell a story which involves me personally very much and my career, and which I think is also relevant to the field of psychology. The story involves the use of an instrument that I developed to assess a child's background and current situation

Previously unpublished. The original 1986 interview transcript was first edited by Rogers following the interview. It has been further edited here for greater readability and to eliminate extraneous material. The informal conversational style is retained.

and to help plan his future. It was an assessment based on the past, but looking toward the future. Then, the story involves the use of that instrument to see if it might predict the future behavior of young delinquents. It involves findings which were so astonishing to me that I didn't believe them. So the study was laid on the shelf for a while. Then it involves the replication of that study two years later (and I think replication of social science research is not very ordinary)—a replication which confirmed all the major findings. By that time, I was ready to believe the findings. The findings were of a nature which, if taken seriously, would greatly change a lot of our social policies. And, finally, the findings helped to focus my career on the field of psychotherapy. So those are some of the reasons why I wanted to tell this story.

The Method: Its Development and Early Use

It must have been in the early 1930s that I developed a system for assessing the quality of the child's situation. I called it the Component Factor Method, and its purpose was to provide a better means of diagnosing the child's behavior than the labeling which seemed to me pretty useless and futile. It was based on a study of case history material and the rating of eight factors. The ratings were to indicate whether the individual factor was destructive of the child's welfare, or whether it was in the direction of healthy and normal adjustment and behavior.

Some of the factors involved were: the quality of family life and influence; the health history or constitution of the child; the economic and cultural background and influence; the intellectual development of the child; the social experience that the youngster had had; the hereditary factor; and the educational influence.

I realize that, at that time, I was quite deterministic in my views. It seemed to me that these seven factors really accounted for behavior. However, I did include one other internal factor —the degree of the child's self-understanding, self-insight; the realistic acceptance of self and the realistic appraisal of the situation in which he found himself; and the acceptance of responsibility for oneself. All those were included in that eighth factor.

The Component Factor Method had the unusual element of not only assessing the child's situation, but taking the further step of indicating which factors were changeable and which were not, thereby helping to develop a treatment plan. Although we could not do much about the child's heredity, we might be able to do something about the social experience the child was having. We might be able to do something about the family environment. We hopefully could do something about self-understanding. So that in the individual case, we could decide, well, this factor really couldn't be changed, apparently, but this other factor could. I still feel that it was a very sensible way of analyzing the possibilities for the individual. It never was picked up much. I'm not sure that we ever used it a great deal, even in the Child Study Department of Rochester, where I developed it. Well, so much for the development of the instrument itself. I wrote it up quite thoroughly in 1937. It was published in 1939 in my book *The Clinical Treatment of the Problem Child.*

Perhaps, though, before I leave the instrument, I should try to give a little bit of the flavor of it. For example, I remember the ratings were from − 3 to + 3, with 0 being the average. There was an attempt to give examples of the different ratings to help the rater to standardize his or her ratings. On heredity, for example, the − 3 rating was exemplified by the statement, "Both parents feeble-minded." On social experience, − 3 ratings were given for this: "Does not get along well with sibs or school companions; quarrelsome; mistreats other children and cruel to small children and animals; not successful in trial social adjustment opportunities." I presume that last refers to foster home placement — I'm not sure. On the other hand, a + 2 rating of social experience might be given for this: "Plays on a team; friends are not delinquents; good mixer; liked by others in the neighborhood and school; has a good stamp collection; has three very close friends." I'm not quite sure what the stamp collection had to do with that, but perhaps this gives some feeling for how these were rather crude ratings in a sense, and yet they were overall assessments of the situation.

Here are some examples of actual case ratings on the factor of self-insight. − 3: "Refuses to discuss his delinquencies; will not or cannot discuss problems arising out of family conflicts;

denies his share of responsibility, even when confronted with the facts." + 2 rating on self-insight: "Freely admits her delinquencies; recognizes and accepts the basis of parental antagonism and rejection; planful and cooperative; responsible when placed on her own; tells the facts frankly; recognizes and understands mother's instability and her own need for personal responsibility; responsive and cooperative in behavior and in making future plans." Perhaps that gives a little bit of a notion of the kind of material on which the ratings were based. Now the next step was the use of the instrument in research.

Initial Research

It must have been in my very early days at Ohio State that Bill Kell decided he wanted to use the Component Factor Method for his master's research. He decided to see if the instrument would predict the future behavior of delinquent boys. He had quite a remarkable source of information: the Bureau of Juvenile Research in Columbus. They had kept records over many years of their study of delinquents and the later probation reports. Without reference to the follow-up information, Kell examined the initial studies of a hundred and fifty-five delinquents and rated them according to the Component Factor Method. Then he turned to the follow-up material. The follow-up material was inadequate in more than half of the cases, but it left him with seventy-five cases with initial study and adequate follow-up information.

Using the follow-up information, he made ratings of the adjustment over the subsequent two to three years following the initial study. The ratings, I think, in that respect were quite obvious. A − 3 rating was for those whose delinquencies had continued and worsened. The + 3 was for those who were making a satisfactory, even perhaps outstanding social adjustment, educational adjustment, and so forth. Then he put the two together. I might say that, overall, the relationship between the total scores on the Component Factor analysis and the follow-up material was a very positive relationship, showing that it did have some merit.

There's no doubt that we both entered the study with certain notions of what would come out. I was quite convinced that family environment was probably the most important determining factor in predicting future behavior. I think Bill thought that, or that social experience might be the determining factor. But the outstanding finding and the one which really bowled us over was that this rather crude rating of self-insight was the one that was most predictive of future behavior. It correlated an astonishing .84 with future behavior, a finding which had less than one possibility in a hundred of being due to chance. Social experience was second, I think, with a .55 correlation, and family influence correlated .36 with future behavior.

At that time, I was simply unprepared to believe that. That fascinates me, too. It indicates that, in the early 1940s, although I was getting very involved in "treatment interviews," I still must have thought that the major factors in a child's behavior were external factors. It was the outside forces that determined what a person's going to do. I simply felt that there must be some flaw in the study.

One reason for concern was that we had made a small study of the reliability of those ratings — I think six psychologists rated the same cases — and on most of the factors, the reliability was reasonable. It wasn't astonishingly high, but it was reasonable. The lowest reliability was on self-insight, which again predisposed me to think that that would not turn out to be very predictive. So, like other researchers before me, I had the findings there and I simply refused to believe them. I thought there must be some flaw in the study. I laid it on the shelf. I certainly didn't forget it. I was impressed by it.

Verification

Bill completed his master's study in 1942, and two years later, Helen McNeil, who was looking for a research topic at that time, decided to replicate his study. She went to the same bureau. She took a new group of cases, entirely different from Bill's. She went through exactly the same steps in rating the background, in collecting her data, and in rating the later behavior. Incidentally, I don't think I've said these were delinquent boys and girls, though boys were predominant in number, as is usually the case with delinquents. The comparison of her sample to that of Kell showed no significant differences in the age. The average age was between fourteen and fifteen; the range went about eight to seventeen. And the other elements were similar.

Her findings confirmed Bill's in all the major respects. The correlations she got were much lower, and that puzzled me at the time. I'm now free to say that I think the real reason was that she was not as perceptive a rater. All her ratings tended to cluster, and so she didn't get as high correlations. But, again, self-insight came out at the top, and social experience next; then there was some difference down the line.

I suppose, by that time, Virginia Axline was doing play therapy, and I was much impressed by her talents and gifts in what she was achieving. I was doing more counseling and had become convinced of the efficacy of that. At any rate, I was now prepared to believe the findings. It interests me, though, and I have no memory of why this was, that I didn't write up the combined studies right away. It was published in 1948 (Rogers, Kell, and McNeil); that was after I had gone to Chicago. So I now had two studies which indicated that the degree of self-understanding, the degree of self-acceptance, the degree to which the child could accept the reality of his or her situation, the degree to which the child was taking responsibility for self—that these factors predicted future behavior.

Yet, because I believed so strongly that family environment was the determining factor—a lot of these kids came from very poor homes, and because of that many of them were moved to foster home placement—I thought, "Ah, there's the explanation. Let's study the group that came from poor homes and remained in those homes during the follow-up period." Well, to my astonishment and disbelief, it was still true that self-understanding was more predictive, even in those cases, than the family environment.

I'm proud of that research because it's real research. The findings were not those I expected. They really taught me something very important, although for a time I wasn't able to believe the findings.

Significance

I want to stress some of the reasons why that whole chain of circumstances seemed so important to me. It was important to me personally because it was one of the few times in my life when I have disbelieved my own research findings. It is an important thing in science, where a scientist turns up something that is so unexpected he or she doesn't believe the findings at the time. It was an important lesson to me to realize that sometimes the findings knew better than I did. It was also important because it was one factor, certainly, in causing me to continue focusing my career on psychotherapy, the factor that seemed most significant in predicting future behavior. Then, I am impressed by that chain of circumstances, because I feel it was socially very important — in fact, somewhat revolutionary in its social implications.

I think that most attempts to change behavior — children's behavior and that of adults — tend to focus on changing the environment. That's what my book *The Clinical Treatment of the Problem Child* was mostly about — how you change the home environment, the school environment, the recreational situation — with special classes, special tutoring, and so forth. There's no doubt that all of those elements do have importance. Yet I think if we made any cost analysis of the way in which we treat children or adults, we would find that the great bulk of the expense goes for changing the environment and a relatively small portion goes for efforts to alter the individual's self-concept. We haven't assimilated the fact that the way that the person looks at him- or herself is the most important factor in predicting future behavior, because along with a realistic self-concept goes a realistic perception of external reality and the situation in which the individual finds him- or herself. So, to put it quite bluntly, if these findings were confirmed (though I don't believe that other research studies have been done of this critical a nature), we would greatly alter our means of dealing with individuals in trouble, problem children, delinquents, criminals, and social deviants of any kind.

Then, another aspect that's socially important: many studies have been made of delinquents, recidivism, and so forth, and most of those studies are quite depressing. They show that children from bad neighborhoods and broken homes tend to repeat their delinquencies. It just seems as though it's a recital of depressing facts that show little hope for the future. These findings, on the other hand, are socially very hopeful. Admitting that you can't do a great deal about a lot of the external factors, here's something that is amenable to change, either by methods we haven't thought of, or by group therapy, by individual therapy, by better attitudes of teachers in the classroom. There are a lot of ways in which we know how to alter the concept of self, self-confidence, belief in self, and self-esteem; so that here is a socially hopeful way of looking at and dealing with deviant and delinquent behavior.

To illustrate this point, I have marked a couple of passages from the published findings that I thought I would read. Talking about the studies of recidivism and the depressing story of what happened to delinquents (and I should add that the present studies do not flatly contradict this conclusion), we wrote: "It is true that a poor heredity and the presence of destructive organic factors and a culturally deprived background all predispose to some degree toward a less adequate adjustment. But the significant fact is that the element which above all others should be the most subject to natural change or planned alteration — the individual's acceptance of himself and of reality — is also the most important determinant of his future behavior. . . . Rather than feeling that a person is inevitably doomed by unalterable forces which have shaped him, this study suggests that the most potent influence in his future behavior is one which is certainly alterable to some degree without any change in his physical or social heredity or in his present environment. The most powerful determinant would appear to lie in the attitudes of the person himself.

"The final implication carried by the results of this study is that if the individual's view of himself and reality is so important — the degree of his defensiveness, the degree of acceptance of himself, his realistic appraisal of reality, his degree of independence and planfulness, his ability to be objectively self-critical — then a great deal of research is needed in this area."

REFERENCES

Rogers, C. R. *The Clinical Treatment of the Problem Child.* Boston: Houghton Mifflin, 1939.
Rogers, C. R., Kell, B. L. and H. McNeil, The role of self-understanding

in the prediction of behavior. *Journal of Consulting Psychology*, 1948, *12*, 174–186.

15
The Use of Electrically Recorded Interviews in Improving Psychotherapeutic Techniques

At Ohio State University it has been possible to install equipment which permits electrical recording of counseling interviews on phonograph records, thus preserving an absolutely accurate account of every word spoken in the interview, and also the inflections and tone of voice. These recorded interviews have proven extremely valuable in the training of advanced students in the field of clinical psychology and counseling. It has helped in a number of ways to equip these clinicians for the responsibilities they will face as counselors and therapists in their psychological work.

The equipment consists of a concealed nondirectional microphone in the clinic interviewing room, which is connected to a double turntable recording machine in another room. This permits continuous recording of the interview on blank phonograph discs. Acetate discs with a metal base have been used, although there are several satisfying varieties. We have made considerable direct use of these records playing them back for one or for a group of counselors. For the most intensive study, however, it has been found best to have a typescript made of the interview, so that each response can be studied more closely. For this purpose we have devised a machine which enables the stenographer to type the material as she would from a dictaphone, listening to the record through earphones. A foot pedal allows her to raise or lower the needle at will, so that she can listen to a sentence, type it, and then listen to the next sentence as on a dic-

American Journal of Orthopsychiatry, Vol. 12, 1942, 429–434. Copyright © 1942 by the American Orthopsychiatric Association, Inc. Reprinted with permission.

taphone transcriber. A full description of the equipment is
contained in two articles recently published (Covner, 1942).

It has been possible to make recordings of a variety of types
of counseling and therapeutic interviews. (Thus far little study
has been made of purely diagnostic interviews.) Counseling interviews with college students, both in regard to study problems
and personal maladjustments, therapeutic interviews with problem parents and problem children, and play therapy contacts
with younger children have all been recorded. Some of this counseling has been done by clinicians in training, some by experienced psychologists, so that various levels of proficiency are
represented. In all, we have phonographic and typescript accounts of nearly one hundred interviews.

Usefulness in Teaching Psychotherapeutic Concepts

These completely recorded interviews have been useful in different ways. In the first place, they give a vivid and clear-cut
picture of various client attitudes which is much more meaningful than anything the counselor can obtain through abstract descriptions. Students may, for example, find it difficult to believe
that play therapy can offer a genuine outlet for feelings of hostility and aggression, but the phonographic record of a play
contact with ten-year-old Jimmy dispels any doubt. His running
comments as he plays with a clay image of his father — an image
which he sometimes refers to as Satan — can only be fully appreciated through the inflections of the phonographic record.
"Huh, I'll take a piece of ya off, that'll fix ya!" is one theme which
recurs several times. Another theme centers around the boy's
struggle to make his father get up, in which Jimmy plays both
roles with appropriate voices. "Get up, get up, get up, get up,
come on, come on dad, get up! . . ." "I won't!" "Then you'll take
that, and that, all day long!" (pounding the image into a shape-
less mass, whistling gleefully the while). Even the student psychologist who has never had any contact with play therapy gains
from this one recording a clear understanding of the fact that
such therapy often serves as a release for the most violent feelings.

In studying a topic such as client resistance, the recordings
are extremely important. They allow the most minute study of

responses, and one finds many indications of minor resistance before that resistance is recognized by the counselor. In fact, study of our recordings has led us to a new concept of resistance in therapy. We have come to feel that resistance to the therapist is entirely due to too much probing, or too rapid interpretation on the part of the counselor and that it is neither a desirable nor a constructive part of therapy. An illustration of this is given in a subsequent section of this paper. It is sufficient here to point out that through study of the typescripts, and through listening to recorded inflections, the counselors not only develop a much clearer concept of the meaning of resistance, but become much more alert to the first "Yes, but—" rather than recognizing client resistance only when an appointment is broken.

An elusive concept such as insight can be carefully and clearly traced through these recordings. The gradual development of self-understanding is well illustrated. The progressive and constructive changes in the client's ways of perceiving himself can be accurately studied, as he expresses changing self-percepts in successive interviews.

MR. B.: In the last analysis it comes down to this, that I enjoy the neurotic symptoms more, but respect them less.

COUNSELOR: Yes, that's a good way of—

MR. B.: Or to use other words, I suppose I'm beginning to value self-respect more now, otherwise I wouldn't give a damn.

The manner in which insight, when it is genuine, becomes translated into positive action directed toward the new life goals is also well illustrated in a number of our records. In regard to Mr. B., the insight described above is followed by two interviews in which he is genuinely undecided as to whether he wishes to be neurotic or healthy, whether he wishes to remain on his present level, or take the hard way of growth. He wants the counselor to cure him first, then he will go out and meet life situations in a healthy manner. But by the seventh interview he has achieved the courage to undertake the task himself. Speaking of the conviction that has developed in his own mind since the last interview, Mr. B. says: "I got a definite feeling—I said, 'Well now you know that you're not going to cure yourself in a vacuum. You can only achieve growth by meeting real situations.' I said,

'Now that's just the bunk, what you are saying the other time [about wanting the counselor to cure him]. What you're looking for there is a way of avoiding situations, not a way of cure.' " After further positive planning he sums up his newfound orientation and his decision in regard to action as follows: "Well, then, to sum all this up, I think I should seek out every and all healthy situations and enter into them." That this was no empty resolve is well indicated by his later healthy actions.

These brief illustrations may serve to point out the way in which vague therapeutic concepts can be given life and meaning and definition through presenting them, not in abstract form, not from the point of view of a biased observer, the counselor, but in a completely factual manner as mechanically recorded.

Recordings as a Means of Teaching the Counseling Process

Probably the most significant use of our recordings is in the process of supervision. It is the unanimous testimony of counselors that they have gained a great deal and have been able to correct many mistakes after listening to the recordings of their interviews, even without supervisory comment. The most effective use of such recordings, however, has been in connection with a practicum for psychologists who are completing their clinical training. In this practicum each psychologist carries on intensive therapeutic work with one case. Whenever possible the contacts are recorded. These recorded interviews are carefully analyzed, and the approach which the counselor is using is thoroughly discussed by the group. That striking improvement in counseling techniques can be achieved through this procedure is attested by recordings taken before and after such supervisory discussions.

These analytical discussions of counseling procedures have enriched our thinking in many ways. There are three points which might be mentioned specifically. The first is that most counselors are far more directive than they suppose. Although the stated aim of most counselors is to refrain from imposing their own direction upon the interview, and to permit the client the greatest freedom in expressing feeling and choosing courses of action, their recorded interviews indicate that they frequently violate this purpose. Probably one of the greatest gains of the recording is that it enables the clinician to discover the points at which he asked directive questions, or blocked the spontaneous flow of feeling, or endeavored to make suggestions or provide solutions for the client. One counselor of some experience wrote the following comments after reading the typescript of two of his recorded interviews. "Not until the counselor read these interviews did he realize the deep dark depths to which his counseling had fallen. He could hardly believe that he had actually said such things. The assumption is made that he knew better. He thinks that he can recognize many of his errors, even though he evidently didn't, during the interview."

A second point worthy of comment is that the recorded interviews almost always give the clue to resistances, antagonisms, or slumps which occur during the interview. Every counselor has felt, after some interview, "We were making real progress up to a point, and then something happened to interfere." The recorded interview, and even more the typescript, almost invariably makes it possible to locate the cause of the difficulty. A probing, directive question, an interpretation given too early, remarks which push the client into expressing repressed attitudes, some unintentional advice or suggestions, a failure to recognize an ambivalence which was expressed — these are some of the mistakes which may block therapeutic progress. Often they stand out so clearly that it is difficult for the counselor to understand how he could have made the blunder.

An example is given from a second interview with a maladjusted high school boy, who is talking about his mother in complaining fashion.

BOY: She is a social worker, by the way. She drives everybody nuts talking about her clients all the time.

COUNSELOR: You feel that perhaps she pays more attention to them than to you?

BOY: Well, I — ah — more or less. Oh, I don't know — it doesn't bother me or anything like that.

Here the counselor has endeavored to point out an attitude which the boy himself has not yet been able to express, with the result that he gets first an admission of the feeling, and then a denial of it. This is the beginning of a resistance which grows stronger as the interview continues. The counselor makes the same type of mistake when the boy speaks of his father.

BOY: I know from experience that he just doesn't get along with people, while my mother does. That's strange, too, because his work is dealing with people. But I think he tends to look down on people.

COUNSELOR: That makes you resent him because he looks down on you.

BOY: I don't think he looks down on — well, he looks down on me some, but not like he does on the majority of people. Why, he speaks as if the majority of people were just imbeciles or something. I don't know — that kind of gets me, because, well, I don't dislike anybody, except one or two people. Everybody has something, you know.

COUNSELOR: But you rather thoroughly dislike him, don't you?

BOY: No, I don't think I dislike him exactly, but he just doesn't give me much else to do.

We may be quite sure that in the ordinary reporting of this interview by the counselor, the cause of the boy's resistance would be difficult to determine. The phonographic recording indicates that on every occasion in which the counselor went beyond the feeling which the boy himself had expressed, the response clearly showed a lack of acceptance. It is not surprising that in the next interview the boy frankly stated that he did not want to talk about his problems. Careful study of this excerpt shows the counselor very clearly the way in which he has blundered and enables him to work toward overcoming this tendency in subsequent contacts.

On the other hand, the recorded interviews show equally clearly those techniques which lead toward insight and reorientation. The way in which catharsis deepens and basic attitudes are verbalized, if the counselor simply recognizes and clarifies the feelings which have been expressed, is clearly evident. The manner in which insight comes spontaneously, providing the clinician does not impose interpretations, praise, criticism, or advice, but concentrates on helping the client clearly to see and accept those feelings which he is able to express, is also plain. The growth of courage, the tentative steps in positive directions, and the increasing independence which makes therapy no longer necessary, can also be minutely studied. Such close analysis of these interviews gives to the inexperienced and experienced counselor alike a new understanding of the therapeutic process. This new understanding necessarily vitalizes and improves their treatment interviewing.

The Use of Recorded Interviews in Research

Not only is this material valuable in teaching basic concepts and in improving counseling techniques, but it is priceless raw material for research. It offers the first opportunity for an adequate study of counseling and therapeutic procedures, based upon thoroughly objective data. A number of possibilities will suggest themselves. Three studies completed or under way may be mentioned.

The first of these (Porter, 1941) developed a scale which is useful in the evaluation of counseling. The scale provides some twenty categories in which all counselor responses may be classified. These may be grouped according to their function in therapy — developing the problem situation, developing insight, fostering client activity, or defining the interview relationship. Or they may be grouped into directive and nondirective techniques. Some of the tentative conclusions of this study are of interest. It was found that the instrument devised was a helpful and reliable method of evaluating interviews. It was also found that a given counselor has a distinctive pattern of the types of techniques he tends to use, and this profile is very similar in his contacts with different clients. Directive and nondirective counselors may be sharply differentiated on the basis of techniques used. In the small group studied, the directive counselors talked nearly three times as much as the client, the nondirective counselors talked less than half as much as the client. These tentative findings open up many new research possibilities.

A second research study is under way undertaking the classification of all client responses into meaningful categories. It will then be possible to study interactions and patterns of counselor and client response. For example, what type of counselor statement is most likely to be followed by statements of the client's feeling about himself? What type of counselor statement is most likely to be followed by resistance? By acceptance? We are well aware that the answers to these questions will not be simple, nor is it likely that one research will answer them. The significant point is that for the first time we have adequate data with which to approach such problems.

A third study under way is concerned with the accuracy of ordinary interview reporting. Counselors, both experienced and inexperienced, conducted interviews and almost immediately afterward wrote accounts of the interview for the case record. These subjective accounts are compared with the phonographic recording. Our data enable us to study omissions and distortions of all sorts. This study is not yet completed, but it is already possible to say that the material which the professional worker includes in writing an account of the interview is relatively accurate. The omissions, however, are far more numerous than the inclusions, and highly significant material as well as unimportant items may be omitted. When completed, this study should have significant implications for all casework professions.

These brief and incomplete descriptions of the various aspects of our program of recording will, it is hoped, arouse interest in this type of approach to the problems of psychotherapy. The use of these relatively new mechanical devices provides for the first time a sound basis for the investigation of therapeutic processes, and the teaching and improvement of psychotherapeutic techniques. Therapy need no longer be vague, therapeutic skill need no longer be an intuitive gift. Psychotherapy can become a process based upon known and tested principles, with tested techniques for implementing those principles. The recording program here described has given us a beginning understanding of the basic elements of therapy, has opened the door to highly significant research, and has enabled us to train psychologists to become much more adequate as therapists.

REFERENCES

Covner, Bernard J., *Studies in phonographic recordings of verbal material*: I. The use of phonographic recordings in counseling practice and research. II. A device for transcribing phonographic recordings of verbal material. *Journal of Consulting Psychology*, Vol. 6, 1942, 105–113 and 149–151.

Porter, E. H., The development and evaluation of a measure of counseling interview procedures. Unpublished Ph.D. dissertation, Ohio
State University, Columbus, Ohio, 1941.

16
The Necessary and Sufficient Conditions of Therapeutic Personality Change

For many years I have been engaged in psychotherapy with
individuals in distress. In recent years I have found myself increasingly concerned with the process of abstracting from that
experience the general principles which appear to be involved
in it. I have endeavored to discover any orderliness, any unity
which seems to inhere in the subtle, complex tissue of interpersonal relationships in which I have so constantly been immersed
in therapeutic work. One of the current products of this concern
is an attempt to state, in formal terms, a theory of psychotherapy,
of personality, and of interpersonal relationship which will encompass and contain the phenomena of my experience. What I
wish to do in this paper is to take one very small segment of that
theory, spell it out more completely, and explore its meaning
and usefulness.

THE PROBLEM

The question to which I wish to address myself is this: Is it
possible to state, in terms which are clearly definable and measurable, the psychological conditions which are both necessary
and sufficient to bring about constructive personality change?
Do we, in other words, know with any precision those elements
which are essential if psychotherapeutic change is to ensue?

Before proceeding to the major task let me dispose very briefly
of the second portion of the question. What is meant by such
phrases as "psychotherapeutic change," "constructive personality change"? This problem also deserves deep and serious con-

Journal of Consulting Psychology, Vol. 21, No. 2, 1957, 95–103.

sideration, but for the moment let me suggest a commonsense type of meaning upon which we can perhaps agree for purposes of this paper. By these phrases is meant: change in the personality structure of the individual, at both surface and deeper levels, in a direction which clinicians would agree means greater integration, less internal conflict, more energy utilizable for effective living; change in behavior away from behaviors generally regarded as immature and toward behaviors regarded as mature. This brief description may suffice to indicate the kind of change for which we are considering the preconditions. It may also suggest the ways in which this criterion of change may be determined.*

THE CONDITIONS

As I have considered my own clinical experience and that of my colleagues, together with the pertinent research which is available, I have drawn out several conditions which seem to me to be *necessary* to initiate constructive personality change, and which, taken together, appear to be *sufficient* to inaugurate that process. As I have worked on this problem I have found myself surprised at the simplicity of what has emerged. The statement which follows is not offered with any assurance as to its correctness, but with the expectation that it will have the value of any theory, namely that it states or implies a series of hypotheses which are open to proof or disproof, thereby clarifying and extending our knowledge of the field.

Since I am not, in this paper, trying to achieve suspense, I will state at once, in several rigorous and summarized terms, the six conditions which I have come to feel are basic to the process of personality change. The meaning of a number of the terms is not immediately evident, but will be clarified in the explanatory sections which follow. It is hoped that this brief statement will have much more significance to the reader when he has completed the paper. Without further introduction let me state the basic theoretical position.

---

*That this is a measurable and determinable criterion has been shown in research already completed. See (7), especially chapters 8, 13, and 17.

For constructive personality change to occur, it is necessary that these conditions exist and continue over a period of time:

1. Two persons are in psychological contact.
2. The first, whom we shall term the client, is in a state of incongruence, being vulnerable or anxious.
3. The second person, whom we shall term the therapist, is congruent or integrated in the relationship.
4. The therapist experiences unconditional positive regard for the client.
5. The therapist experiences an empathic understanding of the client's internal frame of reference and endeavors to communicate this experience to the client.
6. The communication to the client of the therapist's empathic understanding and unconditional positive regard is to a minimal degree achieved.

No other conditions are necessary. If these six conditions exist, and continue over a period of time, this is sufficient. The process of constructive personality change will follow.

A Relationship

The first condition specifies that a minimal relationship, a psychological contact, must exist. I am hypothesizing that significant positive personality change does not occur except in a relationship. This is of course a hypothesis, and it may be disproved.

Conditions 2 through 6 define the characteristics of the relationship which are regarded as essential by defining the necessary characteristics of each person in the relationship. All that is intended by this first condition is to specify that the two people are to some degree in contact, that each makes some perceived difference in the experiential field of the other. Probably it is sufficient if each makes some "subceived" difference, even though the individual may not be consciously aware of this impact. Thus it might be difficult to know whether a catatonic patient perceives a therapist's presence as making a difference to him — a difference of any kind — but it is almost certain that at some organic level he does sense this difference.

Except in such a difficult borderline situation as that just mentioned, it would be relatively easy to define this condition in operational terms and thus determine, from a hard-boiled research point of view, whether the condition does, or does not, exist. The simplest method of determination involves simply the awareness of both client and therapist. If each is aware of being in personal or psychological contact with the other, then this condition is met.

The first condition of therapeutic change is such a simple one that perhaps it should be labeled an assumption or a precondition in order to set it apart from those that follow. Without it, however, the remaining items would have no meaning, and that is the reason for including it.

The State of the Client

It was specified that it is necessary that the client be "in a state of incongruence, being vulnerable or anxious." What is the meaning of these terms?

Incongruence is a basic construct in the theory we have been developing. It refers to a discrepancy between the actual experience of the organism and the self picture of the individual insofar as it represents that experience. Thus a student may experience, at a total or organismic level, a fear of the university and of examinations which are given on the third floor of a certain building, since these may demonstrate a fundamental inadequacy in him. Since such a fear of his inadequacy is decidedly at odds with his concept of himself, this experience is represented (distortedly) in his awareness as an unreasonable fear of climbing stairs in this building, or any building, and soon an unreasonable fear of crossing the open campus. Thus there is a fundamental discrepancy between the experienced meaning of the situation as it registers in his organism and the symbolic representation of that experience in awareness in such a way that it does not conflict with the picture he has of himself. In this case to admit a fear of inadequacy would contradict the picture he holds of himself; to admit incomprehensible fears does not contradict his self-concept.

Another instance would be the mother who develops vague illnesses whenever her only son makes plans to leave home. The actual desire is to hold on to her only source of satisfaction. To perceive this in awareness would be inconsistent with the picture she holds of herself as a good mother. Illness, however, is consistent with her self-concept, and the experience is symbolized in this distorted fashion. Thus again there is a basic incongruence between the self as perceived (in this case as an ill mother needing attention) and the actual experience (in this case the desire to hold on to her son).

When the individual has no awareness of such incongruence in himself, then he is merely vulnerable to the possibility of anxiety and disorganization. Some experience might occur so suddenly or so obviously that the incongruence could not be denied. Therefore, the person is vulnerable to such a possibility.

If the individual dimly perceives such an incongruence in himself, then a tension state occurs which is known as anxiety. The incongruence need not be sharply perceived. It is enough that it is subceived — that is, discriminated as threatening to the self without any awareness of the content of that threat. Such anxiety is often seen in therapy as the individual approaches awareness of some element of his experience which is in sharp contradiction to his self-concept.

It is not easy to give precise operational definition to this second of the six conditions, yet to some degree this has been achieved. Several research workers have defined the self-concept by means of a Q-sort by the individual of a list of self-referent items. This gives us an operational picture of the self. The total experiencing of the individual is more difficult to capture. Chodorkoff (2) has defined it as a Q-sort made by a clinician who sorts the same self-referent items independently, basing his sorting on the picture he has obtained of the individual from projective tests. His sort thus includes unconscious as well as conscious elements of the individual's experience, thus representing (in an admittedly imperfect way) the totality of the client's experience. The correlation between these two sortings gives a crude operational measure of incongruence between self and experience, low or negative correlation representing of course a high degree of incongruence.

The Therapist's Genuineness in the Relationship

The third condition is that the therapist should be, within the confines of this relationship, a congruent, genuine, integrated person. It means that within the relationship he is freely and deeply himself, with his actual experience accurately represented by his awareness of himself. It is the opposite of presenting a façade, either knowingly or unknowingly.

It is not necessary (nor is it possible) that the therapist be a paragon who exhibits this degree of integration, of wholeness, in every aspect of his life. It is sufficient that he is accurately himself in this hour of this relationship, that in this basic sense he is what he actually is, in this moment of time.

It should be clear that this includes being himself even in ways which are not regarded as ideal for psychotherapy. His experience may be "I am afraid of this client" or "My attention is so focused on my own problems that I can scarcely listen to him." If the therapist is not denying these feelings to awareness, but is able freely to be them (as well as being his other feelings), then the condition we have stated is met.

It would take us too far afield to consider the puzzling matter as to the degree to which the therapist overtly communicates this reality in himself to the client. Certainly the aim is not for the therapist to express or talk out his own feelings, but primarily that he should not be deceiving the client as to himself. At times he may need to talk out some of his own feelings (either to the client, or to a colleague or supervisor) if they are standing in the way of the two following conditions.

It is not too difficult to suggest an operational definition for this third condition. We resort again to Q-technique. If the therapist sorts a series of items relevant to the relationship (using a list similar to the ones developed by Fiedler [3, 4] and Bown [1]), this will give his perception of his experience in the relationship. If several judges who have observed the interview or listened to a recording of it (or observed a sound movie of it) now sort the same items to represent *their* perception of the relationship, this second sorting should catch those elements of the therapist's behavior and inferred attitudes of which he is unaware, as well as those of which he is aware. Thus a high correlation between the therapist's sort and the observer's sort would represent in crude form an operational definition of the therapist's congruence or integration in the relationship; and a low correlation, the opposite.

Unconditional Positive Regard

To the extent that the therapist finds himself experiencing a warm acceptance of each aspect of the client's experience as being a part of that client, he is experiencing unconditional positive regard. This concept has been developed by Standal (8). It means that there are no *conditions* of acceptance, no feeling of "I like you only *if* you are thus and so." It means a "prizing" of the person, as Dewey has used that term. It is at the opposite pole from a selective evaluating attitude — "You are bad in these ways, good in those." It involves as much feeling of acceptance for the client's expression of negative, "bad," painful, fearful, defensive, abnormal feelings as for his expression of "good," positive, mature, confident, social feelings, as much acceptance of ways in which he is inconsistent as of ways in which he is consistent. It means a caring for the client, but not in a possessive way or in such a way as simply to satisfy the therapist's own needs. It means a caring for the client as a *separate* person, with permission to have his own feelings, his own experiences. One client describes the therapist as "fostering my possession of my own experience . . . that [this] is *my* experience and that I am actually having it: thinking what I think, feeling what I feel, wanting what I want, fearing what I fear: no 'ifs,' 'buts,' or 'not reallys.' " This is the type of acceptance which is hypothesized as being necessary if personality change is to occur.

Like the two previous conditions, this fourth condition is a matter of degree,* as immediately becomes apparent if we attempt to define it in terms of specific research operations. One such method of giving it definition would be to consider the Q-sort for the relationship as described under condition 3. To the

---

*The phrase "unconditional positive regard" may be an unfortunate one, since it sounds like an absolute, an all-or-nothing dispositional concept. It is probably evident from the description that completely unconditional positive regard would never exist except in theory. From a clinical and experiential point of view I believe the most accurate statement is that the effective therapist experiences unconditional positive regard for the client during many moments of his contact with him, yet from time to time he experiences only a conditional positive regard — and perhaps at times a negative regard, though this is not likely in effective therapy. It is in this sense that unconditional positive regard exists as a matter of degree in any relationship.

extent that items expressive of unconditional positive regard are sorted as characteristic of the relationship by both the therapist and the observers, unconditional positive regard might be said to exist. Such items might include statements of this order: "I feel no revulsion at anything the client says"; "I feel neither approval nor disapproval of the client and his statements — simply acceptance"; "I feel warmly toward the client — toward his weaknesses and problems as well as his potentialities"; "I am not inclined to pass judgment on what the client tells me"; "I like the client." To the extent that both therapist and observers perceive these items as characteristic, or their opposites as uncharacteristic, condition 4 might be said to be met.

Empathy

The fifth condition is that the therapist is experiencing an accurate, empathic understanding of the client's awareness, of his own experience. To sense the client's private world as if it were your own, but without ever losing the "as if" quality — this is empathy, and this seems essential to therapy. To sense the client's anger, fear, or confusion as if it were your own, yet without your own anger, fear, or confusion getting bound up in it, is the condition we are endeavoring to describe. When the client's world is this clear to the therapist, and he moves about in it freely, then he can both communicate his understanding of what is clearly known to the client and can also voice meanings in the client's experience of which the client is scarcely aware. As one client described this second aspect: "Every now and again, with me in a tangle of thought and feeling, screwed up in a web of mutually divergent lines of movement, with impulses from different parts of me, and me feeling the feeling of its being all too much and suchlike — then whomp, just like a sunbeam thrusting its way through cloudbanks and tangles of foliage to spread a circle of light on a tangle of forest paths, came some comment from you. [It was] clarity, even disentanglement, an additional twist to the picture, a putting in place. Then the consequence — the sense of moving on, the relaxation. These were sunbeams." That such penetrating empathy is important for therapy is indicated by Fiedler's research (3) in which items such as the following placed high in the description of relationships created by experienced therapists:

The therapist is well able to understand the patient's feelings.

The therapist is never in any doubt about what the patient means.

The therapist's remarks fit in just right with the patient's mood and content.

The therapist's tone of voice conveys the complete ability to share the patient's feelings.

An operational definition of the therapist's empathy could be provided in different ways. Use might be made of the Q-sort described under condition 3. To the degree that items descriptive of accurate empathy were sorted as characteristic by both the therapist and the observers, this condition would be regarded as existing.

Another way of defining this condition would be for both client and therapist to sort a list of items descriptive of client feelings. Each would sort independently, the task being to represent the feelings which the client had experienced during a just completed interview. If the correlation between client and therapist sortings were high, accurate empathy would be said to exist, a low correlation indicating the opposite conclusion.

Still another way of measuring empathy would be for trained judges to rate the depth and accuracy of the therapist's empathy on the basis of listening to recorded interviews.

The Client's Perception of the Therapist

The final condition as stated is that the client perceives, to a minimal degree, the acceptance and empathy which the therapist experiences for him. Unless some communication of these attitudes has been achieved, then such attitudes do not exist in the relationship as far as the client is concerned, and the therapeutic process could not, by our hypothesis, be initiated.

Since attitudes cannot be directly perceived, it might be somewhat more accurate to state that therapist behaviors and words are perceived by the client as meaning that to some degree the therapist accepts and understands him.

An operational definition of this condition would not be difficult. The client might, after an interview, sort a Q-sort list of items referring to qualities representing the relationship between himself and the therapist. (The same list could be used as for condition 3.) If several items descriptive of acceptance and empathy are sorted by the client as characteristic of the relationship, then this condition could be regarded as met. In the present state of our knowledge the meaning of "to a minimal degree" would have to be arbitrary.

Some Comments

Up to this point the effort has been made to present, briefly and factually, the conditions which I have come to regard as essential for psychotherapeutic change. I have not tried to give the theoretical context of these conditions nor to explain what seem to me to be the dynamics of their effectiveness. Such explanatory material will be available, to the reader who is interested, in the document already mentioned (see Reference 7).

I have, however, given at least one means of defining, in operational terms, each of the conditions mentioned. I have done this in order to stress the fact that I am not speaking of vague qualities which ideally should be present if some other vague result is to occur. I am presenting conditions which are crudely measurable even in the present state of our technology, and have suggested specific operations in each instance even though I am sure that more adequate methods of measurement could be devised by a serious investigator.

My purpose has been to stress the notion that in my opinion we are dealing with an if-then phenomenon in which knowledge of the dynamics is not essential to testing the hypotheses. Thus, to illustrate from another field: if one substance, shown by a series of operations to be the substance known as hydrochloric acid, is mixed with another substance, shown by another series of operations to be sodium hydroxide, then salt and water will be products of this mixture. This is true whether one regards the results as due to magic, or whether one explains it in the most adequate terms of modern chemical theory. In the same way it is being postulated here that certain definable conditions precede certain definable changes and that this fact exists independently of our efforts to account for it.

THE RESULTING HYPOTHESES

The major value of stating any theory in unequivocal terms is that specific hypotheses may be drawn from it which are capable of proof or disproof. Thus, even if the conditions which have been postulated as necessary and sufficient conditions are more incorrect than correct (which I hope they are not), they could still advance science in this field by providing a base of operations from which fact could be winnowed out from error.

The hypotheses which would follow from the theory given would be of this order:

> If these six conditions (as operationally defined) exist, then constructive personality change (as defined) will occur in the client.
>
> If one or more of these conditions is not present, constructive personality change will not occur.
>
> These hypotheses hold in any situation, whether it is or is not labeled "psychotherapy."
>
> Only condition 1 is dichotomous (it either is present or is not), and the remaining five occur in varying degree, each on its continuum. Since this is true, another hypothesis follows, and it is likely that this would be the simplest to test:
>
> If all six conditions are present, then the greater the degree to which conditions 2 to 6 exist, the more marked will be the constructive personality change in the client.

At the present time the above hypothesis can only be stated in this general form — which implies that all of the conditions have equal weight. Empirical studies will no doubt make possible much more refinement of this hypothesis. It may be, for example, that if anxiety is high in the client, then the other conditions are less important. Or if unconditional positive regard is high (as in a mother's love for her child), then perhaps a modest degree of empathy is sufficient. But at the moment we can only speculate on such possibilities.

SOME IMPLICATIONS

Significant Omissions

If there is any startling feature in the formulation which has been given as to the necessary conditions for therapy, it probably lies in the elements which are omitted. In present-day clinical practice, therapists operate as though there were many other conditions in addition to those described, which are essential for psychotherapy. To point this up it may be well to mention a few of the conditions which, after thoughtful consideration of our research and our experience, are not included.

For example, it is *not* stated that these conditions apply to one type of client, and that other conditions are necessary to bring about psychotherapeutic change with other types of client. Probably no idea is so prevalent in clinical work today as that one works with neurotics in one way, with psychotics in another; that certain therapeutic conditions must be provided for compulsives, others for homosexuals, etc. Because of this heavy weight of clinical opinion to the contrary, it is with some "fear and trembling" that I advance the concept that the essential conditions of psychotherapy exist in a single configuration, even though the client or patient may use them very differently.*

It is *not* stated that these six conditions are the essential conditions for client-centered therapy, and that other conditions are essential for other types of psychotherapy. I certainly am heavily influenced by my own experience, and that experience has led me to a viewpoint which is termed "client centered." Nevertheless my aim in stating this theory is to state the conditions which apply to *any* situation in which constructive personality change occurs, whether we are thinking of classical psychoanalysis, or any of its modern offshoots, or Adlerian psychotherapy, or any other. It will be obvious then that in my judgment much of what is considered to be essential would not be found, empirically, to be essential. Testing of some of the stated hypotheses would throw light on this perplexing issue. We may of course find that various therapies produce various types of personality change,

---

*I cling to this statement of my hypothesis even though it is challenged by a just completed study by Kirtner (5). Kirtner has found, in a group of twenty-six cases from the Counseling Center at the University of Chicago, that there are sharp differences in the client's mode of approach to the resolution of life difficulties, and that these differences are related to success in psychotherapy. Briefly, the client who sees his problem as involving his relationships, and who feels that he contributes to this problem and wants to change it, is likely to be successful. The client who externalizes his problem, feeling little self-responsibility, is much more likely to be a failure. Thus the implication is that some other conditions need to be provided for psychotherapy with this group. For the present, however, I will stand by my hypothesis as given, until Kirtner's study is confirmed, and until we know an alternative hypothesis to take its place.

and that for each psychotherapy a separate set of conditions is necessary. Until and unless this is demonstrated, I am hypothesizing that effective psychotherapy of any sort produces similar changes in personality and behavior, and that a single set of preconditions is necessary.

It is *not* stated that psychotherapy is a special kind of relationship, different in kind from all others which occur in everyday life. It will be evident instead that for brief moments, at least, many good friendships fulfill the six conditions. Usually this is only momentarily, however, and then empathy falters, the positive regard becomes conditional, or the congruence of the "therapist" friend becomes overlaid by some degree of façade or defensiveness. Thus the therapeutic relationship is seen as a heightening of the constructive qualities which often exist in part in other relationships, and an extension through time of qualities which in other relationships tend at best to be momentary.

It is *not* stated that special intellectual professional knowledge—psychological, psychiatric, medical, or religious—is required of the therapist. Conditions 3, 4, and 5, which apply especially to the therapist, are qualities of experience, not intellectual information. If they are to be acquired, they must, in my opinion, be acquired through an experiential training — which may be, but usually is not, a part of professional training. It troubles me to hold such a radical point of view, but I can draw no other conclusion from my experience. Intellectual training and the acquiring of information has, I believe, many valuable results — but becoming a therapist is not one of those results.

It is *not* stated that it is necessary for psychotherapy that the therapist have an accurate psychological diagnosis of the client. Here too it troubles me to hold a viewpoint so at variance with my clinical colleagues. When one thinks of the vast proportion of time spent in any psychological, psychiatric, or mental hygiene center on the exhaustive psychological evaluation of the client or patient, it seems as though this *must* serve a useful purpose insofar as psychotherapy is concerned. Yet the more I have observed therapists, and the more closely I have studied research such as that done by Fiedler and others (4), the more I am forced to the conclusion that such diagnostic knowledge is not essential to psychotherapy.* It may even be that its defense as a necessary prelude to psychotherapy is simply a protective alternative to the admission that it is, for the most part, a colossal waste of time. There is only one useful purpose I have been able to observe which relates to psychotherapy. Some therapists cannot feel secure in the relationship with the client unless they possess such diagnostic knowledge. Without it they feel fearful of him, unable to be empathic, unable to experience unconditional regard, finding it necessary to put up a pretense in the relationship. If they know in *advance* of suicidal impulses they can somehow be more acceptant of them. Thus, for some therapists, the security they perceive in diagnostic information may be a basis for permitting themselves to be integrated in the relationship, and to experience empathy and full acceptance. In these instances a psychological diagnosis would certainly be justified as adding to the comfort and hence the effectiveness of the therapist. But even here it does not appear to be a basic precondition for psychotherapy.†

Perhaps I have given enough illustrations to indicate that the conditions I have hypothesized as necessary and sufficient for psychotherapy are striking and unusual primarily by virtue of what they omit. If we were to determine, by a survey of the behaviors of therapists, those hypotheses which they appear to regard as necessary to psychotherapy, the list would be a great deal longer and more complex.

Is This Theoretical Formulation Useful?

Aside from the personal satisfaction it gives as a venture in abstraction and generalization, what is the value of a theoretical

---

*There is no intent here to maintain that diagnostic evaluation is useless. We have ourselves made heavy use of such methods in our research studies of change in personality. It is its usefulness as a precondition to psychotherapy which is questioned.

†In a facetious moment I have suggested that such therapists might be made equally comfortable by being given the diagnosis of some other individual, not of this patient or client. The fact that the diagnosis proved inaccurate as psychotherapy continued would not be particularly disturbing, because one always expects to find inaccuracies in the diagnosis as one works with the individual.

statement such as has been offered in this paper? I should like to spell out more fully the usefulness which I believe it may have.

In the field of research it may give both direction and impetus to investigation. Since it sees the conditions of constructive personality change as general, it greatly broadens the opportunities for study. Psychotherapy is not the only situation aimed at constructive personality change. Programs of training for leadership in industry and programs of training for military leadership often aim at such change. Educational institutions or programs frequently aim at development of character and personality as well as at intellectual skills. Community agencies aim at personality and behavioral change in delinquents and criminals. Such programs would provide an opportunity for the broad testing of the hypotheses offered. If it is found that constructive personality change occurs in such programs when the hypothesized conditions are not fulfilled, then the theory would have to be revised. If however the hypotheses are upheld, then the results, both for the planning of such programs and for our knowledge of human dynamics, would be significant. In the field of psychotherapy itself, the application of consistent hypotheses to the work of various schools of therapists may prove highly profitable. Again the disproof of the hypotheses offered would be as important as their confirmation, either result adding significantly to our knowledge.

For the practice of psychotherapy the theory also offers significant problems for consideration. One of its implications is that the techniques of the various therapies are relatively unimportant except to the extent that they serve as channels for fulfilling one of the conditions. In client-centered therapy, for example, the technique of "reflecting feelings" has been described and commented on (6, pp. 26–36). In terms of the theory here being presented, this technique is by no means an essential condition of therapy. To the extent, however, that it provides a channel by which the therapist communicates a sensitive empathy and an unconditional positive regard, then it may serve as a technical channel by which the essential conditions of therapy are fulfilled. In the same way, the theory I have presented would see no essential value to therapy of such techniques as interpretation of personality dynamics, free association, analysis of dreams, analysis of the transference, hypnosis, interpretation of lifestyle, suggestion, and the like. Each of these techniques may, however, become a channel for communicating the essential conditions which have been formulated. An interpretation may be given in a way which communicates the unconditional positive regard of the therapist. A stream of free association may be listened to in a way which communicates an empathy which the therapist is experiencing. In the handling of the transference an effective therapist often communicates his own wholeness and congruence in the relationship. Similarly for the other techniques. But just as these techniques *may* communicate the elements which are essential for therapy, so any one of them may communicate attitudes and experiences sharply contradictory to the hypothesized conditions of therapy. Feeling may be "reflected" in a way which communicates the therapist's lack of empathy. Interpretations may be rendered in a way which indicates the highly conditional regard of the therapist. Any of the techniques may communicate the fact that the therapist is expressing one attitude which is denied to his own awareness. Thus one value of such a theoretical formulation as we have offered is that it may assist therapists to think more critically about those elements of their experience, attitudes, and behaviors which are essential to psychotherapy, and those which are nonessential or even deleterious to psychotherapy.

Finally, in those programs — education, correctional, military, or industrial — which aim toward constructive changes in the personality structure and behavior of the individual, this formulation may serve as a very tentative criterion against which to measure the program. Until it is much further tested by research, it cannot be thought of as a valid criterion, but, as in the field of psychotherapy, it may help to stimulate critical analysis and the formulation of alternative conditions and alternative hypotheses.

SUMMARY

Drawing from a larger theoretical context, six conditions are postulated as necessary and sufficient conditions for the initiation of a process of constructive personality change. A brief explanation is given of each condition, and suggestions are made as to how each may be operationally defined for research purposes. The implications of this theory for research, for psychotherapy, and for educational and training programs aimed at constructive personality change, are indicated. It is pointed out that many of the conditions which are commonly regarded as necessary to psychotherapy are, in terms of this theory, nonessential.

REFERENCES

1. Bown, O. H. An investigation of therapeutic relationship in client-centered therapy. Unpublished Ph.D. dissertation, University of Chicago, 1954.
2. Chodorkoff, B. Self-perception, perpetual defense, and adjustment. *J. abnorm. soc. Psychol.*, 1954, *49*, 508–512.
3. Fiedler, F. E. A comparison of therapeutic relationships in psychoanalytic, non-directive and Adlerian therapy. *J. consult. Psychol.*, 1950, *14*, 436–445.
4. Fiedler, F. E. Quantitative studies on the role of therapists' feelings toward their patients. In O. H. Mowrer (Ed.), *Psychotherapy: theory and research.* New York: Ronald Press, 1953.
5. Kirtner, W. L. Success and failure in client-centered therapy as a function of personality variables. Unpublished master's thesis, University of Chicago, 1955.
6. Rogers, C. R. *Client-centered therapy.* Boston: Houghton Mifflin, 1951.
7. Rogers, C. R., and Dymond, Rosalind F. (Eds.). *Psychotherapy and personality change.* Chicago: University of Chicago Press, 1954.
8. Standal, S. The need for positive regard: a contribution to client-centered theory. Unpublished Ph.D. dissertation, University of Chicago, 1954.

17
A Theory of Therapy, Personality, and Interpersonal Relationships, As Developed in the Client-Centered Framework

THE GENERAL STRUCTURE OF OUR SYSTEMATIC THINKING

Before proceeding to the detailed statement of some of our theoretical views, I believe it may be helpful to describe some of the interrelationships between various portions of our theoretical formulations.

The earliest portion, most closely related to observed fact, most heavily supported by evidence, is the theory of psychotherapy and personality change which was constructed to give order to the phenomena of therapy as we experienced it.

In this theory there were certain hypotheses regarding the nature of personality and the dynamics of behavior. Some of these were explicit, some implicit. These have been developed more fully into a theory of personality. The purpose has been to provide ourselves with a tentative understanding of the human organism and its developing dynamics—an attempt to make sense of this person who comes to us in therapy.

Implicit in the theories of therapy and of personality are certain hypotheses regarding the outcomes of therapy—hence, hypotheses regarding a more socially constructive or creative individual. In the last few years we have endeavored to spell out the picture of the theoretical end point of therapy, the maximally creative, self-actualizing, or fully functioning person.

In another direction, our understanding of the therapeutic relationship has led us to formulate theoretical statements regarding all interpersonal relationships, seeing the therapeutic relationship simply as one special case. This is a very new and tentative development, which we believe has promise.

Finally, it has seemed that if our views of therapy have any

In Koch, S. (Ed.), *Psychology: A Study of a Science*, Vol. 3. *Formulations of the Person and the Social Context*. New York: McGraw-Hill, 1959, 184–256.

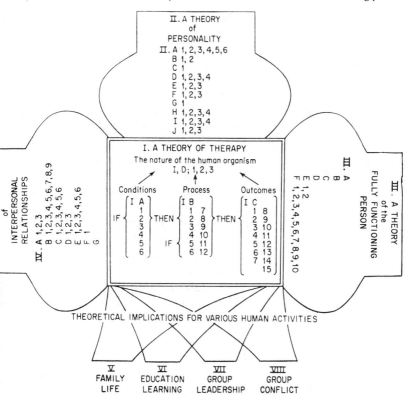

FIGURE 1

validity they have application in all those fields of human experience and endeavor which involve (*a*) interpersonal relationships and (*b*) the aim or potentiality of development or change in personality and behavior. Consequently a cluster of partially developed theories exists in relation to such fields as family life, education, group leadership, and situations of group tension and conflict.

The accompanying chart may help the reader to see and understand these relationships between different aspects of our theories. It should be clear that the chart reads from the center, and that the developments have taken place in the four directions indicated. It should also be remembered that the possibility of magnification of error in the theory increases as one goes out from the center. By and large, there is less evidence available in these peripheral areas than in the center. Entered in the chart are the identifying numbers of the various propositions which follow, so that in reading any specific portion of the theory the reader may refer back to see its organic relationship to other parts of the theoretical structure.

Before proceeding to set forth something of the theories themselves, I should like gratefully to stress the extent to which this is basically a group enterprise. I have drawn upon specific written contributions to theory made by Victor Raimy, Richard Hogan, Stanley Standal, John Butler, and Thomas Gordon. Many others have contributed to my thinking in ways known and unknown, but I would particularly like to mention the valuable influence of Oliver Bown, Desmond Cartwright, Arthur Combs, Eugene Gendlin, A. H. Maslow, Julius Seeman, John Shlien, and Donald Snygg on the theories which I am about to present. Yet these individuals are by no means to be held responsible for what follows, for their own attempts to order experience have often led them into somewhat different channels of thinking.

I. A THEORY OF THERAPY AND PERSONALITY CHANGE

This theory is of the if-then variety. If certain conditions exist (independent variables), then a process (dependent variable) will occur which includes certain characteristic elements. If this process (now the independent variable) occurs, then certain personality and behavioral changes (dependent variables) will occur. This will be made specific.

In this and the following sections the formal statement of the theory is given briefly, in smaller type. The italicized terms or phrases in these formal statements have been defined in the previous section and are to be understood as defined. The remaining paragraphs are explanatory and do not follow the rigorous pattern of the formal statements.

A. Conditions of the Therapeutic Process

For therapy to occur it is necessary that these conditions exist.

1. That two persons are in *contact*.
2. That the first person, whom we shall term the client, is in a state of *incongruence*, being *vulnerable*, or *anxious*.

3. That the second person, whom we shall term the therapist, is *congruent in the relationship.*

4. That the therapist is *experiencing unconditional positive regard* toward the client.

5. That the therapist is *experiencing* an *empathic* understanding of the client's *internal frame of reference.*

6. That the client *perceives*, at least to a minimal degree, Conditions 4 and 5, the *unconditional positive regard* of the therapist for him, and the *empathic* understanding of the therapist.

Evidence. Confirmatory evidence, particularly of item 5, is found in the studies by Fiedler (19, 20) and Quinn (52). Fiedler's study showed that experienced therapists of different orientations created relationships in which one of the most prominent characteristics was the ability to understand the client's communications with the meaning these communications had for the client. Quinn found that the quality of the therapist communication was of crucial significance in therapy. These studies add weight to the importance of empathic understanding.

Seeman (75) found that increase in the counselor's liking for the client during therapy was significantly associated with therapeutic success. Both Seeman and Lipkin (44) found that clients who felt themselves to be liked by the therapist tended to be more successful. These studies tend to confirm condition 4 (unconditional positive regard) and condition 6 (perception of this by the client).

Though clinical experience would support condition 2, the client's vulnerability or anxiety, there is little research which has been done in terms of these constructs. The study by Gallagher (21) indicates that less anxious clients tend never to become involved in therapy, but drop out.

B. The Process of Therapy

When the preceding conditions exist and continue, a process is set in motion which has these characteristic directions:

1. The client is increasingly free in expressing his *feelings*, through verbal and/or motor channels.

2. His expressed feelings increasingly have reference to the *self*, rather than nonself.

3. He increasingly differentiates and discriminates the objects

of his *feelings* and *perceptions*, including his environment, other persons, his *self*, his *experiences*, and the interrelationships of these. He becomes less *intensional* and more *extensional* in his *perceptions*, or to put it in other terms, his experiences are more *accurately symbolized*.

4. His expressed *feelings* increasingly have reference to the *incongruity* between certain of his *experiences* and his *concept of self*.

5. He comes to experience in awareness the threat of such *incongruence*.

   a. This *experience* of *threat* is possible only because of the continued *unconditional positive regard* of the therapist, which is extended to *incongruence* as much as to *congruence*, to *anxiety* as much as to absence of *anxiety*.

6. He *experiences* fully, in *awareness*, feelings which have in the past been *denied to awareness*, or *distorted in awareness*.

7. His *concept of self* becomes reorganized to assimilate and include these *experiences* which have previously been *distorted in* or *denied to awareness*.

8. As this reorganization of the *self-structure* continues, his *concept of self* becomes increasingly *congruent* with his *experience*; the *self* now including *experiences* which previously would have been too *threatening* to be in *awareness*.

   a. A corollary tendency is toward fewer perceptual *distortions in awareness,* or *denials to awareness,* since there are fewer *experiences* which can be *threatening*. In other words, *defensiveness* is decreased.

9. He becomes increasingly able to *experience*, without a feeling of *threat*, the therapist's unconditional positive regard.

10. He increasingly feels an *unconditional positive self-regard*.

11. He increasingly *experiences* himself as the *locus of evaluation*.

12. He reacts to *experience* less in terms of his *conditions of worth* and more in terms of an *organismic valuing process*.

Evidence. There is confirming evidence of varying degrees of relevance for a number of these items describing the therapeutic process. Item 2 (increasing self-reference) is supported by our many recorded therapeutic cases, but has not been reduced to a statistical finding. Stock's study (82) supports item 3, indicating that client self-referent expressions become more objective, less strongly emotional. Mitchell (47) shows that clients become more extensional.

Objective clinical evidence supporting items 4, 5, and 6 is provided in the form of recordings from a case by Rogers (67).

The findings of Vargas (85) are relevant to item 7, indicating the way the self is reorganized in terms of emergent new self-perceptions. Hogan (36) and Haigh (29) have studied the decrease in defensiveness during the process, as described in item 8a, their findings being confirmatory. The increased congruence of self and experience is supported in an exhaustive single case investigation by Rogers (67). That such congruence is associated with lack of defensiveness is found by Chodorkoff (10).

Item 10, the increase in the client's positive self-regard, is well attested by the studies of Snyder (79), Seeman (76), Raimy (55), Stock (82), Strom (83), Sheerer (78), Lipkin (44). The client's trend toward experiencing himself as the locus of evaluation is most clearly shown by Raskin's research (56), but this is supported by evidence from Sheerer (78), Lipkin (44), Kessler (41).

C. Outcomes in Personality and Behavior

There is no clear distinction between process and outcome. Items of process are simply differentiated aspects of outcome. Hence the statements which follow could have been included under process. For reasons of convenience in understanding, there have been grouped here those changes which are customarily associated with the terms *outcomes*, or *results*, or are observed outside of the therapeutic relationship. These are the changes which are hypothesized as being relatively permanent:

1. The client is more *congruent*, more *open to his experience*, less *defensive*.
2. He is consequently more realistic, objective, *extensional* in his *perceptions*.
3. He is consequently more effective in problem solving.
4. His *psychological adjustment* is improved, being closer to the optimum.
   a. This is owing to, and is a continuation of, the changes in *self-structure* described in *B*7 and *B*8.

5. As a result of the increased *congruence of self* and *experience* ($C4$ above) his *vulnerability* to *threat* is reduced.

6. As a consequence of $C2$ above, his perception of his *ideal self* is more realistic, more achievable.

7. As a consequence of the changes in $C4$ and $C5$ his *self* is more *congruent* with his *ideal self*.

8. As a consequence of the increased *congruence* of *self* and *ideal self* ($C6$) and the greater *congruence* of *self* and *experience*, tension of all types is reduced — physiological tension, psychological tension, and the specific type of psychological tension defined as *anxiety*.

9. He has an increased degree of *positive self-regard*.

10. He *perceives* the *locus of evaluation* and the locus of choice as residing within himself.

    a. As a consequence of $C9$ and $C10$ he feels more confident and more self-directing.

    b. As a consequence of $C1$ and $C10$, his values are determined by an *organismic valuing process*.

11. As a consequence of $C1$ and $C2$, he *perceives* others more realistically and accurately.

12. He *experiences* more *acceptance* of others, as a consequence of less need for distortion of his perceptions of them.

13. His behavior changes in various ways.

    a. Since the proportion of *experience* assimilated into the *self-structure* is increased, the proportion of behaviors which can be "owned" as belonging to the *self* is increased.

    b. Conversely, the proportion of behaviors which are disowned as *self-experiences*, felt to be "not myself," is decreased.

    c. Hence his behavior is *perceived* as being more within his control.

14. His behavior is perceived by others as more socialized, more *mature*.

15. As a consequence of $C1$, 2, 3, his behavior is more creative, more uniquely adaptive to each new situation, and each new problem, more fully expressive of his own purposes and values.

Evidence. There is much confirmatory and some ambiguous or non-confirming evidence of the theoretical statement of outcomes. Grummon and John (28) find a decrease in defensiveness, basing judgments on the TAT. Hogan (36) and Haigh (29) also supply some scanty evidence on this point. As to the greater extensionality of perceptions (item 2), Jonietz (38) finds that therapy produces changes in perceptions, and Mitchell (47) finds these changes to be in the direction of extensionality.

Item 4, stating that adjustment is improved, is supported by evidence based upon TAT, Rorschach, counselor rating, and other indexes, in the studies of Dymond (15, 16), Grummon and John (28), Haimowitz and Morris (30), Muench (49), Mosak (48), Cowen and Combs (13). Carr (8), however, found no evidence of change in the Rorschach in nine cases.

Rudikoff (73) found that the self-ideal becomes more achievable, as stated in item 6. The increased congruence of self and ideal has been confirmed by Butler and Haigh (7), Hartley (33), and its significance for adjustment supported by Hanlon, Hofstaetter, and O'Connor (32).

The decrease in physiological tension over therapy is attested by the studies of Thetford (84) and Anderson (1). The reduction in psychological tension as evidenced by the Discomfort-Relief Quotient has been confirmed by many investigators: Assum and Levy (4), Cofer and Chance (12), Kaufman and Raimy (39), N. Rogers (72), Zimmerman (86).

The increase in positive self-regard is well attested, as indicated in I*B*, Evidence. The shift in the locus of evaluation and choice is supported in the evidence provided by Raskin (56) and Sheerer (78). Rudikoff (73) presents evidence which suggests that others may be perceived with greater realism. Sheerer (78) and Stock (82) and Rudikoff (73) show that others are perceived in a more acceptant fashion as postulated in item 11. Gordon and Cartwright (25) provide evidence which is complex but in general nonconfirming on this point. Haimowitz and Morris (30) also have findings which seem to indicate that nonacceptance of minority groups may be more openly expressed.

The behavior changes specified in items 13 and 14 find support in the Rogers study (68) showing that in improved cases both the client and his friends observe greater maturity in his behavior. Hoffman (35) finds that the behavior the client describes in the interviews becomes more mature. Jonietz's study of (38) of perception of ink blots might lend some support to the postulate of item 15.

II. A THEORY OF PERSONALITY

In endeavoring to order our perceptions of the individual as he appears in therapy, a theory of the development of personality, and of the dynamics of behavior, has been constructed. It may be well to repeat the warning previously given, and to note that the initial propositions of this theory are those which are furthest from the matrix of our experience and hence are most suspect. As one reads on, the propositions become steadily closer to the experience of therapy. As before, the defined terms and constructs are italicized, and are to be understood as previously defined.

A. Postulated Characteristics of the Human Infant

It is postulated that the individual, during the period of infancy, has at least these attributes.

1. He perceives his *experience* as reality. His *experience* is his reality.
   a. As a consequence he has greater potential *awareness* of what reality is for him than does anyone else, since no one else can completely assume his *internal frame of reference*.
2. He has an inherent tendency toward *actualizing* his organism.
3. He interacts with his reality in terms of his basic *actualizing* tendency. Thus his behavior is the goal-directed attempt of the organism to satisfy the experienced needs for *actualization* in the reality as *perceived*.
4. In this interaction he behaves as an organized whole, as a gestalt.
5. He engages in an *organismic valuing process*, valuing *experience* with reference to the *actualizing tendency* as a criterion. *Experiences* which are *perceived* as maintaining or enhancing the organism are valued positively. Those which are *perceived* as negating such maintenance or enhancement are valued negatively.
6. He behaves with adience toward positively valued *experiences* and with avoidance toward those negatively valued.

B. The Development of the Self

1. In line with the tendency toward differentiation which is a part of the *actualizing tendency*, a portion of the individual's *experience* becomes differentiated and *symbolized* in an *awareness* of being, *awareness* of functioning. Such awareness may be described as *self-experience*.

2. This representation in *awareness* of being and functioning, becomes elaborated, through interaction with the environment, particularly the environment composed of significant others, into a *concept of self*, a perceptual object in his *experiential field*.

C. The Need for Positive Regard

1. As the awareness of self emerges, the individual develops a *need for positive regard*. This need is universal in human beings, and in the individual is pervasive and persistent. Whether it is an inherent or learned need is irrelevant to the theory. Standal (80), who formulated the concept, regards it as the latter.

   a. The satisfaction of this need is necessarily based upon inferences regarding the experiential field of another.

      (1) Consequently it is often ambiguous.

   b. It is associated with a very wide range of the individual's *experiences*.

   c. It is reciprocal, in that when an individual discriminates himself as satisfying another's need for *positive regard*, he necessarily experiences satisfaction of his own need for *positive regard*.

      (1) Hence it is rewarding both to satisfy this need in another, and to experience the satisfaction of one's own need by another.

   d. It is potent, in that the *positive regard* of any social other is communicated to the total *regard complex* which the individual associates with that social other.

      (1) Consequently the expression of positive regard by a significant social other can become more compelling than the *organismic valuing process*, and the individual becomes more adient to the *positive regard* of such others than toward

experiences which are of positive value in *actualizing* the organism.

D. The Development of the Need for Self-Regard

1. The positive regard satisfactions or frustrations associated with any particular *self-experience* or group of *self-experiences* come to be *experienced* by the individual independently of *positive regard* transactions with social others. *Positive regard experienced* in this fashion is termed *self-regard*.

2. A *need for self-regard* develops as a learned need developing out of the association of *self-experiences* with the satisfaction or frustration of the *need for positive regard*.

3. The individual thus comes to *experience positive regard* or loss of *positive regard* independently of transactions with any social other. He becomes in a sense his own significant social other.

4. Like *positive regard*, *self-regard* which is *experienced* in relation to any particular *self-experience* or group of *self-experiences*, is communicated to the total *self-regard complex*.

E. The Development of Conditions of Worth

1. When *self-experiences* of the individual are discriminated by significant others as being more or less worthy of *positive regard*, then *self-regard* becomes similarly selective.

2. When a *self-experience* is avoided (or sought) solely because it is less (or more) worthy of *self-regard*, the individual is said to have acquired a *condition of worth*.

3. If an individual should *experience* only *unconditional positive regard*, then no *conditions of worth* would develop, *self-regard* would be unconditional, the needs for *positive regard* and *self-regard* would never be at variance with *organismic evaluation*, and the individual would continue to be *psychologically adjusted*, and would be fully functioning. This chain of events is hypothetically possible, and hence important theoretically, though it does not appear to occur in actuality.

F. The Development of Incongruence Between Self and Experience

1. Because of the need for *self-regard*, the individual *perceives* his *experience* selectively, in terms of the *conditions of worth* which have come to exist in him.

   a. Experiences which are in accord with his *conditions of worth* are *perceived* and *symbolized* accurately in *awareness*.
   b. Experiences which run contrary to the *conditions of worth* are *perceived* selectively and distortedly as if in accord with the *conditions of worth*, or are in part or whole *denied to awareness*.
2. Consequently some experiences now occur in the organism which are not recognized as *self-experiences*, are not accurately *symbolized*, and are not organized into the *self-structure* in accurately symbolized form.
3. Thus from the time of the first selective *perception* in terms of *conditions of worth*, the states of *incongruence between self* and *experience*, of *psychological maladjustment* and of *vulnerability*, exist to some degree.

G. The Development of Discrepancies in Behavior
1. As a consequence of the incongruence between self and experience described in *F*, a similar incongruence arises in the behavior of the individual.
   a. Some behaviors are consistent with the *self-concept* and maintain and actualize and enhance it.
   (1) Such behaviors are *accurately symbolized in awareness*.
   b. Some behaviors maintain, enhance, and actualize those aspects of the experience of the organism which are not assimilated into the *self-structure*.
   (1) These behaviors are either unrecognized as *self-experiences* or *perceived* in distorted or selective fashion in such a way as to be *congruent* with the *self*.

H. The Experience of Threat and the Process of Defense
1. As the organism continues to *experience*, an *experience* which is incongruent with the self-structure (and its incorporated *conditions of worth*) is *subceived* as *threatening*.
2. The essential nature of the *threat* is that if the *experience* were *accurately symbolized* in *awareness*, the *self-concept* would no longer be a consistent gestalt, the *conditions of worth* would be violated, and the *need for self-regard* would be frustrated. A state of *anxiety* would exist.

3. The process of *defense* is the reaction which prevents these events from occurring.

   a. This process consists of the selective *perception* or *distortion* of the *experience* and/or the *denial to awareness* of the *experience* or some portion thereof, thus keeping the total *perception* of the *experience* consistent with the individual's *self-structure*, and consistent with his *conditions of worth*.

4. The general consequences of the process of *defense*, aside from its preservation of the above consistencies, are a rigidity of *perception*, due to the necessity of distorting *perceptions*, an inaccurate *perception* of reality, due to distortion and omission of data, and *intensionality*.

I. The Process of Breakdown and Disorganization

Up to this point the theory of personality which has been formulated applies to every individual in a lesser or greater degree. In this and the following section certain processes are described which occur only when certain specified conditions are present.

1. If the individual has a large or significant degree of *incongruence between self and experience* and if a significant experience demonstrating this *incongruence* occurs suddenly, or with a high degree of obviousness, then the organism's process of *defense* is unable to operate successfully.

2. As a result *anxiety* is *experienced* as the *incongruence* is subceived. The degree of *anxiety* is dependent upon the extent of the *self-structure* which is *threatened*.

3. The process of *defense* being unsuccessful, the *experience* is *accurately symbolized* in *awareness*, and the gestalt of the *self-structure* is broken by this *experience* of the *incongruence* in *awareness*. A state of disorganization results.

4. In such a state of disorganization the organism behaves at times in ways which are openly consistent with experiences which have hitherto been distorted or denied to awareness. At other times the self may temporarily regain regnancy, and the organism may behave in ways consistent with it. Thus in such a state of disorganization, the tension between the concept of self (with its included distorted perceptions) and the

experiences which are not accurately symbolized or included in the concept of self, is expressed in a confused regnancy, first one and then the other supplying the "feedback" by which the organism regulates behavior.

J. The Process of Reintegration

In the situations described under sections *G* and *H*, (and probably in situations of breakdown as described under *I*, though there is less evidence on this) a process of reintegration is possible, a process which moves in the direction of increasing the *congruence* between *self* and *experience*. This may be described as follows:

1. In order for the process of *defense* to be reversed — for a customarily *threatening experience* to be *accurately symbolized* in *awareness* and assimilated into the *self-structure*, certain conditions must exist.
   a. There must be a decrease in the *conditions of worth*.
   b. There must be an increase in *unconditional self-regard*.
2. The communicated *unconditional positive regard* of a significant other is one way of achieving these conditions.
   a. In order for the *unconditional positive regard* to be communicated, it must exist in a context of *empathic* understanding.
   b. When the individual *perceives* such *unconditional positive regard*, existing *conditions of worth* are weakened or dissolved.
   c. Another consequence is the increase in his own *unconditional positive self-regard*.
   d. Conditions 2*a* and 2*b* above thus being met, *threat* is reduced, the process of *defense is reversed*, and *experiences* customarily *threatening* are *accurately symbolized* and integrated into the *self-concept*.
3. The consequences of 1 and 2 above are that the individual is less likely to encounter *threatening experiences*; the process of *defense* is less frequent and its consequences reduced; *self* and *experience* are more *congruent*; *self-regard* is increased; *positive regard* for others is increased; *psychological adjustment* is increased; the *organismic valuing process* becomes increasingly the basis of regulating behavior; the individual becomes nearly fully functioning.

III. A THEORY OF THE FULLY FUNCTIONING PERSON

Certain directional tendencies in the individual ($1D$ and $IIA2$) and certain needs (IIC, D) have been explicitly postulated in the theory thus far presented. Since these tendencies operate more fully under certain defined conditions, there is already implicit in what has been given a concept of the ultimate in the actualization of the human organism. This ultimate hypothetical person would be synonymous with "the goal of social evolution," "the end point of optimal psychotherapy," etc. We have chosen to term this individual the fully functioning person.

Although it contains nothing not already stated earlier under I and II, it seems worthwhile to spell out this theoretical concept in its own right.

A. The individual has an inherent tendency toward *actualizing* his organism.

B. The individual has the capacity and tendency to *symbolize experiences* accurately in *awareness*.

  1. A corollary statement is that he has the capacity and tendency to keep his *self-concept* congruent with his *experience*.

C. The individual has a *need for positive regard*.

D. The individual has a *need for positive self-regard*.

E. Tendencies A and B are most fully realized when needs C and D are met. More specifically, tendencies A and B tend to be most fully realized when

  1. The individual *experiences unconditional positive regard* from significant others.

  2. The pervasiveness of this *unconditional positive regard* is made evident through relationships marked by a complete and communicated *empathic* understanding of the individual's *frame of reference*.

F. If the conditions under E are met to a maximum degree, the individual who experiences these conditions will be a fully functioning person. The fully functioning person will have at least these characteristics:

  1. He will be *open to his experience*.

    a. The corollary statement is that he will exhibit no *defensiveness*.

2. Hence all *experiences* will be *available to awareness*.
3. All *symbolizations* will be as accurate as the experiential data will permit.
4. His *self-structure* will be congruent with his *experience*.
5. His *self-structure* will be a fluid gestalt, changing flexibly in the process of assimilation of new *experience*.
6. He will *experience* himself as the *locus of evaluation*.

    a. The *valuing process* will be a continuing *organismic* one.

7. He will have no *conditions of worth*.

    a. The corollary statement is that he will *experience unconditional self-regard*.

8. He will meet each situation with behavior which is a unique and creative adaptation to the newness of that moment.
9. He will find his *organismic valuing* a trustworthy guide to the most satisfying behaviors, because

    a. All available experiential data will be available to *awareness* and used.

    b. No datum of *experience* will be *distorted in*, or *denied to*, *awareness*.

    c. The outcomes of behavior in *experience* will be available to *awareness*.

    d. Hence any failure to achieve the maximum possible satisfaction, because of lack of data, will be corrected by this effective reality testing.

10. He will live with others in the maximum possible harmony, because of the rewarding character of reciprocal *positive regard* (IIC1c).

IV. A THEORY OF INTERPERSONAL RELATIONSHIP

The most recent extension of our theoretical constructs has been the attempt to formulate the order which appears to exist in all interpersonal relationships and interpersonal communication. This formulation springs, as will be evident, primarily from the theory of therapy, viewing the therapeutic relationship as simply one instance of interpersonal relationship. For clarity of presentation the conditions, process, and outcome of a deteriorating relationship and a deepening or improving relationship will be set forth separately. Actually these are two points or spaces on a continuum.

E. The Process of an Improving Relationship

1. The communication of X′ to Y′ is characterized by congruence of *experience, awareness*, and communication.
2. Y′ *experiences* this *congruence* as clear communication. Hence his response is more likely to express a *congruence* of his own *experience* and *awareness*.
3. Since X′ is *congruent* and not *vulnerable* in the area related to his communication, he is able to *perceive* the response of Y′ in an accurate and *extensional* manner, *with empathy* for his *internal frame of reference*.
4. Feeling understood, Y′ *experiences* some satisfaction of his *need for positive regard*.
5. X′ *experiences* himself as having made a positive difference in the *experiential field* of Y′.
   a. Hence reciprocally, X′ tends to increase in *feeling of positive regard* for Y′.
   b. Since X′ is not *vulnerable* in the area of the communication, the *positive regard* he feels for Y′ tends to be an *unconditional positive regard*.
6. Y′ *experiences* himself in a *relationship* which, at least in the area of communication, is characterized by congruence on the part of X′, an *empathic* understanding by X′ of the *internal frame of reference*, and an *unconditional regard*. (See IA3, 4, 5.)
   a. Hence all the characteristics of the process of therapy (1*B*) are initiated, within the confines of the subject of communication.
   b. Because Y′ has less need of any of his *defenses* in this *relationship*, any need for *distortion of perception* is decreased.
   c. Hence he *perceives* the communications of X′ more accurately.
7. Hence communication in both directions becomes increasingly *congruent*, is increasingly accurately *perceived*, and contains more reciprocal *positive regard*.

V. THEORIES OF APPLICATION

To spell out in detail the various theories of application which have been partially developed, would be too repetitious of what has gone before. Hence only a descriptive suggestion will be given in each area of the aspects of theory which would be applicable.

Family life. The theoretical implications would include these:

1. The greater the degree of *unconditional positive regard* which the parent experiences toward the child:
   a. The fewer the *conditions of worth* in the child.
   b. The more the child will be able to live in terms of a continuing *organismic valuing process*.
   c. The higher the level of *psychological adjustment* of the child.
2. The parent experiences such *unconditional positive regard* only to the extent that he *experiences unconditional self-regard*.
3. To the extent that he *experiences unconditional self-regard*, the parent will be congruent in the relationship.
   a. This implies genuineness or congruence in the expression of his own *feelings* (positive or negative).
4. To the extent that conditions 1, 2, and 3 exist, the parent will realistically and *empathically* understand the child's *internal frame of reference* and *experience an unconditional positive regard* for him.
5. To the extent that conditions 1 through 4 exist, the theory of the process and outcomes of therapy (I*B*, *C*), and the theory of the process and outcomes of an improving relationship (IV*E*, *F*), apply.

Group tension and conflict

A. *Conditions of Reduction in Group Conflict*

Group conflict and tension will be reduced if these conditions exist.

1. A person (whom we term a facilitator) is in *contact* with X, Y, and Z.
2. The facilitator is *congruent* within himself in his separate *contacts* with X, Y, and Z.
3. The facilitator experiences toward X, Y, and Z, separately:

    a. An *unconditional positive regard*, at least in the area in which the members of the group are communicating.

    b. An *empathic* understanding of the *internal frame of reference* of X, Y, Z, at least in the area in which the members of the group are communicating.

4. X, Y, and Z *perceive*, at least to a minimal degree, conditions 3a and 3b. (This is generally because 3b is communicated verbally.)

B. The Process of Reduction of Group Conflict
If the above conditions exist and continue, then:

1. The various elements of the process of therapy (IB) take place to some degree, at least within the area involved in the group communication.

    a. One of the important elements of this process is the increase in differentiated *perceptions* and in *extensionality*.

    b. Another important element is the reduction of *threat* (see IB8, 8a) in the experience of X, Y, Z.

2. Consequently the communications of Y to X or Z to X, are less *defensive*, and more nearly *congruent* with the *experience* of Y, and with the *experience* of Z.

3. These communications are perceived with increasing accuracy and *extensionality* by X.

    a. Consequently X *experiences* more *empathic* understanding of Y and Z.

4. Because he is *experiencing* less *threat* from Y and Z and more *empathy* with their *internal frame of reference*:

    a. X now symbolizes in awareness *incongruencies* which formerly existed between *experience* and *awareness*.

    b. Consequently his *defensive* distortions of his own *experience* are reduced.

    c. Hence his communication to Y and Z becomes a more *extensional* expression of his own total *experience* in regard to the area of communication.

5. The conditions now exist for the process of an improving relationship, and the phenomena described in IVE occur.

---

*Because this chapter is excerpted from a longer monograph, not all the original references are included here.

REFERENCES*

1. Anderson, R. An investigation of the relationship between verbal and physiological behavior during client-centered therapy. Unpublished doctoral dissertation, Univer. of Chicago, 1954.
and physiological behavior during client-centered therapy. Unpublished doctoral dissertation, Univer. of Chicago, 1954.

4. Assum, A. L., & Levy, S. J. Analysis of a non-directive case with follow-up interview. *J. abnorm. soc. Psychol.*, 1948, *43*, 78–89.

7. Butler, J. M., & Haigh, G. V. Changes in the relation between self-concepts and ideal concepts consequent upon client-centered counseling. In [70, chap. 4].

8. Carr, A. C. Evaluation of nine psychotherapy cases by the Rorschach. *J. consult. Psychol.*, 1949, *13* (3), 196–205.

10. Chodorkoff, B. Self-perception, perceptual defense, and adjustment. *J. abnorm. soc. Psychol.*, 1954, *49* (4), 508–512.

12. Cofer, C. N., & Chance, J. The discomfort-relief quotient in published cases of counseling and psychotherapy. *J. Psychol.*, 1950, *29*, 219–224.

13. Cowen, E. L., & Combs, A. W. Followup study of 32 cases treated by nondirective psychotherapy. *J. abnorm. soc. Psychol.*, 1950, *45*, 232–258.

15. Dymond, Rosalind F. Adjustment changes over therapy from self-sorts. In [70, chap. 5].

16. Dymond, Rosalind F. Adjustment changes over therapy from Thematic Apperception Test ratings. In [70, chap. 8].

19. Fiedler, F. E. A comparative investigation of early therapeutic relationships created by experts and non-experts of the psychoanalytic, non-directive and Adlerian schools. Unpublished doctoral dissertation, Univer. of Chicago, 1949.

20. Fiedler, F. E. A comparison of therapeutic relationships in psychoanalytic, non-directive and Adlerian therapy. *J. consult. Psychol.*, 1950, *14*, 436–445.

21. Gallagher, J. J. The problem of escaping clients in non-directive counseling. In W. U. Snyder (Ed.), *Group report of a program of research in psychotherapy*. Psychotherapy Research Group, Pennsylvania State Univer., 1953. Pp. 21–38.

25. Gordon, T., & Cartwright, D. The effects of psychotherapy upon certain attitudes toward others. In [70, chap. 11].

28. Grummon, D. L., & John, Eve S. Changes over client-centered therapy evaluated on psychoanalytically based Thematic Apperception Test scales. In [70, chap. 11].

29. Haigh, G. V. Defensive behavior in client-centered therapy. *J. consult. Psychol.*, 1949, *13* (3), 181–189.

30. Haimowitz, Natalie Reader, & Morris, L. Personality changes in client-centered therapy. In W. Wolff (Ed.), *Success in psychotherapy.* New York: Grune & Stratton, 1952. Chap. 3.

32. Hanlon, T. E., Hofstaetter, P. R., & O'Connor, J. P. Congruence of self and ideal self in relation to personality adjustment. *J. consult. Psychol.*, 1954, *18* (3), 215–218.

33. Hartley, Margaret. Changes in the self-concept during psychotherapy. Unpublished doctoral dissertation, Univer. of Chicago, 1951.

35. Hoffman, A. E. A study of reported behavior changes in counseling. *J. consult. Psychol.*, 1949, *13*, 190–195.

36. Hogan, R. The development of a measure of client defensiveness in the counseling relationship. Unpublished doctoral dissertation, Univer. of Chicago, 1948.

38. Jonietz, Alice. A study of phenomenological changes in perception after psychotherapy as exhibited in the content of Rorschach percepts. Unpublished doctoral dissertation, Univer. of Chicago, 1950.

39. Kauffman, P. E., & Raimy, V. C. Two methods of assessing therapeutic progress. *J. abnorm. soc. Psychol.*, 1949, *44*, 379–385.

41. Kessler, Carol. Semantics and non-directive counseling. Unpublished master's thesis, Univer. of Chicago, 1947.

44. Lipkin, S. Clients' feelings and attitudes in relation to the outcome of client-centered therapy. *Psychol. Monogr.*, 1954, *68*, No. 1 (Whole No. 372).

47. Mitchell, F. H. A test of certain semantic hypotheses by application to client-centered counseling cases: intensionality-extensionality of clients in therapy. Unpublished doctoral dissertation, Univer. of Chicago, 1951.

48. Mosak, H. Evaluation in psychotherapy: a study of some current measures. Unpublished doctoral dissertation, Univer. of Chicago, 1950.

49. Muench, G. A. An evaluation of non-directive psychotherapy by means of the Rorschach and other tests. *Appl. Psychol. Monogr.*, 1947, No. 13, 1–463.

52. Quinn, R. D. Psychotherapists' expressions as an index to the quality of early therapeutic relationships established by representatives of the nondirective, Adlerian, and psychoanalytic schools. Unpublished doctoral dissertation, Univer. of Chicago, 1950.

55. Raimy, V. C. Self reference in counseling interviews. *J. consult. Psychol.*, 1948, *12*, 153–163.

56. Raskin, N. J. An objective study of the locus of evaluation factor in psychotherapy. Unpublished doctoral dissertation, Univer. of Chicago, 1949.

67. Rogers, C. R. The case of Mrs. Oak: a research analysis. In [70, chap. 15].
68. Rogers, C. R. Changes in the maturity of behavior as related to therapy. In [70, chap. 13].
70. Rogers, C. R., & Dymond, R. F. (Eds.). *Psychotherapy and personality change*. Chicago: University of Chicago Press, 1954.
72. Rogers, Natalie. Measuring psychological tension in non-directive counseling. *Personal Counselor*, 1948, *3*, 237–264.
73. Rudikoff, Esselyn C. A comparative study of the changes in the concept of the self, the ordinary person, and the ideal in eight cases. In [70, chap. 11].
75. Seeman, J. Counselor judgments of therapeutic process and outcome. In [70, chap. 11].
76. Seeman, J. A study of the process of non-directive therapy. *J. consult. Psychol.*, 1949, *13*, 157–168.
78. Sheerer, Elizabeth T. The relationship between acceptance of self and acceptance of others. *J. consult. Psychol.*, 1949, *13* (3), 169–175.
79. Snyder, W. U. An investigation of the nature of non-directive psychotherapy. *J. genet. Psychol.*, 1945, *33*, 193–223.
80. Standal, S. The need for positive regard: a contribution to client-centered theory. Unpublished doctoral dissertation, University of Chicago, 1954.
82. Stock, Dorothy. The self concept and feelings toward others. *J. consult. Psychol.*, 1949, *13* (3), 176–180.
83. Strom, K. A re-study of William U. Snyder's "An investigation of the nature of non-directive psychotherapy." Unpublished master's thesis, Univer. of Chicago, 1948.
84. Thetford, W. N. An objective measure of frustration tolerance in evaluating psychotherapy. In W. Wolff (Ed.), *Success in psychotherapy*. New York: Grune & Stratton, 1952. Chap. 2.
85. Vargas, M. Changes in self-awareness during client-centered therapy. In [70, chap. 10].
86. Zimmerman, J. Modification of the discomfort-relief quotient as a measure of progress in counseling. Unpublished master's thesis, Univer. of Chicago, 1950.

A HUMAN SCIENCE

Having achieved international acclaim for his scientific research on psychotherapy and having written and edited two substantial books on his research methods and results (Rogers and Dymond, 1954; Rogers et al., 1967), in the second half of his career Rogers went on to question some of the very assumptions of the scientific paradigm that had brought him such acclaim.

Actually, his concern about the underlying assumption of "the growing behavioral sciences" took two forms. The first was the social and political context in which the behavioral sciences operated. In 1956 his famous symposium with B. F. Skinner, the leading scientist of the behavioral school of psychology, defined the issues of the debate for decades to come. Skinner argued persuasively for the intelligent and hopefully humane use of reinforcement theory to direct the course of the individual's and society's development. In any event, Skinner argued, freedom and choice are merely illusions; it is solely our previous reinforcements that determine our current behavior. Rogers, with equal eloquence, argued that freedom and choice were not illusory but real phenomena, and that a science that dehumanizes the individual and attempts to control human development only by outside reinforcement paves the way for dictators and despots to move society inexorably toward a totalitarian, Orwellian future.

While this first encounter between the two leading voices of the behaviorist and humanist models of psychology attracted widespread attention throughout the helping professions, Rogers and Skinner continued their exchange in two lesser-known meetings over the following decade. Their third and longest dialogue is reprinted in the companion volume to this one, *Carl Rogers: Dialogues* (Kirschenbaum and Henderson, eds., 1989).

Along with his concern over society's current and future utilization of psychology and the behavioral sciences, Rogers gradually became interested in the philosophical and methodological assumptions of the behavioral sciences. As knowledge of human growth and development, human relations, and behavioral change and control grew so rapidly, he believed it was important to reexamine many of the scientific assumptions of these fields. In particular, he questioned whether the scientific research methods of the "hard sciences" could or should automatically be applied to the behavioral sciences as the only valid scientific model.

To further this line of thought, he and William Coulson, his colleague at the Western Behavioral Sciences Institute, planned a small, invitational conference to explore the foundations of the behavioral sciences. It was held in La Jolla in 1966. Michael Polanyi, Jacob Bronowski, Jonas Salk, and other leading scientists and scholars from many countries presented papers and participated in the discussions, later published in book form as *Man and the Science of Man* (Coulson and Rogers, 1968). "Some Thoughts Regarding the Current Presuppositions of the Behavioral Sciences" is Rogers's opening address to the conference.

Having suggested that the behavioral sciences should begin pursuing avenues of scientific research more suitable to a humanistic psychology than the strict, logical positivist, experimental approaches typically thought of as "the scientific method," Rogers himself was beyond the point where he personally wished to engage in active research. Unlike other stages of his career, he was advocating an activity that he himself was not engaged in, although he encouraged and supported others along these lines when he could. Still, he continued to speak and write on the topic and eventually saw a new wave of scientific activity in the behavioral sciences which he believed was the beginning of that movement he had advocated a generation earlier. In "Toward a More Human Science of the Person," written two years before his death, Rogers describes many of these "new and human investigations" which he regarded as an important new development in the field.

It remains to be seen whether this apparently growing interest in a "more human science" is a temporary phenomenon or, as Rogers suggested, the dawning of a new age for the behavioral sciences.

18
Some Thoughts Regarding the Current Presuppositions of the Behavioral Sciences

Introduction

Due to circumstances which seem odd to me, my writings regarding practice, theory, and research in the field of interpersonal relationships appear to have significance in fields as diverse as education and psychotherapy, executive development and pastoral psychology, personality theory and sensitivity training. Consequently, there are demands on me from all these fields. I already feel that my efforts are spread too wide and too thin. By what right, then, do I interest myself in the philosophy of the behavioral sciences? Why would I initiate a conference such as this? Am I simply a dilettante in every field? I can assure you that I ask myself this question with as much seriousness as any of you might ask it of me.

I have interested myself in the philosophical assumptions which underlie the behavioral sciences because I feel a great concern for what is happening in my own science: the field of psychology. I hope that my remarks will make clear the nature of my concern.

Behavioral Science As a Fundamental Issue

Psychology and the other behavioral sciences are without doubt coming into their own. There is a vastly increased degree of public acceptance and public acclaim. The behavioral sciences are now a part of the hope of the modern world. In Washington, D.C., a psychologist heads up an important commission regard-

In Coulson, W. and Rogers, C. R. (Eds.), *Man and the Science of Man*. Columbus, Ohio: Charles E. Merrill, 1968, 55–72.

ing international tensions. A psychologist has been head of the enormous Department of Health, Education, and Welfare. In industry, there are leaders of sensitivity groups and many other types of professionals and consultants who base their work on the behavioral sciences. In education, programmed learning plays an increasing role. In personal life, the individual or the group in search of help turns to psychotherapy. There is no doubt that the behavioral sciences and their applications play a part hitherto unknown in the history of mankind, serving many important and valued functions.

At the same time, the behavioral sciences constitute one of the bugaboos of the modern world. Skinner's *Walden Two*, the most honest and straightforward account of what the present trends in the behavioral sciences would mean if applied to the social world, has received and is receiving a great deal of fearful attention. The possibility of the control of human behavior through the knowledge gained in the behavioral sciences is of increasing interest to large groups of people, and is seen as a real threat. It has come clear that psychology, like physics, can be used to enrich or to destroy our lives.

Since the behavioral sciences are a boon to society; since we are growing to be a respected area of science; since we are a fearful threat to our culture; since we are a group of rapidly developing disciplines, perhaps this is a good time to consider some of our foundations. Perhaps it is a time to try to examine at the most fundamental level possible, and in the freshest possible way, the presuppositions which underlie our whole field of work and its relation to life and living. Perhaps we can anticipate some of the problems which in the not-too-distant future will face us and our society by asking ourselves some of the deeper questions: How do we know? What is "true"? What are the identifying characteristics of a scientist? What is science? What is the special nature of behavioral science?

I am well aware of my lack of qualifications for so fundamental an inquiry. I am a therapist, a student of interpersonal relationships, not a philosopher of science.

The Controversy As It Exists in Me

As with many other issues which have seemed to me to be of general importance, I feel the disputes within myself. I sometimes think that if I have a contribution to make to the behavioral sciences, it is that the deepest current conflicts in that field all take place in me, as well as in the more open arena of professional and scientific life and discussion. Since I believe that even our most abstract and philosophical views spring from an intensely personal base, I would like to give you some of the tensions as I feel them in myself—the tensions which have made me turn to the simple but basic questions which I have just stated.

In the first place, let me speak of me as scientist. I love the precision and the elegance of science. The simple law of the lever: that the weight times distance to the fulcrum at one end equals the weight times the distance to the fulcrum at the other end, fascinates me. This whole question of balance and leverage has so intrigued me that I love to build large floating mobiles which, in their movement and balance, express some of the beauty of the law of the lever. I can lose myself in the contemplation of this elegance.

I like to create hypotheses and I like to test them against hard reality. I dislike fuzzy and personal emotional statements when they are given out as general truths, even when I respect them as expressions of the person. I am fascinated when I feel that I am close to an understanding of some principle of nature; an understanding which gives an opportunity for control of natural events by attuning with these discovered principles. (This, of course, is as close as we ever come to *control* of nature. We never control it in an arbitrary sense; we simply endeavor to put ourselves in accord with its underlying principles.)

I believe that psychological science will advance along the lines of discovering the lawful order which exists in human behavior and experience—in interpersonal relationships, in learning, in perception, in those experiences denied to awareness, and other psychological events. As a psychologist, I am always looking for the invariant relationship, the statement that X always precedes Y, or is related to it in some highly probable manner. I am sure that if these definite relationships exist and are discoverable, they can give us a deeper understanding of psychological events.

What I am trying to say is that I have, deep within me, a feeling for science—for that relatively new invention in human history by which we have come to have a partial understanding of the awesome order of our physical and psychological universe.

Consequently, I value the concepts which underlie the behavioral sciences. The concern with observable behavior, the casting of all variables in operational terms, the adequate testing of hypotheses, and the use of increasingly sophisticated design and statistics all have meaning to me. I try continuously to see that my own research is conducted in a precise fashion with adequate controls and with sophisticated research design and statistical methodology, so that the findings are not deceiving. I mention all these personal attitudes because I definitely am a scientist.

But I am also a therapist, a person who has lived deeply in human relationships. Here, I come up with some other values and views which have equally deep meaning to me.

I value the person. Of all the incredible forms of life and non-life which exist in the universe, the individual human being seems to me to have the most exciting potential, the greatest possibilities for an expanding development, the richest capacities for self-aware living. I cannot prove that the individual is most to be valued. I can only say that my experience leads me to place a primary value on him.

I am well aware that other views are possible; that one can, for example, place a primary value upon society, and only a secondary value upon the individual. But only in the individual does awareness exist. Only in the individual can alternative courses of action be most deeply and consciously tested as to their enriching or destructive consequences. The whole history of mankind, it seems to me, shows a gradually increasing emphasis upon the significance and worth of each individual. I not only observe this trend, I concur in it.

As a consequence, it is not surprising that I object to the process of depersonalization and dehumanization of the individual which I see in our culture. I regret that the behavioral sciences seem to me to be promoting and reinforcing this trend. I am concerned when so astute an observer as Clifton Fadiman says, in speaking of the newspapers, that "this machine [the newspaper] . . . mediates between Technological Man (of whom we are the faint foreshadowing) and the Technological Order of which we will eventually be the Computable Factors" (*Holiday*, 1963). I do not look forward to being no more than a computable factor in such an order. It appears to me that many of the modern trends would indicate that we are moving inexorably toward a world in which men will be no more than conditioned ants in a gigantic anthill. I do not appreciate this prospect.

I have come to place a high value on personal, subjective choice. My experience in psychotherapy confirms me in the belief that such choice, made openly by an individual who is aware both of what is going on within him, and aware also of his personal environment, is highly significant. I think of the confused psychotic man hospitalized for years, whose turn toward improvement was probably best predicted when he muttered, "I don't know *what* I'm going to do, but *I'm* going to do it." In short, I believe that such terms as *personal freedom*, *choice*, *purpose*, or *goal*, have profound and significant meaning. I cannot agree with the view that the behavioral sciences have made not only such terms, but the concept of meaning itself, meaningless.

I have tried to give something of this continuing dialogue within myself simply to indicate that, as a person, I stand in both camps: the world of the precise, hard scientist; and the world of the sensitive, subjective person. I hope this may provide a background for a better understanding of some of the ideas that I would like to put forth in an attempt to answer some of the naive questions which I initially raised.

HOW DO WE KNOW?

In recent years I have attempted, with the aid of colleagues and students, to think and probe more deeply into some of these issues. Let me turn first to the question "How do we know?" When we first encounter this question, we are apt to think of some of the impressive machinery of science. The more one pursues this question, the more one is forced to realize that in the last analysis, knowledge rests on the subjective: I *experience*; in this experiencing, I *exist*; in thus existing, I in some sense *know*, I have a "felt assurance." All knowledge, including all scientific knowledge, is a vast inverted pyramid resting on this tiny, personal, subjective base.

If this seems to you to be an unwarranted undercutting of the solidity of our knowledge, I would add that such modern philosophers of science as Polanyi reinforce this view. I think that it is not too much to say that knowing, even in the hardest sciences, is a risky, uncertain, subjective leap even when it is most "objective." We do no one a service by pretending it is not this. Instead, we might look with awe at the scientific, philosophical, and artistic achievements which man has been able to build upon this very shaky base of personal experience. It speaks well for the essential trustworthiness of his functioning.

If it seems hard or difficult to give up the certainty of knowing which has customarily been related to science, perhaps we should recognize that the statements I am making put a firm emphasis upon science as a *process*, rather than upon science as a result. I believe there is a great deal of evidence to indicate that in many aspects of our culture, including science, we are moving toward a process conception of all aspects of living and life. Even in the teaching of high school science as the conduct of inquiry, we are endeavoring to facilitate an understanding of science as a subjectively guided *process*. To me, it appears that our security is in this process; not in the scientific results which may at any time be contradicted.

One of the best statements of the character of knowing, and also of the true scientist, is given not by a philosopher of science, but by a choreographer. Agnes de Mille has this to say about the gaining of knowledge:

> The moment one knows how, one begins to die a little. Living is a form of not being sure, of not knowing what next or how. And the artist before all others never entirely knows. He guesses, and he may be wrong. But then how does one know whom to befriend or, for that matter, to marry? One can't go through life on hands and knees. One leaps in the dark. For this reason creative technique reduces itself basically to a recognition and a *befriending* of one's self. "Who am I?" the artist asks, and he devotes his entire career to answering.
>
> There is one clue: what moves him is his. What amuses or frightens or pleases him becomes by virtue of his emotional participation a part of his personality and history; conversely what neither moves nor involves him, what brings him no joy, can be reckoned as spurious. An artist begins to go wrong exactly at the point where he begins to pretend. But it is difficult sometimes to accept the truth. He has to learn who he in fact is, not who he would like to be, nor even who it would be expedient or profitable to be. (1958)

The parallel with truly scientific thinking is profound. The scientist, like the artist, trusts himself and his experiencing, or as she puts it so charmingly, "befriends" himself, as he searches for the perceptions of truth which are his, which really belong to *him*, which constitute his basis for taking the subjective leap. This process is beautifully illustrated by none other than Dr. B. F. Skinner, in his subjective account of his process of becoming a scientist. Here his story is studded by such phrases as, "This was, of course, the kind of thing I was looking for"; "I can easily recall the excitement of "; "Of course, I was working on a basic assumption" (1961). These phrases indicate the kind of intuitive trust which he placed in his own experiencing, and the fact that it was those experiences which moved him, subjectively, and guided his scientific directions.

WHAT IS SCIENCE?

But let us turn away from these comments on the personal process of knowing, to the larger conception of science as a whole. How do we pursue truth? How do we discover new or generalized knowledge? What is it like to be a scientist? What is the essence of science? I should like to set forth a few statements as a basis for discussion.

It appears that if I wish to become a scientist, the first step is to immerse myself in the phenomena of the particular field in which I have developed an interest. The more complete the immersion, the longer it lasts, the more I love and prize the whole field, the more open I am to all the subtleties of my experiencing, the more likely I am to discover new knowledge. This means a tolerance for ambiguity and contradiction, a resistance to the need for closure, the valuing of unbridled curiosity. It means soaking up experience like a sponge, so that it is taken in in all its complexity, with my total organism freely participating in the experiencing of the phenomena; not simply my conscious mind.

The Emergence of a Sense of Pattern

Out of this immersion in the phenomena, certain things "come to mind." I may find some sense of pattern, or rhythm, or relationship emerging. As I read the history of science, this subjective sense of pattern is something to be nourished, no matter how absurd it may seem when scrutinized by conscious thought. I need to recognize that my conscious thought is full of fixed constructs which may interfere with the perception of an underlying pattern. It appears that the discoverer of knowledge feels a trust in *all* his avenues of knowing: unconscious, intuitive, and conscious.

It is this intuitive sensing of a pattern which is all-important in true science. If I can lay aside rigidly held preconceptions, and forget for a moment the "truth," or the clear-cut constructs already known, then the pattern may shine through more clearly. Here is an excellent statement of the attitude I am describing. "What you have to do is let go, let go every thought of your own, wipe your mind clean, fresh, innocent, newborn, sensitive as unexposed film to take up the impressions around you, and let what will come in. This is the pregnant void, the fertile state of no-mind. This is nonpreconception, the beginning of discovery" (1960). This could certainly have come from a scientist. Actually, it is a statement by a gifted creator of documentary films, Francis Flaherty.

The great scientists — men like Kepler, Einstein, and others — have learned to trust this intuitive sensing. It may be clearly wrong, and yet fundamentally right. For example, I have chuckled at the natives in the Caribbean who would not think of planting their crops except at the time of the new moon, when "the moon is right." All of us "know" that the moon cannot possibly affect this seed that is placed in the ground. The native is acting on a ridiculous hypothesis. Now, however, centuries after the natives formulated their adages, scientists find to their puzzlement that rainfall during the week following the new moon is significantly greater all over the world than rainfall during the other portions of the moon's cycle. In other words, the hypothesis that the moon affected the seed is as wrong as we in our superior knowledge thought that it was. But the sensing of the pattern, by natives immersed for a lifetime in the growing of crops, was correct! This accords very deeply with my belief that the human organism, when operating freely and nondefensively, is perhaps the best scientific tool in existence, and is able to sense a pattern long before it can consciously formulate one.

Bronowski sees these patterns or rhythms as "hidden likenesses"; that is, as similarities between two objects or events which on the surface would seem to be totally unrelated. He says,

> All science is the search for unity in hidden likenesses. . . . The scientist looks for order in the appearances of nature by exploring such likenesses, for order does not display itself of itself; if it can be said to be there at all it is not there for the mere looking. There is no way of pointing a finger or a camera at it; order must be discovered and in a deep sense it must be created. What we see as we see it is mere disorder. . . . We remake nature by the act of discovery in the poem or in the theorem. (1956, pp. 23–24, 32)

One of the great mistakes in the behavioral sciences today, in my judgment, is that since our science must deal in observables — the movement of a needle on a polygraph, a mark on paper, a sound emitted, a movement of a limb — we have assumed that the pattern we sense must also have to do with observables. This is where the freely functioning human organism is confined in its operation and permitted only a distorted perception. It appears to me that when a pattern is sensed, it must be perceived in its *own* terms; whether those terms are internal, ineffable, subjective, and invisible; or whether they are external, tangible, and visible.

If I develop some sense of pattern regarding the perceptions and visions of individuals who have taken the drug LSD, my first perception of that pattern can best be cast in terms of the visions and hallucinations (which no observer can see) rather than in terms of the emitted words, tears, groans, and writhings of the individuals involved. We need not be fearful of perceiving the pattern in terms which are natural to it. Later, in testing hypotheses, we may have to limit ourselves to observable elements, but this is a different matter.

I sum up this point about pattern by saying that I have come to realize that all science is based on a recognition — usually prelogical, intuitive, involving all the capacities of the organism — of a dimly sensed gestalt: a hidden reality. This gestalt or pattern appears to give meaning to disconnected phenomena. The more that this total apprehension of a pattern is free from cultural values and is free from past scientific values, the more adequate it is likely to be. The more that it is based on all sensory avenues, upon unconscious intuitions as well as cognitive insights, the more adequate it is likely to be. I regard this sensing of a pattern of relationships as perhaps the heart of all true science.

The Characteristics of a Fruitful Pattern

Since I have laid such stress upon this sensing of a pattern, I should like to indicate some of the elements that would be likely to discriminate a significant and fruitful pattern from one that is simply an illusion or a misperception. The more that the pattern is based on some of the following elements, the more likely it is, I believe, to prove fruitful and productive in a scientific sense:

- a keen and alert intelligence;
- a dedicated immersion over time in a broad range of related phenomena;
- a disciplined personal commitment by the scientist to his search — to finding out;
- a fresh, nondefensive openness to all of the phenomena and their interrelationships. This is an openness to the field of study, laying aside so far as possible all previous knowledge and previous conceptions, or at least holding such knowledge and concepts very lightly;
- an openness to all avenues of knowledge — previous studies in the field, the insights of nonscientists, the experiencing of others who are involved in the same field — and a willingness to take in any bit of seemingly relevant data;
- a trust in the total organismic sensing which is based on the above and which is deeper than, but includes, the cognitive perceptions;
- a recognition that the beauty or elegance of the perceived pattern is at least one clue to its fruitfulness;
- the recognition that the more the pattern reveals a unity in nature, the more likely it is to be fruitful. (It should be obvious that both the beauty or elegance of the pattern and its recognition of a unity in nature can be artificial and misleading. Nonetheless, it is true that all significant scientific

discoveries do have these qualities of both elegance and the introduction of a hitherto unperceived unity.)

Perhaps a quotation from Dr. Polanyi would be in order here. He says,

> To say that the discovery of objective truth in science consists in the apprehension of a rationality which commands our respect and arouses our contemplative admiration; that such discovery, while using the experience of our senses as clues, transcends this experience by embracing the vision of a reality beyond the impression of our senses, a vision which speaks for itself in guiding us to an ever deeper understanding of reality—such an account of scientific procedure would be generally shrugged aside as outdated Platonism: a piece of mystery mongering unworthy of an enlightened age. Yet it is precisely on this conception of objectivity that I wish to insist. (1958)

Putting the Pattern to Test

Important as is the "vision of reality"—this sensing of a pattern—it is not in itself sufficient for the discovery of new truth. The hypothesis must be put to the test. Here I would say that operationism, as I understand it, seems, for me, to be the most satisfactory mode of testing a hypothesis and confirming, modifying, or disconfirming it. I have a deep respect for the methodology which scientists have developed.

I do not propose to expand on this point because I believe that the operational approach is fairly well understood. I will simply give an example from my own experience which could be duplicated, I am sure, in the experience of any scientist. I have made the assertion that certain describable attitudinal sets in the psychotherapist—genuineness, acceptance, a sensitive empathic understanding—are the necessary and sufficient conditions of change in the client or patient who is involved with the therapist in psychotherapy. Simply as an assertion, this has about the same status as the assertion that the moon is made of green cheese. When it is recognized that the assertion grows out of some thirty years of therapeutic experience it has a slightly better, but not greatly better, status. Unless I am willing to define these terms operationally, to design a research which will put them to test, or to encourage others to design such researches;

and unless the various extraneous variables are controlled, and the findings support the hypotheses, then we are only in the realm of pattern perception and not of confirmation.

Perhaps, however, the methodology of science and all its enormous, modern sophistication is placed in a more suitable perspective if we clearly recognize that it is simply the machinery by which we try to determine whether we have deceived ourselves in the pattern which we have sensed in nature.

Even in the realm of confirmation, the personal element enters. In a recent discussion with Lancelot Whyte, the physicist who has become a historian of ideas and a philosopher of science, I was surprised to find that, for him, the truth value of a statement, even in science, could in the last analysis be evaluated by one criterion only. If I understood him correctly, that criterion is: How deeply acquainted with the phenomena, how nondefensive, how truly open to all facets of his experiencing, is the scientist who perceived the pattern and put it to test? After our conversation, I realized that if I tried to state the judgment of this physicist in my own terminology, it would be that the more nearly the individual comes to being a fully functioning person (Rogers, 1963), the more trustworthy he is as a discoverer of truth.

In the behavioral sciences, I think that one of our problems is that the methods of testing hypotheses come to be regarded as dogmas. These are, or should be, as unwelcome as dogmas in any other field. Our rules and methods for testing hypotheses are creations of the scientists themselves, and should be recognized as such. Thus, we should realize that there is no special virtue to any one procedure. Some hypotheses can best be tested on a single individual. One such famous hypothesis had to do with the circulation of the blood, and the testing of it involved no statistics. Others can only be satisfactorily tested on a large population using all of the most elaborate statistical methods. Some very pioneering hypotheses should first be tested in rough ways before they are put to refined tests. In all instances, the method of testing should be appropriate to the hypothesis, the pattern, the "vision of reality."

Perhaps it will help us in achieving a proper perspective on our methodology if we recognize that we are always dealing with labels in our research work; never with the phenomenon itself.

No one has ever seen a stimulus or a response or a reinforcement, for example, any more than we have ever seen a negative self-concept. We do observe behavior which we *interpret* to be a stimulus or a response or a reinforcement to the animal or the human being, just as we can observe behaviors which seem to be reasonably interpreted as indicators of a negative self-concept. But it is always true that the measures which we adopt or devise are based on external clues. We try to choose measures which bring us as close as possible to the underlying phenomena in which we are actually interested, but our research methods never utilize those phenomena—only an external clue or interpretation of them. This is true in all the sciences, *especially* in the sciences we so admire as the "hard" sciences.

Some Implications of This View for the Behavioral Sciences

If we look at the behavioral sciences in the light of what I have been saying, certain questions come naturally to mind. Are the behavioral scientists immersing themselves in their true field of study? Or are they endeavoring to work in detachment from it? In recent years, I have heard much criticism of those who teach clinical psychology in the universities. The statement is often made that they are so intent on doing research in the field that they do no clinical work. But if what I have been saying is true, their only hope of doing *significant* research is to be immersed in clinical work. I think we might ask of all behavioral scientists whether they are permitting themselves to live deeply, fully, openly, in interpersonal relationships, in deep contact with individuals and with the culture which helps to shape them. Or are they quickly, and sometimes fearfully, abstracting themselves from the very groundwork of their science? If the latter is true, it is unlikely that they can be very creative as scientists.

Are we creating a climate in our graduate schools and laboratories in which a confrontation with the mystery of the real in human personality and behavior can exist? Is the atmosphere such as to permit dimly perceived patterns to emerge and be tested? In the graduate departments which I know best, I would say that such a climate does not exist. We have a good environment for training technicians, but not a good climate for scientists.

Is it clear to us as behavioral scientists that our true task is to discern the patterns, rhythms, and relationships which cut so deeply into the rationality of nature that the implications of our perceptions will only be fully evident many decades hence? Granted that such perceptions cannot be forced, and must emerge naturally, is it clear that this is our central purpose? It appears to me that all too often the behavioral sciences are marked by a shallowness which bodes ill. When one small technical study is piled on top of many others, this is not science in its true sense. We seem, all too frequently, to have forgotten the nature of science.

Are we willing for the model and the methods of our science to emerge naturally from the problems of our science? Can we work at the central issues — whether a question of brain function, memory storage, response to love, the influence of the group on attitudes, the significance of values in behavior, or whatever — and simply evolve methods pertinent and relevant to those issues? Can we build a *psychological* science, or a *behavioral* science which grows out of the problems encountered in the study of the whole man in his subjective and objective being? Or must we feel that our science can only be a copy of Newtonian science — a model already outdated in its own field?

Some Possible Changes in the Behavioral Sciences

Let me bring my remarks to a close. It may seem that the statements I have been making about knowing and science, and the behavioral sciences in particular, add very little to our present conceptions. Yet, I should like to indicate some of the effects that such a view of science might have, particularly if imparted to our graduate students and to the younger men in the field.

1. It would tend to do away with the fear of creative subjective speculation. As I talk with graduate students in psychology, this fear is a very deep one. It cuts them off from any significant discovery. They would be shocked by the writings of a Kepler in his mystical and fanciful searching for likenesses and patterns in nature. They do not recognize that often it is out of such fanciful thinking that true science emerges. As Bronowski says, "To us the analogies by which Kepler listened for the movement of the planets and the music of the spheres are far-fetched. But are they more so than the wild leap by which Rutherford and

Bohr found a model for the atom in, of all places, the planetary system?" (1956, pp. 22–23). We are badly in need of a course on "The Care and Nurture of Infant Ideas." In our desire to be rigorous, we so often strangle the newborn idea, rather than nourishing its growth and development.

2. It would place a stress on disciplined commitment, disciplined *personal* commitment; not methodology. It would be a very healthy emphasis in the behavioral sciences if we could recognize that it is the dedicated, personal search of a disciplined, open-minded individual which discovers and creates new knowledge. No refinement of laboratory or statistical method can do this.

3. It would do away with many of the "oughts" in selecting hypotheses. For example, it is deeply imbedded in most behavioral scientists that we "ought" to be concerned only with the observables in behavior. Until recently, this has tended to inhibit work on dreams, on fantasy, on creative thinking. It has made most psychologists small-caliber scientists, involved only with the simplest problems in the science of man.

4. It would permit a free rein to phenomenological thinking in behavioral science, our effort to understand man and, perhaps, even the animals from the inside. It would recognize that no type of hypothesis has any special virtue in science save only in its relationship to a meaningful pattern which exists in the universe. Thus, a phenomenologically based hypothesis would have as much place in the behavioral sciences as a chemically based, genetically based, or behaviorally based hypothesis. We would develop a broader science (Rogers, 1964).

5. It would do away with those hypotheses which are selected simply because there are tools to measure the variables involved.

6. It would put the machinery of confirmation, the machinery of empirical testing of hypotheses, in its proper place. Method would not occupy a central place as the core of behavioral science.

7. It would put the stress on meaning; not simply on statistical significance at the .01 level.

8. More generally, if the picture of science I have tried to suggest gains some general acceptance in our field, it would give a new dignity to the science of man and to the scientist who

commits himself to that field. It would keep the scientist as a human being in the picture at all times, and we would recognize that science is but the lengthened shadow of dedicated human beings.

9. Perhaps most important of all, it would keep the subject of the investigation of the behavioral sciences in the picture as a subjective human being; not simply as a machine, not simply as an object or a determined sequence of cause and effect. We would not be fearful of looking at man as an existing human being, to use Kierkegaard's term, with more to his life than can be compressed into a machine model. Unless we can make progress in this direction, the behavioral sciences have, I fear, the capacity for becoming a threat to society more extreme and more devastating than the physical sciences have been.

REFERENCES

Bronowski, J. *Science and Human Values.* New York: Harper Torchbooks, 1956.

de Mille, Agnes B. *And Promenade Home.* Boston: Little, Brown and Company, 1958, pp. 190–191.

Fadiman, C. "Party of One." *Holiday,* 34 (5), November, 1963, p. 14.

Flaherty, Frances. *The Odyssey of a Film-Maker.* Urbana, Illinois: Beta Phi Mu, 1960, p. 20.

Kline, M. *Mathematics in Western Culture.* New York: Oxford University Press, 1953.

Polanyi, M. *Personal Knowledge.* Chicago: University of Chicago Press, 1958, p. 6.

Rogers, C. R. "The Concept of the Fully Functioning Person." *Psychotherapy: Theory, Research, and Practice.* Vol. 1 (1), 1963, 17–26.

———. "Toward a Science of the Person," in T. W. Wann (ed.), *Behaviorism and Phenomenology: Contrasting Bases for Modern Psychology.* University of Chicago Press, 1964, 109–140.

Skinner, B. F. *Cumulative Record.* New York: Appleton-Century Crofts, 1961.

19
Toward a More Human Science
of the Person

I would like to take you with me on the path of thought and study that I have followed in preparing for this meeting. It has been an exceedingly educational journey for me, and I hope I can convey something of the surprise and excitement that I experienced. The path starts with a concern that I have had for a long time. Humanistic psychology has not had a deep or significant impact on mainstream psychology in the United States, as it exists in our universities and colleges. If you need evidence for this statement, you need only look at almost any introductory textbook in psychology, where you will find "sensation," "perception," "motivation," and all the other parts of the human psyche, but where the living, acting, whole human being has very little place.

Another bit of evidence surprised me. I have been unable to find any humanistically oriented program of graduate study that has been approved by the American Psychological Association as a program leading to the doctorate in psychology. I have also been unable to find humanistically oriented internships that have APA approval. All this, in spite of the fact that in the criteria for APA approval there is a definite place for nonlaboratory research carried on in natural settings, and for nonexperimental forms of research.

I believe that one of the main factors in this disregard of humanistic psychology by academic psychologists is that we are

AUTHOR'S NOTE: In preparing for this article I asked for help from a number of individuals and received a generous flood of ideas, examples, materials, data— a real education for me and far more material than I could possibly use. I wish to give special thanks to Richard Farson, Clark Moustakas, Roy Fairfield, Larry Smith, Desmond Cartwright, Debora Brink, Maureen O'Hara, Donald Polkinghorne, Hallock Hoffman, and Michael Patton.

Journal of Humanistic Psychology, Vol. 25, No. 4, Fall 1985, 7–24. Reprinted by permission of Sage Publications, Inc.

not seen as having made significant scientific contributions to the field of knowledge in psychology. So we are perceived as having relatively little importance.

On the other hand, humanistic psychology has had a tremendous impact on our culture through its emphasis on experiential learning and experiential knowledge. Through intensive groups, through differing forms of psychotherapy, through a variety of means of learning, through self-expression, experiential learning has changed the lives of thousands, if not millions, of people. Our culture is very different because of humanistic psychology. One has only to visit countries unfamiliar with this development to discover the hunger for such interpersonal communication and experiential learning that exists in those who have not had the opportunities we have had.

It should be recognized, however, that experiential knowledge, no matter how valuable, cannot be communicated directly. We can communicate *about* it, or we can create the conditions that facilitate it, but it cannot be communicated directly. Consequently, it has not become a part of the mainstream of psychological knowledge. Also, academic psychologists are generally fearful of any personal involvement that might bring about change in them. They are threatened by events that involve experiential learning and tend to avoid them.

Why is it that humanistic psychologists have not been noted for activities that would lead to the discovery and development of new cognitive and scientific knowledge in the psychological realm? I believe they have been held back by a number of factors.

In the first place, they do not find the operationalism — based in logical positivism — of the conventional science in which they were trained particularly suitable for or congenial to the study of the human condition. This is not to say that it cannot be used constructively. Reinhard and Anne-Marie Tausch (Tausch, 1978) and their students in West Germany, for example, have contributed notably, using modifications of a conventional research approach. Likewise David Aspy and Flora Roebuck (Aspy and Roebuck, 1983) have made remarkable contributions in the field of humanistic education, also using a conventional approach. In both cases hypotheses of humanistic psychology, and especially hypotheses of a person-centered approach, have been tested and significantly confirmed. So the conventional methods are not to be thrown out, but they are often inappropriate for questions we wish to study.

Another factor in this picture is that humanistic psychologists tend to go into clinical practice or service occupations rather than into faculty positions in major universities. Because of this, there are not many graduate students who are doing their work under the guidance of humanistically oriented faculty members, and graduate students are the primary source of all research. These factors combined explain why humanistic psychology has had a minimal influence on psychology as it exists in our educational institutions.

The Need for a New Science

I have been one of those who, over the past several decades, have pointed out the need for new models of science more appropriate to human beings. In the early 1950s (published later), I wrote,

> There is a rather widespread feeling in our group that the logical positivism in which we were professionally reared is not necessarily the final philosophical word in an area in which the phenomenon of subjectivity plays such a vital and central part. . . . Is there some view, possibly developing out of an existentialist orientation, which might . . . find more room for the existing subjective person . . . ? This is a highly speculative dream of an intangible goal. (Rogers, 1959, p. 251)

Later, Maslow and I and others spoke in much stronger terms, challenging the traditional view (Maslow, 1966; Rogers, 1964, 1968). But we felt like David challenging Goliath — a small voice of protest against a massive and solid system.

But the world of thought has been changing. There are new developments in the philosophy of science, spearheaded perhaps by Michael Polanyi (1958). There are new developments in theoretical physics that make for a different view of the cosmos and a new understanding of the limitations of science.

New Models

As I have been looking into this whole matter, I have been most pleasantly surprised. I find that in recent years there has been a burgeoning of books and articles that, without apology, develop and present new models of science that are much more appropriate to a human science. I wish to mention a few of these because they deserve to be more widely known.

There is, first of all, a most comprehensive article by Manicas and Secord (1983), which makes it clear that the straitjacket of logical empiricism no longer constrains us. They observe that "in recent decades a virtual Copernican Revolution has taken place in the philosophy of science" (p. 399). They maintain, among other things, that only in the laboratory can we even approach closure or certainty. In the life experiences and behaviors that psychologists, especially humanistic psychologists, wish to investigate there will necessarily be varying degrees of imprecision in the knowledge we gain. They also point out that "to understand a person we must grasp the person's meanings and understandings . . . motivations and intentions" (p. 409), a clear indication that we must see the person from within and recognize that this is a person with choice and will.

I would also like to speak of a book, *Human Inquiry: A Sourcebook of New Paradigm Research*, edited by two British psychologists, Reason and Rowan, and published in 1981. It is an excellent collection of papers exploring the philosophical and methodological aspects of the new alternative scientific models. It is a gold mine for anyone undertaking this new type of research.

Then there is the recent book by Polkinghorne, *Methodology for Human Sciences: Systems of Inquiry* (1983). This is a very thorough, scholarly book which traces the history of the debate, points out the reasons for the decline of logical positivism, and describes many new alternative modes of research. One of the book's concluding sentences gives a sense of its general tone: "What is called for is getting on with the development of a science without certainty, that deepens our understanding of human existence." All of these alternative methods provide new knowledge, some findings being better and more reliable than others, yet all of them contributing to our understanding of the person.

A somewhat earlier book, by Michael Q. Patton, *Utilization-Focused Evaluation* (1978), is another valuable guide for researchers. Perhaps particularly pertinent is Chapter 10 of this volume, "The Methodology Dragon: Alternative Paradigms of Evaluation Measurement and Design." Patton gives an excellent and persuasive presentation of new paradigms, new alternatives in doing research. He also has a later book, *Qualitative Evaluation Methods* (1980), which is a more specific manual of useful methods.

Still another book, by Matthew Miles and A. M. Huberman, is well described by its title: *Qualitative Data Analysis: A Sourcebook of New Methods* (1984). The theory of phenomenological research is brought up to date, and a number of research studies using such methodology are presented in a recent volume edited by Giorgi (1984).

Very recently, Douglass and Moustakas (1985) make a persuasive case for heuristic research. Heuristics is presented as a philosophical and conceptual orientation out of which grows a special type of inquiry. While close to a phenomenological approach, a heuristic search is characterized as a passionate, highly personal, self-searching commitment to inner truth. It has its own criteria and its own process. It is, in my judgment, a disciplined but intuitive search that explores, by every possible subjective means, the essence of personal experience, thus generating personal truth that may later be further tested by some of the means already described.

Finally, I will mention a difficult book by Bleicher on contemporary hermeneutics (1980), if only because it gives me the opportunity to bring in a word that is being more and more used. My understanding of hermeneutics is that it grew out of the effort to improve the interpretation of ancient or sacred writings and texts. Its central point is that, for a proper interpretation of such ancient material, one must immerse oneself in the history of the time, the customs, the values, the beliefs, the symbols, the ways of expressing meaning. Then the text can speak to us in its own terms. The interpretation will be closer to the author's meaning at the time. Hermeneutics has become more complex and sophisticated, but it is well to be aware of its origin. It is another of the new methodologies.

It is interesting that there is a parallel to these new developments in science appearing in mathematics and computer science. As computers deal with real-life human problems, they find that imperfections must be accepted. The title of a recent article in *Discover* gives an amusing thumbnail sketch of this new way of mathematical thinking. The title is "Fuzzy Means to Logical Ends: Can Precision Be a Vice and Vagueness a Virtue? Yes, say a new breed of logicians whose way of thinking is anything but Aristotelian" (McKean and Dworetsky, 1985). As computers are used more and more in all research, this different mathematical logic may be found useful in fields in which we are interested.

Some Common Elements

As I surveyed these books and similar materials, I began to sense that they had certain themes in common, certain statements they were all making in somewhat different ways.

It was the first of these that I found most astonishing. It might be summarized by saying, "The debate is over!" What I mean by this is that the authors no longer feel the need to argue the case between the long-held orthodox view of psychological science and the new broader view. The Newtonian, mechanistic, reductionistic, linear cause-effect, behaviorist view of science is not thrown out but it is seen as simply one aspect of science, a perfectly good way of investigating certain questions, but decidedly inappropriate for others. The conventional view of science no longer reigns supreme.

A second element that runs through these volumes is that there is no longer the illusion that we can gain *certain* knowledge. Instead, by a variety of means and methods, we can gain new knowledge and this new knowledge has a degree of truth value that depends on the methods and circumstances of the particular research study. It is refreshing to find that we need to use our judgment to discriminate between those findings and conclusions that have a high degree of validity and those that have a lesser degree of validity. There is a full recognition that we will never have certain knowledge.

A further point of agreement is that there is no one method that is best. The methodology chosen must be appropriate to the question being asked. This is very important, because, if taken seriously, it will prevent new rigidities from developing. Phenomenological studies, for example, are an excellent way of investigating certain issues, but phenomenological methods are not *the* best tool of research, but simply one tool appropriate to some kinds of situations.

An important characteristic that further links all these new methodologies could be described by Polanyi's term "indwelling" (1958). The scientist develops a mode of indwelling in the perceptions, or the attitudes, or the feelings, or the experience, or the behaviors of the participant. The knowledge gained from this deep empathic indwelling can then be organized in logical and meaningful fashion, so as to yield new discoveries, new approximations to the truth.

Another point of similarity in most of these writings is that there are no longer "subjects" of research, but "coresearchers," "research partners," "participants." Mearns and McLeod (1984) carry this to an extreme. In their paper they advocate having these research partners involved in every step of the study — the planning, the data gathering, the analysis, the interpretation, the conclusions. They make psychological science a cooperative enterprise in which everything is aboveboard, a participatory endeavor.

A Fantasy

Perhaps I can best illustrate the difference between the conventional view of psychological science and this modern view by a fantasy sequence I have had about Piaget.

Suppose that Piaget approached a psychology department a decade ago (or even today in many departments) with his plan. He says,

> I am a candidate for a doctoral degree. I hope to make a contribution to psychological knowledge. I hope you will award me a doctor's degree when I have carried through my plan. I propose to observe children deeply and carefully, especially my two daughters, over a period of several years. By such careful observation, I hope to gain an understanding of the inner workings of the child's mind. I expect to discover some of the ways in which children reason, the ways in which cognition and conceptualization develop. I believe I may learn much more than we now know about the development of thought processes. I believe that meanings will emerge from my collected observations which will have real significance.

The faculty members consider this. They tell him,

> You have no theory from which to draw hypotheses. You have
> no hypothesis for your study. You have no research design. You
> have no control group. You have an N of two, which is totally
> unsuitable for statistical manipulation. Your so-called research is
> completely unacceptable for a doctor's degree. Your candidacy is
> rejected.

Now let us suppose that Piaget approaches any one of several
humanistically oriented universities that have come to understand the new view of science. He presents his hopes and his
plan in the same way. The faculty members consider what he
has said. Then they say to him: "We have several important
questions we want you to consider very seriously. We will list
them."

> Can you approach these children with a well-informed mind, but
> an open mind? By this we mean, can you be well acquainted with
> the previous studies and the literature in the field and yet hold
> this knowledge in abeyance so that you can make your observa-
> tions with minimal bias?

> Can you so immerse yourself in the child's life that you see as the
> child sees, feel as the child feels, think as the child thinks, ex-
> perience as the child experiences? In short, can you, as an adult,
> let yourself sense the child's world, indwell in it, without losing
> the ability to withdraw into your adult world, in order to make
> observations about the child's experience?

> Can you immerse yourself in all the observations you have col-
> lected, live with them until patterns begin to emerge, themes and
> concepts begin to be evident? Can you do this without coming to
> premature conclusions, without imposing on the data the pattern
> of some previous study?

> Can you articulate the patterns that you have discovered, the
> learnings that have impressed themselves on you, and set them
> forth clearly in organized form?

> If, as you make your study, you can give a positive answer to each
> one of these questions, we believe that you will make a significant
> contribution to psychological knowledge, a contribution that is
> worthy of a doctoral degree.

Some Examples

Thus far I have spoken of the differing methodologies available, but I have not named them. I wish to remedy that deficiency by giving a number of examples — from the past and present — illustrating some of the models that have been used. These are in no particular order, as I wish to emphasize that the method must fit the question.

Many years ago Adrian van Kaam made what I think of as a classical phenomenological investigation. He studied the experience of "really feeling understood." He gathered written descriptions of the experience from 365 high school and college students. Three researchers, working independently, studied the data and the themes that emerged. The findings were based on a consensus of the three. Nine elements were experienced by an overwhelming majority, including feeling good, experiencing relief from loneliness, and feeling oneself safe in a communicative relationship. Van Kaam points out that this study is replicable, which is not true of all the studies I will cite. This research is published (Van Kaam, 1959), unlike the more recent ones to follow.

Colleen McNally used her own experience and that of others to investigate the experience of "really feeling sensitive." Through a process of "immersion, incubation, illumination, explication, and creative synthesis," she was able to analyze and describe the two main aspects of the experience — being open and being touched. She considers her study to be based on a phenomenological-existential model (McNally, n.d.).

Marcine Johnson (1980) hypothesized that the level of discontent (based on Maslow's hierarchy of needs) would rise as one result of psychotherapy. As lower-level needs were satisfied, the person might still be discontent, because higher-level needs are not fulfilled. Using Q-technique, she developed an instrument measuring levels of discontent. Thirty women sorted the items before and after brief, "effective" psychotherapy. The hypothesis was upheld. There was more high-level discontent at the conclusion of therapy. The implications of this study for psychotherapy research are profound. A client may have changed significantly and still be as dissatisfied as at the beginning of therapy, but the nature of that dissatisfaction needs to be evaluated. "I'm not realizing all my potential" is quite different from "I can't stand my job." The method used by Johnson could be classed as using a structured phenomenological instrument.*

Debora Brink (1968), in a study made before these new models of science had been clearly presented, combined a phenomenological approach with a simple statistical analysis to investigate the concept of meaningfulness. Graduate students — forty-five in psychology, forty-five in physics — were asked to describe intellectual experiences that had been highly meaningful for them, and to explain the factors that accounted for their personal meaningfulness. Fifty-eight such factors were found, and the groups were compared. There was much similarity, but interesting differences. For psychologists the experience was significant when it involved such factors as increased self-awareness, or helping others in face-to-face contact. For physicists it was when the experience related to finding ultimate answers, or when it revealed an underlying simplicity. A most interesting difference was that for physicists the experience might be significant when it allowed for a playful approach or was aesthetically pleasing. Psychologists did not mention playfulness or the aesthetic quality.

It is obvious that an important aspect of life — the meaningfulness of experience — cannot possibly be adequately studied by conventional empirical methods. The approach must be from within.

Sara Wolinsky (n.d.) studied the behavior of a fourteen-year-

---

*It would seem that structured instruments, which give an objective picture of the individual's perceptions, should be revived and more widely used. The Q-technique (Stephenson, 1953) is one of these. Its usefulness in illuminating the changes in the perceived self and the desired self during and after therapy is clearly shown in an earlier research (Rogers and Dymond, 1954). It could be used for many other purposes as well, and a computer program could almost eliminate the tedious aspects of the computations.

Another such instrument is the Relationship Inventory of Barrett-Lennard (1962, 1978). It has been used in scores of researches, studying the facilitative conditions involved in therapist-client relationships, teacher-pupil, spouse-spouse. The findings have shed light on the degree to which the quality of the relationship affects other variables. It is a most useful instrument for measuring one person's perception of the extent to which growthful qualities are present in his or her relationship to another.

old boy who had learning difficulties and was in special education. Eight observers, rotating in shifts, recorded forty variables of social action. Analysis showed the social actions occurred in six directions and could be classified as harmonious or disharmonious. The study showed that differing factors in different environments brought out very different styles of behavior — emotionally disordered, intellectually precocious, and normal. The study has many implications for those involved in special education. The methodology could be classed as intense observation, and as a single case study.

Kathleen Lisowski (1980) was able to communicate with deaf people through sign language, so she spent eleven months observing and interviewing twelve older adults who were profoundly deaf. Her findings threw new light on the personality and coping mechanisms of the deaf. Her methodologies would be categorized as participant observation and in-depth interviewing.

Sally Wood (1981) studied the transformation of a man and a woman from being a couple to being a family. For a period of three months, beginning one month before the birth of their first child, she spent six hours a week observing them as they went about their daily lives — at home, at work, and elsewhere. She recorded her observations, transcribed and studied them, to understand the process of change. She analyzed her material, describing five phases: anticipation, passage, absorption, adaptation, and synthesis. She suggests that the period of absorption following the birth, with its sleeplessness, disorientation, and disruptiveness, may actually speed the transition to parenthood. Clearly, this is a study based on naturalist observation. Piaget would be the outstanding example of this method.

Suzanne Shaw (1979) focused on a medical school to determine whether a week-long encounter group retreat, including students, faculty, administrators, and support staff, had any significant impact. Two years after the intensive experience, she interviewed sixty-five participants and some thirty who had chosen not to participate. The interviews were transcribed (an enormous task) and she read and reread the material, seeking the themes and categories that emerged. She had three colleagues spot-check this analysis for its validity.

In spite of the fact that the group program was flawed in its implementation and that the school was administratively chaotic during the two years following, the program was found to have had a major impact. Of the participants, 60 percent reported positive interpersonal changes, compared with 20 percent of the nonparticipants. The greatest change occurred in family relationships, followed by closer relations of faculty to students, students to faculty. Peer relationships also were improved, in both faculty and students. But there followed little or no change in organizational policy or structure. The administrators reported interpersonal changes, but the experience did not seem to affect their organizational behavior.

I was close to this study, and remember how difficult it was for Dr. Shaw to find writings that would justify her use of a phenomenological approach. Now a flood of books and articles could be cited.

To indicate the range of research being done, let me list a few more, by title only: "The Meaning of Being Ill" (Mann, 1980); "The Heroin Experience — Users' Recollections of Heroin's Attractive Effects" (Dichner, 1983); "Moments of Meeting: A Study of Dialogic Meeting Between Adult and Child" (Oppenheimer, 1982); "Psychological Dimensions of Mystery" (Varani, n.d.); "A Heuristic Study of Solitude" (Brechenser, 1983); "Themes in the Lives of Well Siblings of Schizophrenics" (Chase, 1983).

Why have I presented so many examples? It is because I wish to point up the variety and richness of topics being studied, questions that could not possibly be dealt with by conventional psychological science. Here are graduate student researchers thinking creatively about questions of personal and professional importance. It is heartening to note that they are not confined to a single methodology, but choose appropriate methods, freely combining methods to obtain further insights.

I also wish to point to the exciting new body of knowledge to which they are contributing — knowledge quite different in kind from that found in most psychological journals.

The Issue of Publication

It is encouraging to know that we now have ample presentations, from different points of view, of new models of science that are appropriate to the study of human beings in all their complexity. It is also encouraging to realize that research is being done utilizing these new models. So then, our problem is solved. Right? Wrong! I have examined abstracts of two master's theses and nearly a score of doctoral dissertations that have been selected and recommended to me because they were using these new methodologies. I find no evidence that any one of these has been published or is even on its way to publication. (I don't, of course, mean publication of the whole dissertation, but an article based on the dissertation.)

I am puzzled by this lack of publication, because a number of these seem worthy of presentation to the professional public. Is it that we still doubt the worth of such studies, feeling that they are somehow inferior to research based on statistical analysis? I feel it is most unfortunate that these investigations simply sit in their institutional files without being known to our profession. Instead of "Publish or perish," our slogan should be "Don't hide your light under a bushel!"

Can We Strengthen Humanistic Universities?

I have other suggestions to make. It is unlikely that conventional universities will be quick to adopt these new paradigms and methodologies for scientific research. Consequently, if they are to flourish, they will need to be fostered and encouraged in the institutions that already have a humanistic orientation. For the most part, these are institutions with programs of independent study. Ones with which I am most familiar are Union Graduate School, which is now fully accredited, Saybrook Institute, Fielding Institute, the Center for Humanistic Studies in Detroit, Walden University in Florida, and Duquesne University in Pittsburgh. There may well be others. These institutions now have solid records of achievement and have shown they maintain high standards. It would be highly desirable that they be more adequately funded. Whether donors will be willing to make large donations to institutions that are invested primarily in the process of learning rather than in buildings and laboratories is a question that only time can answer. It is a challenge to be faced. It is to be hoped that better opportunities and better salaries can be offered for faculty members so that these institutions can more successfully compete with private practice. Modest grants to students to support their research activities would be highly desirable.

Student Interaction

The independent study program leading to the doctorate has one major weakness. It is that graduate students have very little opportunity to educate one another. In the graduate programs of the conventional university, the dialogues and interaction among the students, both in and out of seminars, is one of the primary means for stimulating thinking and testing out ideas. In independent study programs this kind of interaction is limited to brief colloquia in which students and faculty meet together for a relatively short period of time. Yet perhaps even this obstacle can be overcome.

In this modern computer age it is not too much to suggest that each student have access to a computer and to significant computer terminals. A program can be set up whereby they can quickly and easily engage in conversation and dialogue — student to faculty, student to student, and student to outside resource persons, as well as student to library and other facilities. This would vastly improve the speed and the depth of communication and learning. This is not an idle dream. Fielding Institute developed such a plan and came very close to putting it into effect this past year. Western Behavioral Sciences Institute in La Jolla has such a plan in action, although the members of the group are not graduate students, but business executives embarked on a program of leadership training. It has been their experience that these dialogues become very significant, stimulating learning and leading to personal bonds of closeness.

Such a computer network would be initially costly, but it seems likely that in the long run it would be worthwhile. Certainly, the experiment is worth a trial.

A Shift of Focus

It is clear that the basic elements are already present that would permit a much-increased productive flow of new and human investigations. We need to sharpen our vision of what is possible and to shift some of the intensity of our interest from service to that most fascinating of all enterprises — the unearthing, the discovery, the pursuit of significant new knowledge. There seems no doubt that we can cast new light on the living human person and how he or she functions and grows and changes.

To help bring about this shift, we need to revamp our reward system so that it will be as rewarding to teach and inspire and supervise graduate students as to carry on private practice or a consulting service. It is very important that we make this shift if humanistic psychology is to be a viable part of the ongoing stream of psychology today.

To some extent, this change is already under way. One of the most exciting and encouraging aspects of my work on this paper has been to discover that graduate students are turning out research based on new scientific models. They are using methods that enable them to study and explore aspects of human thought, feeling, and behavior that simply could not be investigated by an operationalist methodology.

It is most gratifying to see in the researches I have described, and in others that I have examined, that these new methodologies are having just the effects that I hoped for so many years ago. It is clear that creative thinking has been released, that much of this research is based on an indwelling in the reality of each participant, and that the researchers are personally committed to their studies in a way that can only increase the dignity of all involved.

It is pleasant to live long enough to see some dreams coming true, thanks to the dedicated efforts of others who are younger.

REFERENCES

Aspy, D., and Roebuck, F. N. (1983). Researching person-centered issues in education. In C. R. Rogers (Ed.), *Freedom to learn for the '80's*. Columbus, OH: Charles Merrill.

Barrett-Lennard, G. T. (1962). Dimensions of therapist response as causal factors in therapeutic change. *Psychological Monographs, 76* (43, 562).

Barrett-Lennard, G. T. (1978). *The relationship inventory: Later developments and adaptations*. West Perth, Australia: Centre for Studies in Human Relations.

Bleicher, J. (1980). *Contemporary hermeneutics: Hermeneutics as method, philosophy, and critique*. London: Routledge & Kegan Paul.

Brechenser, D. M. (1983). *A heuristic study of solitude.* Unpublished Ph.D. dissertation, Saybrook Institute.

Brink, D. C. (1968). *The characteristics of personally meaningful intellectual experience.* Unpublished Ph.D. dissertation, Columbia University.

Chase, L. P. (1983). *Themes in the lives of well siblings of schizophrenics.* Unpublished Ph.D. dissertation, Saybrook Institute.

Dichner, M. D. (1983). *The heroin experience: Users' recollections of heroin's attractive effects.* Unpublished Ph.D. dissertation, Saybrook Institute.

Douglass, B. G., and Moustakas, C. (1985). Heuristic inquiry: The internal search to know. *Journal of Humanistic Psychology,* 25 (3).

Giorgi, A. (Ed.). (1984). *Phenomenology and psychological research.* Pittsburgh: Duquesne University Press.

Johnson, M. M. (1980). *Psychotherapy as a precipitant of high level discontent.* Unpublished Ph.D. dissertation, Saybrook Institute.

Lisowski, K. (1980). *A naturalistic study of the experience of living as a deaf person.* Unpublished Ph.D. dissertation, Saybrook Institute.

Manicas, P. T., and Secord, P. F. (1983). Implications for psychology of the new philosophy of science. *American Psychologist,* 38, 399–413.

Mann, S. (1980). *The meaning of being ill.* Unpublished Ph.D. dissertation, Saybrook Institute.

Maslow, A. (1966). *The psychology of science: A reconnaissance.* South Bend, IN: Gateway Editions.

McKean, and Dworetzky, T. (1985). Fuzzy means to logical ends. *Discover,* 6 (2), 70–73.

McNally, C. (n.d.). *The experience of being sensitive.* Unpublished Ph.D. dissertation, Union Graduate School.

Mearns, D. J., and McLeod, J. (1984). A person-centered approach to research. In R. F. Levant and J. Shlien (Eds.), *Client-centered therapy and the person-centered approach: New directions in theory, research and practice* (pp. 370–389). New York: Praeger.

Miles, M. B., and Huberman, A. M. (1984). *Qualitative data analysis: A sourcebook of new methods.* Beverly Hills, CA: Sage.

Oppenheimer, R. (1982). *Moments of meeting: A study of dialogic meeting between adult and child.* Unpublished master's thesis, Center for Humanistic Studies.

Patton, M. Q. (1978). *Utilization-focused evaluation.* Beverly Hills, CA: Sage.

Patton, M. Q. (1980). *Qualitative evaluation methods.* Beverly Hills, CA: Sage.

Polanyi, M. (1958). *Personal knowledge.* Chicago: University of Chicago Press.

Polkinghorne, D. (1983). *Methodology for human sciences: Systems of inquiry.* Albany: State University of New York Press.

Reason, P., and Rowan, J. (Eds.). (1981). *Human inquiry: A sourcebook of new paradigm research.* New York: John Wiley.

Rogers, C. R. (1959). A theory of therapy, personality, and interpersonal relationships as developed in the client-centered framework. In S. Koch (Ed.), *Psychology: A study of a science, Vol. III* (pp. 184–256). New York: McGraw-Hill.

Rogers, C. R. (1964). Toward a science of the person. In T. W. Wann (Ed.), *Behaviorism and phenomenology: Contrasting bases for modern psychology.* Chicago: University of Chicago Press.

Rogers, C. R. (1968). Some thoughts regarding the current assumptions of the behavioral sciences. In W. Coulson & C. R. Rogers (Eds.), *Man and the science of man.* Columbus, OH: Charles Merrill.

Rogers, C. R., and Dymond, R. F. (Eds.). (1954). *Psychotherapy and personality change.* Chicago: University of Chicago Press.

Shaw, S. (1979). *Human dimensions in medical education as a change intervention at Eastern Virginia Medical School: A phenomenological approach to the study of change.* Unpublished Ph.D. dissertation, Fielding Institute.

Stephenson, W. (1953). *The study of behavior: Q-technique and its methodology.* Chicago: University of Chicago Press.

Tausch, R. (1978). Facilitative dimensions in interpersonal relations: Verifying the theoretical assumptions of Carl Rogers in school, family education, client-centered therapy and encounter groups. *College Student Journal, 12*, 2–11.

Van Kaam, A. L. (1959). Phenomenal analysis: Exemplified by a study of the experience of "really feeling understood." *Journal of Individual Psychology, 15*, 66–72.

Varani, J. (n.d.). *Psychological dimensions of mystery: A phenomenological-heuristic investigation.* Unpublished Ph.D. dissertation, Union Graduate School.

Wolinsky, S. (1983). *An observational study of an atypical learner in special education.* Unpublished Ph.D. dissertation, Saybrook Institute.

Wood, S. M. (1981). *Family transformation: A naturalistic study of the arrival of the first child.* Unpublished Ph.D. dissertation, Saybrook Institute.

EDUCATION

After twenty years in various college, university, and other educational settings, by the late forties Rogers had developed his own, unique style of teaching. Not surprisingly, that style was a natural outgrowth of his nondirective counseling method. This parallel occurred throughout his career, with his evolving views on teaching mirroring his growing understanding of the therapeutic process.

In "Personal Thoughts on Teaching and Learning," one of his shortest and most famous essays, Rogers states his nondirective teaching philosophy. It was first presented in 1952, at Harvard, as part of a demonstration session on "Classroom Approaches to Influencing Human Behavior." It was his goal to present a short, provocative statement and then to facilitate the lively discussion he hoped would follow. It was the demonstration of the student-centered discussion method that was most important to him, rather than his own brief comments.

While his remarks did, indeed, spark a heated and meaningful discussion, his brief paper also had a lasting impact on the participants. Though Rogers did not attempt to have it published ("My views on psychotherapy had already made me a 'controversial figure' among psychologists and psychiatrists. I had no desire to add educators to the list"), his paper was widely circulated until it was finally published in 1957. Since then, it has become one of his most frequently reprinted essays.

As he came to understand that the therapist's facilitative attitudes were more important than the particular method he employed, Rogers also began to recognize that it was the same facilitative attitudes of the teacher that were most effective in producing significant, independent learning by the student. And as he recognized that the person-to-person *relationship* in therapy resulted from the successful implementation of those facilitative attitudes, he saw a comparable relationship develop in the classroom. "The Interpersonal Relationship in the Facilitation of Learning" illustrates Rogers's later thinking on the teaching process, or as he would say, the *learning* process. It was first published in 1967 in *Humanizing Education,* one of the popular annual yearbooks of the influential Association for Supervision and Curriculum Development, and later reprinted in Rogers's own book on education, *Freedom to Learn* (1969).

In the 1970s Rogers began to understand and explore the wider political implications of his person-centered framework. He saw how systemwide educational change was resisted, even when some individual teachers began altering instructional practices in their own classrooms, because student-centered teaching, like client-centered therapy, transfers power from the teacher to the student, from the professional to the client. Any transfer of power in one part of the system has reverberations throughout the system. So Rogers began exploring the political implications of his views, as in "The Politics of Education," included here.

He did more than explore the politics of education. In several major experiments in the seventies, he and his colleagues attempted to change entire educational systems, such as the Louisville, Kentucky, public schools and Immaculate Heart College. Using primarily the encounter group technique (see following section), the Rogers group immersed faculty and administrators in often powerful group-centered learning experiences. Many of these professionals, in turn, took the student-centered methods back to their own classrooms and department meetings. While significant short-run changes took place throughout these systems amidst great tumult and controversy, long-term educational improvement was difficult to document.

Whether the problem was that large educational systems are simply too resistant to redistributing power between staff and students or whether it was the shortcomings in Rogers's own approach to systemwide change, or some of both, is a question that only future experiments in large-scale educational change will clarify.

20

Personal Thoughts on Teaching and Learning

I wish to present some very brief remarks, in the hope that if they bring forth any reaction from you, I may get some new light on my own ideas.

I find it a very troubling thing to *think*, particularly when I think about my own experiences and try to extract from those experiences the meaning that seems genuinely inherent in them. At first, such thinking is very satisfying, because it seems to discover sense and pattern in a whole host of discrete events. But then it very often becomes dismaying, because I realize how ridiculous these thoughts, which have so much value to me, would seem to most people. My impression is that if I try to find the meaning of my own experience it leads me, nearly always, in directions regarded as absurd.

So in the next few minutes, I will try to digest some of the meanings which have come to me from my classroom experience and the experience I have had in individual therapy and group experience. They are in no way intended as conclusions for someone else, or a guide to what others should do or be. They are the very tentative meanings, as of April 1952, which my experience has had for me, and some of the bothersome questions which their absurdity raises. I will put each idea or meaning in a separate lettered paragraph, not because they are in any particular logical order, but because each meaning is separately important to me.

a. I may as well start with this one in view of the purposes of this conference. *My experience has been that I cannot teach another person how to teach.* To attempt it is for me, in the long run, futile.

Merrill-Palmer Quarterly, Vol. 3, Summer 1957, 241–243. Reprinted by permission of Wayne State University Press.

b. *It seems to me that anything that can be taught to another is relatively inconsequential and has little or no significant influence on behavior.* That sounds so ridiculous I can't help but question it at the same time that I present it.

c. *I realize increasingly that I am only interested in learnings which significantly influence behavior.* Quite possibly this is simply a personal idiosyncrasy.

d. *I have come to feel that the only learning which significantly influences behavior is self-discovered, self-appropriated learning.*

e. *Such self-discovered learning, truth that has been personally appropriated and assimilated in experience, cannot be directly communicated to another.* As soon as an individual tries to communicate such experience directly, often with a quite natural enthusiasm, it becomes teaching, and its results are inconsequential. It was some relief recently to discover that Søren Kierkegaard, the Danish philosopher, had found this too, in his own experience, and stated it very clearly a century ago. It made it seem less absurd.

f. As a consequence of the above, *I realize that I have lost interest in being a teacher.*

g. When I try to teach, as I do sometimes, I am appalled by the results, which seem a little more than inconsequential, because sometimes the teaching appears to succeed. When this happens I find that the results are damaging. It seems to cause the individual to distrust his own experience, and to stifle significant learning. *Hence I have come to feel that the outcomes of teaching are either unimportant or hurtful.*

h. When I look back at the results of my past teaching, the real results seem the same — either damage was done — or nothing significant occurred. This is frankly troubling.

i. As a consequence, *I realize that I am only interested in being a learner, preferably learning things that matter, that have some significant influence on my own behavior.*

j. *I find it very rewarding to learn,* in groups, in relationships with one person as in therapy, or by myself.

k. *I find that one of the best, but most difficult, ways for me to learn is to drop my own defensiveness, at least temporarily, and to try to understand the way in which his experience seems and feels to the other person.*

l. I find that another way of learning for me is to state my own uncertainties, to try to clarify my puzzlements, and thus get closer to the meaning that my experience actually seems to have.

m. This whole train of experiencing, and the meanings that I have thus far discovered in it, seem to have launched me on a process which is both fascinating and at times a little frightening. *It seems to mean letting my experiences carry me on, in a direction which appears to be forward, toward goals that I can but dimly define, as I try to understand at least the current meaning of that experience.* The sensation is that of floating with a complex stream of experience, with the fascinating possibility of trying to comprehend its ever-changing complexity.

I am almost afraid I may seem to have gotten away from any discussion of learning, as well as teaching. Let me again introduce a practical note by saying that by themselves these interpretations of my experience may sound queer and aberrant, but not particularly shocking. It is when I realize the *implications* that I shudder a bit at the distance I have come from the commonsense world that everyone knows is right. I can best illustrate this by saying that if the experiences of others had been the same as mine, and if they had discovered similar meanings in it, many consequences would be implied:

a. Such experience would imply that we would do away with teaching. People would get together if they wished to learn.
b. We would do away with examinations. They measure only the inconsequential type of learning.
c. We would do away with grades and credits for the same reason.
d. We would do away with degrees as a measure of competence partly for the same reason. Another reason is that a degree marks an end or a conclusion of something, and a learner is only interested in the continuing process of learning.
e. We would do away with the exposition of conclusions, for we would realize that no one learns significantly from conclusions.

I think I had better stop there. I do not want to become too fantastic. I want to know primarily whether anything in my inward thinking, as I have tried to describe it, speaks to anything in your experience of the classroom as you have lived it, and if so, what the meanings are that exist for you in *your* experience.

21

The Interpersonal Relationship in the Facilitation of Learning

We are, in my view, faced with an entirely new situation in education where the goal of education, if we are to survive, is the *facilitation of change and learning*. The only man who is educated is the man who has learned how to learn; the man who has learned how to adapt and change; the man who has realized that no knowledge is secure, that only the process of *seeking* knowledge gives a basis for security. Changingness, a reliance on *process* rather than upon static knowledge, is the only thing that makes any sense as a goal for education in the modern world.

So now with some relief I turn to an activity, a purpose, which really warms me—the facilitation of learning. When I have been able to transform a group—and here I mean all the members of a group, myself included—into a community of *learners*, then the excitement has been almost beyond belief. To free curiosity; to permit individuals to go charging off in new directions dictated by their own interests; to unleash the sense of inquiry; to open everything to questioning and exploration; to recognize that everything is in process of change—here is an experience I can never forget. I cannot always achieve it in groups with which I am associated, but when it is partially or largely achieved, then it becomes a never-to-be-forgotten group experience. Out of such a context arise true students, real learners, creative scientists and scholars, and practitioners, the kind of individuals who can live in a delicate but ever-changing balance between what is presently known and the flowing, moving, altering problems and facts of the future.

In Leeper, R. (Ed.), *Humanizing Education*. Alexandria, VA: Association for Supervision and Curriculum Development, 1967, 1–18.

Here then is a goal to which I can give myself wholeheartedly. I see *the facilitation of learning* as the *aim* of education, the way in which we might develop the learner, the way in which we can learn to live as individuals in process. I see the facilitation of learning as the function that may hold constructive, tentative, changing *process* answers to some of the deepest perplexities that beset humankind today.

But do we know how to achieve this new goal in education or is it a will-o'-the-wisp that sometimes occurs, sometimes fails to occur, and thus offers little real hope? My answer is that we possess a very considerable knowledge of the conditions that encourage self-initiated, significant, experiential, "gut-level" learning by the whole person. We do not frequently see these conditions put into effect because they mean a real revolution in our approach to education and revolutions are not for the timid. But we do, as we have seen in the preceding chapters, find examples of this revolution in action.

We know — and I will briefly mention some of the evidence — that the initiation of such learning rests not upon the teaching skills of the leader, not upon scholarly knowledge of the field, not upon curricular planning, not upon use of audiovisual aids, not upon the programmed learning used, not upon lectures and presentations, not upon an abundance of books, though each of these might at one time or another be utilized as an important resource. No, the facilitation of significant learning rests upon certain attitudinal qualities that exist in the personal *relationship* between the facilitator and the learner.

We came upon such findings first in the field of psychotherapy, but now there is evidence that shows these findings apply in the classroom as well. We find it easier to think that the intensive relationship between therapist and client might possess these qualities, but we are also finding that they *may* exist in the countless interpersonal interactions between the teacher and pupils.

QUALITIES THAT FACILITATE LEARNING

What are these qualities, these attitudes, that facilitate learning? Let me describe them very briefly, drawing illustrations from the teaching field.

Realness in the Facilitator of Learning

Perhaps the most basic of these essential attitudes is realness or genuineness. When the facilitator is a real person, being what she is, entering into a relationship with the learner without presenting a front or a façade, she is much more likely to be effective. This means that the feelings that she is experiencing are available to her, available to her awareness, that she is able to live these feelings, be them, and able to communicate them if appropriate. It means that she comes into a direct personal encounter with the learner, meeting her on a person-to-person basis. It means that she is *being* herself, not denying herself.

Seen from this point of view it is suggested that the teacher can be a real person in her relationship with her students. She can be enthusiastic, can be bored, can be interested in students, can be angry, can be sensitive and sympathetic. Because she accepts these feelings as her own, she has no need to impose them on her students. She can like or dislike a student product without implying that it is objectively good or bad or that the student is good or bad. She is simply expressing a feeling for the product, a feeling that exists within herself. Thus, she is a person to her students, not a faceless embodiment of a curricular requirement nor a sterile tube through which knowledge is passed from one generation to the next.

It is obvious that this attitudinal set, found to be effective in psychotherapy, is sharply in contrast with the tendency of most teachers to show themselves to their pupils simply as roles. It is quite customary for teachers rather consciously to put on the mask, the role, the façade of being a teacher and to wear this façade all day, removing it only when they have left the school at night.

But not all teachers are like this. Take Sylvia Ashton-Warner, who took resistant, supposedly slow-learning primary school Maori children in New Zealand, and let them develop their own reading vocabulary. Each child could request one word — whatever word he wished — each day, and she would print it on a card and give it to him. *Kiss, ghost, bomb, tiger, fight, love, daddy* — these are samples. Soon they were building sentences, which they could also keep. "He'll get a licking." "Pussy's frightened." The children simply never forgot these self-initiated learnings. But it is not my purpose to tell you of her methods. I want instead to give you a glimpse of her attitude, of the passionate realness that must have been as evident to her tiny pupils as to her readers. An editor asked her some questions, and she responded: "A few cool facts you asked me for. . . . I don't know that there's a cool fact in me, or anything else cool for that matter, on this particular subject. I've got only hot long facts on the matter of Creative Teaching, scorching both the page and me" (3, p. 26).

Here is no sterile façade. Here is a vital *person*, with convictions, with feelings. It is her transparent realness that was, I am sure, one of the elements that made her an exciting facilitator of learning. She doesn't fit into some neat educational formula. She *is*, and students grow by being in contact with someone who really and openly *is*.

Take another very different person, Barbara Shiel, whose exciting work in facilitating learning in sixth-graders has been described earlier. She gave her pupils a great deal of responsible freedom, and I will mention some of the reactions of her students later. But here is an example of the way she shared herself with her pupils — not just sharing feelings of sweetness and light, but anger and frustration. She had made art materials freely available, and students often used these in creative ways, but the room frequently looked like a picture of chaos. Here is a report of her feelings and what she did with them.

> I find it maddening to live with the mess — with a capital M! No one seems to care except me. Finally, one day I told the children . . . that I am a neat, orderly person by nature and that the mess was driving me to distraction. Did they have a solution? It was suggested there were some volunteers who could clean up. . . . I said it didn't seem fair to me to have the same people clean up all the time for others — but it would solve it for me. "Well, some people like to clean," they replied. So that's the way it is. (13)

I hope this example puts some lively meaning into the phrases I used earlier, that the facilitator "is able to live these feelings, be them, and able to communicate them if appropriate." I have chosen an example of negative feelings because I think it is more difficult for most of us to visualize what this would mean. In this instance, Miss Shiel is taking the risk of being transparent in her angry frustrations about the mess. And what happens? The same thing that, in my experience, nearly always happens. These young people accept and respect her feelings, take them into account, and work out a novel solution that none of us, I believe, would have suggested. Miss Shiel wisely comments, "I used to get upset and feel guilty when I became angry. I finally realized the children could accept *my* feelings too. And it is important for them to know when they've 'pushed' me. I have my limits, too" (13).

Just to show that positive feelings, when they are real, are equally effective, let me quote briefly a college student's reaction, in a different course:

> . . . Your sense of humor in the class was cheering; we all felt relaxed because you showed us your human self, not a mechanical teacher image. I feel as if I have more understanding and faith in my teachers now. I feel closer to the students too.

Another says:

> . . . You conducted the class on a personal level and therefore in my mind I was able to formulate a picture of you as a person and not as merely a walking textbook.

Another student in the same course:

> . . . It wasn't as if there was a teacher in the class, but rather someone whom we could trust and identify as a "sharer." You were so perceptive and sensitive to our thoughts, and this made it all the more "authentic" for me. It was an "authentic" *experience*, not just a class. (7)

I trust I am making it clear that to be real is not always easy, nor is it achieved all at once, but it is basic to the person who wants to become that revolutionary individual, a facilitator of learning.

Prizing, Acceptance, Trust

There is another attitude that stands out in those who are successful in facilitating learning. I have observed this attitude. I have experienced it. Yet, it is hard to know what term to put to it, so I shall use several. I think of it as prizing the learner, prizing her feelings, her opinions, her person. It is a caring for the learner, but a nonpossessive caring. It is an acceptance of this other individual as a separate person, having worth in her own right. It is a basic trust—a belief that this other person is somehow fundamentally trustworthy. Whether we call it prizing, acceptance, trust, or by some other term, it shows up in a variety of observable ways. The facilitator who has a considerable degree of this attitude can be fully acceptant of the fear and hesitation of the student as she approaches a new problem as well as acceptant of the pupil's satisfaction in achievement. Such a teacher can accept the student's occasional apathy, her erratic desires to explore byroads of knowledge, as well as her disciplined efforts to achieve major goals. She can accept personal feelings that both disturb and promote learning—rivalry with a sibling, hatred of authority, concern about personal adequacy. What we are describing is a prizing of the learner as an imperfect human being with many feelings, many potentialities. The facilitator's prizing or acceptance of the learner is an operational expression of her essential confidence and trust in the capacity of the human organism.

I would like to give some examples of this attitude from the classroom situation. Here any teacher statements would be properly suspect, since many of us would like to feel we hold such attitudes and might have a biased perception of our qualities. But let me indicate how this attitude of prizing, of accepting, of trusting appears to the student who is fortunate enough to experience it.

Here is a statement from a college student in a class with Dr. Morey Appell:

> Your way of being with us is a revelation to me. In your class I feel important, mature, and capable of doing things on my own. I want to think for myself and this need cannot be accomplished through textbooks and lectures alone, but through living. I think you see me as a person with real feelings and needs, an individual. What I say and do are significant expressions from me, and you recognize this. (1)

College students in a class with Dr. Patricia Bull describe not only these prizing, trusting attitudes, but the effect these have had on their other interactions.

> ... I still feel close to you, as though there were some tacit understanding between us, almost a conspiracy. This adds to the in-

class participation on my part because I feel that at least one person in the group will react, even when I am not sure of the others. It does not matter really whether your reaction is positive or negative, it just *IS*. Thank you.

. . . I appreciate the respect and concern you have for others, including myself. . . . As a result of my experience in class, plus the influence of my readings, I sincerely believe that the student-centered teaching method does provide an ideal framework for learning; not just for the accumulation of facts, but more important, for learning about ourselves in relation to others. . . . When I think back to my shallow awareness in September compared to the depth of my insights now, I know that this course has offered me a learning experience of great value which I couldn't have acquired in any other way.

. . . Very few teachers would attempt this method because they would feel that they would lose the students' respect. On the contrary. You gained our respect, through your ability to speak to us on our level, instead of ten miles above us. With the complete lack of communication we see in this school, it was a wonderful experience to see people listening to each other and really communicating on an adult, intelligent level. More classes should afford us this experience. (7)

I am sure these examples show that the facilitator who cares, who prizes, who trusts the learner creates a climate for learning so different from the ordinary classroom that any resemblance is purely coincidental.

Empathic Understanding
A further element that establishes a climate for self-initiated, experiential learning is empathic understanding. When the teacher has the ability to understand the student's reactions from the inside, has a sensitive awareness of the way the process of education and learning seems *to the student*, then again the likelihood of significant learning is increased.

This kind of understanding is sharply different from the usual evaluative understanding, which follows the pattern of "I understand what is wrong with you." When there is a sensitive empathy, however, the reaction in the learner follows something of this pattern: "At last someone understands how it feels and seems to be *me* without wanting to analyze me or judge me. Now I can blossom and grow and learn."

This attitude of standing in the other's shoes, of viewing the world through the student's eyes, is almost unheard of in the classroom. One could listen to thousands of ordinary classroom interactions without coming across one instance of clearly communicated, sensitively accurate, empathic understanding. But it has a tremendously releasing effect when it occurs.

Let me take an illustration from Virginia Axline, dealing with a second-grade boy. Jay, age seven, has been aggressive, a troublemaker, slow of speech and learning. Because of his "cussing," he was taken to the principal who paddled him, unknown to Miss Axline. During a free work period, Jay fashioned very carefully a man of clay down to a hat and a handkerchief in his pocket. "Who is that?" asked Miss Axline. "Dunno," replied Jay. "Maybe it is the principal. He has a handkerchief in his pocket like that." Jay glared at the clay figure. "Yes," he said. Then he began to tear the head off and looked up and smiled. Miss Axline said, "You sometimes feel like twisting his head off, don't you? You get so mad at him." Jay tore off one arm, another, then beat the figure to a pulp with his fists. Another boy, with the perception of the young, explained, "Jay is mad at Mr. X because he licked him this noon." "Then you must feel lots better now," Miss Axline commented. Jay grinned and began to rebuild Mr. X (5, pp. 521–533).

The other examples I have cited also indicate how deeply appreciative students feel when they are simply *understood* — not evaluated, not judged, simply understood from their *own* point of view, not the teacher's. If any teacher set herself the task of endeavoring to make one nonevaluative, acceptant, empathic response per day to a student's demonstrated or verbalized feeling, I believe she would discover the potency of this currently almost nonexistent kind of understanding.

WHAT ARE THE BASES OF FACILITATIVE ATTITUDES?

A "Puzzlement"

It is natural that we do not always have the attitudes I have been describing. Some teachers raise the question, "But what if I am *not* feeling empathic, do *not*, at this moment, prize or accept or like my students. What then?" My response is that realness is the most important of the attitudes mentioned, and it is not accidental that this attitude was described first. So if one has little understanding of the student's inner world and a dislike for the students or their behavior, it is almost certainly more constructive to be *real* than to be pseudoempathic or to put on a façade of caring.

But this is not nearly as simple as it sounds. To be genuine, or honest, or congruent, or real means to be this way about *oneself*. I cannot be real about another because I do not *know* what is real for him. I can only tell, if I wish to be truly honest, what is going on in me.

Let me take an example. Early in this chapter I reported Miss Shiel's feelings about the "mess" created by the art work. Essentially she said, "I find it maddening to live with the mess! I'm neat and orderly and it is driving me to distraction." But suppose her feelings had come out somewhat differently in the disguised way that is much more common in classrooms at all levels. She might have said, "You are the messiest children I've ever seen! You don't take care about tidiness or cleanliness. You are just terrible!" This is most definitely *not* an example of genuineness or realness, in the sense in which I am using these terms. There is a profound distinction between the two statements, which I should like to spell out.

In the second statement she is telling nothing of herself, sharing none of her feelings. Doubtless the children will *sense* that she is angry, but because children are perceptively shrewd, they may be uncertain as to whether she is angry at them or has just come from an argument with the principal. It has none of the honesty of the first statement in which she tells of her *own* upsetness, of her *own* feeling of being driven to distraction.

Another aspect of the second statement is that it is all made up of judgments or evaluations, and like most judgments, they are all arguable. Are these children messy, or are they simply excited and involved in what they are doing? Are they *all* messy, or are some as disturbed by the chaos as she? Do they care nothing about tidiness, or is it simply that they don't care about it every day? If a group of visitors were coming, would their attitude be different? Are they terrible, or simply children? I trust it is evident that when we make judgments, they are almost never fully accurate and hence cause resentment and anger as well as guilt and apprehension. Had she used the second statement, the response of the class would have been entirely different.

I am going to some lengths to clarify this point because I have found from experience that to stress the value of being real, of *being* one's feelings, is taken by some as a license to pass judgments on others, to project on others all the feelings that one should be "owning." Nothing could be further from my meaning.

Actually the achievement of realness is most difficult, and even when one wishes to be truly genuine, it occurs but rarely. Certainly it is not simply a matter of the *words* used, and if one is feeling judgmental, the use of a verbal formula that sounds like the sharing of feelings will not help. It is just another instance of a façade, of a lack of genuineness. Only slowly can we learn to be truly real. For first of all, one must be close to one's feelings, capable of being aware of them. Then one must be willing to take the risk of sharing them as they are, inside, not disguising them as judgments, or attributing them to other people. This is why I so admire Miss Shiel's sharing of her anger and frustration, without in any way disguising it.

A Trust in the Human Organism

It would be most unlikely that one could hold the three attitudes I have described, or could commit herself to being a facilitator of learning, unless she has come to have a profound trust in the human organism and its potentialities. If I distrust the human being, then I *must* cram her with information of my own choosing lest she go her own mistaken way. But if I trust the capacity of the human individual for developing her own potentiality, then I can provide her with many opportunities and permit her to choose her own way and her own direction in her learning.

It is clear, I believe, that the teachers whose works are described in the preceding chapters rely basically upon the tendency toward fulfillment, toward actualization, in their students. They are basing their work on the hypothesis that students who are in real contact with problems that are relevant to them wish to learn, want to grow, seek to discover, endeavor to master, desire to create, move toward self-discipline. The teacher is attempting to develop a quality of climate in the classroom and a quality of personal relationship with students that will permit these natural tendencies to come to their fruition.

Living the Uncertainty of Discovery

I believe it should be said that this basically confident view of the human being and the attitudes toward students that I have described do not appear suddenly, in some miraculous manner, in the facilitator of learning. Instead, they come about through taking risks, through *acting* on tentative hypotheses. This is most obvious in the chapter describing Miss Shiel's work, where, acting on hypotheses of which she is unsure, risking herself uncertainly in new ways of relating to her students, she finds these new views confirmed by what happens in her class. The same is definitely true of Mrs. Swenson. I am sure the others went through the same type of uncertainty. As for me, I can only state that I started my career with the firm view that individuals must be manipulated for their own good; I only came to the attitudes I have described and the trust in the individual that is implicit in them because I found that these attitudes were so much more potent in producing learning and constructive change. Hence, I believe that it is only by risking herself in these new ways that the teacher can *discover*, for herself, whether or not they are effective, whether or not they are for her.

I will then draw a conclusion, based on the experiences of the several facilitators and their students that have been included up to this point. When a facilitator creates, even to a modest degree, a classroom climate characterized by all that she can achieve of realness, prizing, and empathy; when she trusts the constructive tendency of the individual and the group; then she discovers that she has inaugurated an educational revolution. Learning of a different quality, proceeding at a different pace, with a greater degree of pervasiveness, occurs. Feelings — positive, negative, confused — become a part of the classroom experience. Learning becomes life and a very vital life at that. The student is on the way, sometimes excitedly, sometimes reluctantly, to becoming a learning, changing being.

The Evidence

The research evidence for the statements in the last paragraph is now very convincing indeed. It has been most interesting to watch that evidence accumulate to a point where it seems irrefutable.

First, in the 1960s, several studies in psychotherapy and in education led to some tentative conclusions. Let me summarize them briefly, without presenting the methods used. (These can be learned from consulting the references given.)

When clients in therapy perceived their therapists as rating high in genuineness, prizing, and empathic understanding, self-learning and therapeutic change were facilitated. The significance of these therapist attitudes was supported in a classic research by Barrett-Lennard (6).

Another study focused on teachers. Some teachers see their urgent problems as "Helping children think for themselves and be independent"; "Getting students to participate"; etc. These teachers were regarded as the "positively oriented" group. Other teachers saw their urgent problems as "Getting students to listen"; "Trying to teach children who don't even have the ability to learn"; etc. These were termed the negatively oriented group. It was found that their students perceived the first group as exhibiting far more of empathy, prizing, and realness than the second group. The first group showed a high degree of facilitative attitudes, the second did not (8).

An interesting study by Schmuck (12) showed that when teachers are empathically understanding, their students tend to like each other better. In an understanding classroom climate, every student tends to feel liked by all the others, has a more positive attitude toward self, and a positive attitude toward school. This ripple aspect of the teacher's attitude is provocative and significant. To extend an empathic understanding to students has effects that go on and on.

The foregoing are samples of the many small studies that began to pile up. But it could still be asked, does the student actually *learn* more when these attitudes are present? Back in 1965, David Aspy (4) did a careful study of six classes of third-graders. He found that in the three classes where the teacher's facilitative attitudes were highest, the pupils showed a significantly greater gain in their reading achievement than in those classes with a lesser degree of these qualities.

Aspy and a colleague, Flora Roebuck, later enlarged this research into a program that extended for more than a decade.

The overwhelming evidence that they accumulated is presented in a later section, "What Are the Facts?" Their study makes it very clear that the attitudinal climate of the classroom, as created by the teacher, is a major factor in promoting or inhibiting learning.

Evidence from Students

Certainly before the research evidence was in, students were making it clear by their reactions to student-centered or person-centered classrooms that an educational revolution was under way. This kind of evidence persists to the present day.

The most striking learnings of students exposed to such a climate are by no means restricted to greater achievement in the three R's. The significant learnings are the more personal ones — independence, self-initiated and responsible learning, release of creativity, a tendency to become more of a person. I can only illustrate this by picking, almost at random, statements from students whose teachers have endeavored to create a climate of trust, of prizing, of realness, of understanding, and above all, of freedom.

Again I must quote from Sylvia Ashton-Warner one of the central effects of such a climate. "The drive is no longer the teacher's, but the children's own. . . . The teacher is at last with the stream and not against it, the stream of children's inexorable creativeness" (3, p. 93).

If you need verification of this, here is one of a number of statements made by students in a course on poetry led (not taught) by Dr. Samuel Moon.

> In retrospect, I find that I have actually enjoyed this course, both as a class and as an experiment, although it had me quite unsettled at times. This, in itself, made the course worthwhile since the majority of my courses this semester merely had me bored with them and the whole process of "higher education." Quite aside from anything else, due mostly to this course, I found myself devoting more time to writing poetry than to writing short stories, which temporarily interfered with my writing class.
>
> . . . I should like to point out one very definite thing which I have gained from the course; this is an increased readiness on my part to listen to and to seriously consider the opinions of my fellow

students. In view of my past attitude, this alone makes the course valuable. I suppose the real result of any course can be expressed in answer to the question, "Would you take it over again?" My answer would be an unqualified "Yes." (9, p. 227)

I should like to add to this several comments from Dr. Bull's sophomore students in a class in adolescent psychology. The first two are midsemester comments.

This course is proving to be a vital and profound experience for me. . . . This unique learning situation is giving me a whole new conception of just what learning is. . . . I am experiencing a real growth in this atmosphere of constructive freedom. . . . The whole experience is challenging.

I feel that the course had been of great value to me. . . . I'm glad to have had this experience because it has made me think. . . . I've never been so personally involved with a course before, especially *outside* the classroom. It has been frustrating, rewarding, enjoyable, and tiring!

The other comments are from the end of the course:

. . . This course is not ending with the close of the semester for me, but continuing. . . . I don't know of any greater benefit which can be gained from a course than this desire for further knowledge.

. . . I feel as though this type of class situation has stimulated me more in making me realize where my responsibilities lie, especially as far as doing required work on my own. I no longer feel as though a test date is the criterion for reading a book. I feel as though my future work will be done for what *I* will get out of it, not just for a test mark.

I think that now I am acutely aware of the breakdown in communications that does exist in our society from seeing what happened in our class. . . . I've grown immensely. I know that I am a different person than I was when I came into that class. . . . It has done a great deal in helping me understand myself better. . . . Thank you for contributing to my growth.

If you wish to know what this type of course seems like to a sixth-grader, let me give you a sampling of the reactions of Miss Shiel's youngsters, misspellings and all.

I feel that I am learning self abilty [*sic*]. I am learning not only school work but I am learning that you can learn on your own as well as someone can teach you.

I like this plan because there is a lot of freedom. I also learn more this way than the other way you don't have to wate [*sic*] for others you can go at your own speed rate it also takes a lot of responsibility. (13)

Or from Dr. Appell's graduate class:

. . . You follow no plan, yet I'm learning. Since the term began I seem to feel more alive, more real to myself. I enjoy being alone as well as with other people. My relationships with children and other adults are becoming more emotional and involved. Eating an orange last week, I peeled the skin off each separate orange section and liked it better with the transparent shell off. It was juicier and fresher tasting that way. I began to think, that's how I feel sometimes, without a transparent wall around me, really communicating my feelings. I feel that I'm growing, how much, I don't know. I'm thinking, considering, pondering and learning. (1)

I can't read these student statements — sixth-grade, college, graduate level — without being deeply moved. Here are teachers, risking themselves, *being* themselves, *trusting* their students, adventuring into the existential unknown, taking the subjective leap. And what happens? Exciting, incredible *human* events. You can sense persons being created, learnings being initiated, future citizens rising to meet the challenge of unknown worlds. If only one teacher out of one hundred dared to risk, dared to be, dared to trust, dared to understand, we would have an infusion of a living spirit into education that would, in my estimation, be priceless.

THE EFFECT UPON THE INSTRUCTOR

Let me turn to another dimension that excites me. I have spoken of the effect upon the *student* of a climate that encourages significant, self-reliant, personal learning. But I have said nothing about the reciprocal effect upon the instructor. When she has been the agent for the release of such self-initiated learning, the faculty member finds herself changed as well as her students. One such says:

To say that I am overwhelmed by what happened only faintly reflects my feelings. I have taught for many years but I have never experienced anything remotely resembling what occurred. I, for my part, never found in a classroom so much of the whole person coming forth, so deeply involved, so deeply stirred. Further, I question if in the traditional setup, with its emphasis on subject matter, examinations, grades, there is, or there can be a place for the "becoming" person with his deep and manifold needs as he struggles to fulfill himself. But this is going far afield. I can only report to you what happened and to say that I am grateful and that I am also humbled by the experience. I would like you to know this for it has enriched my life and being. (11, p. 313)

Another faculty member reports as follows:

Rogers has said that relationships conducted on these assumptions mean "turning present day education upside down." I have found this to be true as I have tried to implement this way of living with students. The experiences I have had have plunged me into relationships which have been significant and challenging and beyond compare for me. They have inspired me and stimulated me and left me at times shaken and awed with their consequences for both me and the students. They have led me to the fact of what I can only call . . . the tragedy of education in our time — student after student who reports this to be his first experience with total trust, with freedom to be and to move in ways most consistent for the enhancement and maintenance of the core of dignity which somehow has survived humiliation, distortion, and corrosive cynicism. (1)

TOO IDEALISTIC?

Some readers may feel that the whole approach of this chapter — the belief that teachers can relate as persons to their students — is hopelessly unrealistic and idealistic. They may see that in essence it is encouraging both teachers and students to be creative in their relationship to each other and in their relationship to subject matter, and feel that such a goal is quite impossible. They are not alone in this. I have heard scientists at leading schools of science and scholars in leading universities arguing that it is absurd to try to encourage all students to be creative — we need hosts of mediocre technicians and workers, and if a few creative scientists and artists and leaders emerge, that will be enough. That may be enough for them. It may be enough to suit you. I want to go on record as saying it is *not* enough to suit me. When I realize the incredible potential in the ordinary student, I want to try to release it. We are working hard to release the incredible energy in the atom and the nucleus of the atom. If we do not devote equal energy—yes, and equal money—to the release of the potential of the individual person, then the enormous discrepancy between our level of physical energy resources and human energy resources will doom us to a deserved and universal destruction.

I'm sorry I can't be coolly scientific about this. The issue is too urgent. I can only be passionate in my statement that people count, that interpersonal relationships *are* important, that we know something about releasing human potential, that we could learn much more, and that unless we give strong positive attention to the human interpersonal side of our educational dilemma, our civilization is on its way down the drain. Better courses, better curricula, better coverage, better teaching machines will never resolve our dilemma in a basic way. Only persons acting like persons in their relationships with their students can even begin to make a dent on this most urgent problem of modern education.

SUMMARY

Let me try to state, somewhat more calmly and soberly, what I have said with such feeling and passion.

I have said that it is most unfortunate that educators and the public think about, and focus on, *teaching*. It leads them into a host of questions that are either irrelevant or absurd so far as real education is concerned.

I have said that if we focused on the facilitation of *learning*—how, why, and when the student learns, and how learning seems and feels from the inside—we might be on a much more profitable track.

I have said that we have some knowledge, and could gain more, about the conditions that facilitate learning, and that one of the most important of these conditions is the attitudinal quality of the interpersonal relationship between facilitator and learner.

Those attitudes that appear effective in promoting learning can be described. First of all is a transparent realness in the facilitator, a willingness to be a person, to be and live the feelings and thoughts of the moment. When this realness includes a prizing, a caring, a trust and respect for the learner, the climate for learning is enhanced. When it includes a sensitive and accurate empathic listening, then indeed a freeing climate, stimulative of self-initiated learning and growth, exists. The student is *trusted* to develop.

I have tried to make plain that individuals who hold such attitudes, and are bold enough to act on them, do not simply modify classroom methods — they revolutionize them. They perform almost none of the functions of teachers. It is no longer accurate to call them *teachers*. They are catalyzers, facilitators, giving freedom and life and the opportunity to learn, to students.

I have brought in the accumulating research evidence that suggests that individuals who hold such attitudes are regarded as effective in the classroom; that the problems that concern them have to do with the release of potential, not the deficiencies of their students; that they seem to create classroom situations in which there are not admired children and disliked children, but in which affection and liking are a part of the life of every child; that in classrooms approaching such a psychological climate, children learn more of the conventional subjects.

But I have intentionally gone beyond the empirical findings to try to take you into the inner life of the student — elementary, college, and graduate — who is fortunate enough to live and learn in such an interpersonal relationship with a facilitator, in order to let you see what learning feels like when it is free, self-initiated, and spontaneous. I have tried to indicate how it even changes the student-student relationship — making it more aware, more caring, more sensitive, as well as increasing the self-related learning of significant material. I have spoken of the change it brings about in the faculty member.

Throughout, I have tried to indicate that if we are to have citizens who can live constructively in this kaleidoscopically changing world, we can *only* have them if we are willing for them to become self-starting, self-initiating learners. Finally, it has been my purpose to show that this kind of learner develops best, so far as we now know, in a growth-promoting, facilitative relationship with a *person*.

REFERENCES

1. Appell, Morey L. "Selected Student Reactions to Student-centered Courses." Unpublished manuscript, Indiana State University, 1959.
2. Appell, Morey L. "Self-understanding for the Guidance Counselor." *Personnel & Guidance Journal*, October 1963, pp. 143–48.
3. Ashton-Warner, Sylvia. *Teacher*. New York: Simon and Schuster, 1963.
4. Aspy, David N. "A Study of Three Facilitative Conditions and Their Relationship to the Achievement of Third Grade Students." Unpublished Ph.D. dissertation, University of Kentucky, 1965.
5. Axline, Virginia M. "Morale on the School Front." *Journal of Educational Research*, 1944, 521–33.
6. Barrett-Lennard, G. T. "Dimensions of Therapist Response as Causal Factors in Therapeutic Change." *Psychological Monographs*, 76 (Whole No. 562), 1962.
7. Bull, Patricia. "Student Reactions, Fall, 1965." Unpublished manuscript, New York State University College, 1966.
8. Emmerling, F. C. "A Study of the Relationships Between Personality Characteristics of Classroom Teachers and Pupil Perceptions." Unpublished Ph.D. dissertation, Auburn University, Auburn, Alabama, 1961.
9. Moon, Samuel F. "Teaching the Self." *Improving College and University Teaching, 14* (Autumn 1966):213–29.
10. Rogers, Carl R. "The Interpersonal Relationship in the Facilitation of Learning." In *Humanizing Education*, edited by R. Leeper, pp. 1–18. Washington, D.C.: NEA, 1967. Copyright by Association for Supervision and Curriculum Development.
11. Rogers, Carl R. *On Becoming a Person*. Boston: Houghton Mifflin, 1961, p. 313.
12. Schmuck, R. "Some Aspects of Classroom Social Climate." *Psychology in the Schools 3* (1966): 59–65; and "Some Relationships of Peer Liking Patterns in the Classroom to Pupil Attitudes and Achievements." *The School Review 71* (1963): 337–59.
13. Shiel, Barbara J. "Evaluation: A Self-directed Curriculum, 1965." Unpublished manuscript, n.p. 1966.

22

The Politics of Education

A humanistically oriented teacher often finds that she simply does not fit into a conventional school. The humanistic teacher may feel herself to be an alien being in a conventional system. This is not surprising, because there are two sharply different approaches to the learning process. I would like to consider these in more detail.

Traditional education and person-centered education may be thought of as the two poles of a continuum. I think that every educational effort, every teacher, every institution of learning could locate itself at some appropriate point on this scale. You may wish to think of yourself or the school or educational enterprise with which you are connected and consider its fitting placement on this continuum.

The Traditional Mode

I believe that the following are the major characteristics of conventional education, as we have known it for a long time in this country and as it is experienced by students and faculty.

The teacher is the possessor of knowledge, the student the expected recipient. The teacher is the expert who knows the field. The student sits with poised pencil and notebook, waiting for the words of wisdom. There is a great difference in the status level between the instructor and student.

The lecture, the textbook, or some other means of verbal intellectual instruction are the major methods of getting knowledge into the recipient. The examination measures the extent to which the student has received it. These are the central elements of this kind of education. Why the lecture is regarded as a major means of instruction is a mystery. It made sense before books were published, but its current ra-

Journal of Humanistic Education, Vol. 1, No. 1, 1977, 6–22. Reprinted by permission of the Association for Humanistic Education.

tionale is almost never explained. The increasing stress on the examination is also mysterious. Certainly its importance in this country has increased enormously in the last couple of decades. It has come to be regarded as the most important aspect of education, the goal toward which all else is directed.

The teacher is the possessor of power, the student the one who obeys. The administrator is also the possessor of power, and both the teacher and the student are the ones who obey. Control is always exercised downward.

Rule by authority is the accepted policy in the classroom. New elementary school teachers are often advised, "Make sure you get control of your students the very first day." Another common maxim, expressing the grimness of this control, is, "Don't smile at your kids before Christmas." The authority figure—the instructor—is very central in this education. Whether greatly admired as a fountain of knowledge or despised as a dictator, the teacher is always the center.

Trust is at a minimum. Most notable is the teacher's distrust of the student. The student cannot be expected to work satisfactorily without the teacher's constant supervision. The student's distrust of the teacher is more diffuse—a lack of trust in teacher's motives, honesty, fairness, competence. There may be a real rapport between an entertaining lecturer and those who are being entertained. There may be admiration for the instructor, but mutual trust is not a noticeable ingredient.

The subjects (students) are best governed by being kept in an intermittent or constant state of fear. Today there is not as much physical punishment in schools, but public criticism and ridicule and a constant fear of failure are even more potent. In my experience, this state of fear appears to increase as we go up the educational ladder because the student has more to lose. The individual in elementary school may be an object of scorn or regarded as stupid. In high school there is added to this the fear of failure to graduate, with its vocational, economic, and educational disadvantages. In college all these consequences are magnified and intensified. In graduate school sponsorship by one professor offers even greater opportunities for extreme punishment due to autocratic whim. Many graduate students have failed to receive their degrees because they have refused to conform to every wish of their major professor. Their position is often analogous to that of some slave, subject to the life-and-death power of an Oriental despot.

Democracy and its values are ignored and scorned in practice. Students do not participate in choosing the goals, the curriculum, or the manner of working. These things are chosen for the students. Students have no part in the choice of teaching personnel, nor any voice in educational policy. Likewise the teachers often have no choice in choosing their administrative officers. Often they, too, have no part in forming educational policy. All this is in striking contrast to all the teaching about the virtues of democracy, the importance of the "free world," and the like. The political practices of the school stand in the most striking contrast to what is taught. While being taught that freedom and responsibility are the glorious features of our democracy, students are experiencing themselves as powerless, as having little freedom, and as having no opportunity to exercise choice or carry responsibility.

There is no place for the whole person in the educational system, only for her intellect. In elementary school the bursting curiosity of the normal child and the youngster's excess of physical energy are curbed and, if possible, stifled. In secondary school the one overriding interest of all the students is sex and the emotional and physical relationships between the sexes. Teachers almost totally ignore this interest and certainly do not regard it as a major area for learning. There is very little place for emotions in the secondary school. In college the situation is even more extreme — only the rational *mind* is welcomed.

The Politics of Conventional Education

In discussing the politics of this traditional mode, I use the term *politics* in its sociological sense, as in "the politics of the family," the "politics of psychotherapy," or "sexual politics." In this sense, politics has to do with control and with the making of choices. It has to do with the strategies and maneuvers by which one carries on these functions. Briefly, it is the process of gaining, using, sharing, or relinquishing power and decision-making. It is also the process of the complex interactions and effects of these elements as they exist in relationships between persons, between a person and a group, or between groups.

Looked at from this perspective, the politics of traditional education is exceedingly clear. Decisions are made at the top. "Power over" is the important concept. The strategies for holding and exercising this power are (1) the rewards of grades and vocational opportunities; and (2) the use of such aversive, punitive, and fear-creating methods as failure on exams, failure to graduate, and public scorn.

It is the politics of a "jug and mug" theory of education, wherein the faculty (the jug) possess the intellectual and factual knowledge and cause the student to be the passive recipient (the mug) so that the knowledge can be poured in.

We see this concept of conventional education practiced all around us. It is not often openly defended as the *best* system. It is simply accepted as the inevitable system. Occasionally, however, it acquires a spokesperson, as in the case of Dr. Jay Michael, vice president of the University of California. Michael strongly opposed two recommendations that have been made to the legislature. One recommendation was that a small percentage of the budget be set aside for innovation in education. This suggestion was completely unacceptable to him. The other recommendation was that education should include *both* affective and cognitive learning. Of this, Michael said, "There is knowledge that exists separate and apart from how a person feels . . . and that accumulation of knowledge is *cognitive*. It can be transmitted, it can be taught and learned." To include affective learning would, he feared, reduce the importance of cognitive learning "to a level unacceptable to scholars."* Here is explicit support for the politics of the jug and mug theory. Teachers know best what is to be transmitted to the student.

The Person-Centered Mode

The person-centered approach is at the opposite end of the scale. It is sharply different in its philosophy, its methods, and its politics. In our present educational culture, it cannot exist unless there is one precondition. If this precondition exists, then the other features listed may be experienced or observed at any educational level, from kindergarten through graduate school.

---

*As reported in Los Angeles *Times*, 3 December 1974.

The precondition is: a leader or a person who is perceived as an authority figure in the situation is sufficiently secure within herself and in her relationship to others that she experiences an essential trust in the capacity of others to think for themselves, to learn for themselves. She regards human beings as trustworthy organisms. If this precondition exists, then the following aspects become possible, and tend to be implemented.

The facilitative teacher shares with the others — students, and possibly also parents or community members — the responsibility for the learning process. Curricular planning, the mode of administration and operation, the funding, the policy making, are all the responsibility of the particular group involved. Thus, a class may be responsible for its own curriculum, but the total group may be responsible for overall policy. In any case, responsibility is shared.

The facilitator provides learning resources, from within herself and her own experience, from books or materials or community experiences. She encourages the learners to add resources of which they have knowledge, or in which they have experience. She opens doors to resources outside the experience of the group.

The student develops her own program of learning, alone or in co-operation with others. Exploring one's own interests, facing this wealth of resources, the student makes the choices as to her own learning direction and carries the responsibility for the consequences of those choices.

A facilitative learning climate is provided. In meetings of the class or of the school as a whole, an atmosphere of realness, of caring, and of understanding listening is evident. This climate may spring initially from the person who is the perceived leader. As the learning process continues, it is more and more often provided by the learners for each other. Learning from each other becomes as important as learning from books or films or work experiences.

It can be seen that *the focus is primarily on fostering the continuing process of learning.* The content of the learning, while significant, falls into a secondary place. Thus, a course is successfully ended not when the student has "learned all she needs to know," but when she has made significant progress in learning *how to learn* what she wants to know.

The discipline necessary to reach the student's goal is a self-discipline and is recognized and accepted by the learner as being her own responsibility. Self-discipline replaces external discipline.

The evaluation of the extent and significance of the student's learning is made primarily by the learner, although this self-evaluation may be influenced and enriched by caring feedback from other members of the group and from the facilitator.

In this growth-promoting climate, the learning tends to be deeper, proceeds at a more rapid rate, and is more pervasive in the life and behavior of the student than is learning acquired in the traditional classroom. This comes about because the direction is self-chosen, the learning is self-initiated, and the whole person (with feelings and passions as well as intellect) is invested in the process.

The Politics of Person-Centered Education

Consider the political implications of person-centered education. Who has the essential power and control? It is clear that it is the learner, or the learners as a group, including the facilitator-learner.

Who is attempting to gain control over whom? The student is in the process of gaining control over the course of her own learning and her own life. The facilitator relinquishes control over others, retaining only control over herself.

I see two strategies used in relation to power. The facilitator provides a psychological climate in which the learner is able to take responsible control. The facilitator also helps to de-emphasize static or content goals and, thus, encourages a focus on the process, on *experiencing* the way in which learning takes place.

The decision-making power is in the hands of the individual or individuals who will be affected by the decision. Depending on the issue, the choice may be up to the individual student, the students and facilitators as a group, or may include administrators, parents, members of the local government, or community members. Deciding what to learn in a particular course may be entirely in the hands of each student and the facilitator. Whether to build a new building affects a much larger group and would be so dealt with.

Each person regulates the modes of feeling, thought, behavior, and values through her own self-discipline.

It is obvious that the growing, learning person is the politically powerful force in such education. The *learner* is the center. This process of learning represents a revolutionary about-face from the politics of traditional education.

The Threat

I have slowly realized that it is in its *politics* that a person-centered approach to learning is most threatening. The teacher who considers using such an approach must face up to the fearful aspects of sharing her power and control. Who knows whether students can be trusted and whether a process can be trusted? One can only take the risk; and risk is frightening.

Person-centered education is threatening to the student. It is much easier to conform and complain than to take responsibility, make mistakes, and live with the consequences. In addition, students have been directed for so many years that they long for the continuance of the security of being told what to do. Just this week, a faculty member told me of sharing with students the responsibility for learning in a course on marriage and the family. Even in a course with such an enormous potential for significant personal development, the initial student reactions were largely ones of alarm. "How will we be graded?" "How many exams?" "How much of the text are we supposed to study?" Clearly, responsible choice is frightening, a fact we do not always recognize.

I hardly need to mention the threat to the administrator. Time and again I have observed that if one teacher in a traditional system, without talk or fanfare, institutes a person-centered process of learning in *one* classroom, that teacher becomes a threat to the whole system. The ferment of responsible freedom and shared power is recognized for what it is — a *revolutionary force* — and is suppressed if possible.

Naturally, the conventional members of the system do not *say* that they are opposed to a democratic process or to responsible freedom. The most frequent reaction to the threat is, "This idealistic notion is very commendable as a dream, but it just wouldn't and couldn't work in practice."

The Evidence

This last statement implies that person-centered education is neither practical nor effective. The statement is completely contradicted by the facts. Some evidence has been presented in previous chapters, but the overwhelming research confirmation will be found in the section "What Are the Facts?"

The day is now past when teachers or administrators can dismiss the person-centered approach as an impossible mode of conducting education or as ineffective in promoting learning. The facts are all on the side of a person-centered approach. The superiority of this mode of education has been clearly demonstrated in many countries and in solid research studies, especially in the United States and Germany.

The Political Implications of the Evidence

The "facilitative conditions" studied make a profound change in the power relationships of the educational setting. To respect and prize the student, to understand what the student's school experience means to her, and to be real as a human being in relation to the pupil is to move the school a long way from its traditional authoritarian stance. These conditions make of the classroom a human, interactive situation, with much more emphasis upon the student as the important figure who is responsible for the evaluation of her own experience. And the research demonstrates that politics of this humane sort foster all kinds of constructive learning, both personal and intellectual. Furthermore, a lack of such a humane environment works against such learning and is associated with *less* than normal progress. Under a sharply and measurably defined humane politics, students improve in their way of perceiving themselves and in their social behavior. All this is a striking affirmation of the value of a person-centered approach in education.

Can We Influence a Profession?

Would it be possible to move a whole profession toward a more humanistic, person-centered approach? Obviously if we were to attempt this, the strategic approach would be to provide person-centered experiences for those who were involved in the preparation of the professionals. We have seen in the preceding chapter how individual teacher-training institutions may make a difference. But there exists an interesting example of an effort to involve a whole profession, the medical field. The story is one from which we may learn.

More than ten years ago Orienne Strode-Maloney, a member of our center, whose former husband had been a physician until his death, initiated a plan for helping physicians to be more human in their relationships. She elicited support and encouragement from the dean of Johns Hopkins University Medical School and from others, including me. A program was developed; it was aimed at medical educators, the persons most responsible for the attitudes of young physicians.

The first four-day workshop on Human Dimensions in Medical Education was held in June 1972. We had been apprehensive that high-status medical personnel would not respond to a program carried on by a nonmedical staff. Consequently, we were surprised and pleased that more than fifty chose to come, a large proportion being deans of medical schools or chairmen of departments. We found the attendees to be generally dubious that the experience would be worthwhile. For a few, the program was not very profitable, but the great majority left the workshop with many new personal and professional learnings. We also included some medical students and interns, so that the viewpoint of the physician-in-training would be represented. This proved to be a very wise move.

The staff was surprised to find that those attending this conference and the succeeding ones felt that they gained more of what they wanted from the small, often highly personal intensive groups than from the sessions on how institutions might be changed. Consequently, the small groups were made more of a central focus of the conferences.

What did the participants gain? I think it might be best to let a few of them speak for themselves through their letters and questionnaire responses.

> Enjoy "teaching" more—don't feel the fantastically unreal drive to "keep up" or "get ahead" or get "one-up" as much—don't feel guilty when haven't read the latest. Relate on a much more human level to students, faculty, and personnel. (Faculty member)

> In these weeks since our experience, I'm still gaining drive, understanding, warmer relations at home, an urge to know colleagues better, an ability to relate to others. . . . It works! I sense a closeness to my group members that has rarely happened before. (Medical school dean)

It gave me a far greater awareness of students as persons. (Professor)

My experience there was the most meaningful and valuable part of my medical education to this date. The exposure to genuine, dynamic interactions between people from the medical community has sustained me throughout the process of becoming a physician. (Third-year medical student)

To say it in a few words, I learned a lot. Medicine and medical education desperately need what sessions like this have to offer. On the plane coming back I decided to build a requirement for training in human relations into our surgical internship and residency program as we develop it. (Chairman, department of surgery)

Notice that many of these responses indicate a freer communication and a greater sharing of power.

Since that beginning, the program has grown very rapidly. There have now been many of these four-day conferences with more than one thousand participants. Nearly every medical school in the United States has been represented, and members of foreign schools are beginning to attend.

A number of those attending wished they might have more extensive training in group facilitation so that they could be more effective "back home." As a consequence, a number of ten-day conferences have been held. Somewhat more cognitive material has been presented in them, although the best training for a facilitator is still the experience of learning to be more of oneself with a group.

A frequent reaction was the wish that others in one's department or medical school attend. Consequently, team attendance was encouraged. A number of medical schools have had five to fifteen educators attend. They constitute a support group for each other when they return to their school.

Most important of all have been the many requests to hold similar conferences in the medical school itself.

I would be interested in pursuing the idea of a cooperative venture between your group and perhaps four medical schools to set up a specific program aimed toward the development of the whole physician and a more humanistic approach to the teaching and practice of medicine. (Chairman, department of surgery)

A number of medical schools have now initiated such humanistic programs, adopting different forms suitable to the situation, but having a common goal of turning out doctors with experience and training in effective interpersonal relationships.

In one of these medical schools, a unique and pioneering program was strongly supported by the dean, who had himself attended one of the early workshops. This school recently held a four-day conference, involving intensive group experience, for all of their incoming students, the thirty faculty members who will be dealing with those students and the school staff (registrar, secretaries, librarians). The facilitators of the intensive groups were physicians from other medical schools in the region who had attended our ten-day programs. Deep levels of communication were achieved among faculty, students, and staff. Can you imagine a situation in which ninety incoming students and spouses are on a first-name basis with all of their teaching faculty, having shared as equals their hopes, dreams, anxieties, concerns, fears — interacting as *persons* in their classes, not as roles? The situation constitutes a revolution in professional education! Feedback from all levels has been enthusiastic. This same group of students and their teaching faculty will be meeting in a two-day, off-campus conference every six months throughout their medical school career. Another revolution!

This whole program for humanizing medical education has led to dramatic changes in curricular thinking in a number of schools. It is bringing about in faculty and students the very attitudes we have described as being effective in promoting a humanized process of learning. It is creating a person-centered context for turning out physicians who are both competent *and* human.

Conclusion

I ask myself why such a program is growing so rapidly in medical education, while there is no comparable program, nor so far as I know any desire for such a program, in our schools of education and teacher-training institutions. I believe there are several answers. In the first place, physicians are accustomed to changing their practice as new knowledge and new ways of treatment develop. A doctor eagerly seizes upon the newest, most effective way of dealing with an old disease and is rewarded for so doing. I believe there are very few rewards in the teacher-training field for educators who are trying out new ways. Another element is that the physician is continually exposed to feedback and is accustomed to learning from mistakes. An autopsy tells her she made a mistaken diagnosis. A patient who develops a damaging side effect from some new drug confronts her with the necessity of fresh learning. It is to her political advantage to be open-minded and changing. But long-term feedback is very rare in education. An educator almost never learns of the curiosity she has killed or the persons she has damaged. Feedback is too politically threatening.

My conclusion is that we may see a person-centered approach to education developing strong roots in alternative schools, in universities-without-walls, and in specialized situations such as medical education, before it has a major impact on our larger teacher-training institutions. A rigid power structure in most of these schools of education is resistant to the political threat posed by change.

Yet the challenge and the possibility remain. Clearly, steps could be taken in teacher education, not unlike those beginning to have a real influence on physician education, with the purpose of bringing about a more human and effective learning climate in our classrooms. Do we, as educators, wish to take those steps, or will the politics of traditional education continue to stand in the way?

THE HELPING PROFESSIONS

Psychologists, social workers, ministers, medical practitioners, and other professionals all have occasions to help their clients work through difficult situations, changes, emotions, and decisions in their lives. Rogers's influence extended to so many of these fields, because the basic, one-to-one relationship he described so eloquently could be employed by all these helping professionals.

The application of the client-centered approach to the broader helping professions occurred in three stages. Initially, Rogers addressed himself exclusively to counselors and psychotherapists. Other professionals simply read and applied his work to their own fields. Next, in works mostly geared toward counselors and therapists, Rogers began to include some chapters or sections in which he applied his own work to a wider professional context. Finally, from the 1960s on, feeling confident of the broad applicability of his work, Rogers wrote a number of articles and books addressed not primarily to counselors and therapists, but to all professionals (and laypersons) interested in helping relationships.

In the three chapters of this section, Rogers addresses issues of concern to all the helping professions. The first relates to the widespread use, in the sixties and seventies, of the small, intensive group, known variously as the encounter group, human relations training group, T-group, group therapy, Synanon group, and so forth. Rather than rely on one-to-one relationships to facilitate growth, many professions had come to recognize how working with small groups could both reach a wider number of people and provide growth and learning opportunities not available in the one-to-one relationship.

Rogers was one early pioneer in the small-group movement. Characteristically, he applied his theories and methods for counseling and psychotherapy to the small-group setting. In subsequent years, he found the opportunity to test these theories in numerous groups. Out of this wealth of experience came the book *Carl Rogers On Encounter Groups* (1970). We have selected a chapter from that book presenting his views of facilitative leadership in a group, as well as some comments on what he deemed to be nonfacilitative leadership behavior.

Presented first as an address to the American Psychological Association in 1972, the next chapter challenges widespread attitudes and practices throughout the helping professions. As well as being an appeal for a more authentic professionalism, it is a call to more creativity and wholeness on the part of the professionals themselves. For Rogers, professionalism had less to do with licensing than with competence. He once related a story about a participant in one of his workshops,

> a man [whose] district was so poor that they appointed him school director, even though he was not technically qualified. He took a very disorderly, unprofitable school and by enlisting the parents, the teachers and the students, and trusting them to set the guidelines and policies for the school, made it into a splendid place for learning. One of the tragedies of bureaucracies of education to me is the fact that when the district became economically more sound and was able to hire a director, he was fired because he did not have the paper qualifications.

In the mid-1970s, Rogers was asked about the politics of client-centered therapy. The suggestion that the person-centered approach might be political in nature took him by surprise. It led him to explore more deeply the underlying meanings in his approach to psychotherapy and in his way of being in relationship, whether the relationship was therapeutic, teacher to student, parent to child, leader to group, spouse to spouse, or almost any other human relationship. This led to comparisons with political implications of other approaches in the behavioral sciences and to his reiteration and reformulation of deeply held principles about relationships — where power resides, who is in control, who makes decisions, who evaluates — issues that are of fundamental significance in the person-centered approach. Rogers's thinking on this topic achieved its fullest expression in *Carl Rogers on Personal Power* (1977), the first chapter of which is excerpted here.

23
Can I Be a Facilitative Person in a Group?

I want to write as openly as I am able about my efforts to be a facilitative person in a group, to express what I can of my strengths, weaknesses, and uncertainties as I try to engage effectively in the honest artistry of interpersonal relations.

Background of Philosophy and Attitudes

One does not enter a group as a tabula rasa. So I would like to state some of the attitudes and convictions I bring with me.

I trust the group, given a reasonably facilitating climate, to develop its own potential and that of its members. For me, this capacity of the group is an awesome thing. Perhaps as a corollary of this, I have gradually developed a great deal of trust in the group process. This is undoubtedly similar to the trust I came to have in the process of therapy in the individual, when it was facilitated rather than directed. To me the group seems like an organism, having a sense of its own direction even though it could not define that direction intellectually. This is reminiscent of a medical motion picture which once made a deep impression on me. It was a photomicrographic film showing the white blood corpuscles moving very randomly through the blood stream, until a disease bacterium appeared. Then, in a fashion which could only be described as purposeful, they moved toward it.

Carl Rogers on Encounter Groups. New York: Harper and Row, 1970, 43–59 and 64–68.

They surrounded it and gradually engulfed and destroyed it, then moved on again in their random way. Similarly, it seems to me, a group recognizes unhealthy elements in its process, focuses on them, clears them up or eliminates them, and moves on toward becoming a healthier group. This is my way of saying that I have seen the "wisdom of the organism" exhibited at every level from cell to group.

This is not to say that every group is "successful"* or that the process is always identical. One group may start at a very rapid, inexpressive level and move a few small steps toward greater freedom. Another may start at a very spontaneous, feelingful level and move a long way toward developing their potential to the fullest. Both of these movements seem to me part of the group process, and I trust each group equally, though my personal enjoyment of the two may be quite different.

Another attitude has to do with aims. I usually have no specific goal for a particular group and sincerely want it to develop its own directions. There are times when, because of some personal bias or anxiety, I *have* had a specific goal for a group. When this has happened, either the group has carefully defeated that aim or has spent enough time dealing with me so that I have truly regretted having a specific goal in mind. I stress the negative aspects of *specific* goals because, at the same time as I hope to avoid them, I also hope there will be some sort of process movement in the group, and even think I can predict some of the probable generalized directions, though not any specific direction. For me this is an important difference. The group will *move* — of this I am confident — but it would be presumptuous to think that I can or should *direct* that movement toward a *specific* goal.

In no basic philosophical way, so far as I can see, does this approach differ from that which I have adopted for years in

---

*What is "successful"? For the present I will settle for the simplest sort of definition. If, a month after the group is over, a number of the participants feel that it was a meaningless, dissatisfying experience, or a hurtful one from which they are still recovering, then for them this was certainly not a successful group. If, on the other hand, most or all of the members still feel that it was a rewarding experience which somehow moved them forward in their own growth, then for me it deserves the label of a successful group.

individual therapy. However, my behavior is often quite different in a group from what it used to be in a one-to-one relationship. I attribute this to the personal growth experienced in groups.

Ordinarily the question of how my style of facilitation looks to another person is not important to me. In that sense I usually feel reasonably competent and comfortable. On the other hand, I know from experience that I can be at least temporarily jealous of a co-leader who seems more facilitative than myself.

My hope is gradually to become as much a participant in the group as a facilitator. This is difficult to describe without making it appear that I am consciously playing two different roles. If you watch a group member who is honestly being himself, you will see that at times he expresses feelings, attitudes, and thoughts primarily directed toward facilitating the growth of another member. At other times, with equal genuineness, he will express feelings or concerns which have as their obvious goal the opening of himself to the risk of more growth. This describes me too, except that I know I am likely to be the second, or risking, kind of person more often in the later than in the earlier phases of the group. Each facet is a real part of me, not a role.

Perhaps another brief analogy will be useful here. If I am trying to explain some scientific phenomenon to a five-year-old, my terminology and even attitude will be very different from those I display if I am explaining the same thing to a bright sixteen-year-old. Does this mean that I am playing two roles? Of course not—it simply means that two facets or expressions of the real me have been brought into play. In the same way, in one moment I really want to be facilitative toward some person, and in another, to risk exposing some new aspect of myself.

I believe that the way I serve as facilitator has significance in the life of the group, but that the group process is much more important than my statements or behavior, and will take place if I do not get in the way of it. I certainly feel responsible *to* the participants, but not *for* them.

In any group to some degree, but especially in a so-called academic course I am conducting in encounter group fashion, I want very much to have the *whole* person present, in both his affective and cognitive modes. I have not found this easy to achieve since most of us seem to choose one mode rather than the other at any given instant. Yet this still remains a way of being which has much value for me. I try to make progress in myself, and in groups I facilitate, in permitting the whole person, with his ideas as well as his feelings — with feelings permeated with ideas and ideas permeated with feelings — to be fully present. In a recent seminar, for reasons I do not fully understand, this was achieved by all of us to a most gratifying degree.

Climate-Setting Function

I tend to open a group in an extremely unstructured way, perhaps with no more than a simple comment: "I suspect we will know each other a great deal better at the end of these group sessions than we do now," or "Here we are. We can make of this group experience exactly what we wish," or "I'm a little uneasy, but I feel somewhat reassured when I look around at you and realize we're all in the same boat. Where do we start?" In a recorded discussion with a group of other facilitators I stated this view as follows.

> Partly because I do trust the group, I can usually be quite loose and relaxed in a group even from the first. That's overstating it somewhat, for I always feel a little anxiety when a group starts, but by and large I feel, "I don't have any idea what's going to happen, but I think what's going to happen will be all right," and I think I tend to communicate nonverbally, "Well, none of us seem to know what's going to happen, but it doesn't seem to be something to worry about." I believe that my relaxation and lack of any desire to guide may have a freeing influence on others.

I listen as carefully, accurately, and sensitively as I am able, to each individual who expresses himself. Whether the utterance is superficial or significant, I *listen*. To me the individual who speaks is worthwhile, worth understanding; consequently *he* is worthwhile for having expressed something. Colleagues say that in this sense I "validate" the person.

There is no doubt that I am selective in my listening, hence "directive" if people wish to accuse me of this. I am centered in the group member who is speaking, and am unquestionably much less interested in the details of his quarrel with his wife, or of his difficulties on the job, or his disagreement with what has just been said, than in the *meaning* these experiences have for him now and the *feelings* they arouse in him. It is to these meanings and feelings that I try to respond.

I wish very much to make the climate psychologically safe for the individual. I want him to feel from the first that if he risks saying something highly personal, or absurd, or hostile, or cynical, there will be at least one person in the circle who respects him enough to hear him clearly and listen to that statement as an authentic expression of himself.

There is a slightly different way in which I also want to make the climate safe for the member. I am well aware that one cannot make the experience safe from the pain of new insight or growth, or the pain of honest feedback from others. However, I would like the individual to feel that whatever happens *to* him or *within* him, I will be psychologically very much *with* him in moments of pain or joy, or the combination of the two which is such a frequent mark of growth. I think I can usually sense when a participant is frightened or hurting, and it is at those moments that I give him some sign, verbal or nonverbal, that I perceive this and am a companion to him as he lives in that hurt or fear.

The Acceptance of the Group

I have a great deal of patience with a group and with the individual within it. If there is one thing I have learned and relearned in recent years, it is that it is ultimately very rewarding to accept the group exactly where it *is*. If a group wishes to intellectualize, or discuss quite superficial problems, or is emotionally very closed, or very frightened of personal communication, these tendencies rarely "bug" me as much as they do some other leaders. I am well aware that certain exercises, tasks set up by the facilitator, can practically force the group to more of a here-and now communication or more of a feelings level. There are leaders who do these things very skillfully, and with good effect at the time. However, I am enough of a scientist-clinician to make many casual follow-up inquiries, and I know that frequently the lasting result of such procedures is not nearly as satisfying as the immediate effect. At its best it may lead to discipleship (which I happen not to like): "What a marvelous leader he is to have *made* me open up when I had no intention of doing it!" It can also lead to a rejection of the whole experience. "Why did I do those silly things he asked me to?" At worst, it can make the person feel that his private self has been in some way violated, and he will be careful never to expose himself to a group again. From my experience I know that if I attempt to push a group to a deeper level it is not, in the long run, going to work.

So for me, I have found that it pays off to live with the group exactly where it is. Thus I have worked with a cluster of very inhibited topnotch scientists — mostly in the physical sciences — where feelings were rarely expressed openly and personal encounter at a deep level was simply not seen. Yet this group became much more free, expressive, and innovative, and showed many positive results of our meetings.

I have worked with high-level educational administrators — probably the most rigid and well-defended group in our culture — with similar results. This is not to say it is always easy for me. In one particular group of educators there had been much superficial and intellectual talk, but gradually they moved to a deeper level. Then in an evening session the talk became more and more trivial. One person asked, "Are we doing what we *want* to do?" And the answer was an almost unanimous "No." But within moments the talk again became social chatter about matters in which I had no interest. I was in a quandary. In order to allay a considerable early anxiety in the group, I had stressed in the first session that they could make of it exactly what they wished, and operationally they seemed to be saying very loudly, "We want to spend expensive, hard-won weekend time talking of trivia." To express my feelings of boredom and annoyance seemed contradictory to the freedom I had given them.* After wrestling within myself for a few moments, I decided that they had a perfect right to talk trivia, and I had a perfect right not to endure it. So I walked quietly out of the room and went to bed. After I left, and the next morning, the reactions were as

---

*Had I said in the first meeting, "*We* can make of this what we wish," which would have been preferable and probably more honest, I would have felt free to say, "I don't like what we are making of it." But I was quite certain that in my attempt at reassurance I had said, "You can make of it what you wish." We always pay for our blunders.

varied as the participants. One felt rebuked and punished, another felt I had played a trick on them, a third felt ashamed of their time-wasting, others felt as disgusted as I at their trivial interchanges. I told them that, to the best of my awareness, I was simply trying to make my behavior match my contradictory feelings, but that they were entitled to their own perceptions. At any rate, after that the interactions were far more meaningful.

Acceptance of the Individual

I am willing for the participant to commit or not to commit himself to the group. If a person wishes to remain psychologically on the sidelines, he has my implicit permission to do so. The group itself may or may not be willing for him to remain in this stance but personally I am willing. One skeptical college administrator said that the main thing he had learned was that he could withdraw from personal participation, be comfortable about it, and realize that he would not be coerced. To me, this seemed a valuable learning and one which would make it much more possible for him actually to participate at the next opportunity. Recent reports on his behavior, a full year later, suggest that he gained and changed from his seeming nonparticipation.

Silence or muteness in the individual are acceptable to me providing I am quite certain it is not unexpressed pain or resistance.

I tend to accept statements at their face value. As a facilitator (as in my function as therapist) I definitely prefer to be a gullible person; I will believe that you are telling me the way it is in you. If not, you are entirely free to correct your message at a later point, and are likely to do so. I do not want to waste my time being suspicious, or wondering, "What does he *really* mean?"

I respond *more* to present feelings than to statements about past experiences but am willing for both to be present in the communication. I do not like the rule "We will only talk about the here and now."

I try to make clear that whatever happens will happen from the choices of the group, whether these are clear and conscious, gropingly uncertain, or unconscious. As I become increasingly a member of the group, I willingly carry my share of *influence*, but do not *control* what happens.

I am usually able to feel comfortable with the fact that in eight hours we can accomplish eight hours' worth and in forty hours we can accomplish forty hours' worth—while in a one-hour demonstration session we can accomplish one hour's worth.

Empathic Understanding

My attempt to understand the exact meaning of what the person is communicating is the most important and most frequent of my behaviors in a group.

For me, it is a part of this understanding that I try to delve through complications and get the communication back onto the track of the *meaning* that it has to the *person*. For example, after a very complicated and somewhat incoherent statement by a husband I respond, "And so, little by little, you have come to hold back things that previously you would have communicated to your wife? Is that it?"

"Yes."

I believe this is facilitative, since it clarifies the message for the speaker and helps the group members to understand and not waste time asking questions about or responding to the complicated details he has presented.

When talk is generalized or intellectualizing, I tend to select the self-referent meanings to respond to out of the total context. Thus I might say, "Though you are speaking of all this in general terms of what everybody does in certain situations, I suspect you are speaking very much for yourself in saying that. Is that right?" Or, "You say we all do and feel thus and so. Do you mean that *you* do and feel these things?"

At the beginning of one group, Al said some rather meaningful things. John, another member, started questioning and questioning him about what he had said, but I heard more than questions. I finally said to John, "OK, you keep trying to get at what he said and what he meant, but I think you're trying to say something *to* him and I'm not sure what that is." John thought for a moment and then began to speak for *himself*. Up to that moment, he had apparently been trying to get Al to articulate his (John's) feelings for him, so that he wouldn't have to voice them as coming from himself. This seems quite a common pattern.

I very much want my understanding to extend to both sides of a difference in feeling which is being expressed. Thus, in one group which was discussing marriage, two people held very different views. I responded, "This is a real difference between the two of you, because you, Jerry, are saying, 'I like smoothness in a relationship. I like it to be nice and tranquil,' and Winnie is saying, 'To hell with that! I like communication.'" This helps to sharpen and clarify the significance of differences.

Operating in Terms of My Feelings

I have learned to be more and more free in making use of my own feelings as they exist in the moment, whether in relation to the group as a whole, or to one individual, or to myself. I nearly always feel a genuine and present concern for each member and for the group as a whole. It is hard to give any reason for this. It is just a fact. I value each person; but this valuing carries no guarantee of a permanent relationship. It is a concern and feeling which exists *now*. I think I feel it more clearly because I am not saying it is or will be permanent.

I believe I am quite sensitive to moments when an individual is feeling a readiness to speak or is close to pain or tears or anger. Thus one might say, "Let's give Carlene a chance," or "You look as though you are really troubled about something. Do you want to let us in on it?"

It is probably particularly to hurt that I respond with empathic understanding. This desire to understand, and to stand psychologically with the person in pain, probably grows in part out of my therapeutic experience.

I endeavor to voice any *persisting* feelings which I am experiencing toward an individual or toward the group, in any significant or continuing relationship. Obviously such expressions will not come at the very beginning, since feelings are not yet persistent ones. I might, for example, take a dislike to someone's behavior during the first ten minutes the group is together, but would be unlikely to voice it at that time. If the feeling persists, however, I would express it.

In discussing this point, one facilitator said, "I've been trying to follow an eleventh commandment, 'You shall always express the feelings you are experiencing.'" Another discussant came back, "You know how I react to that? That we should always have the *choice*. Sometimes I choose to express my feelings; other times I choose not to."

I find myself much more in agreement with the second statement. If one can only be *aware* of all the complexity of one's feelings in any given moment—if one is listening to oneself adequately—then it is possible to *choose* to express attitudes which are strong and persistent, or not to express them at this time if that seems highly inappropriate.

I *trust* the feelings, words, impulses, fantasies, that emerge in me. In this way I am using more than my conscious self, drawing on some of the capacities of my whole organism. For example, "I suddenly had the fantasy that you are a princess, and that you would love it if we were all your subjects." Or, "I sense that you are the judge as well as the accused, and that you are saying sternly to yourself, 'You are *guilty* on every count.'"

Or the intuition may be a bit more complex. While a responsible business executive is speaking, I may suddenly have the fantasy of the small boy he is carrying around within himself—the small boy that he was, shy, inadequate, fearful—a child he endeavors to deny, of whom he is ashamed. And I am wishing that he would love and cherish this youngster. So I may voice this fantasy—not as something true, but as a fantasy in me. Often this brings a surprising depth of reaction and profound insights.

I want to be as expressive of positive and loving feelings as of negative or frustrated or angry ones. There may be a certain risk in this. In one instance I think I hurt the group process by being too expressive, early in the sessions, of warm feelings toward a number of members of the group. Because I was still perceived as the facilitator, this made it more difficult for others to bring out some of their negative and angry feelings, which were never voiced until the last session, bringing the group to a definitely unhappy ending.

I find it difficult to be easily or quickly aware of angry feelings in myself. I deplore this, and am slowly learning in this respect.

It would be good to be unselfconsciously expressive of the feelings of the moment. There was one encounter group which was recorded—a group in which there was a great deal of movement. I did not hear the recordings until about two years later, and was amazed at some of the feelings I had expressed — toward others particularly. If a member of the group had said to me (after two years), "You expressed this feeling toward me," I'm sure I would have flatly denied it. Yet here was the evidence that, without weighing every word or thinking of possible consequences, I had, as a person in the group, unselfconsciously voiced whatever feeling I had in the moment. I felt good about this.

I seem to function best in a group when my "owned" feelings — positive or negative — are in immediate interaction with those of a participant. To me this means that we are communicating on a deep level of personal meaning. It is the closest I get to an I-Thou relationship.

When asked a question, I try to consult my own feelings. If I sense it as being real and containing no other message than the question, then I will try my best to answer it. I feel no social compulsion, however, to answer simply because it is phrased as a question. There may be other messages in it far more important than the question itself.

A colleague has told me that I "peel my own onion," that is, express continuously deeper layers of feeling as I become aware of them in a group. I can only hope that this is true.

Confrontation and Feedback

I tend to confront individuals on specifics of their behavior. "I don't like the way you chatter on. Seems to me you give each message three or four times. I wish you would stop when you've completed your message." "To me you seem sort of like silly putty. Someone seems to reach you, to make a dent in you, but then it all springs back into place as though you hadn't been touched."

And I like to confront another person only with feelings I am willing to claim as my own. These may at times be very strong. "Never in my life have I been so pissed off at a group as I am at this one." Or, to one man in this group, "I woke up this morning feeling, 'I never want to see you again.' "

To attack a person's defenses seems to me judgmental. If one says, "You're hiding a lot of hostility," or "You are being highly intellectual, probably because you are afraid of your own feelings," I believe such judgments and diagnoses are the opposite of facilitative. If, however, what I perceive as the person's coldness frustrates me, or his intellectualizing irritates me, or his brutality to another person angers me, then I would like to face him with the frustration or the irritation or the anger that exists in *me*. To me this is *very* important.

Often in confronting someone I use quite specific material, given previously by the participant. "Now you're being what you called the 'pore lil ole country boy' once more." "Now it seems to me you are doing it again — the very thing you described — being the child who wants approval at any cost."

If a person seems distressed by my confrontation or that of others, I am very willing to help him "get off the hook" if he so desires. "You look as though you have had about all you want to take. Would you like us to let you alone for the time being?" One can only be guided by the response, learning that sometimes he wants the feedback and confrontation to continue, even though it is painful for him.

Expression of Own Problems

If I am currently distressed by something in my own life, I am willing to express it in the group, but I do have some sort of professional conscience about this, for if I am paid to be a facilitator, then severe problems I feel I should work out in a staff group or with some therapist rather than taking group time. I am probably too cautious about this. In one instance — a slow-moving faculty group meeting once a week — I feel I really cheated them. At a certain point I was much upset about a personal problem, but felt that it did not concern the group and refrained from talking about it. As I look back, I think nothing would have more facilitated the group process than to articulate my upsetness; I believe it would have helped them to be more expressive.

If I do not feel free to express my personal problems, this has two unfortunate consequences. In the first place, I do not listen as well. In the second, I know from various experiences that the group is apt to perceive that I am upset and think *they* are at fault in some unknown way.

Avoidance of Planning and "Exercises"

I try to avoid using any procedure that is *planned*; I have a real "thing" about artificiality. If any planned procedure is tried, the group members should be as fully in on it as the facilitator, and should make the choice themselves as to whether they want to use that approach. On rare occasions, when frustrated or when a group has seemed to reach a plateau, I have tried what I think of as devices, but they rarely work. Probably this is because I myself lack faith that they are really useful.

It is possible to outline a procedure to group members, but what happens is up to them. In one apathetic group I suggested that we try to get out of our doldrums by doing as other groups had done: forming an inner circle and an outer one, with the person in the outer circle prepared to speak up for the real feelings of the individual in front of him. The group paid absolutely no attention to the suggestion and went on as though it had never been made. But within an hour, one man picked up the central aspect of this device and used it, saying, "I want to speak for John and say what I believe he is *actually* feeling." At least a dozen times in the next day or two, others used it — but in their own spontaneous way, not as a crude or stiff device.

To me nothing is a "gimmick" if it occurs with real spontaneity. Thus, one may use role playing, bodily contact, psychodrama, exercises such as I have described, and various other procedures when they seem to express what one is actually feeling at the time.

This leads me to say that spontaneity is the most precious and elusive element I know. I do something very spontaneously, and it is highly effective. Then in the next group I may be strongly tempted to do it again — "spontaneously" — and I have some difficulty in understanding why it falls flat. Obviously it has not been truly spontaneous.

Avoidance of Interpretive or Process Comments

I make comments on the group process very sparingly. They are apt to make the group self-conscious; they slow it down, giving members the sense that they are under scrutiny. Such comments also imply that I am not seeing them as persons but as sort of a lump or conglomeration, and that is not the way I want to be with them. Comments on the group process best come naturally from the member, if at all.

I feel much the same about process comments on the individual. To me, the *experience* of feeling competitive, for example, and experiencing that feeling openly, is more important than to have the facilitator put a label on this behavior. For some reason, I have no objection when a participant does something of this sort. For example, a faculty member was complaining about students who *always* want their questions answered, and *continually* ask questions. He felt they just weren't adequately self-reliant. He kept insistently asking me, over and over, what to do about such behavior. A group member finally said, "You seem to be giving us a good example of just what you are complaining about." This seemed very helpful.

I tend not to probe into or comment on what may be behind a person's behavior. To me, an interpretation as to the *cause* of individual behavior can never be anything but a high-level guess. The only way it can carry weight is when an authority puts his experience behind it. But I do not want to get involved in this kind of authoritativeness. "I think it's because you feel inadequate as a man that you engage in this blustering behavior," is not the kind of statement I would ever make.

The Therapeutic Potentiality of the Group

If a very serious situation arises in a group, when an individual seems to be exhibiting psychotic behavior or is acting in a bizarre way, I have learned to rely on the members of the group to be as therapeutic or more therapeutic than I am myself. Sometimes as a professional one gets caught up in labels and feels, for example, "This is straight paranoid behavior!" As a consequence, one tends to withdraw somewhat and deal with the person more as an object. The more naive group member, however, continues to relate to the troubled person as a *person*, and this is in my experience far more therapeutic. So, in situations in which a member is showing behavior which is clearly pathological, I rely on the wisdom of the group more than on my own, and am often deeply astonished at the therapeutic ability of the members. This is both humbling and inspiring. It makes me realize what incredible potential for helping resides in the ordinary untrained person, if only he feels the freedom to use it.

Physical Movement and Contact

I express myself in physical movement as spontaneously as possible. My background is not such as to make me particularly free in this respect. But if I am restless I get up and stretch and move around; if I want to change places with another person, I ask him if he is willing. One may sit or lie on the floor if that meets one's physical needs. I do not particularly attempt, however, to promote physical movement in others, though there are facilitators who can do this beautifully and effectively.

Slowly I have learned to respond with physical contact when this seems real and spontaneous and appropriate. When a young woman was weeping because she had had a dream that no one in the group loved her, I embraced her and kissed and comforted her. When a person is suffering and I feel like going over and putting my arm around him, I do just that. Again, I do not try consciously to *promote* this kind of behavior. I admire the younger people who are looser and freer in this respect.

Some Faults of Which I Am Aware

I am much better in a group in which feelings are being expressed — any kind of feelings — than in an apathetic group. I am not particularly good in provoking a relationship, and have real admiration for some facilitators I know who can readily provoke a real and meaningful relationship, which then continues to develop. I frequently choose such a person as a co-facilitator.

As I noted briefly above, I am often slow to sense and express my own anger. Consequently, I may only become aware of it and express it later. In a recent encounter group I was at different times very angry with two individuals. With one I was not conscious of it until the middle of the night and had to wait until the next morning to express it. With the other, I was able to realize and express it in the session in which it occurred. In both instances it led to real communication — to a strengthening of the relationship and gradually to the feeling of genuine liking for each other. But I am a slow learner in this area and consequently have a real appreciation of what others go through as they try to relax their defenses sufficiently to let immediate feelings of the moment seep through into awareness.

A Special Problem

In recent years I have had to deal with a problem which is special to anyone who has become rather widely known through writings and through being taught about in classrooms. People come into a group with me with all kinds of expectations — from a halo over my head to sprouting horns. I try to dissociate myself as rapidly as possible from these hopes or fears. In dress, manner, and by expressing my wish that they get to know me as a person — not simply as a name or a book or a theory — I try to *become* a person to the members of the group. It is always refreshing to find myself in a gathering — for example, of high school girls, or sometimes of businessmen — for whom I am not a "name" and where I have to "make it" all over again simply as the person I am. I could have kissed the young girl who said challengingly at the start of a group, "I think this sounds like kind of a risky thing. What are your qualifications for doing this?" I replied that I had had some experience in working with groups and hoped they would find me qualified, but that I could certainly understand her concern, and they would have to form their own judgment of me.

Behavior Which I Believe to Be Nonfacilitative*

Though I stressed at the outset of this chapter that there are many effective styles of working with a group, there are also a number of people who conduct groups whom I do not recommend, because some of their approach seems to me nonfacilitative, or even damaging, to a group and its members. I cannot conclude this discussion in an honest way without listing some of these behaviors. Research is in such an infant stage in this field that one cannot pretend that opinions such as those expressed below are factually based or supported by research findings. These are simply opinions which have grown out of my experience, and are expressed as such.

---

*In writing this section I have profited by discussion with many individuals, but particularly Ann Dreyfuss and William R. Coulson.

1. I am definitely suspicious of the person who appears to be exploiting the present interest in groups. Because of the enormously expanding interest, a number of workers seem to me to have as their slogans "Get publicity fast!" "Get on the bandwagon!" When such traits appear in individuals who are working with people, I am deeply offended.

2. A facilitator is less effective when he pushes a group, manipulates it, makes rules for it, tries to direct it toward his own unspoken goals. Even a slight flavor of this kind can either diminish (or destroy) the group's trust in him, or — even worse — make the members his worshipful followers. If he has specific goals, he had best make them explicit.

3. Then there is the facilitator who judges the success or failure of a group by its dramatics — who counts the number of people who have wept or those who have been "turned on." For me, this leads toward a highly spurious evaluation.

4. I do not recommend a facilitator who believes in some one single line of approach as the *only* essential element in the group process. For one, "attacking defenses" is the sine qua non. For another, "drawing out the basic rage in every person" is his one-note song. I have a great deal of respect for Synanon and the effectiveness of their work with drug addicts, but am repelled by their hastily formed dogma that unrelenting attack, whether based on real or spurious felings, is the criterion by which a group is to be judged successful or unsuccessful. I want hostility or rage to be expressed when it is present, and want to express them myself when they are genuinely present in me, but there are *many* other feelings, and they have equal significance in living and in the group.

5. I cannot recommend as facilitator a person whose own problems are so great and pressing that he needs to center the group on himself and is not available to, or deeply aware of, others. Such a person might well be a participant in a group, but it is unfortunate when he carries the label of "facilitator."

6. I do not welcome as facilitator a person who frequently gives interpretations of motives or causes of behavior in members of the group. If these are inaccurate they are of no help; if deeply accurate, they may arouse extreme defensiveness, or even worse, strip the person of his defenses, leaving him vulnerable and possibly hurt as a person, particularly after the group ses-

sions are over. Such statements as "You certainly have a lot of latent hostility," or "I think you're compensating for your essential lack of masculinity" can fester in an individual for months, causing great lack of confidence in his own ability to understand himself.

7. I do not like it when a facilitator introduces exercises or activities with some such statement as, "Now we will all—" This is simply a special form of manipulation, but very difficult for the individual to resist. If exercises are introduced, I think any member should have the opportunity, clearly stated by the facilitator, to opt out of the activity.

8. I do not like the facilitator who withholds himself from personal emotional participation in the group—holding himself aloof as the expert, able to analyze the group process and members' reactions through superior knowledge. This is often seen in individuals who make their living by conducting groups, but seems to show both a defensiveness in themselves and a deep lack of respect for the participants. Such a person denies his own spontaneous feelings and provides a model for the group —that of the overly cool analytical person who never gets involved—which is the complete antithesis of what I believe in. That is what each participant will then naturally aim to achieve: the exact opposite of what I should hope for. Nondefensiveness and spontaneity—not the defense of aloofness—are what I personally hope will emerge in a group.

Let me make clear that I do not object at all to the qualities I have mentioned in any *participant* in the group. The individual who is manipulative, or overinterpretative, or totally attacking, or emotionally aloof, will be very adequately handled by the group members themselves. They will simply not permit such behaviors to continue persistently. But when the facilitator exhibits these behaviors, he tends to set a norm for the group before the members have learned that they can confront and deal with him as well as with each other.

Conclusion

I have tried here to describe the manner in which I would like to behave as the perceived facilitator of a group. I do not always succeed in carrying out my own personal aims, and then the experience tends to be less satisfying to the group members and to myself. I have also described some of the behaviors which I regard as nonfacilitative. I sincerely hope that this presentation will encourage others to speak for their own styles of group facilitation.

24
Some New Challenges to the Helping Professions

I appreciate being invited to address psychologists. It has been a long time indeed since I have attended an APA convention. I have a temptation to reminisce, to think and talk about the forty-five years I have been engaged in clinical psychology or work that is related to it—helping troubled individuals, conducting research in this field, promoting personal growth and development in individuals and groups, endeavoring to work with organizations such as our educational systems, even voicing my concerns about our very sick society and the near fatal illnesses of our culture.

Such reminiscences would cover such things as the strenuous effort that was necessary to make a place for that small infant, clinical psychology, in the APA—a struggle that seems ludicrous now; the struggle to prove that psychologists could actually and legally carry on psychotherapy, involving various professional struggles with psychiatry; the attempt to open up therapy to detailed scrutiny and empirical research; the effort to build a theoretical formulation that would release clinical work from the dying orthodoxy of psychoanalytic dogma, and promote diversified and creative thinking; the efforts to broaden the scope and the vision of clinical and other psychologists; and perhaps finally the effort to help psychologists become true change agents, not simply remedial appliers of psychic Band-Aids. Each one of those phrases could be a long story in itself.

But I do not wish to yield to this temptation. I prefer to look

American Psychologist, Vol. 28, No. 5, May 1973, 379–387. Copyright © 1973 by the American Psychological Association. Reprinted by permission of the publisher.

ahead, to try to describe some of the challenges that are currently facing us, or will, in my judgment, face us in the near future.

I am afraid that these challenges have little or no logical sequence. They are the dilemmas that I perceive as most significant. For this reason, what follows may seem disjointed, just as I think life rather ruthlessly presents us with many divergent issues, some of which we would sweep under the rug if we conveniently could. Here are some that I think cannot be wished away.

DARE WE DEVELOP A HUMAN SCIENCE?

The first challenge I wish to mention is not particularly new, but it is definitely unmet. It is this: Does our profession dare to develop the new conception of science which is so necessary if we are to have a true *psychological* science? Or will we continue as a pseudoscience? Let me explain my meaning, in terms which are full of personal meaning to me.

Psychology, for all its thousands of experiments, its multitude of white rats, its vast enterprises involving laboratories, computers, electronic equipment, highly sophisticated statistical measures, and the like, is in my estimation slipping backward as a significant science. We have failed dismally to heed Robert Oppenheimer's (1956) warning, addressed to the APA, when he pointed out that the worst thing psychology might do would be "to model itself after a physics which is not there anymore, which has been outdated" (p. 134). But we have determinedly tied ourselves to this old Newtonian conception of science, seemingly unaware of the changes in the views of science that have been taking place in theoretical physics and in various other "hard" as well as "soft" sciences. I and others have endeavored to spell out some of these changes (Koch, 1959; Rogers, 1955, 1964; Schultz, 1970) and I do not wish to repeat those formulations here. For me the heart of the change is best summed up in a paragraph by my friend, Michael Polanyi (1958). It is a complex thought:

> To say that the discovery of objective truth in science consists in the apprehension of a rationality which commands our respect and arouses our contemplative admiration; that such discovery,

while using the experience of our senses as clues, transcends this experience by embracing the vision of a reality beyond the impressions of our senses, a vision which speaks for itself in guiding us to an ever deeper understanding of reality—such an account of scientific procedure would be generally shrugged aside as outdated Platonism: a piece of mystery-mongering unworthy of an enlightened age. Yet it is precisely on this conception of objectivity that I wish to insist. (p. 5)

A beautiful example of Polanyi's view of a man being pulled, by his subjective vision, into a deeper and more significant view of reality is contained in the account of how he became a scientist by none other than B. F. Skinner (1959). It is a human, private, inner view. It is full of the use of such subjective clues as "when you run onto something interesting, drop everything else and study it" (p. 363). It is unfortunate that Skinner now regards this beautiful personal account as no more than an epiphenomenon, insignificant in itself. Yet I have had the same kind of story from prominent scientists at Caltech—the dream, the vision, the hunch as to the structure of the nucleus of the atom or some other mystery, and the valuable work which has been guided by that informed but vaguely transcending dream. Hans Reichenbach (Schilpp, 1959) reports a conversation with Albert Einstein: "When I, on a certain occasion, asked Professor Einstein how he found his theory of relativity, he answered that he found it because he was so strongly convinced of the harmony of the universe" (p. 292). He had, in other words, a subjectively formed guiding vision.

I myself (Coulson and Rogers, 1968) have tried to sum up this newer view:

All of this which we [psychologists] have known as science becomes but one modest *part* of science. It can be seen as imbedded in an impressive personal context in which personal and group judgment of plausibility becomes as important as statistical significance. The model of a precise, beautifully built, and unassailable science (which most of us hold, consciously or unconsciously) becomes, then, a limited and distinctly human construction, incapable of precise perfection. Openness to experiences can be seen as being fully as important a characteristic of the scientist as the understanding of research design. And the whole enterprise of science can be seen as but one portion of a larger field of knowledge in which truth is pursued in many equally meaningful ways, science being one of those ways. (p. 8)

These quotations indicate the kind of challenge that faces psychologists if they are to develop a science of man. (See also Dagenais, 1972, and Schultz, 1970.) It will become a science based on careful observation of inner cognitive processes, such as we find in Piaget. It will involve the exploration of inner, personal, emotionalized meanings, such as I and my colleagues have pioneered. It will be based upon understanding the phenomenological world of man, as well as his external behavior and reactions. This trend toward convergent lines of confirmation has been evident in research in psychotherapy. It also shows up dramatically in the increasingly sophisticated work on dreams by numerous investigators, tying together the completely subjective irrational dream world of the individual with his responses on various electronic measuring devices. Here, indeed, one of the most ancient subjective realities — the dream — is linked to the most modern technology. It is to be noted that in all of these trends toward a newer science, we do not push the individual into some contrived situation to investigate some hypothesis we have imposed on him. We are instead opening our minds and our whole selves to learning *from* him.

Why is this important? Because otherwise, man becomes but an object to us. Hanna (1971) states it well:

> Man *uses* that which he perceives to be *unlike* himself, but he searches for a *common understanding and common harmony* with that which he perceives to be *like* himself. The former perception leads to manipulation and authentic technology; the latter perception leads to understanding and authentic science.

I believe that until we develop this authentic human science, we are but developing a technology for the use of planners and dictators, not a true understanding of the human condition. Perhaps our graduate departments, those bastions of traditionalism, have kept us from bringing about this change. The Ph.D. thesis has, in most universities, become a travesty of its true purpose. To follow one's informed curiosity into the mysteries of some aspect of human nature, and out of that rigorous, personal, independent search to come up with a significant contribution to knowledge — this is the true picture of the Ph.D.; but this is *not* an accurate description of most doctoral dissertations today. We have settled for safe mediocrity, and frowned on creativity. If our concept of science is to change, our departments must change. If that change does not come about, psychology will become more and more irrelevant to the search for the truth of man.

DO WE DARE TO BE DESIGNERS?

Another great challenge of our times to the psychologist is to develop an approach that is focused on constructing the new, not repairing the old; that is, designing a society in which problems will be less frequent, rather than putting poultices on those who have been crippled by social factors. The question is whether our group can develop a future-oriented preventive approach, or whether it will forever be identified with a past-oriented remedial function.

Let me give a few examples. Will the school psychologist be content with the attempt to diagnose and remedy the individual ills created by an obsolete educational system with an irrelevant curriculum; or will he insist on having a part in designing an opportunity for learning in which the student's curiosity can be unleashed and in which the joy of learning replaces the assigned tasks of the prisons we now know as schools?

To work in such a way demands that the psychologist be a radical in the true sense of that word. It means that he leaves his secure little office and works — often at great risk, I know — with school administrators, teachers, and community leaders to plan and design a learning environment. His task will no longer be to try to assuage the pain of the victims of the old system, for whom failure has become a daily experience; he will, instead, have embarked on the broader task of building a flexible institution — if such is possible — with students as the core and all others as the servants of the learners. As clinicians, we have seen our task in such degrading ways that I do not know whether we can lift our view enough to see the function we might be serving.

Why are psychologists not at the heart of designing environments—cities, schools, homes, cultures—that enhance rather than degrade, that utilize technology rather than becoming its slaves? To their credit, let it be said that there are a few psychologists so employed, but they are *very* few.

Take one example of which I have some personal knowledge. A psychologist—I suppose he would be termed a consulting psychologist—is working with a large firm in its efforts to design an enormous new plant. He is working to plan for the satisfactoriness of human relationships in that plant, so he deals with the architects, with the technicians designing the automation, with the labor-union leaders, with the production-line specialists, with teams of all of these. His effort is not simply to modify or soften the deadening human effects of such a plant. He sees his job as putting the person at the heart of the whole enterprise, trying to discover whether a large modern unit of production can be so constructed, so organized, as to enhance the human spirit, to enrich the lives of the persons involved. I believe he is engaged in an attempt to build a system that is, first of all, human. To the extent that the whole team can be successful, we will not need to speak of the dehumanizing effects of modern industry, of the enormous damage done to the human psyche. To be sure, he may lose, or he may win. But he is engaged in the preventive effort to *construct* a human enterprise. Would that more psychologists were similarly engaged!

The same comment applies if we are thinking of developing whole new communities from the start. The one with which I have some familiarity is Columbia, Maryland. To build a community for persons—without regard to their race, cultural background, or economic level—is an exciting experiment. I know they have already made mistakes, and will undoubtedly make more, but it is an attempt to build for persons, not simply to make profits for the developer. How many social scientists were involved I do not know, but not enough. How much attention is being given to building continuing relationships within the community? Far too little. But this is the kind of area in which, in my judgment, there lies an important place for psychologists, if they can be creative as well as down-to-earth, if they can free themselves from their traditionalism as well as their professionalism, and work imaginatively with others from all pertinent fields—physicians and architects and plumbers and educators —to build a new unit of a new society.

In another area, can we be of significant help in improving relationships between minority groups—blacks, Chicanos, Indians, women—and the so-called Establishment? Here is the kind of relevant, risky field that offers great opportunities. I know, and I am sure you do too, of individual psychologists, black, white, Chicano, and female, who have been highly influential in bringing about improved communication in crucial interface situations. Some have worked with ghetto members and police; some with the health-consuming poor and the medical establishment; some with the drug culture and the community. We, as psychologists, have available many of the skills for facilitating communication and problem-solving procedures between these often bitter and alienated groups and the culture which has mistreated them. We can help both sides to find solutions that constitute a quiet revolution without violence. Will we do so? Will we receive any backing whatsoever from our university roots, our professional societies, and our governmental agencies set up to serve the public, when we do engage in such activities? It is too soon to know, but it is not too soon to make a concerted gamble.

DARE WE DO AWAY WITH PROFESSIONALISM?

The third challenge I wish to raise, especially for clinical and social psychologists, is the radical possibility of sweeping away our procedures for professionalization. I know what heresy that idea is, what terror it strikes in the heart of the person who has struggled to become a "professional." But I have seen the moves toward certification and licensure, the attempts to exclude charlatans, from a vantage point of many years, and it is my considered judgment that they fail in their aims. I helped the APA to form the ABEPP* (as it was then known) in 1947 when I was president of the APA. I was ambivalent about the move then. I wish now that I had taken a stand against it.

---

*American Board of Examiners in Professional Psychology, now named the American Board of Professional Psychology.

I am not in any way impugning the motives, the integrity, and the efforts of those who aim toward certification and all that follows from it. I sympathize deeply. I wish there were a way to separate the qualified from the unqualified, the competent worker from the opportunist, the exploiter, and the charlatan. But let's look at a few facts.

As soon as we set up criteria for certification—whether for clinical psychologists, for NTL group trainers, for marriage counselors, for psychiatrists, for psychoanalysts, or, as I heard the other day, for psychic healers—the first and greatest effect is to freeze the profession in a past image. This is an *inevitable* result. What can you use for examinations? Obviously, the questions and tests that have been used in the past decade or two. Who is wise enough to be an examiner? Obviously, the person who has ten or twenty years of experience and who therefore started his training fifteen to twenty-five years previously. I know how hard such groups try to update their criteria, but they are always several laps behind. So the certification procedure is always rooted in the rather distant past and defines the profession in those terms.

The second drawback I state sorrowfully: there are as many *certified* charlatans and exploiters of people as there are uncertified. If you had a good friend badly in need of therapeutic help, and I gave you the name of a therapist who was a Diplomate in Clinical Psychology, with no other information, would you send your friend to him? Of course not. You would want to know what he is like as a person and a therapist, recognizing that there are many with diplomas on their walls who are not fit to do therapy, lead a group, or help a marriage. Certification is *not* equivalent to competence.

The third drawback is that the urge toward professionalism builds up a rigid bureaucracy. I am not personally aware of such bureaucracy at the national level, but it certainly occurs frequently at the state level. Bureaucratic rules become a substitute for sound judgment. A person is disqualified because he has 150 hours of supervised therapy, while another is approved because he has the required 200. No attention is given to the *effectiveness* of either therapist, or the quality of his work, or even the quality of the supervision he received. Another person might be disqualified because his excellent psychological thesis was done in a graduate department that is not labeled "psychology." I won't multiply the examples. The bureaucrat is beginning to dominate the scene in ways that are all too familiar, setting the profession back enormously.

Then there is the other side of the coin. I think of the "hot-line" workers whom I have been privileged to know in recent years. Over the phone, they handle bad drug trips, incipient suicides, tangled love affairs, family discord, all kinds of personal problems. Most of these workers are college students or those just beyond this level, with minimal intensive "on-the-job" training. And I know that in many of these crisis situations they use a skill and judgment that would make a professional green with envy. They are completely "unqualified," if we use conventional standards. But they *are*, by and large, both dedicated and *competent*.

I think also of my experience in groups, where the so-called naive member often has an inner wisdom in dealing with difficult individuals and situations which far outclasses that of myself or of any other professional facilitator. It is a sobering experience to observe this. Or, when I think of the best leaders I know for dealing with groups of married couples, I think of a man and a woman, neither of whom has even the beginning of satisfactory paper credentials. Very well qualified people exist outside the fence of credentials.

But you may protest, "How are you going to stop the charlatans who exploit persons psychologically, often for great financial gain?" I respect this question, but I would point out that the person whose purpose is to exploit others can do so without calling himself a psychologist. Scientology (from which we might have learned some things, had we been less concerned about credentials) now goes its merry and profitable way as a religion! It is my considered judgment that tight professional standards do not, to more than a minimal degree, shut out the exploiters and the charlatans. If we concentrated on developing and giving outstanding personal help, individuals would come to us, rather than to con artists.

We must face the fact that in dealing with human beings a certificate does not give much assurance of real qualification. If we were less arrogant, we might also learn much from the "un-certified" individual, who is sometimes unusually adept in the area of human relationships.

I am quite aware that the position I am taking has disadvantages and involves risks. But so does the path to certification and licensure. And I have slowly come to the conclusion that if we did away with "the expert," "the certified professional," "the licensed psychologist," we might open our profession to a breeze of fresh air, a surge of creativity, such as it has not known for years.

In every area — medicine, nursing, teaching, bricklaying, or carpentry — certification has tended to freeze and narrow the profession, has tied it to the past, has discouraged innovation. If we ask ourselves how the American physician acquired the image of being a dollar-seeking reactionary, a member of the tightest union in the country, opposed to all progress and change, and especially opposed to giving health care where it is most needed, there is little doubt that the American Medical Association has slowly, even though unintentionally, built that image in the public mind. Yet the primary initial purpose of the AMA was to certify and license qualified physicians and to protect the public against the quack. It hurts me to see psychology beginning to follow that same path.

The question I am humbly raising, in the face of what I am sure will be great shock and antagonism, is simply this: Can psychology find a new and better way? Is there some more creative method of bringing together those who need help and those who are truly excellent in offering helping relationships?

I do not have a final answer, but I would point to one suggestive principle, first enunciated for me by my colleague Richard Farson (personal communication, 1966): "The population which has the problem possesses the best resources for dealing with the problem." This has been shown to be true in many areas. Drug addicts, or former drug addicts, are most successful in dealing with individuals who have drug problems; similarly, ex-alcoholics help alcoholics, ex-convicts help prisoners — all of them probably more effectively than professionals. But if we certify or otherwise give these individuals superior status as helpers, their helpfulness declines. They then become "professionals," with all the exclusiveness and territoriality that mark the professional.

So, though I know it must sound horrendous, I would like to see all the energy we put into certification rules, qualifications, licensure legislation, and written and oral examinations rechanneled into assisting clinical psychologists, social psychologists, and group leaders to become so effective, so devoted to human welfare, that they would be chosen over those who are *actually* unqualified, whether or not they possess paper credentials.

As a supplement to guide the public, we might set up the equivalent of a Consumer Protective Service. If one complaint comes in about ineffective or unethical behavior, it might well be explained away. But if many complaints come in about an individual's services to the public, then his name should be made available to the public, with the suggestion "Let the buyer beware."

Meanwhile, let us develop our learning processes in psychology in such new ways that we are of significantly more service to the public than the "instant gurus," the developers of new and untried fads, the exploiters who feed on a public obviously hungry to be dependent on someone who claims to have *the* answer to all human problems. When our own lasting helpfulness is clearly evident, then we will have no need for our elaborate machinery for certifying and licensing.

CAN WE PERMIT OURSELVES TO BE WHOLE MEN AND WOMEN?

Now I wish to move on to a quite different, yet perhaps not unrelated, challenge. Most of us spent twenty or more years in educational institutions where the intellect was *all*. Anything that counted, anything of any importance, occurred above the neck — in absorbing and memorizing, in thought and expression. Yet in life, in therapy, in marriage, in parent-child and other intimate relationships, in encounter groups, in university faculty meetings, we were forced to learn that feelings were an equally important part of living. But, due largely to our education, we still tend to dichotomize these two aspects. I have observed this so strongly in groups: if the group is assembled for an intellectual task, feelings are denied, though they are often painfully evident; if the group is assembled for personal encounter, ideas are often strongly rejected as having no place in such a group. It seems that we live on an either-or basis. We are aware of, and express, what we think; or we are aware of, and express, our emotional reactions. Almost never are the two sides of our life brought together.

The state of clinical psychology is an interesting indication of the depth of this division. Training is usually separated into courses — the straight intellectual effort — and practicum experience, in which one deals with the emotions of others, and occasionally with one's own. But the rift is most clearly indicated if I present a hypothetical example. One student states that for his dissertation he wishes to measure, with all sophisticated precaution, the differences between group A and group B. He believes he will find this intellectually stimulating and valuable. Another states that for his dissertation he wishes to present, in appropriate form and thoughtfully viewed, the most important learning in all his graduate years: the deeply insightful self-learning in his relationship with a difficult client with whom he discovered mutual growth, bringing about lasting changes in his own and his client's behavior. We all know that the first plan would be accepted without question. The second would not only be rejected, but probably angrily and summarily rejected. Who does the student think he is, trying to bring in his feelings, his understanding of his and his client's gut-level reactions, together with his thoughts about these? This would be regarded as a ridiculous subject for a dissertation.

Although this seems only normal educational procedure to the older generation, the younger generation is more and more frequently refusing to accede. I think of a weekend encounter between faculty and students at a strife-torn university. It ended inconclusively. I thought one student summed up the dilemma accurately when he finally told the faculty: "I don't know if our two worlds can *ever* meet — because our world has feelings in it." For me, this said it.

Why are so many of our best students leaving universities? Because they find no place for the whole person. Why are so many young people finding life perplexing, without meaning? Partly because they do not know that it is possible to live as a person of thought united with passion, of feeling suffused with intellect and curiosity. Thomas Hanna (1970), in his excellent book *Bodies in Revolt*, puts up a strong plea for the soma, a beautiful unity of the pulsing human organism in all of its manifestations. About the feelings of many young people about our "absurd" world, he says: "The experience of 'meaninglessness' is a living accusation of that hypertrophy of one aspect of our somas: namely conscious attention and rational effort" (p. 227). I could not agree with him more. It is the overstress on the conscious and the rational and the underestimation of the wisdom of our total reacting organism that prevent us from living as unified, whole human beings.

Yet I can testify from personal experience that it is not easy for people whose lives have been dichotomized for decades to achieve this unity. I have conducted courses in which the whole group, including myself, have agreed that our feelings are as important a part of the curriculum as our ideas. Yet, if a member starts exploring some highly emotionalized experiences into which he is beginning to gain understanding, other members hesitate to bring up anything but feeling reactions. And if one person starts a class meeting excitedly propounding the ideas involved in a budding theory he is just beginning to develop, that session tends to be intellectual in focus. Only occasionally has a group been able to *be* whole persons in the experience. Yet, when they have achieved this, the results have been unforgettable. Some members turn in highly original and scholarly papers; others express their deepest learnings in poetry or creative writing; still another brings to the final meeting a painted wooden "construction" in which he has tried artistically to set forth what his learnings have been; and still another has written a sardonic and dramatic play, very pertinent to the course. For the traditional grade-bound instructor, this would be chaos. For one who is interested in expressions of learning by the total and unified person, this is heartwarming.

But in spite of such innovative efforts — and they are increasingly frequent — dichotomized persons are still an overwhelming majority. We still go to our universities for ideas, and to encounter groups or therapy to emit any "primal scream" of our pent-up emotions.

Yet if we are truly aware, we can hear the *silent* screams of denied feelings echoing off every classroom wall and university corridor. And if we are sensitive enough, we can hear the creative thoughts and ideas that often emerge during and from the open expression of our feelings. Most of us consist of two separated parts, trying desperately to bring themselves together into an integrated soma, where the distinctions between mind and body, feelings and intellect, would be obliterated.

Who can bring into being this whole person? From my experience I would say that the least likely are university faculty members. Their traditionalism and smugness approach the incredible. I remember with something approaching horror the statement of a Columbia University professor shortly after buildings were seized and campus turmoil erupted among the students, who could not be heard in any other way. This professor told me, "There's no problem of communication at Columbia. Why, I speak to students almost every day." He sounded like a southern slaveowner in the 1850s.

No, I think that if change is to come about in dealing with ourselves and others as complete somas with thought and feeling intertwined, it will be the younger generation who achieve it. They are throwing off the shackles of tradition. They have largely discarded the religious dogmas that proclaimed the body evil and only the mind and spirit capable of good. They are a strong hope against the dichotomized, dehumanized being who can drop bombs on Vietnamese civilians, and handle this quite comfortably at the intellectual level. (In his mind, he has not murdered people, or torn flesh from bone: he has only engaged in "a protective reaction strike.") Only the younger generation, I believe, can help us to see the awful dehumanization we have bred in our educational system by separating thoughts, which are to be approved, from feelings, which are somehow seen as animal in origin. Perhaps the young can make us whole again. God knows we need once more to be unified organisms, responsive to *all* of ourselves and *all* of our environment.

IS THIS THE ONLY REALITY?

Finally, I must mention a challenge that is, I believe, the most dreadfully threatening to psychologists. It is the very strong possibility that there is more than one "reality," that there may indeed be a number of realities. This is far from a new thought. William James (1928) said that "our normal waking consciousness is but one special type of consciousness. . . . Parted from it by the filmiest of screens there lie potential forms of consciousness entirely different." He concluded that the facts then available to him "forbid our premature closing of accounts with reality."

Now, with knowledge of many types of drug-induced states of expanded consciousness and changed reality, with all the years of careful study of ESP, with the international studies of psi phenomena, with serious theorists such as LeShan (1969) explicating such phenomena, we will have a harder and harder time closing our eyes to the possibility of another reality (or realities), operating on rules quite different from our well-known commonsense empirical reality, the only one known to most psychologists.

I would like to make this a bit more personal. I have never had a mystical experience, nor any type of experience of a paranormal reality, nor any drug-induced state that gave me a glimpse of a world different from our secure "real" world. Yet, the evidence grows more and more impressive. One could pass off as inadequate reporting such books as *Psychic Discoveries Behind the Iron Curtain* (Ostrander and Schroeder, 1971), yet there are some aspects of that which are hard to brush aside. One could regard James's thinking as just an aberration of an otherwise great psychologist. One could try to dismiss the mystics of many ages and countries, were it not for remarkable similarities in their accounts, quite separate from the religious views they held. One would have a harder time with the closely reasoned arguments of Lawrence LeShan (1969), in which, starting out to destroy the myth of other realities, he gradually found himself building a theory that points in the opposite direction. He shows the astonishingly close relationship of the person "sensitive" to paranormal phenomena, the mystic of all periods, and surprisingly enough, the modern theoretical physicist. A reality in which time and space have vanished, a world in which we cannot live, but whose laws we can learn and perceive, a reality that is based not on our senses but on our inner perceptions, is common to all of these. The fact that he is continually devising ingenious ways to test his theory adds to his credibility.

I would have to say that the most vividly convincing documents

I have read come from one man, Carlos Castaneda (1968, 1971). Beginning with a thoroughgoing skepticism worthy of a university-trained anthropologist, his excursion into a new way of knowing as practiced by a wise old Yaqui Indian becomes a truly exciting and hair-raising adventure. Then his attempt to reduce all of this to acceptable rational ways of thinking (probably to obtain his Ph.D.) is simply ludicrous (1968). Obviously, he was too frightened to admit, as he does in his second book, that there is "a separate reality" (1971).

Why is this idea of another reality so threatening to psychologists? I believe it is because we are one of the most insecure of the sciences. We do not *dare* to investigate the mysterious. Yet, I think of a notably prominent physicist, very well read in psychology, who was thinking of transferring his interest and changing his profession to the field of psychology because he felt he was too old to make further contributions to theoretical physics (he was thirty-two!). The major question he wished to consult me on concerned the areas of "greatest mystery" in psychology, since it was to those he would wish to devote his time. I could not help but think that I had never heard of a psychologist aiming his work toward areas of "greatest mystery." It is only the secure scientist who can do that.

I am not suggesting that we "know" there is a separate reality (or realities). What I am saying is that we would not be demeaning ourselves if we became open-minded to such a possibility and started investigating it, as the Russians and British are doing.

To be sure, much more study is needed. I would wish to see a replication of the experiment on the mother rabbit and her litter. The mother rabbit, her brain hooked up to electrodes, was kept on shore. Her infants, far off at sea in a submarine, were killed one at a time at varying periods by the investigators. At each synchronized instant of the death of one of her babies, the mother rabbit reportedly showed clearly registered electronic reactions (Ostrander and Schroeder, 1971, pp. 33–34). What do we make of this?

A clairvoyant woman picks up an envelope which she has never seen before (containing a fragment of an ancient cuneiform tablet) and begins to describe "a girl associated with this," giving completely the portrait and life history of a secretary who had assisted in packing the object. Her report was so detailed that not one other woman in a thousand would have matched it. Yet, she said not one word that could be construed as having anything to do with the tablet. Here is a double kind of mystery which LeShan (1969, pp. 53–54) thinks he begins to understand. Yet, similar studies and the testing of his theory are certainly necessary.

And what of the various instances of precognition or simultaneous cognition of the pain or death of a loved one far away? Or telepathic communication by which a hypnotist, out of sight and at a distance, can put to sleep a trained hypnotic subject simply by concentrating on the message he wishes to get across to her (Ostrander and Schroeder, 1971, p. 104)? And finally, what do we make of the strange and unearthly experiences of Carlos Castaneda (1968, 1971)?

Perhaps in the coming generations of younger psychologists, hopefully unencumbered by university prohibitions and resistances, there will be a few who will dare to investigate the possibility that there is a lawful reality which is not open to our five senses; a reality in which present, past, and future are intermingled, in which space is not a barrier, and time has disappeared; a reality which can be perceived and known only when we are passively receptive, rather than actively bent on knowing. This is one of the most exciting challenges posed to psychology.

CONCLUSIONS

When I began this discussion, I stated that the various issues I was raising had little logical connection, but were simply diverse challenges. As I have worked over the material, I do see — from my own bias, I am sure — a certain unity to the questions I have raised. I am far from sure that I have raised the most important issues. I may be greatly deceived in the way I perceive these challenges. But let me try to restate them in fresh ways and then indicate the thread that, for me, binds them together.

I have raised the question of whether psychology will remain a narrow technological fragment of a science, tied to an outdated philosophical conception of itself, clinging to a security blanket of observable behaviors only; or whether it can possibly become a truly broad and creative science, rooted in subjective vision, open to all aspects of the human condition, worthy of the name of a mature science.

I have raised the question of whether we dare to turn from being a past-oriented remedial technology to focusing on future-oriented planning, taking our part in a chaotic world to build environments where human beings can choose to learn, where minorities can choose to remake the establishment through relating to it, where people can learn to live cooperatively together. Will psychologists continue to be peripheral to our society, or will we risk the dangers of being a significant social factor?

I have pointed out that perhaps the safety, the prestige, the vestments of traditionalism that can be earned through certification and licensure may not be worth the cost. I have wondered aloud if we would dare to rest our confidence in the quality and competence we have as persons, rather than the certificates we can frame on our walls.

I have questioned—a bit despairingly, I fear—whether we could possibly see the day when faculty and students and psychologists in general could function as whole persons—not as minds walking around on stilts, or headless feelings muttering wild cries to one another. Could we accept ourselves as total organisms, with wisdom in every pore—if we would but hear and be aware of that wisdom?

I have hesitantly pointed out that the reality we are so sure of, the reality so plainly shown to us by our senses, may not be the only reality open to humankind. I have raised the query as to whether we would ever be willing to take the frightening risk of investigating this possibility, without prejudgment.

As I mull over these issues, I believe that if psychology—as a science and a profession—gave a clear affirmative answer to each of these questions, gave a positive response to each of these challenges, it would be moving forward.

So the thread that I see in the issues I have raised is that each one represents a possible move toward the enhancement, the deepening, the enrichment of our profession. Each issue, in a word, represents for psychology a step toward self-actualization. If my perceptions have been even approximately correct, then the final question I would leave with you is, Do we dare?

REFERENCES

Castaneda, C. *The teachings of Don Juan: A Yaqui way of knowledge.* New York: Ballantine Books, 1968.

Castaneda, C. *A separate reality: Further conversations with Don Juan.* New York: Simon & Schuster (A Touchstone Book), 1971.

Coulson, W. R., & Rogers, C. R. (Eds.). *Man and the science of man.* Columbus, Ohio: Charles E. Merrill, 1968.

Dagenais, J. J. *Models of man.* The Hague, Netherlands: Martinus Nimhoff, 1972.

Hanna, T. *Bodies in revolt: A primer in somatic thinking.* New York: Holt, Rinehart, & Winston, 1970.

Hanna, T. The project of somatology. Paper presented at the annual meeting of the Association for Humanistic Psychology, Washington, D.C., September 1971.

James, W. *The varieties of religious experience.* London: Longmans, Green, 1928.

Koch, S. Epilogue. In S. Koch (Ed.), *Psychology: A study of a science* (Vol. 3). New York: McGraw-Hill, 1959.

LeShan, L. *Toward a general theory of the paranormal.* New York: Parapsychology Foundation, 29 W. 57th Street, New York, 1969.

Oppenheimer, R. Analogy in science. *American Psychologist,* 1956, *11*, 127–135.

Ostrander, S., and Schroeder, L. *Psychic discoveries behind the Iron Curtain.* New York: Bantam Books, 1971.

Polanyi, M. *Personal knowledge.* Chicago: University of Chicago Press, 1958.

Rogers, C. R. Persons or science? A philosophical question. *American Psychologist,* 1955, *10*, 267–278.

Rogers, C. R. Toward a science of the person. In T. W. Wann (Ed.), *Behaviorism and phenomenology: Contrasting bases for modern psychology.* Chicago: University of Chicago Press, 1964.

Schilpp, P. A. (Ed.) *Albert Einstein: Philosopher-scientist.* New York: Harper Torchbooks, 1959.

Schultz, D. P. (Ed.). *The science of psychology: Critical reflections.* New York: Appleton-Century-Crofts, 1970.

Skinner, B. F. A case history in scientific method. In S. Koch (Ed.), *Psychology: A study of a science* (Vol. 2). New York: McGraw-Hill, 1959.

25
The Politics of the Helping Professions

Three years ago I was first asked about the politics of the client-centered approach to psychotherapy. I replied that there was no politics in client-centered therapy, an answer which was greeted with a loud guffaw. When I asked my questioner to explain, he replied, "I spent three years of graduate school learning to be an expert in clinical psychology. I learned to make accurate diagnostic judgments. I learned the various techniques of altering the subject's attitudes and behavior. I learned subtle modes of manipulation, under the labels of interpretation and guidance. Then I began to read your material, which upset everything I had learned. You were saying that the power rests not in my mind but in his organism. You completely reversed the relationship of power and control which had been built up in me over three years. And then you say there is no politics in the client-centered approach!"

This was the beginning—perhaps a late beginning—of my education regarding the politics of interpersonal relationships. The more I thought and read, and the more I sensed the present-day concern with power and control, the more new facets I experienced in my relationships in therapy, in intensive groups, in families, and among friends. Gradually I realized my experience ran parallel to the old story of the uneducated man and his first exposure to a course in literature. "You know," he told his friends later, "I've found out I've been speaking prose all my life and never knew it." In similar vein I could now say "I've been practicing and teaching politics all my professional life and never realized it fully until now." So I am no longer surprised when Farson, in an appraisal of my work, says, "Carl Rogers is not known for his politics. People are more likely to associate his name with widely acclaimed innovations in counseling technique, personality theory, philosophy of science, psychotherapy research, encounter groups, student-centered teaching. . . . But

Carl Rogers On Personal Power. New York: Delacorte Press, 1977, 3–28.

in recent years, I have come to think of him more as a political figure, a man whose cumulative effect on society has made him one of the . . . social revolutionaries of our time."[1] It is not just that I am a slow learner, that I have only recently realized my political impact. It is partly that a new concept has been in the process of construction in our language. It is not just a new label. It brings together a cluster of meanings into a powerful new concept.

The use of the word *politics* in such contexts as "the politics of the family," "the politics of therapy," "sexual politics," "the politics of experience" is new. I have not found any dictionary definition that even suggests the way in which the word is currently utilized. *The American Heritage Dictionary* still gives definitions only of this sort: **politics:** "The methods or tactics involved in managing a state or government."[2]

Yet the word has acquired a new set of meanings. Politics, in present-day psychological and social usage, has to do with *power and control*: with the extent to which persons desire, attempt to obtain, possess, share, or surrender power and control over others and/or themselves. It has to do with *the maneuvers, the strategies and tactics, witting or unwitting*, by which such power and control over one's own life and others' lives is sought and gained — or shared or relinquished. It has to do with the *locus of decision-making power*: who makes the decisions which, consciously or unconsciously, regulate or control the thoughts, feelings, or behavior of others or oneself. It has to do with the *effects of these decisions and these strategies*, whether proceeding from an individual or a group, whether aimed at gaining or relinquishing control upon the person himself, upon others, and upon the various systems of society and its institutions.

In sum it is the process of gaining, using, sharing or relinquishing power, control, decision-making. It is the process of the highly complex interactions and effects of these elements as they exist in relationships between persons, between a person and a group, or between groups.

This new construct has had a powerful influence on me. It has caused me to take a fresh look at my professional life work. I've had a role in initiating the person-centered approach. This view developed first in counseling and psychotherapy, where it was known as client-centered, meaning a person seeking help was not treated as a dependent patient but as a responsible client. Extended to education, it was called student-centered teaching. As it has moved into a wide variety of fields, far from its point of origin — intensive groups, marriage, family relationships, administration, minority groups, interracial, intercultural, and even international relationships — it seems best to adopt as broad a term as possible: person-centered.

It is the psychological dynamics of this approach that has interested me — how it is seen by and how it affects the individual. I have been interested in observing this approach from a scientific and empirical point of view; what conditions make it possible for a person to change and develop, and what are the specific effects or outcomes of these conditions. But I have never given careful consideration to the interpersonal politics set in motion by such an approach. Now I begin to see the revolutionary nature of those political forces. I have found myself compelled to reassess and reevaluate all my work. I wish to ask what are the *political* effects (in the new sense of political) of all that I, and my many colleagues throughout the world, have done and are doing.

What is the impact of a client-centered point of view on the issues of power and control in individual psychotherapy? We shall explore the politics of various approaches to helping people, whether through one-to-one therapy, or through encounter or other intensive groups. We shall confront openly a subject not often discussed: the issue of power and control in the so-called helping professions.

In 1940 I began to try to change what I would now call the politics of therapy. Describing an emerging trend, I said,

> This newer approach differs from the older one in that it has a genuinely different goal. It aims directly toward the greater independence and integration of the individual rather than hoping that such results will accrue if the counselor assists in solving the problem. The individual and not the problem is the focus. The aim is not to solve one particular problem but to assist the individual to *grow*, so that he can cope with the present problem and with later problems in a better integrated fashion. If he can gain enough integration to handle one problem in more independent,

more responsible, less confused, better organized ways, then he will also handle new problems in that manner.

If this seems a little vague, it may be made more specific. . . . It relies much more heavily on the individual drive toward growth, health, and adjustment. Therapy is not a matter of doing something *to* the individual, or of inducing him to do something about himself. It is instead a matter of freeing him for normal growth and development, of removing obstacles so that he can again move forward.[3]

When they were enunciated first in 1940, great furor was aroused by these statements. I had described various counseling techniques much in use at that time — such as suggestions, advice, persuasion, and interpretation — and had pointed out that these rested on two basic assumptions: that "the counselor knows best," and that he can find techniques by which to move his client most efficiently to the counselor-chosen goal.

I see now that I had dealt a double-edged political blow. I had said that most counselors saw themselves as competent to control the lives of their clients. And I had advanced the view that it was preferable simply to free the client to become an independent, self-directing person. I was making it clear that if they agreed with me, it would mean the complete disruption and reversal of their personal control in their counseling relationships.

Over the years, the point of view I advanced so tentatively in 1940 became enlarged, deepened, and reinforced, both by clinical experience and research. It became known as client-centered psychotherapy, and in the intervening years it has been buttressed by more empirical studies than any other therapeutic approach.

From the perspective of politics, power, and control, person-centered therapy is based on a premise which at first seemed risky and uncertain: a view of man as at core a trustworthy organism. This base has over the years been strengthened by experience with troubled individuals, psychotic persons, small intensive groups, students in classes, and staff groups. It has become more and more firmly established as a basic stance, though each person must learn it step by step for himself, to be convinced of its soundness. I have recently described it as "the gradually formed and tested hypothesis that the individual has within himself vast resources for self-understanding, for altering his self-concept, his attitudes, and his self-directed behavior — and that these resources can be tapped if only a definable climate of facilitative psychological attitudes can be provided."[4]

Is there any basis for this premise other than wishful thinking and the experience of a few people? I believe so. Biologists, neurophysiologists, and other scientists, including psychologists, have evidence that adds up to one conclusion. There is in every organism, at whatever level, an underlying flow of movement toward constructive fulfillment of its inherent possibilities. There is a natural tendency toward complete development in man. The term that has most often been used for this is the actualizing tendency, and it is present in all living organisms. It is the foundation on which the person-centered approach is built.

The actualizing tendency can of course be thwarted, but it cannot be destroyed without destroying the organism. I remember that in my boyhood the potato bin in which we stored our winter supply of potatoes was in the basement, several feet below a small basement window. The conditions were unfavorable, but the potatoes would begin to sprout — pale white sprouts, so unlike the healthy green shoots they sent up when planted in the soil in the spring. But these sad, spindly sprouts would grow two or three feet in length as they reached toward the distant light of the window. They were, in their bizarre, futile growth, a sort of desperate expression of the directional tendency I have been describing. They would never become a plant, never mature, never fulfill their real potentiality. But under the most adverse circumstances they were striving to become. Life would not give up, even if it could not flourish. In dealing with clients whose lives have been terribly warped, in working with men and women on the back wards of state hospitals, I often think of those potato sprouts. So unfavorable have been the conditions in which these people have developed that their lives often seem abnormal, twisted, scarcely human. Yet the directional tendency in them is to be trusted. The clue to understanding their behavior is that they are striving, in the only ways available to them, to move toward growth, toward becoming. To us the results may seem bizarre and futile, but they are life's desperate attempt to become itself. It is this potent tendency which is the underlying basis of client-centered therapy and all that has grown out of it.

It is obvious that even this premise of client-centered therapy, without going further, has enormous political implications. Our educational system, our industrial and military organizations, and many other aspects of our culture take the view that the nature of the individual is such that he cannot be trusted — that he must be guided, instructed, rewarded, punished, and controlled by those who are wiser or higher in status. To be sure, we give lip service to a democratic philosophy in which all power is invested in the people, but this philosophy is "honored more in the breach than in the observance." Hence simply describing the fundamental premise of client-centered therapy is to make a challenging political statement.

The politics of the client-centered approach is a conscious renunciation and avoidance by the therapist of all control over, or decision-making for, the client. It is the facilitation of self-ownership by the client and the strategies by which this can be achieved. The placing of the locus of decision-making and the responsibility for the effects of these decisions are politically centered in the client.

Client-centered therapy has forever changed the politics of psychotherapy by the recording and publishing of transcribed therapeutic interviews. The mysterious, unknowable operations of the therapist are now wide open for all to see. This has let a breath of fresh air and common sense pervade the therapeutic world. The individual is able at least to choose a school of therapy that appears congenial to him. And where, at first, only client-centered interviews were available for discussion and criticism, there are now available on tape recordings expert therapists of a variety of orientations.[5]

Tom Hanna summarizes well the effect of this, and places a person-centered psychotherapy in a broader context.

> Humanistic psychology has served to demystify the nature of therapy. Both the theory and the practice of therapeutic change should be made public, so that this knowledge can be shared in common by both the patient and the therapist. . . . It is not a matter of the therapist following the old authoritarian medical

model of keeping the patient in the dark as a patriarch might treat a child. . . . It is a matter of the habituated, unhappy individual regaining self-control and self-maintenance of his own wholeness and health.

Of course, this is a most "unprofessional" procedure, for it gives away the authority, the secrecy and the unquestionability of the professional healer and therapist. And it gives these things away to the patient. The center of the therapeutic action is not, therefore, considered to be within the therapist's decisions but within the patient's decisions.[6]

It is hardly necessary to say that the person-centered view drastically alters the therapist-patient relationship, as previously conceived. The therapist becomes the "midwife" of change, not its originator. She places the final authority in the hands of the client, whether in small things such as the correctness of a therapist response, or large decisions like the course of one's life direction. The locus of evaluation, of decision, rests clearly in the client's hands.

A person-centered approach is based on the premise that the human being is basically a trustworthy organism, capable of evaluating the outer and inner situation, understanding herself in its context, making constructive choices as to the next steps in life, and acting on those choices.

A facilitative person can aid in releasing these capacities when relating as a real person to the other, owning and expressing her own feelings; when experiencing a nonpossessive caring and love for the other; and when acceptantly understanding the inner world of the other. When this approach is made to an individual or a group, it is discovered that, over time, the choices made, the directions pursued, the actions taken are increasingly constructive personally and tend toward a more realistic social harmony with others.

So familiar has this humanistic, person-centered concept become — more familiar in the realm of the intellect than in actual practice — that we sometimes forget what a blow it struck at the views then current. It has taken me years to recognize that the violent opposition to a client-centered therapy sprang not only from its newness, and the fact that it came from a psychologist rather than a psychiatrist, but primarily because it struck such an outrageous blow to the therapist's *power*. It was in its *politics* that it was most threatening.

Freud shows his degree of distrust of the basic nature of man when he says, speaking of the need for superego control: "Our mind, that precious instrument by whose means we maintain ourselves alive, is no peacefully self-contained unity. It is rather to be compared with a modern State in which a mob, eager for enjoyment and destruction, has to be held down forcibly by a prudent superior class."[7]

To the end of his days, Freud still felt that if man's basic nature were released, nothing but destruction could be expected. The need for control of this beast within man was a matter of the greatest urgency.

> The core of our being, then, is formed by the obscure id. . . . The one and only endeavor of these instincts is toward satisfaction. . . . But an immediate and regardless satisfaction of instinct, such as the id demands, would often enough lead to perilous conflicts with the external world and to extinction. . . . The id obeys the inexorable pleasure principle . . . and it remains a question of the greatest theoretical importance, and one that has not yet been answered, when and how it is ever possible for the pleasure principle to be overcome.[8]

As for the question of power and control in the everyday world, Freud took a very authoritarian stance: "The great majority of people have a strong need for authority which they can admire, to which they can submit, and which dominates and sometimes even ill-treats them. We have learned from the psychology of the individual whence comes this need of the masses. It is the longing for the father that lives in each of us from his childhood days."[9]

Freud's view of groups is equally pessimistic and startling. It would almost seem that Hitler must have studied and adopted these views:

> A group is extraordinarily credulous and open to influence, it has no critical faculty, and the improbable does not exist for it. . . . Inclined as it itself is to all extremes, a group can only be excited by an excessive stimulus. Anyone who wishes to produce an effect upon it needs no logical adjustment in his arguments; he must

paint in the most forcible colors, he must exaggerate, and he must repeat the same thing again and again. . . . It respects force and can only be slightly influenced by kindness, which it regards merely as a form of weakness. . . . It wants to be ruled and oppressed, and to fear its masters. . . . And, finally, groups have never thirsted after truth. They demand illusions, and cannot do without them. They constantly give what is unreal precedence over what is real; they are almost as strongly influenced by what is untrue as by what is true. They have an evident tendency not to distinguish between the two. . . . A group is an obedient herd, which could never live without a master. It has such a thirst for obedience that it submits instinctively to anyone who appoints himself as its master.[10]

For a therapist who was guided by Freud's thinking, client-centered views such as the following must have seemed not only heretical but highly dangerous: that the human organism is, at its deepest level, trustworthy; that man's basic nature is not something to be feared, but to be released in responsible self-expression; that small groups (in therapy or in classrooms) can responsibly and sensitively build constructive interpersonal relationships and choose wise individual and group goals; that all of the foregoing will be achieved if a facilitative person assists by creating a climate of realness, understanding, and caring. Now that I review again Freud's views I can better understand why I was solemnly warned at the Menninger Clinic, around 1950, about the results of my views. I was told I would produce a dangerous psychopath because there would be no one to control her innately destructive core.

Over the years, Freudian analysts have softened their views of the politics of therapy. Along with Gestalt therapists, Jungians, rational emotive therapists, advocates of transactional analysis, and many other new therapies, they now take a middle-of-the-road view. The expert is at times definitely the authority (as in the Gestalt therapist dealing with the person in the "hot seat"), but there is also a recognition of the right of the individual to be responsible for himself. There has been no attempt to rationalize these contradictions. These therapists take a paternalistic stance, or follow the medical model, believing that at times control is best vested in the therapist, at other times (to be decided by the therapist) control and responsibility are best placed in the client's, or patient's, hands.

One approach which has been very definite in the politics of relationships is behaviorism. Its clear purpose is outlined in Skinner's famous *Walden Two*.[11] For the good of the person (individually or collectively), an elitist technocracy of behaviorists sets the goals that will make the person happy and productive. It then shapes her behavior by operant conditioning (with or without the "subject's" knowledge) to achieve those goals. One's behavior is, after all, *completely* determined by environment, and this might better be planned so as to make one happy, socialized, and moral. Who is it that sets the environment for the *planners* so that their completely determined behavior causes them to operate as such a wise and good elite is a question always deftly avoided. Nevertheless it is assumed that their goals will be constructively social, and the shaping of behavior will be for the good of the person as well as society.

Yet at times, when applied to aberrant behavior, this approach seems a little startling. In "Criminals Can Be Brainwashed—Now," McConnell says: "We'd assume that a felony was clear evidence that the criminal had somehow acquired a full-blown social neurosis and needed to be cured, not punished. We'd send him to a rehabilitation center where he'd undergo positive brainwashing until we were quite sure he had become a law-abiding citizen who would not again commit an antisocial act. We'd probably have to restructure his entire personality."[12] McConnell seems completely oblivious to the political implications of what he is saying. Clearly psychologists who believe as he does would be the first to be subsidized and employed by a dictator, who would be very happy to have them "cure" various "felonies" that threatened the state.

In fairness to behaviorists it should be said that many of them have come to adopt a greatly changed view of the politics of relationships. In the commune Twin Oaks, patterned initially after Walden Two, the residents often choose for themselves which behaviors they wish to change, and select the rewards which will be most reinforcing. Clearly this is completely opposed to the politics of the strict behaviorist, since it is self-initiated, self-evaluated change. It is not the environment shaping the individual's behavior, but the individual choosing to shape the environment for her own personal development.

Some behaviorists have gone even further. Several recent books depart completely from the basic Skinnerian view. Rather than controlling the individual, they are helping the person learn to achieve her own betterment. The title of the latest book to come to my attention is sufficient in itself to show that its philosophy is far removed from that of Walden Two. The title is *Self-Control: Power to the Person!*[13] In its politics this is the reverse of strict behaviorism.

The foregoing paragraphs may give the impression that therapists, in the interpersonal politics of their therapies, are gradually drifting toward a more humanistic view, and may not actually differ very much from each other in the pattern of their relationships. Nothing could be further from the truth, as is dramatically illustrated by a landmark study by Raskin,[14] begun more than a decade ago but only recently appearing in published form.

Raskin took six recorded interviews, conducted by six widely known and experienced therapists, each from a different school of thought. Each therapist approved a selected segment of his interview as being representative of his way of working. These segments were rated by eighty-three therapists, who classified themselves as belonging to twelve different therapeutic orientations. The segments were rated on many variables drawn from differing therapeutic theories and practices. Looked at politically, those who rated high on such variables as "therapist-directed" or "systematically reinforces" are clearly therapists whose behavior is controlling, and who make important choices for the client. Those who rate high on such variables as "warm and giving," "equalitarian," and "empathic" obviously leave power and choice in the hands of the client.

When these eighty-three therapists used the same variables to give their picture of the "ideal" therapist, there was very substantial agreement, and the outstanding characteristics were all *non*controlling. In other words they *desire* to behave in ways that treat the client as an autonomous person.

Yet in practice the picture is very different. Of the six expert therapists rated, only two—the client-centered and experiential therapists—showed any great similarity to the ideal therapist. The other four—including the rational emotive, the psychoanalytic, the Jungian—correlated negatively with the ideal, some sharply so. In other words, in *practice* four of the six were more opposite to than like the ideal therapist as perceived by the eighty-three practicing therapists. The politics of the therapeutic relationship thus not only differs sharply from therapist to therapist, but in the same therapist may show a sharp difference between the professed ideal of the group and the way she actually behaves.

Most procedures in psychotherapy may be placed on a scale having to do with power and control. At one end of the scale stand orthodox Freudians and orthodox behaviorists, believing in a politics of authoritarian or elitist control of persons "for their own good," either to produce better adjustment to the status quo or happiness or contentment or productivity or all of these. In the middle are most of the contemporary schools of psychotherapy, confused, ambiguous, or paternalistic in the politics of their relationships (though they may be very clear regarding their therapeutic strategies). At the other end of the scale is the client-centered, experiential, person-centered approach, consistently stressing the capacity and autonomy of the person, her right to choose the directions she will move in her behavior, and her ultimate responsibility for herself in the therapeutic relationship, with the therapist's person playing a real but primarily catalytic part in that relationship.[15]

This same scale can be applied to the interpersonal relationships in intensive groups. These are so multiform—T-groups, encounter groups, sensitivity training, sensory awareness groups, Gestalt groups, and the like—that generalization is well-nigh impossible. The outstanding fact is that different group leaders vary enormously in the way of relating. Some are highly authoritarian and directive. Others make maximum use of exercises and games to reach goals they have chosen. Others feel little responsibility toward group members: "I do my thing and you do your thing." Others, including me, endeavor to be facilitative, but in no way controlling.[16] Each leader should probably be considered as an individual if we are to assess the politics of her approach.

One new approach appears to be sweeping the country. This is the Erhard Seminars Training, founded by Werner Erhard, and better known as "est." It is the extreme of the leader-dominated type of group. Members are held to an absolute discipline, subjected to long hours of ridicule and abuse. All their beliefs are "bullshit," and they themselves are "assholes." This leads to such confusion that eventually the unquestioned authority of the leader is established. The final damning statement is that "You are nothing but a goddamn machine! And you can't be anything but what you are." Then comes the optimistic revelation that "if you accept the nature of your mind . . . and take responsibility for having created all the . . . mechanisms it comprises, then in effect you have freely chosen to do everything you have ever done and to be precisely what you are. In that instant you become exactly what you always wanted to be!"[17]

A great many of the group experience conversion-type experiences and feel their lives have been greatly changed for the better. From the point of view of interpersonal politics, two things impress me. One is the leader's assumption of absolute control. Though some resent this, the majority who surrender to the will of the leader indicates what a large proportion of persons desires to be dependent on a guru. The second point is that in Erhard's voluminous speeches, where he describes in many ways the outcomes of his work, he never once refers to the authoritarian *process* by which these changes are brought about. As in all authoritarian approaches, the end justifies the means. In the person-centered approach, the *process* is all-important, and the changes are only partially predictable.

While est is an extreme example, there is much political significance in the increasing use of games and exercises in all types of intensive groups. There must by now be hundreds of such exercises, and many who are active in the intensive group movement use them constantly.

There are many varieties of the fantasy trip. "I'm going to play some music, and I want each of you to have a fantasy while you listen. Then we can each share our fantasies with the others." There are also many exercises involving touching. Here is one that involves both touching and feedback. "One at a time, go around the circle. Touch each person, look in his eyes, and tell him what you feel about him." And of course this one: "We will speak only of our feelings in the here and now, with no references to the past or to the outside world."

The politics of these exercises depend very much on how they are used. If the leader describes the game and its purpose, asks the members if they wish to participate, permits individuals to opt out if they desire, it is clearly not a coercive move. On the other hand, if the leader declares "Now we will all . . ." the impact is very different indeed. There is no doubt that in general the use of exercises or games makes the group leader-centered rather than member-centered.

Here is an example that indicates the efficacy of the person-centered approach. Diabasis is a center for dealing with acutely schizophrenic young persons that was established by John W. Perry, M.D., a respected Jungian analyst. Diabasis is a Greek word meaning "crossing over."

Perry had had twenty-five years of experience in dealing with psychotics in various settings. He had become increasingly convinced that most schizophrenic episodes were actually a chaotic but vital attempt at growth and self-healing, and that if such an "Individual" (he dropped the term *patient*) were treated as a person and provided with a close and trusting relationship, she could, in a relatively short time, live through this crisis and emerge stronger and healthier.[19]

Dr. Perry and Dr. Howard Levine, another Jungian analyst, set up Diabasis to implement this view more fully than could be done in a psychiatric hospital. The first step was to select a staff. Paper credentials were disregarded. The criteria for selection consisted of attitudes. They chose people, mostly young, who showed in their training seminars an ability to relate to withdrawn individuals who were preoccupied with events in their inner worlds. Many of these young volunteers were members of the counterculture. They knew what it was to be alienated. Often they had been on drug trips—good and bad. They were not frightened by bizarre thoughts or behavior.

The home that housed Diabasis had room for only six Individuals, plus volunteers and minimal house staff. It "is a non-authoritarian, non-judgmental milieu in which each individual (staff as well as client) is allowed to express himself in whatever modes he chooses, emotionally, artistically, and physically. Clients at every point of their psychosis are regarded as being in a 'legitimate' state and are not compelled . . . to conform to 'rational' modes of behavior."[20] Instead the psychotic individual is accepted in two important ways. He is accepted by everyone in the house as going through a stressful period of growth during which he needs understanding and companionship.

Of equal importance is the special relationship with one staff person, who thoroughly invests herself in building a trusting closeness with the troubled person. Whenever possible the individual selects this special person with whom to work. Dr. Perry describes well the reason for this special staff member.

> The inner journey or renewal process tends to remain scattered, fragmented, and incoherent until the point at which the individual begins to open up to another person enough to entrust to him his inner experience as it unfolds. When this happens the content of his symbolic experience becomes more intensified, and thereupon apparently moves ahead in a more progressive fashion toward its conclusion. It is often surprising how 'psychotic' and yet at the same time coherent the patient's communication can be, providing he feels related to the therapist.[21]

The same point is made by a young man who worked for two years at Diabasis, first as a volunteer, recently on the paid staff. He says:

> We feel that what is called madness can best be understood as a journey of exploration and discovery, regulated by the psyche, in which the various elements of the personality can be reorganized in a more fruitful and self-fulfilling way. This process can only occur, however, in an environment in which these altered states of consciousness are respected as valid ways of being, rather than being derided as "crazy" and of no value.[22]

The contrast with the medical model of treatment of psychosis could scarcely be greater. Under the medical model, this individual is first of all a patient rather than a person. She is diagnosed, and either explicitly or implicitly is given to know that she has an "illness," a craziness, which is to be eliminated by heavy medication or shock therapy, or even restraint if necessary, until her "illness" is eradicated. It is clear that there is something "wrong" with her state, and she must somehow be brought around into a "right" state. "In the traditional settings there is massive use of medication and behavioral restraint in the early phase of the treatment to *suppress* the psychotic material. There is no attempt to see the material as useful to the individual involved. Thus, after *control* of the psychosis has been established, no efforts are made to integrate the material into the ongoing life of the individual."[23] It is a politics of suppression and control by professional power, and it has a very poor record, as indicated by the "revolving door" syndrome of psychiatric hospitals.

In Diabasis, as in any person-centered therapy, the politics is completely reversed. As Perry says,

> The philosophy of therapy is, in this case, not one of imposing order from above downwards by a regimen of strict management, but rather it is a more fluid one of sensitively following the Individual's concerns as they evolve through the process in order to catalyze it. Then a democratic structure of the ward community is the appropriate form, in which ordering and integrating are expected to emerge from the spontaneous concerns and feelings and insights of both resident Individuals and staff together.[24]

This means that the Individual provides the leads, points the directions she needs to go. Empathically, the therapist and the other house staff act as companions in following those leads, without sacrificing their own feelings or their own personhood. "The non-rational concerns of the client are given a full hearing and, to the best of the staff's ability (which increases with experience) are empathically understood, as a necessary and deeply meaningful inner journey."[25] The nurses take their cues from the Individual and these closer staff companions. The psychiatrist aids in helping them all understand the directions they are taking, but in no sense directs the process. Essential power and control thus flow upward from the psychotic person and her needs, to the dedicated house staff, to the nurses and psychiatrists. It is a complete reversal of traditional hierarchical, psychiatric treatment.

This focus on the person is evident in the highly equalitarian atmosphere. Staff and Individuals eat together, dress as they desire. The casual visitor would have no way of knowing who was client and who was staff.

This whole atmosphere has permeated the organization as well. From the first the administration of Diabasis became the province of the whole staff rather than of a director. The power, responsibility, and decision-making are shared by all. "Democracy can be recognized as a state of psychic development in which the ordering and ruling principle is realized as belonging essentially within the psychic life of the individual. . . . The social structure and culture established in the therapeutic milieu should be a reflection of this natural need, a fitting external expression of what is happening in depth."[26] In person-centered therapy, the traditional organization, with power flowing down from the top, becomes totally inappropriate and ridiculous.

The immediate result of this whole program on the psychotic individual is dramatic. "What has been most remarkable and beyond all of our expectations, is that individuals in acutely psychotic turmoils very rapidly settle down and become clear and coherent, usually within a period of a few days to a week, and without the use of medication. Thus severely disturbed behavior becomes manageable when staff relate with feeling to the individual's emotional state."[27]

Although the history of this unique place is brief, the outcomes appear to be good. One indication is that four former clients (Individuals) are already on the staff of a conceptually similar small institution. They are now able to use their own past experience to help others. The cost is far less than in the usual facility. And it seems to have left behind the "revolving door" experience of the state hospital.

It is reasonable to suppose that this innovative, helpful new mode of dealing with the young person during her first psychotic episode would be widely hailed and eagerly supported. Not so. To understand the reasons, we need to look at the politics of Diabasis, and the threat it constitutes to the traditional politics.

It is easy to see why orthodox psychiatrists and even Jungian colleagues look upon Diabasis with uneasiness and criticism. At Diabasis the best therapists often have proven to be relatively untrained paraprofessionals. This is disturbing to the ordinary professional. They are mostly volunteers, thus posing a vague economic threat. There is no strict medical control, in the ordinary sense. This offends physicians. The doctors do not even use their prerogative to prescribe medication. Dr. Perry thinks he has given two tranquilizers in the past ten months! The organization itself is not *directed* by physicians. They are simply facilitators of a process. This is a staggering departure from tradition.

Consequently there is grumbling and criticism about "low standards." Financial support is very difficult to come by. Like all person-centered therapy, it is revolutionary in its implications, and the professional establishment is fearful of it. To see psychiatrists relinquishing control of "patients" and staff, to see them serving only as successful facilitators of personal growth for deeply troubled "insane" persons rather than being in *charge* of these people is, I am sad to say, a very frightening scene to psychiatrists, psychologists, and other mental health professionals. Revolutionaries are seen as dangerous — and there is no doubt that they *are* dangerous to the established order.

A person-centered approach, when utilized to encourage the growth and development of the psychotic, the troubled, or the normal individual, revolutionizes the customary behaviors of members of the helping professions. It illustrates many things: (1) A sensitive person, trying to be of help, becomes more person-centered, no matter what orientation she starts from, because she finds that approach more effective. (2) When you are focused on the person, diagnostic labels become largely irrelevant. (3) The traditional medical model in psychotherapy is discovered to be largely in opposition to person-centeredness. (4) It is found that those who can create an effective person-centered relationship do not necessarily come from the professionally trained group. (5) The more this person-centered approach is implemented and put into practice, the more it is found to challenge hierarchical models of "treatment" and hierarchical methods of organization. (6) The very effectiveness of this unified person-centered approach constitutes a threat to professionals, administrators, and others, and steps are taken — consciously and unconsciously — to destroy it. It is too revolutionary.

REFERENCES

1. R. Farson, "Carl Rogers, Quiet Revolutionary," *Education*, 95, No. 2 (Winter 1974), p. 197.
2. *American Heritage Dictionary*, Boston: Houghton Mifflin, 1982.
3. C. R. Rogers, *Counseling and Psychotherapy*, Boston: Houghton Mifflin, 1942, pp. 28–29.
4. C. R. Rogers, "In Retrospect: 46 Years," *American Psychology*, 29, No. 2 (1974), p. 116.
5. Available from AAP Tape Library, 1040 Woodcock Road, Orlando, Fla. 32803.
6. T. Hanna, *The End of Tyranny*, San Francisco: Freeperson Press, 1975, pp. 162–163.
7. S. Freud, "My Contact with Josef Popper-Lynkeus," in *Character and Culture*, from Collier Books edition of *The Collected Papers of Sigmund Freud*, translated by J. Strachey, New York: Crowell-Collier, 1963 (originally published 1932), p. 303.
8. S. Freud, *Outline of Psychoanalysis*. New York: Norton, 1949, pp. 108–109.
9. S. Freud, *Moses and Monotheism*, New York: Random House, 1955.
10. S. Freud, *Group Psychology and the Analysis of the Ego*. London: Hogarth Press, 1948 (published in the United States by Liveright Publishing Corporation), pp. 15–21.
11. B. F. Skinner, *Walden Two*, New York: Macmillan, 1960.
12. J. McConnell, "Criminals Can Be Brainwashed — Now," *Psychology Today* (April 1970). Cited in W. Anderson, "Politics and the New Humanism," *Journal of Humanistic Psychology*, 14, No. 4 (Fall 1974), p. 21. (Condensed from his book of the same title, Pacific Palisades, Calif.: Goodyear, 1973.)
13. M. J. Mahoney and C. E. Thorense, *Self-Control: Power to the Person*. Monterey, Calif.: Brooks/Cole, 1974.
14. N. Raskin, "Studies of Psychotherapeutic Orientation: Ideology and Practice," *AAP Research Monograph No. 1*, American Academy of Psychotherapists, Orlando, Fla., 1974.
15. This general philosophical stance in relation to therapy is expressed not only in my own writings and others of the client-centered group but by R. D. Laing, *The Politics of Experience*, New York: Ballantine Books, 1968; John W. Perry, *The Far Side of Madness*, Englewood Cliffs: Prentice-Hall, 1974; Thomas S. Szasz, *The Myth of Mental Illness*, rev. ed., New York: Harper & Row, 1974; and other well-known therapists.
16. C. R. Rogers, *Carl Rogers on Encounter Groups*, New York: Harper & Row, 1970.

17. M. Brewer, "Erhard Seminars Training: 'We're Going to Tear You Down and Put You Back Together,'" *Psychology Today*, *9*, No. 3 (August 1975), p. 88.
18. Rogers, *Encounter Groups*, p. 56.
19. J. W. Perry, "Diabasis II," unpublished manuscript, 1975.
20. Perry, "Diabasis II," p. 5.
21. J. W. Perry, personal communication, 1975, p. 3.
22. B. Heller, personal communication, 1975.
23. Perry, "Diabasis II," p. 5.
24. Perry, *The Far Side of Madness*, p. 151.
25. Perry, "Diabasis II," p. 5.
26. Perry, *The Far Side of Madness*, pp. 151–152.
27. Perry, "Diabasis II," p. 5.

A PHILOSOPHY OF PERSONS

The fields of religion, science, art, psychology, or any other discipline of human culture, inevitably confront the perennial dilemmas of the human condition. It is not surprising, therefore, that decades of practicing in-depth psychotherapy would eventually lead Carl Rogers to consider some of the basic questions of human philosophy. "The Nature of Man," the first selection of this section, explores one such question.

What *is* the human being really like at his or her deepest level of being? Rogers's position on this topic was often oversimplified by others. It was generally assumed that he believed that humans were "basically good," and that was that. Freudian psychoanalysts, psychiatrists, theologians, and others often accused Rogers of an overly optimistic view of human nature. Rogers once told an interviewer that existential psychotherapist Rollo May "told the story that I once questioned the existence of tragedy by saying that Romeo and Juliet might have been all right with just a little counseling."

Rogers's actual belief about the nature of man was somewhat more sophisticated than that, although it is accurate to say it *is* a more optimistic view than that held by most of his critics. In fact, his conception of the nature of man is a revolutionary departure from almost all of Western tradition — a more optimistic view than Western culture from the Old Testament through Freud has held on this subject. One might argue that Rogers's voice, combined with those of a number of other modern theologians, psychologists, and writers, has dramatically altered or called into question our traditional concept of the nature of man.

The nature of the "good life" is another long-term question that has preoccupied philosophers. Estranged from his own religious background, Rogers sought the answer to this question not in the ethical or religious mandates of organized religion, but in the empirical evidence he witnessed in the strivings of countless clients seeking a better life for themselves through therapy. Where would the process lead if carried to its end? What would the good life be for the healthy product of successful psychotherapy? Are there common threads among the experiences of most clients that might reveal any universal principles on this question? In "A Therapist's View of the Good Life: The Fully Functioning Person," Rogers presents his own thesis.

Philosophers have often assumed the difficult task of balancing the tenets of religion and science. The organization of the universe, of heaven and hell, of different planes of existence, and the nature of life and death have been among the most perplexing questions about "reality" explored by religion, science, and philosophy through the ages. In later years, Rogers also pondered some of these questions.

This was not a concerted, systematic inquiry into these philosophical questions, but a continuing openness to his experience. In the seventies and eighties, the world around him, particularly in California, was exploring many new and old ideas touching upon the nature of the universe. He was aware of various conferences and publications in which top physicists and mystics were making progress in reconciling traditional Western and Eastern views on the nature of matter and energy in the universe. A number of his own trusted friends and even his dying wife, Helen, reported apparently valid psychic experiences.

In exploring the nature of reality, then, Rogers was not alone, but rather reflected a growing interest within the scientific and intellectual community of the period. As a respected intellectual leader with an impeccable scientific background, Rogers added his voice in probing one of the most basic philosophical questions of all. As usual, he approached it in his own way. Instead of joining with others to try to identify the "real" nature of reality, Rogers simply asked, "Do We Need 'A' Reality?"

Rogers never called himself a philosopher or presented himself as such. Neither did he limit his thinking or writing to the normal parameters of any one profession, but rather explored the implications of his work and thought wherever they led. In so doing, he made some significant contributions to a number of major philosophical questions. In the long run, he may be remembered as much for his influence on how civilization views human nature as for his contributions to any of the helping professions.

26
A Note on "The Nature of Man"

I have read with interest the article by Walker (9) in which he compares Freud's view of the nature of man with my own, and have also been educated by the further discussion by Snyder (9), Gehman (3), Walker (10) and Nosal (4) on this issue. Since my own views are in considerable part the topic of this discussion, perhaps I may be permitted a word of comment.

Walker's thesis may be very briefly summarized. He states that "Freud inherits the tradition of Augustine in his belief that man is basically and fundamentally hostile, anti-social and carnal." On the other hand, "Carl Rogers, in the same sense, is the successor to Rousseau [who observes] that every man comes from the hand of his Maker a perfect being. This pristine splendor is corrupted, said Rousseau, by an imperfect society" (9, p. 89). Walker goes on to point out that Freud and I see the basic nature of the individual in very different ways, and that hence very different considerations flow from these differing views, so far as psychotherapy is concerned. He concludes that since clinicians lean toward Freud's philosophy, and personality theorists take a neutral view of man, and I have this Rousseauian view, it behooves all of us to think of this problem. Snyder and the others offer various valuable and discriminating comments on Walker's presentation.

I feel pleased that such a discussion in print calls attention to the value orientation, to the philosophical substratum, of every

Journal of Counseling Psychology, Vol. 4, No. 3, 1957, 199–203.

form of psychotherapy. One cannot engage in psychotherapy without giving operational evidence of an underlying value orientation and view of human nature. It is definitely preferable, in my estimation, that such underlying views be open and explicit, rather than covert and implicit. I appreciate the emphasis which is given in this discussion to the sharp difference in philosophical views between the Freudian and the client-centered orientation. I have myself tried to call attention to this (6, pp. 56–57; 7, p. 207).

As to the "predecessors" of Freud's thinking and my own I have some question. I am somewhat skeptical of the value of thus putting very different people into the same pigeonhole. I believe it might be of greater value to look separately at Augustine or Freud or Rousseau or myself, rather than to lump any two of them together. However, for what it is worth, I believe one might find more philosophical similarity between Freud and Calvin than between Freud and Augustine. A very perceptive woman who had been much helped by her psychoanalysis told me that she had never fully understood or assimilated her analysis until she came to realize its basically Calvinistic view of the evilness of the natural man. As to myself, whether I am a "successor" to Rousseau I am not competent to say. I can only comment that though it might truthfully be said that my thinking is closer to that of Rousseau than to that of Calvin, I certainly do not think of myself as being in any sense a follower of Rousseau. I can testify that at least there has been no direct influence. My only personal contact with Rousseau's work was the required reading of a portion of his *Emile* for my doctoral language examination in French, and I nearly flunked the exam!

The major point at which I might clarify this whole discussion, however, is by endeavoring to state what I think about the basic characteristics of the human organism. To be sure my own changing and developing views have been presented in partial form in a number of references (6, especially pp. 56–57; 5, especially pp. 56–64, 522–524; 8), but a current formulation might be in order.

My views of man's most basic characteristics have been formed by my experience in psychotherapy. They include certain observations as to what man is *not*, as well as some description of what, in my experience, he *is*. Let me state these very briefly and then endeavor to clarify my meanings.

I do not discover man to be well characterized in his basic nature by such terms as *fundamentally hostile, antisocial, destructive, evil*.

I do not discover man to be, in his basic nature, completely without a nature, a tabula rasa on which *anything* may be written, nor malleable putty which can be shaped into *any* form.

I do not discover man to be essentially a perfect being, sadly warped and corrupted by society.

In my experience I have discovered man to have characteristics which seem inherent in his species, and the terms which have at different times seemed to me descriptive of these characteristics are such terms as *positive, forward-moving, constructive, realistic, trustworthy*.

Let me see if I can take the discussion of these points of view into a fresh area where perhaps we have somewhat fewer preconceived biases. Suppose we turn to the animal world and ask ourselves what is the basic nature of the lion, or the sheep, or the dog, or the mouse. To say that any one or all of these are basically hostile or antisocial or carnal seems to be ridiculous. To say that we view their nature as neutral means either that it is neutral in terms of some unspecified set of values, or that their natures are all alike, all putty waiting to receive a shape. This view seems to me equally ridiculous. I maintain that each has a basic nature, a common set of attributes generally characteristic of the species. Thus the sheep is by far the most gregarious or group-minded, the mouse the most generally timorous. No amount of training — therapeutic or otherwise — will make a lion out of the mouse, or vice versa, even though a wide degree of change is possible. There is a basic substratum of species characteristics which we will do well to accept.

We might take a closer look at some of those characteristics. Since the lion has the most pronounced reputation for being a "ravening beast," let us choose him. What are the characteristics of his common nature, his basic nature? He kills an antelope when he is hungry, but he does not go on a wild rampage of killing. He eats his fill after the killing, but there are no obese lions on the veldt. He is helpless and dependent in his puppyhood, but he does not cling to the dependent relationship. He becomes increasingly independent and autonomous. In the infant state he is completely selfish and self-centered, but as he matures he shows, in addition to such impulses, a reasonable degree of cooperativeness in the hunt. The lioness feeds, cares for, protects, and seems to enjoy her young. Lions satisfy their sexual needs, but this does not mean they go on wild and lustful orgies. His various tendencies and urges come to a continaully changing balance in himself, and in that sense he is very satisfactorily self-controlled and self-regulated. He is in basic ways a constructive, a trustworthy member of the species *Felis leo*. His fundamental tendencies are in the direction of development, differentiation, independence, self-responsibility, cooperation, maturity. In general the expression of his basic nature makes for the continuation and enhancement of himself and his species.

With the appropriate variations, the same sort of statements could be made about the dog, the sheep, the mouse. To be sure, each behaves in ways which from some specific point of view are destructive. We wince to see the lion kill the antelope; we are annoyed when the sheep eats our garden; we complain when the mouse eats the cheese we were saving for our picnic; I regard the dog as destructive when he bites me, a stranger; but surely none of these behaviors justifies us in thinking of any of these animals as basically evil. If I endeavored to explain to you that if the "lion-ness" of the lion were to be released, or the "sheepness" of the sheep, that these animals would then be impelled by insatiable lusts, uncontrollable aggressions, wild and excessive sexual behaviors, and tendencies of innate destructiveness, you would quite properly laugh at me. Obviously, such a view is pure nonsense.

I would like now to consider again the nature of man in the light of this discussion of the nature of animals. I have come to know men most deeply in a relationship which is characterized by all that I can give of safety, absence of threat, and complete freedom to be and to choose. In such a relationship men express all kinds of bitter and murderous feelings, abnormal impulses, bizarre and antisocial desires. But as they live in such a relationship, expressing and being more of themselves, I find that man, like the lion, has a nature. My experience is that he is a basically trustworthy member of the human species, whose deep-

est characteristics tend toward development, differentiation, cooperative relationships; whose life tends fundamentally to move
from dependence to independence; whose impulses tend naturally to harmonize into a complex and changing pattern of self-
regulation; whose total character is such as to tend to preserve
and enhance himself and his species, and perhaps to move it
toward its further evolution. In my experience, to discover that
an individual is truly and deeply a unique member of the human
species is not a discovery to excite horror. Rather I am inclined
to believe that fully to be a human being is to enter into the
complex process of being one of the most widely sensitive, responsive, creative, and adaptive creatures on this planet.

So when a Freudian such as Karl Menninger tells me (as he has,
in a discussion of this issue) that he perceives man as "innately
evil," or more precisely, "innately destructive," I can only shake
my head in wonderment. It leads me to all kinds of perplexing
questions. How could it be that Menninger and I, working with
such a similar purpose in such intimate relationships with individuals in distress, experience people so differently? Perhaps, as
Snyder suggests, these deep differences do not matter if the therapist really cares for his patient or client. But how can the analyst
feel a positive caring for his patient, if his own innate tendency is
to destroy? And even if his own destructive tendencies were
properly inhibited and controlled by *his* analyst, who controlled
the destructiveness of *that* analyst? And so on ad infinitum.

It will be clear that my experience provides no evidence for
believing that if the deepest elements in man's nature were released we would have an uncontrolled and destructive id unleashed in the world.* To me this makes as little sense as to say

---

*Freud seems however to have believed something like this to the end. In his
Outline of Psychoanalysis, brief, precise, and calmly stated, he still indicates that
the core of our being leads to conflicts, even to its own destruction, unless some
means is discovered for its control. "The core of our being, then, is formed by
the obscure id. . . . Within this id the organic instincts operate. . . . The one and
only endeavor of these instincts is toward satisfaction. . . . But an immediate and
regardless satisfaction of instinct, such as the id demands, would often enough
lead to perilous conflicts with the external world and to extinction. . . . The id
obeys the inexorable pleasure principle . . . and it remains a question of the
greatest theoretical importance, and one that has not yet been answered, when

that the "lion-ness" of the lion would be an evil thing. I respect the men who hold such views, but I find no evidence in my experience to support them. I stand by a statement made in an earlier paper:

> I have little sympathy with the rather prevalent concept that man is basically irrational, and that his impulses, if not controlled, will lead to destruction of others and self. Man's behavior is exquisitely rational, moving with subtle and ordered complexity toward the goals his organism is endeavoring to achieve. The tragedy for most of us is that our defenses keep us from being aware of this rationality, so that consciously we are moving in one direction, while organismically we are moving in another. But in our person who is living the process of the good life there would be a decreasing number of such barriers, and he would be increasingly a participant in the rationality of his organism. The only control of impulses which would exist or which would prove necessary is the natural and internal balancing of one need against another, and the discovery of behaviors which follow the vector most closely approximating the satisfaction of all needs. The experience of extreme satisfaction of one need (for aggression, or sex, etc.) in such a way as to do violence to the satisfaction of other needs (for companionship, tender relationships, etc.)—an experience very common in the defensively organized person— would be greatly decreased. He would participate in the vastly complex self-regulatory activities of his organism—the psychological as well as physiological thermostatic controls—in such a fashion as to live in increasing harmony with himself and with others. (8)

I have puzzled as to the reasons for the wide discrepancy between the Freudian view of man's nature and that which has seemed justified by experience in client-centered therapy.* I have two hypotheses which I should like to present for consid-

---

and how it is ever possible for the pleasure principle to be overcome" (2, pp. 108–109).

*Perhaps it is only a difference between early Freudianism and the client-centered view. I have the impression that most modern psychoanalysts hold a view of human nature sharply different from Freud's, but if they have made this explicit, I am not aware of it. And present-day thinkers who have taken their model from Freud continue to hold his dark view. Thus Ludwig von Bertalanffy in a recent article says, "It appears that we cannot change the bête humaine: we can only hope that the brute in man is better controlled" (11, p. 37).

eration, though they may seem shocking to devoted followers of psychoanalysis.

First, it appears to me that Freud was understandably very much excited by his discovery—a tremendous discovery for his time—that beneath a conventional or "good" exterior, man harbored all kinds of aggressive and sexual feelings and impulses which he had successfully hidden from himself as well as from others. This discovery was shocking to the culture of that period and hence both his critics and Freud himself focused on the "evil" feelings in man which lay beneath the surface. This continued to be the focus even though Freud's own experience with his patients must have shown him that once these "evil" feelings were known, accepted, and understood by the individual, he could be trusted to be a normally self-controlled, socialized person. In the furor of the controversy over psychoanalysis this latter point was overlooked, and Freud settled for what is, in my estimation, a too-superficial view of human nature. It was of course a much more deeply informed view than that held by his contemporaries, but it was not so profound a concept as his own experience would have justified.

My second hypothesis would explain why Freud did not assimilate this deeper meaning which he might have perceived in the therapy he carried on. It has been my experience that though clients can, to some degree, independently discover some of their denied or repressed feelings, they cannot on their own achieve full emotional acceptance of these feelings. It is only in a caring relationship that these "awful" feelings are first fully accepted by the therapist and then can be accepted by the client. Freud in his self-analysis was deprived of this warmly acceptant relationship. Hence, though he might come to know and to some extent to understand the hidden and denied aspects of himself, I question whether he could ever come to accept them fully, to embrace them as a meaningful, acceptable, and constructive part of himself. More likely he continued to perceive them as unacceptable aspects of himself—enemies, whom knowing he could control—rather than as impulses which, when existing freely in balance with his other impulses, were constructive. At any rate I regard this as a hypothesis worthy of consideration. It does not, I admit, explain why his followers have continued to accept his view.

In closing I would like to agree with Walker that the view the therapist holds of human nature does have consequences in his therapy. Hence I believe it is important for each therapist to abstract for himself from his own experience those trends or tendencies which seem most deeply characteristic of the human being. I have indicated that for myself man appears to be an awesomely complex creature who can go terribly awry, but whose *deepest* tendencies make for his own enhancement and that of other members of his species. I find that he can be trusted to move in this constructive direction when he lives, even briefly, in a nonthreatening climate where he is free to choose any direction.

REFERENCES

1. Bertalanffy, L. von. A biologist looks at human nature. *Sci. Mon.*, 1956, *82*, 33–41.
2. Freud, S. *Outline of Psychoanalysis.* New York: Norton, 1949.
3. Gehman, W. S. Letter to editor. *J. counsel. Psychol.*, 1956, *3*, 229.
4. Nosal, W. S. Letter to editor. *J. counsel. Psychol.*, 1956, *3*, 299–301.
5. Rogers, C. R. *Client-centered therapy.* Boston: Houghton Mifflin, 1951. Especially pp. 56–64, 522–524.
6. Rogers, C. R. Some of the directions and end points of therapy. In O. H. Mowrer (Ed.), *Psychotherapy; Theory and research.* New York: Ronald Press, 1953. Especially pp. 56–57.
7. Rogers, C. R. Client-centered therapy—a current view. In F. Fromm-Reichmann and J. L. Moreno (Eds.), *Progress in psychotherapy 1956.* New York: Grune & Stratton, 1956, p. 207.
8. Rogers, C. R. A therapist's view of the good life. *The Humanist*, 1957. In press.
9. Walker, D. E. Carl Rogers and the nature of man. *J. counsel. Psychol.*, 1956, *3*, 89–92. (Includes comment by W. U. Snyder.)
10. Walker, D. E. Letter to editor. *J. counsel. Psychol.*, 1956, *3*, 229–230.

27
A Therapist's View of the Good Life: The Fully Functioning Person

My views regarding the meaning of the good life are largely based upon my experience in working with people in the very close and intimate relationship which is called psychotherapy. These views thus have an empirical or experiential foundation, as contrasted perhaps with a scholarly or philosophical foundation. I have learned what the good life seems to be by observing and participating in the struggle of disturbed and troubled people to achieve that life.

I should make it clear from the outset that this experience I have gained comes from the vantage point of a particular orientation to psychotherapy which has developed over the years. Quite possibly all psychotherapy is basically similar, but since I am less sure of that than I once was, I wish to make it clear that my therapeutic experience has been along the lines that seem to me most effective, the type of therapy termed "client-centered."

Let me attempt to give a very brief description of what this therapy would be like if it were in every respect optimal, since I feel I have learned most about the good life from therapeutic experiences in which a great deal of movement occurred. If the therapy were optimal, intensive as well as extensive, then it would mean that the therapist has been able to enter into an intensely personal and subjective relationship with the client—relating not as a scientist to an object of study, not as a physician expecting to diagnose and cure, but as a person to a person. It would mean that the therapist feels this client to be a person of unconditional self-worth: of value no matter what his condition, his behavior, or his feelings. It would mean that the therapist is genuine, hiding behind no defensive façade, but meeting the client with the feelings which organically he is experiencing. It would mean

The Humanist, Vol. 17, 1957. Expanded in *On Becoming a Person*. Boston: Houghton Mifflin, 1961, 184–196.

that the therapist is able to let himself go in understanding this client; that no inner barriers keep him from sensing what it feels like to be the client at each moment of the relationship; and that he can convey something of his empathic understanding to the client. It means that the therapist has been comfortable in entering this relationship fully, without knowing cognitively where it will lead, satisfied with providing a climate which will permit the client the utmost freedom to become himself.

For the client, this optimal therapy would mean an exploration of increasingly strange and unknown and dangerous feelings in himself, the exploration proving possible only because he is gradually realizing that he is accepted unconditionally. Thus he becomes acquainted with elements of his experience which have in the past been denied to awareness as too threatening, too damaging to the structure of the self. He finds himself experiencing these feelings fully, completely, in the relationship, so that for the moment he *is* his fear, or his anger, or his tenderness, or his strength. And as he lives these widely varied feelings, in all their degrees of intensity, he discovers that he has experienced *himself*, that he *is* all these feelings. He finds his behavior changing in constructive fashion in accordance with his newly experienced self. He approaches the realization that he no longer needs to fear what experience may hold, but can welcome it freely as a part of his changing and developing self.

This is a thumbnail sketch of what client-centered therapy comes close to, when it is at its optimum. I give it here simply as a brief picture of the context in which I have formed my views of the good life.

A Negative Observation

As I have tried to live understandingly in the experiences of my clients, I have gradually come to one negative conclusion about the good life. It seems to me that the good life is not any fixed state. It is not, in my estimation, a state of virtue, or contentment, or nirvana, or happiness. It is not a condition in which the individual is adjusted, or fulfilled, or actualized. To use psychological terms, it is not a state of drive reduction, or tension reduction, or homeostasis.

I believe that all of these terms have been used in ways which imply that if one or several of these states is achieved, then the goal of life has been achieved. Certainly, for many people happiness, or adjustment, are seen as states of being which are synonymous with the good life. And social scientists have frequently spoken of the reduction of tension, or the achievement of homeostasis or equilibrium, as if these states constituted the goal of the process of living.

So it is with a certain amount of surprise and concern that I realize that my experience supports none of these definitions. If I focus on the experience of those individuals who seem to have evidenced the greatest degree of movement during the therapeutic relationship, and who, in the years following this relationship, appear to have made and to be making real progress toward the good life, then it seems to me that they are not adequately described at all by any of these terms which refer to fixed states of being. I believe they would consider themselves insulted if they were described as "adjusted," and they would regard it as false if they were described as "happy" or "contented," or even "actualized." As I have known them I would regard it as most inaccurate to say that all their drive tensions have been reduced, or that they are in a state of homeostasis. So I am forced to ask myself whether there is any way in which I can generalize about their situation, any definition which I can give of the good life which would seem to fit the facts as I have observed them. I find this not at all easy, and what follows is stated very tentatively.

A Positive Observation

If I attempt to capture in a few words what seems to me to be true of these people, I believe it will come out something like this:

The good life is a *process*, not a state of being.

It is a direction, not a destination.

The direction which constitutes the good life is that which is selected by the total organism, when there is psychological freedom to move in *any* direction.

This organismically selected direction seems to have certain discernible general qualities which appear to be the same in a wide variety of unique individuals.

So I can integrate these statements into a definition which can at least serve as a basis for consideration and discussion. The good life, from the point of view of my experience, is the process of movement in a direction which the human organism selects when it is inwardly free to move in any direction, and the general qualities of this selected direction appear to have a certain universality.

THE CHARACTERISTICS OF THE PROCESS

Let me now try to specify what appear to be the characteristic qualities of this process of movement, as they crop up in person after person in therapy.

An Increasing Openness to Experience

In the first place, the process seems to involve an increasing openness to experience. The phrase has come to have more and more meaning for me. It is the polar opposite of defensiveness. Defensiveness I have described in the past as being the organism's response to experiences which are perceived or anticipated as threatening, as incongruent with the individual's existing picture of himself, or of himself in relationship to the world. These threatening experiences are temporarily rendered harmless by being distorted in awareness, or being denied to awareness. I quite literally cannot see, with accuracy, those experiences, feelings, reactions in myself which I already possess. A large part of the process of therapy is the continuing discovery by the client that he is experiencing feelings and attitudes which heretofore he has not been able to be aware of, which he has not been able to "own" as being a part of himself.

If a person could be fully open to his experience, however, every stimulus — whether originating within the organism or in the environment — would be freely relayed through the nervous system without being distorted by any defensive mechanism. There would be no need of the mechanism of "subception," whereby the organism is forewarned of any experience threatening to the self. On the contrary, whether the stimulus was the impact of a configuration of form, color, or sound in the environment on the sensory nerves, or a memory trace from the past, or a visceral sensation of fear or pleasure or disgust, the person would be "living" it, would have it completely available to awareness.

Thus, one aspect of this process which I am naming "the good life" appears to be a movement away from the pole of defensiveness toward the pole of openness to experience. The individual is becoming more able to listen to himself, to experience what is going on within himself. He is more open to his feelings of fear and discouragement and pain. He is also more open to his feelings of courage, and tenderness, and awe. He is free to live his feelings subjectively, as they exist in him, and also free to be aware of these feelings. He is more able fully to live the experiences of his organism rather than shutting them out of awareness.

Increasingly Existential Living

A second characteristic of the process which for me is the good life, is that it involves an increasing tendency to live fully in each moment. This is a thought which can easily be misunderstood, and, which is perhaps somewhat vague in my own thinking. Let me try to explain what I mean.

I believe it would be evident that for the person who was fully open to his new experience, completely without defensiveness, each moment would be new. The complex configuration of inner and outer stimuli which exists in this moment has never existed before in just this fashion. Consequently such a person would realize that "What I will be in the next moment, and what I will do, grows out of that moment, and cannot be predicted in advance either by me or by others." Not infrequently we find clients expressing exactly this sort of feeling.

One way of expressing the fluidity which is present in such existential living is to say that the self and personality emerge *from* experience, rather than experience being translated or twisted to fit preconceived self-structure. It means that one becomes a participant in and an observer of the ongoing process of organismic experience, rather than being in control of it.

Such living in the moment means an absence of rigidity, of tight organization, of the imposition of structure on experience. It means instead a maximum of adaptability, a discovery of structure *in* experience, a flowing, changing organization of self and personality.

It is this tendency toward existential living which appears to me very evident in people who are involved in the process of the good life. One might almost say that it is the most essential quality of it. It involves discovering the structure of experience in the process of living the experience. Most of us, on the other hand, bring a preformed structure and evaluation to our experience and never relinquish it, but cram and twist the experience to fit our preconceptions, annoyed at the fluid qualities which make it so unruly in fitting our carefully constructed pigeonholes. To open one's spirit to what is going on *now*, and to discover in that present process whatever structure it appears to have — this to me is one of the qualities of the good life, the mature life, as I see clients approach it.

An Increasing Trust in His Organism

Still another characteristic of the person who is living the process of the good life appears to be an increasing trust in his organism as a means of arriving at the most satisfying behavior in each existential situation. Again let me try to explain what I mean.

In choosing what course of action to take in any situation, many people rely upon guiding principles, upon a code of action laid down by some group or institution, upon the judgment of others (from wife and friends to Emily Post), or upon the way they have behaved in some similar past situation. Yet as I observe the clients whose experiences in living have taught me so much, I find that increasingly such individuals are able to trust their total organismic reaction to a new situation because they discover to an ever-increasing degree that if they are open to their experience, doing what "feels right" proves to be a competent and trustworthy guide to behavior which is truly satisfying.

As I try to understand the reason for this, I find myself following this line of thought. The person who is fully open to his experience would have access to all of the available data in the situation, on which to base his behavior; the social demands, his own complex and possibly conflicting needs, his memories of similar situations, his perception of the uniqueness of this situation, etc., etc. The data would be very complex indeed. But he could permit his total organism, his consciousness participating, to consider each stimulus, need, and demand, its relative intensity and importance, and out of this complex weighing and balancing, discover that course of action which would come closest to satisfying all his needs in the situation. An analogy which might come close to a description would be to compare this person to a giant electronic computing machine. Since he is open to his experience, all of the data from his sense impressions, from his memory, from previous learning, from his visceral and internal states, is fed into the machine. The machine takes all of these multitudinous pulls and forces which are fed in as data, and quickly computes the course of action which would be the most economical vector of need satisfaction in this existential situation. This is the behavior of our hypothetical person.

The defects which in most of us make this process untrustworthy are the inclusion of information which does *not* belong to this present situation, or the exclusion of information which *does*. It is when memories and previous learnings are fed into the computations as if they were *this* reality, and not memories and learnings, that erroneous behavioral answers arise. Or when certain threatening experiences are inhibited from awareness, and hence are withheld from the computation or fed into it in distorted form, this too produces error. But our hypothetical person would find his organism thoroughly trustworthy, because all of the available data would be used, and it would be present in accurate rather than distorted form. Hence his behavior would come as close as possible to satisfying all his needs—for enhancement, for affiliation with others, and the like.

In this weighing, balancing, and computation, his organism would not by any means be infallible. It would always give the best possible answer for the available data, but sometimes data would be missing. Because of the element of openness to experience, however, any errors, any following of behavior which was not satisfying, would be quickly corrected. The computations, as it were, would always be in process of being corrected, because they would be continually checked in behavior.

Perhaps you will not like my analogy of an electronic computing machine. Let me return to the clients I know. As they become more open to all of their experiences, they find it increasingly possible to trust their reactions. If they "feel like" expressing anger they do so and find that this comes out satisfactorily, because they are equally alive to all of their other desires for affection, affiliation, and relationship. They are surprised at their own intuitive skill in finding behavioral solutions to complex and troubling human relationships. It is only afterward that they realize how surprisingly trustworthy their inner reactions have been in bringing about satisfactory behavior.

The Process of Functioning More Fully

I should like to draw together these three threads describing the process of the good life into a more coherent picture. It appears that the person who is psychologically free moves in the direction of becoming a more fully functioning person. He is more able to live fully in and with each and all of his feelings and reactions. He makes increasing use of all his organic equipment to sense, as accurately as possible, the existential situation within and without. He makes use of all of the information his nervous system can thus supply, using it in awareness, but recognizing that his total organism may be, and often is, wiser than his awareness. He is more able to permit his total organism to function freely in all its complexity in selecting, from the multitude of possibilities, that behavior which in this moment of time will be most generally and genuinely satisfying. He is able to put more trust in his organism in this functioning, not because it is infallible, but because he can be fully open to the consequences of each of his actions and correct them if they prove to be less than satisfying.

He is more able to experience all of his feelings, and is less afraid of any of his feelings; he is his own sifter of evidence, and is more open to evidence from all sources; he is completely engaged in the process of being and becoming himself, and thus discovers that he is soundly and realistically social; he lives more completely in this moment, but learns that this is the soundest living for all time. He is becoming a more fully functioning organism, and because of the awareness of himself which flows freely in and through his experience, he is becoming a more fully functioning person.

SOME IMPLICATIONS

Any view of what constitutes the good life carries with it many implications, and the view I have presented is no exception. I hope that these implications may be food for thought. There are two or three of these about which I would like to comment.

A New Perspective on Freedom vs. Determinism

The first of these implications may not immediately be evident. It has to do with the age-old issue of "free will." Let me endeavor to spell out the way in which this issue now appears to me in a new light.

For some time I have been perplexed over the living paradox which exists in psychotherapy between freedom and determinism. In the therapeutic relationship some of the most compelling subjective experiences are those in which the client feels within himself the power of naked choice. He is *free* — to become himself or to hide behind a façade; to move forward or to retrogress; to behave in ways which are enhancing; quite literally free to live or die, in both the physiological and psychological meaning of those terms. Yet as we enter this field of psychotherapy with objective research methods, we are, like any other scientist, committed to a complete determinism. From this point of view every thought, feeling, and action of the client is determined by what preceded it. There can be no such thing as freedom. The dilemma I am trying to describe is no different than that found in other fields — it is simply brought to sharper focus, and appears more insoluble.

This dilemma can be seen in a fresh perspective, however, when we consider it in terms of the definition I have given of the fully functioning person. We could say that in the optimum of therapy the person rightfully experiences the most complete and absolute freedom. He wills or chooses to follow the course of action which is the most economical vector in relationship to all the internal and external stimuli, because it is that behavior which will be most deeply satisfying. But this is the same course of action which from another vantage point may be said to be determined by all the factors in the existential situation. Let us contrast this with the picture of the person who is defensively organized. He wills or chooses to follow a given course of action, but finds that he *cannot* behave in the fashion that he chooses. He is determined by the factors in the existential situation, but these factors include his defensiveness, his denial or distortion of some of the relevant data. Hence it is certain that his behavior will be less than fully satisfying. His behavior is determined, but he is not free to make an effective choice. The fully functioning person, on the other hand, not only experiences, but utilizes, the most absolute freedom when he spontaneously, freely, and voluntarily chooses and wills that which is also absolutely determined.

I am not so naive as to suppose that this fully resolves the issue between subjective and objective, between freedom and necessity. Nevertheless it has meaning for me that the more the person is living the good life, the more he will experience a freedom of choice, and the more his choices will be effectively implemented in his behavior.

Creativity As an Element of the Good Life

I believe it will be clear that a person who is involved in the directional process which I have termed the good life is a creative person. With his sensitive openness to his world, his trust of his own ability to form new relationships with his environment, he would be the type of person from whom creative products and creative living emerge. He would not necessarily be "adjusted" to his culture, and he would almost certainly not be a conformist. But at any time and in any culture he would live constructively, in as much harmony with his culture as a balanced satisfaction of needs demanded. In some cultural situations he might in some ways be very unhappy, but he would continue to move toward becoming himself, and to behave in such a way as to provide the maximum satisfaction of his deepest needs.

Such a person would, I believe, be recognized by the student of evolution as the type most likely to adapt and survive under changing environmental conditions. He would be able creatively to make sound adjustments to new as well as old conditions. He would be a fit vanguard of human evolution.

Basic Trustworthiness of Human Nature

It will be evident that another implication of the view I have been presenting is that the basic nature of the human being, when functioning freely, is constructive and trustworthy. For me this is an inescapable conclusion from a quarter-century of experience in psychotherapy. When we are able to free the individual from defensiveness, so that he is open to the wide range of his own needs, as well as the wide range of environmental and social demands, his reactions may be trusted to be positive, forward moving, constructive. We do not need to ask who will socialize him, for one of his own deepest needs is for affiliation and communication with others. As he becomes more fully himself, he will become more realistically socialized. We do not need to ask who will control his aggressive impulses; for as he becomes more open to all of his impulses, his need to be liked by others and his tendency to give affection will be as strong as his impulses to strike out or to seize for himself. He will be aggressive in situations in which aggression is realistically appropriate, but there will be no runaway need for aggression. His total behavior, in these and other areas, as he moves toward being open to all his experience, will be more balanced and realistic, behavior which is appropriate to the survival and enhancement of a highly social animal.

The Greater Richness of Life

One last implication I should like to mention is that this process of living in the good life involves a wider range, a greater richness, than the constricted living in which most of us find ourselves. To be a part of this process means that one is involved in the frequently frightening and frequently satisfying experience of a more sensitive living, with greater range, greater variety, greater richness. It seems to me that clients who have moved significantly in therapy live more intimately with their feelings of pain, but also more vividly with their feelings of ecstasy; that anger is more clearly felt, but so also is love; that fear is an experience they know more deeply, but so is courage. And the reason they can thus live fully in a wider range is that they have this underlying confidence in themselves as trustworthy instruments for encountering life.

I believe it will have become evident why, for me, adjectives such as *happy, contented, blissful, enjoyable,* do not seem quite appropriate to any general description of this process I have called the good life, even though the person in this process would experience each one of these feelings at appropriate times. But the adjectives which seem more generally fitting are adjectives such as *enriching, exciting, rewarding, challenging, meaningful*. This process of the good life is not, I am convinced, a life for the faint-hearted. It involves the stretching and growing of becoming more and more of one's potentialities. It involves the courage to be. It means launching oneself fully into the stream of life. Yet the deeply exciting thing about human beings is that when the individual is inwardly free, he chooses as the good life this process of becoming.

28
Do We Need "A" Reality?

I believe most educators would agree that a high priority in education is to help individuals to acquire the learning, the information, and the personal growth that will enable them to deal more constructively with the "real world." This is often the theme of commencement addresses, in which one expresses hopes or fears concerning how the new graduates will face and cope with the "real world." It is often a topic in the final hours of intensive encounter groups, when individuals who have learned a great deal about themselves and about their interpersonal relationships are concerned about how they will behave when they return to their "real" lives outside.

What is this "real world"? It is this question that I want to explore, and I believe that the direction in which my thinking has inexorably led me will be best portrayed by giving a number of personal and commonplace examples.

A few weeks ago, I was sitting alone, late at night, on the deck of a beach cottage in northern California. As I sat there for several hours, a bright star on the horizon moved upward into clear view. A brilliant planet moved with the same slow, majestic speed from directly above me to a point well on my right. The star and the planet were accompanied in their movement by the Milky Way and all the other constellations. Obviously, I was the center of the universe, and the heavens were slowly revolving about me. It was a humbling experience (How small I am!) and an uplifting one (How marvelous to be such a focal point!). I was looking at the real world.

Yet, in another corner of my mind, I knew that I, and the earth beneath me, and the atmosphere surrounding me were moving at a breathless speed — faster than a modern jet plane — in the direction I called east, and that the stars and planets were, relative to the earth, comparatively motionless. Although I could not *see* what I've just described, I knew that this — not the more obvious perception — was *really* the real world.

At some other level, I was aware that I was an infinitesimal speck on an insignificant planet in one of the minor galaxies (of which there are millions) in the universe. I knew that each of these galaxies was moving at an incredible speed, often exploding away from the others. Was this reality, too? I was confused.

But at least there was one reality of which I could be sure: the hard wooden chair on which I sat, the solid earth on which the deck rested, the stainless steel pen I held in my hand. This was a reality that could not only be seen, but also felt and touched. These objects could sustain weight and pressure. They were solid.

But no, I knew enough of science to challenge all this. The chair is made up of formerly living cells, intricate in their composition, composed more of space than of matter. The earth is a slowly moving fluid mass, which shudders very frequently as it shrinks and cracks and crinkles. The road over which I drove yesterday had been a part of one of those shudders. One day in 1906, the earth shrugged a little and the road cracked, and the western side of the crack was carried twenty feet north of its continuation on the other side. Solid earth indeed!

And what about the reassuring hardness of my metal pen? They tell me it is composed of invisible atoms, moving at great speed. Each atom has a nucleus, and recent years have brought discoveries of more and more particles in those nuclei. Each particle is endowed with fantastically unbelievable characteristics; it moves in possibly random, possibly orderly trajectories in the great inner space of each atom. My pen is hardly the firm solid object that I so clearly feel and hold. The "real world" seems to be dissolving.

I am reassured, but also perplexed, by the statement of the great physical scientist Sir James Jeans. He says: "The stream of human knowledge is impartially heading toward a nonmechanical reality: the Universe begins to look more like a great *thought* than a great machine." Try that on your practical friend, or your plumber, or your stockbroker. Tell them, "The real world is just a great thought." At any rate, the conception of a real world, obvious to anyone, is rapidly slipping completely out of my grasp.

But at least in the interpersonal world, I know my family and my friends; this knowledge is surely a solid basis on which I can act. But then my memories trip me up. One needs only the simple occasion of a softly facilitated encounter group, where permission is given to express oneself, to discover how shaky our interpersonal knowledge is. Individuals have discovered in their closest friends and family members great realms of hidden feelings. There are previously unknown fears, feelings of inadequacy, suppressed rages and resentments, bizarre sexual desires and fantasies, hidden pools of hopes and dreams, of joys and dreads, of creative urges and unbidden loves. This reality, too, seems as unsure, as full of unknowns, as any yet considered in this chapter.

So the individual is driven back to self: "At least I know who *I* am. I decide what I want to do, and I do it. *That's* for real." But is it? If I talk to the behaviorist, he tells me, "You are nothing but the sum of your stimulus inputs and the conditioned responses you emit. All the rest is illusion." Well, finally we have reality. I am nothing but a mechanical robot. Or is that all? Where do my dreams come from? Perhaps that can be explained too. Then I think of Jean, the woman who told me that her identical twin sister was driving back to her own home at night by a familiar route when Jean awoke in a panic of certainty. She phoned the highway police and told them, "There's been an accident on such-and-such a highway. It's a white car with this license and a lone woman driver." There was a pause, and then the officer said, in a puzzled and slightly suspicious voice, "But how did you know about that, lady? We only got the report of the accident two minutes ago." What do we make of *that* kind of reality?

That little episode opens up a whole train of thought about inner worlds and "separate realities." What do we make of the vision or dream that Carl Jung (1961) had at the age of three? He saw a large mysterious underground cavern, with all the light focused on a great pillar of flesh with something like a head on top, enthroned on a royal chair. Fifty years passed before he fully understood this experience, when he rediscovered this same vision in the phallic rituals of some primitive tribes. How had that vision come to him at the age of three? In what real world does this phenomenon belong?

Read the story of Robert Monroe (1971), a hardheaded businessman and engineer who, after some puzzling experiences, found himself one night floating up to the ceiling of his room, looking down on his own body and that of his wife. His account of these experiences, in which he tells of his initial fright, then his increasing willingness to take journeys out of his body, is startling indeed, and often very convincing. One cannot help but ponder the question: What "reality" can encompass such experiences, as well as the "real" experiences I know?

How about Don Juan, the ageless Yaqui Indian, who opened whole new worlds to the stubbornly skeptical anthropologist Carlos Castaneda? Worlds of magical events, of flights through the air, of a nonordinary reality where death is not different from life, where the "man of knowledge" has a spirit ally, where the impossible is experienced. Rubbish, you say? His own experiences were enough to force Castaneda (1969, 1971) to recognize that there exist separate realities completely alien to the thinking of the modern scientific mind.

I think of John Lilly (1973), a scientist trained at the California Institute of Technology, who went on to study neuroanatomy, medicine, and psychiatry, and who is perhaps best known for his twelve years of work with dolphins, trying to communicate with these animals, who he believes are at least as intelligent as human beings. To trace his path from his beginnings as a scientist who believed only in mechanical models of reality, to his present view that there are various levels of altered consciousness (which he has achieved and helped others to achieve), is mind-boggling. Along the way, he became convinced that the dolphins could read his thoughts. Lilly's experiences in a sensory-deprivation tank — where he floated in warm water with absolutely minimal input of sight, sound, touch, or taste—were fascinating. He discovered that the inner world, without any external stimuli, was incredibly rich, sometimes frightening, often bizarre. In trying to understand this inner world, he experimented with LSD, with both illuminating and terrifying results. This led to meditation, unbidden thought transmission, and higher and higher states of consciousness in which he—like many before him, who were called mystics—experienced the universe as a unity, a unity based on love. Quite a distance from his Caltech training!

These and other accounts cannot simply be dismissed with contempt or ridicule. The witnesses are too honest, their experiences too real. All these accounts indicate that a vast and mysterious universe—perhaps an inner reality, or perhaps a spirit world of which we are all unknowingly a part—seems to exist. Such a universe delivers a final crushing blow to our comfortable belief that "we all know what the real world is."

Where have my thoughts led me in relation to an objective world of reality?

> It clearly does not exist in the objects we can see and feel and hold.
> It does not exist in the technology we admire so greatly.
> It is not found in the solid earth or the twinkling stars.
> It does not lie in a solid knowledge of those around us.
> It is not found in the organizations or customs or rituals of any one culture.
> It is not even in our own known personal worlds.
> It must take into account mysterious and currently unfathomable "separate realities," incredibly different from an objective world.

I, and many others, have come to a new realization. It is this: The only reality I can possibly know is the world as *I* perceive and experience it at this moment. The only reality you can possibly know is the world as *you* perceive and experience it at this moment. And the only certainty is that those perceived realities are different. There are as many "real worlds" as there are people! This creates a most burdensome dilemma, one never before experienced in history.

From time immemorial, the tribe or the community or the nation or the culture has agreed upon what constitutes the real world. To be sure, different tribes or different cultures might have held sharply different world views, but at least there was a large, relatively unified group which felt assured in its knowledge of the world and the universe, and knew that this perception was *true*. So the community frowned upon, condemned, persecuted, even killed those who did not agree, who perceived reality differently. Copernicus, even though he kept his findings secret for many years, was eventually declared a heretic. Galileo established proof of Copernicus's views, but in his seventies he was forced to recant his teachings. Giordano Bruno was burned at the stake in 1600 for teaching that there were many worlds in our universe.

Individuals who deviated in their perception of religious reality were tortured and killed. In the mid-1800s, Ignaz Semmelweis, an intense young Hungarian physician-scientist, was driven insane by his persecutors because he made the then absurd claim that childbed fever, that dread scourge of the maternity room, was carried from one woman to another by invisible germs on the hands and instruments of the doctors. Obvious nonsense, in terms of the reality of his day. In our own American Colonies, those who were even suspected of having psychic powers were considered witches and were hanged or crushed under great stones. History offers a continuing series of examples of the awful price paid by those who perceive a reality different from the agreed-upon real world. Although society has often come around eventually to agree with its dissidents, as in the instances I have mentioned, there is no doubt that this insistence upon a known and certain universe has been part of the cement that holds a culture together.

Today we face a different situation. The ease and rapidity of worldwide communication means that every one of us is aware of a dozen "realities"; even though we may think some of them absurd (like reincarnation) or dangerous (like communism), we cannot help but be aware of them. No longer can we exist in a secure cocoon, knowing that we all see the world in the same way.

Because of this change, I want to raise a very serious question: Can we today afford the luxury of having "*a*" reality? Can we still preserve the belief that there is a "real world" upon whose definition we all agree? I am convinced that this is a luxury we *cannot* afford, a myth we dare not maintain. Only once in recent history has this been fully and successfully achieved. Millions of people were in complete agreement as to the nature of social and cultural reality—an agreement brought about by the mesmerizing influence of Hitler. This agreement about reality nearly marked the destruction of Western culture. I do not see it as something to be emulated.

In Western culture during this century—especially in the United States—there has also been an agreed-upon reality of values. This gospel can be stated very briefly: "More is better, bigger is better, faster is better, and modern technology will achieve all three of these eminently desirable goals." But now that credo is a crumbling disaster in which few believe. It is dissolving in the smog of pollution, the famine of overpopulation, the Damocles' sword of the nuclear bomb. We have so successfully achieved the goal of "a bigger bang for a buck" that we are in danger of destroying all life on this planet.

Our attempts, then, to live in the "real world" which all perceive in the same way have, in my opinion, led us to the brink of annihilation as a species. I will be so bold as to suggest an alternative.

It appears to me that the way of the future must be to base our lives and our education on the assumption that there are as many realities as there are persons, and that our highest priority is to accept that hypothesis and proceed from there. Proceed where? Proceed, each of us, to explore open-mindedly the many, many perceptions of reality that exist. We would, I believe, enrich our own lives in the process. We would also become more able to cope with the reality in which each one of us exists, because we would be aware of many more options. This might well be a life full of perplexity and difficult choices, demanding greater maturity, but it would be an exciting and adventurous life.

The question may well be raised, however, whether we could have a community or a society based on this hypothesis of multiple realities. Might not such a society be a completely individualistic anarchy? That is not my opinion. Suppose my grudging tolerance of your separate world view became a full acceptance of you and your right to have such a view. Suppose that instead of shutting out the realities of others as absurd or dangerous or heretical or stupid, I was willing to explore and learn about those realities? Suppose you were willing to do the same. What would be the social result? I think that our society would be based not on a blind commitment to a cause or creed or view of reality, but on a common commitment to each other as rightfully separate persons, with separate realities. The natural human tendency to care for another would no longer be "I care for you because you are the same as I," but, instead "I prize and treasure you because you are different from me."

Idealistic, you say? It surely is. How can I be so utterly naive and "unrealistic" as to have any hope that such a drastic change could conceivably come about? I base my hope partly on the view of world history so aptly stated by Charles Beard: "When the skies grow dark, the stars begin to shine." So we may see the emergence of leaders who are moving in this new direction.

I base my hope, even more solidly, on the view enunciated by Lancelot Whyte, the historian of ideas, in his final book before his death. It is his theory, in which he is not alone, that great steps in human history are anticipated, and probably brought about, by changes in the unconscious thinking of thousands and millions of individuals during the period preceding the change. Then, in a relatively short space of time, a new idea, a new perspective, seems to burst upon the world scene, and change occurs. He gives the example that before 1914, patriotism and nationalism were unquestioned virtues. Then began the faint unconscious questioning which built an unconscious tradition reversing a whole pattern of thought. This new perspective burst into the open between 1950 and 1970. "My country, right or wrong" is no longer a belief to live by. Nationalistic wars are out of date and out of favor, and even though they continue, world opinion is deeply opposed. Whyte (1974) points out that "at any moment the *unconscious levels are ahead of the conscious* in the task of unifying emotion, thought and action!" (p. 107)

For me, this line of thought is entirely congenial. I have stated that we are wiser than our intellects, that our organisms as a whole have a wisdom and purposiveness which goes well beyond our conscious thought. I believe that this idea applies to the concepts I have been presenting in this chapter. I think that men and women, individually and collectively, are inwardly and organismically rejecting the view of one single, culture-approved reality. I believe they are moving inevitably toward the acceptance of millions of separate, challenging, exciting, informative, *individual* perceptions of reality. I regard it as possible that this view—like the sudden and separate discovery of the principles of quantum mechanics by scientists in different countries—may begin to come into effective existence in many parts of the world at once. If so, we will be living in a totally new universe, different from any in history. Is it conceivable that such a change can come about?

Here lies the challenge to educators—probably the most insecure and frightened among any of the professions—battered by public pressures, limited by legislative restrictions, essentially conservative in their reactions. Can they possibly espouse such a view of multiple realities as I have been describing? Can they begin to bring into being the changes in attitudes, behaviors, and values that such a world view would demand? Certainly, by themselves they cannot. But with the underlying change in what Whyte calls "the unconscious tradition," and with the aid of the new person whom I and many others see emerging in our culture, it is just conceivable that they might succeed.

I conclude that if nations follow their past ways, then, because of the speed of world communication of separate views, each society will have to exert more and more coercion to bring about a forced agreement as to what constitutes the real world and its values. Those coerced agreements will differ from nation to nation, from culture to culture. The coercion will destroy individual freedom. We will bring about our own destruction through the clashes caused by differing world views.

But I have suggested an alternative. If we accept as a basic fact of all human life that we live in separate realities; if we can see those differing realities as the most promising resource for learning in all the history of the world; if we can live together in order to learn from one another without fear; if we can do all this, then a new age could be dawning. And perhaps—just perhaps—humankind's deep organic sensings are paving the way for just such a change.

REFERENCES

Castaneda, C. *The teachings of Don Juan: A Yaqui way of knowledge.* New York: Ballantine Books, 1969.

Castaneda, C. *A separate reality: Further conversations with Don Juan.* New York: Pocket Books, Division of Simon & Schuster, 1971.

Jung, C. G. *Memories, dreams, reflections.* New York: Vintage Books, 1961.

Lilly, J. C. *The center of the cyclone.* New York: Doubleday, 1973.

Monroe, R. A. *Journeys out of the body.* New York: Bantam Books, 1971.

Whyte, L. L. *The universe of experience.* New York: Harper Torchbooks, 1974.

A MORE HUMAN WORLD

While the foundations of Carl Rogers's professional work began with the practice of individual psychotherapy, his focus gradually broadened over a period of many years to many fields beyond psychology. The person-centered approach exerted a significant influence on education, medicine, business, social work, the ministry, and numerous other professions. Eventually, Rogers recognized the potential of applying his philosophy and methods on an even wider social canvas, as he sought to bring together and facilitate communication between opposing groups whose differences involved political, religious, and even international conflicts.

"Social Implications" is a brief, early expression of Rogers's recognition that his work in individual therapy might have important social applications. In "Resolving Intercultural Tensions," excerpted here, he described several examples of how he and others had applied the methods of human relations training to fostering meaningful communication between bitterly antagonistic groups, such as Rogers's own work with Catholics and Protestants from Northern Ireland. In "A Psychologist Looks at Nuclear War," Rogers offers still other examples — from his own experience to President Carter's facilitation of the Sadat-Begin Camp David accords — to illustrate the potency and practicality of applying principles of human communication to situations of intergroup conflict.

So impassioned did he become about the possibilities for applying the person-centered approach on a wider scale that in the last decade of his life, Rogers became a virtual globetrotter, facilitating groups in such widely diverse places as Japan, Mexico, Venezuela, Brazil, Austria, Hungary, Poland, France, Switzerland, Germany, Finland, Italy, Spain, the Soviet Union, England, Ireland, South Africa, and, of course, the United States. At the time of his death, he was planning a trip to Greece, as well as a return trip to South Africa. (He had also accompanied his physician son, David Rogers, on a nonworking trip to the Republic of China.)

Many of the workshops and training programs Rogers and his colleagues conducted were cross-cultural conferences, initiated by his associate Charles M. Devonshire, bringing together people from many countries. Others were indigenous groups who invited Rogers to come and work with individuals around local and regional concerns. For example, in South Africa, Rogers was asked to work with mixed groups including blacks, whites, and coloreds to deal with the pressing issues and problems created by the system of apartheid.

For years Rogers had stated that helping individuals experience and express their fuller range of both emotion and cognition would lead not only to more satisfying living but to more constructive behavior in society. In the seventies and eighties, he saw repeatedly that the expression and acceptance of the whole person in conflicting *groups* also led to constructive awareness and positive, tension-reducing action. Still, Rogers was eager to put his theory to a wider test—the fantasy he had expressed in "Social Implications" many years earlier—to help the *leaders* of conflicting countries communicate in more genuine and trusting ways, to use the behavioral sciences to reduce major world conflicts.

Toward that end, in 1984, with his colleague Gay Leah Swenson, Rogers established what is now the Carl Rogers Institute for Peace, a project of the Center for Studies of the Person in La Jolla, California. The institute was instrumental in convening "The Rust Workshop," described here in Rogers's article. Attended by high-level leaders from many countries, with the focus on reducing tensions in Central America, the Rust workshop was a natural outgrowth, culmination, and tentative validation of all that had gone before.

In the late 1980s, the Soviet Union's new policy of openness and the accompanying improvement of U.S.-Soviet relations were continual and major topics of international news. Carl Rogers made two trips to the Soviet Union in the 1980s, one of which is described vividly in the final chapter of this section. Not only does this essay give a fascinating glimpse into some seldom-seen or -discussed aspects of Soviet life, it illustrates an important part of Rogers's work in his last years.

At Rogers's memorial service in 1987, Richard Farson suggested that Rogers's visits to Russia and his personal exchanges with high-level Soviet officials played a significant role in the Soviet Union's willingness to become more open and trusting in their international relations. How much truth there is in this assertion is impossible to ascertain, for Rogers's visits and dialogues with Soviet officials were but one of many citizen peace initiatives during this period. Nevertheless, there is, at least, much symbolic truth in Farson's assertion. For whatever improvement in U.S.-Soviet relations has occurred — whether from governmental negotiations, cultural and professional exchanges, or citizen diplomacy — has come about because of an increasing and mutual willingness to communicate. This was, after all, the essence of Rogers's life's work — not only a theoretical belief in the ideal of better communication, but an ongoing search for realistic and effective ways of implementing that theory on the intrapersonal, interpersonal, intergroup, and, in the end, international levels of application.

Nominated for the Nobel Peace Prize shortly before his death at age eighty-five, Carl Rogers, in his life and work, played a significant role in influencing much of our perception of the possibilities for using the principles and techniques of the behavioral sciences — particularly the "person-centered approach" — for dealing with some of the major social issues of our time.

29
Social Implications

Let me turn for a moment to some of the social implications of the path of life I have attempted to describe. I have presented it as a direction which seems to have great meaning for individuals. Does it have, could it have, any meaning or significance for groups or organizations? Would it be a direction which might usefully be chosen by a labor union, a church group, an industrial corporation, a university, a nation? To me it seems that this might be possible. Let us take a look, for example, at the conduct of our own country in its foreign affairs. By and large we find, if we listen to the statements of our leaders during the past several years, and read their documents, that our diplomacy is always based upon high moral purposes; that it is always consistent with the policies we have followed previously; that it involves no selfish desires; and that it has never been mistaken in its judgments and choices. I think perhaps you will agree with me that if we heard an individual speaking in these terms we would recognize at once that this must be a façade, that such statements could not possibly represent the real process going on within himself.

Suppose we speculate for a moment as to how we, as a nation, might present ourselves in our foreign diplomacy if we were openly, knowingly, and acceptingly being what we truly are. I do not know precisely what we are, but I suspect that if we were trying to express ourselves as we are, then our communications with foreign countries would contain elements of this sort.

> We as a nation are slowly realizing our enormous strength, and the power and responsibility which go with that strength.
> We are moving, somewhat ignorantly and clumsily, toward accepting a position of responsible world leadership.
> We make many mistakes. We are often inconsistent.
> We are far from perfect.
> We are deeply frightened by the strength of communism, a view of life different from our own.

Excerpted from "A Therapist's View of Personal Goals." *Pendle Hill Pamphlet No. 108*. Wallingford, PA, 1960, 30 pp.

We feel extremely competitive toward communism, and we are angry and humiliated when the Russians surpass us in any field.

We have some very selfish foreign interests, such as in the oil in the Middle East.

On the other hand, we have no desire to hold dominion over peoples.

We have complex and contradictory feelings toward the freedom and independence and self-determination of individuals and countries: we desire these and are proud of the past support we have given to such tendencies, and yet we are often frightened by what they may mean.

We tend to value and respect the dignity and worth of each individual, yet when we are frightened, we move away from this direction.

Suppose we presented ourselves in some such fashion, openly and transparently, in our foreign relations. We would be attempting to be the nation which we truly are, in all our complexity and even contradictoriness. What would be the results? To me the results would be similar to the experiences of a client when he is more truly that which he is. Let us look at some of the probable outcomes.

We would be much more comfortable, because we would have nothing to hide.

We could focus on the problem at hand, rather than spending our energies to prove that we are moral or consistent.

We could use all of our creative imagination in solving the problem, rather than in defending ourselves.

We could openly advance both our selfish interests, and our sympathetic concern for others, and let these conflicting desires find the balance which is acceptable to us as people.

We could freely change and grow in our leadership position, because we would not be bound by rigid concepts of what we have been, must be, ought to be.

We would find that we were much less feared, because others would be less inclined to suspect what lies behind the façade.

We would, by our own openness, tend to bring forth openness and realism on the part of others.

We would tend to work out the solutions of world problems on the basis of the real issues involved, rather than in terms of the façades being worn by the negotiating parties.

In short what I am suggesting by this fantasied example is that nations and organizations might discover, as have individuals, that it is a richly rewarding experience to be what one deeply is. I am suggesting that this view contains the seeds of a philosophical approach to all of life, that it is more than a trend observed in the experience of clients.

30
Resolving Intercultural Tensions

In tension situations, the pattern is simple. *Each* of the parties involved holds, with equal conviction, an identical view: "I am right and you are wrong; I am good and you are bad." This holds for tension between individuals and between groups, where it becomes "*We* are right and you are wrong; *we* are good and you are bad." One of our greatest difficulties in any dispute is to recognize or, even more difficult, to accept that the certitude we feel about our own rightness and goodness is equaled by the certitude of the opposing individual or group about their rightness and goodness. If tension is to be reduced, it is this pattern that must somehow be dissolved. Here is where a person-centered approach is at its most powerful.

Community tensions, racial and otherwise, can be eased by using the person-centered approach to empower the people on both sides of the conflict.

A young minister in a Wyoming town of about nine thousand was disturbed by the sharp division between the Chicanos and Anglos and decided to try to do something about it. The town was divided by a railroad and the Chicanos (about a quarter of the population) lived on the south side and the Anglos on the other. The white Americans thought that everything was fine in the town, because there was no very overt discrimination. The Mexican-Americans, on the other hand, felt that they *were* discriminated against. They felt oppressed, believed that the com-

Excerpted from *Carl Rogers on Personal Power*. New York: Delacorte Press, 1977, 115–140.

munity was not responsive to their needs, and harbored feelings ranging from passive resignation to burning resentment.

Lloyd Henderson, the minister, was able to get a modest grant to finance a program for the improvement of communication. First he chose nine leaders from the community, representing a cross-section — Anglo; Chicano; upper, middle, and lower class; men and women. He invited a facilitator from the Center for Studies of the Person to give an intensive weekend of training to the leaders. It helped them to discover that they were not expected to be leaders in the conventional sense, but facilitators of expression and communication. The groups were to be focused on communication, not on taking action. Then the nine groups were set up, with an attendance of eight to fifteen in each group. They met once a week for twelve weeks and they had an optional weekend together, which some of them chose to utilize and others did not. The groups, too, were cross-sectional; the local judge, in fact, was in with some Chicano youths who had always regarded him as their worst enemy.

First the groups turned to the leaders, expecting them to take responsibility, but gradually they realized that if the groups were to function, they had to take responsibility for themselves and for their own expression. The conversation was personal but focused on community issues. There was talk about unemployment. There was an airing of frustration with the railroad, which was a very central feature in the community. They discussed educational problems that their children were having. Thus, the major topics were community issues but set in a personal framework. The Chicanos were disheartened to be reconfronted with the lack of solidarity in their own group. Although the Anglos often thought of the Chicanos as a united group, the Chicanos themselves were aware of their disunity as a barrier to improving their situation.

One of the most characteristic discoveries in these meetings was that the attitudes of the participants, no matter what their backgrounds or ages, were more similar than they had supposed. When they discussed their children or the need for jobs, feelings were the same on both sides of the track. A look of wonder and awe came over the faces of two mothers, one Anglo and one Chicano, when they discovered how very much alike they were in their hopes for, and their problems with, their children.

Members of the groups were invited to participate on a local television show, telling of what they were doing and the progress they were making. This helped to keep the community in touch with the project and to give it some investment in better communication.

Gradually changes began to occur. Individuals who in the normal course of events would never have met built friendships across cultural and age barriers. The judge came to have a better understanding of the young people he was dealing with in his court. Toward the end, some groups did take action — for example, talking to employers about their hiring practices.

After the sessions had ended, the Chicanos banded together into a group, wrote a proposal, and got a grant from the federal government, which had as its aims reducing school dropouts, providing job training, and taking Mexican-American parents to see the state university, to raise their educational goals. These are samples of the group's activities. They hired a director to manage this program. It was a decided morale booster for the south side of the tracks.

All this was accomplished through a person-centered approach on a budget of less than five thousand dollars. The minister had believed in placing responsibility on the local leadership. Then he had provided these leaders, and himself, with a very brief but intensive training period in listening skills and facilitative skills. He was able to start *enough* groups to create a "critical mass." One group might have been helpful to the individuals involved, but almost certainly would not have affected the community. But nine groups, involving only a little over one hundred persons out of nine thousand, proved to be a sufficient mass to initiate creative social action. The results speak for themselves, indicative of what can be accomplished when tensions are not too great and bitterness not too deep. Individuals on both sides of the track experienced and used their power because they were able to realize their strengths through open expression and personal communication.

I experienced a deep feud when I worked with a group from Belfast, Northern Ireland. It was possible to observe what happens in a group where the bitterness involves generations of economic, religious, and cultural hatred. There were five Protestants — including one Englishman — and four Catholics in the group. The nine were chosen to include extremists and moderates on both sides, men and women, older and younger. The Englishman was a retired army colonel. We wanted to facilitate straightforward communication and to film this interaction.*

In the early sessions the bitterness, horror, and despair of everyday life in Belfast was abundantly clear. Tom's sister was blown to bits by a bomb which might have been thrown by terrorists of either side. Dennis and his family have hidden behind mattresses as bullets struck their home during a wild burst of shooting on their street. Dennis has on several occasions had to help carry away the torn bodies, living and dead, from bomb explosions. Becky spoke repeatedly of the brutality of the British army patrols to her teenaged sons. After one episode where the boy was made to believe he would be shot, "that child came in and I never saw fear like it on anybody's face in my whole life."

Gilda, young and attractive, spoke of the hopelessness. "I just get so full of despair. I just give up, you know." Becky said, "I really feel hopeless. . . . If something is not done the bitterness is just going to keep eating away at those kids and eventually they could become IRA men."

The bitterness was on both sides. Pretty Protestant Gilda said, "If I seen an IRA man lying on the ground — this is the wrong thing I suppose in your eyes — I would *step* on him, because to me he has just went out and taken the lives of innocent people."

All the violent feelings leave their mark. Sean, a sensitive young Catholic teacher, told how he had been forced to pull down a "steel shutter" between his functioning self and the seething feelings within. Otherwise he would go berserk. In a very quiet, soft voice he spoke of this inner wild beast: "Yeah, I know myself. I'm quite aware of this kind of thing, and it scares me to know that it is there. 'Cause it is violent and emotional and daft. . . . I take long walks and let this thing inside of me talk. It isn't quite the same as human feelings — it isn't quite the same as having a beast inside you — some sort of animal feelings, you know."

---

*This film, *The Steel Shutter*, is available for rental through Center for Studies of the Person, 1125 Torrey Pines Road, La Jolla, CA 92037.

The whole mixed stream of hatred and violence, of fear and despair, seems so powerful that to think one weekend could possibly make *any* difference seems incredibly quixotic. Yet changes did occur. One small example composed of two interchanges between Dennis, a Protestant, and Becky, Catholic:

DENNIS (*speaking about Becky*): The general impression back in Belfast is, if she is a Catholic she is a Catholic and you just put her in a wee box and that is the end of it. But you just can't do that. She has communicated to me that she is in a worse position than what I am. . . . I would hate to be sitting in Becky's chair . . . because I feel that she feels the absolute despair that I would feel. I don't know how I would react if I were one of her lads. I would probably go out and get a gun and finish up doing something radical and end up dead.

BECKY (*later*): Words couldn't describe what I feel towards Dennis from the discussion we had at dinner time. We spoke quietly for about ten minutes and I felt that here I have got a friend and that was it.

DENNIS: We sat here at dinner time and had a wee bit of a yarn quietly when you were all away for your dinner—

BECKY: I think he fully understands me as a person.

DENNIS: I do, there is no question about that—

BECKY: And for that reason I am very grateful and I think I have found a friend.

During our sessions the hatreds, the suspicions, the mistrusts of the two feuding groups were very evident, sometimes in covert form, gradually becoming more open in their expression. The individuals were speaking not only for themselves but for generations of resentment and prejudice. There were only sixteen hours of group interaction, yet during that incredibly short period these centuries-old hatreds were not only softened but in some instances deeply changed. It is evidence that facilitative attitudes can create an atmosphere in which open expression can occur. Open expression, in this kind of a climate, leads to communication. Better communication very often leads to understanding, and understanding washes away many of the ancient barriers. So rapid was the progress, so significant the changes, that some of the statements I have quoted here had to be deleted from the film. To show such understanding of the opposition would have endangered the lives of the speakers when it was shown in Belfast.

When the group returned to Belfast, almost all of them continued to meet at the home of the British colonel, whose neighborhood was the safest. After the film was completed they formed teams—one Protestant, one Catholic—and showed the film to many church groups of both sects, and led discussions. None of this had been planned. There were no funds to help out. It was done on their own spontaneous initiative.

For one group to make progress toward reconciliation hasn't ended the killings in Belfast. True, but suppose there had been a thousand or two thousand groups. The expense would be a fraction of what private Catholic armies, the British occupation army, and private Protestant armies have cost. As for facilitators, there are hundreds already sufficiently trained, and with three months' notice, they could be on the job.

This whole view is thoroughly confirmed in a recent interview with two Belfast men, very knowledgeable in the community, who have been acquainted with the project and who have seen the impact of the film on small audiences. They are all for training large numbers of Irish as facilitators. "We've got to get thousands of people involved. Once we do, it gets harder for the two percent of paramilitary gunmen [to control the public mind]. The whole idea of encounter groups—this is it! Encounter groups need to be done at a street-by-street level."

When will this come about? It will happen when the concerned public makes up its mind that the problem is so serious that something *must* be done. It is not experience or personnel or solid evidence that is lacking. It is the public will. The public is not yet convinced that there are any possible solutions, and even if there were, it is not willing—yet—to take the risk. When it is, a humanistic, person-centered approach has something to offer, even in situations of deadly antagonism.

In working with international groups it is fascinating to watch the development of appreciation for the customs and beliefs of very diverse nationalities, races, and cultures. The reactions of the participants and facilitators to the person-centered approach has been overwhelmingly positive. They speak of loss of fear in trying to communicate, a feeling of being heard, and an awareness of the beauty and richness of cultural differences.

One of the most striking things about international groups is that they are so similar to every other encounter group. The national and racial and cultural differences come to seem unimportant as the *person* is discovered. In spite of all the differences, there is a great potential for understanding and closeness in the human issues we are all trying to cope with. The participants in this workshop do not speak much of the cultural issues. Instead they speak of things like "I've found my family again"; "I was not being honest with myself"; "I can cry, show feeling, instead of constantly joking"; "If I am going to change, can change, or dare to change, I don't know yet, but I am surer of myself"; "I am more self-confident"; "I have learned to better trust my feelings." Think of these statements. Which was made by a black, by a German, by a man, by a Swede? It is impossible even to guess. These are *human* statements, and that seems to be the outcome typical of such person-centered groups. It is being human which dissolves the barriers and brings closeness.

This appears to be the result when persons of highly divergent cultures are empowered by being heard and accepted and permitted to be self-directed. This is the interpersonal politics of a cross-cultural application of the person-centered approach.

I hope I have been successful in demonstrating that models do exist for the constructive handling of almost every variety of intergroup tension. Whether we are speaking of religious differences or of bitterness based in poverty versus wealth or mistrust rooted in differing cultural customs or the seething rage growing out of racial discrimination or deadly centuries-old feuds involving a number of these elements, we are not without knowledge of, and experience in, utilizing interpersonal skills which help to resolve these tensions. We need to improve our skills. We need to recognize the problems that will emerge if these efforts are multipled 100- or 1,000-fold. But experience with a person-centered approach indicates that there is no basic reason for despair. We have made progress in setting up test-tube solutions. When the world is ready, we can say tentatively and with humility that we are ready to begin.

Throughout every example there runs a consistent thread of interpersonal politics. The individual is not manipulated by powerful leadership; is not converted by some charismatic figure; is enabled to become more of self, more expressive, more open to feelings, good and bad. And it is out of that more complete and powerful humanness that person touches person, communication becomes real, tensions are reduced, and relationships become expressive and understanding, with an acceptance of the negative as well as the positive. This is the end result of a person-centered politics in intergroup frictions.

31
A Psychologist Looks at Nuclear War

This is an awesome time in the history of the world. It is entirely possible that we are approaching our doom. I wish to speak as a citizen of the United States, loyal to its principles and ideals. I wish to speak as a psychologist devoted to the enhancement of personal growth and the improvement of human relationships. I want to voice my deep concern regarding the growing likelihood of nuclear war.

First, I will point to some of the dreadful possibilities. Fritjof Capra is a highly respected theoretical physicist. In his new book, *The Turning Point* (1982), he says that an all-out nuclear war with Russia would mean that there would be a half billion dead after the first exchange. The entire war would be over in thirty to sixty minutes and almost no living thing would survive its consequences. The Pentagon plan for this war is known in the Defense Department as "Mutually Assured Destruction." The initials accurately describe it: MAD. Capra's information leads him to believe that the Pentagon has plans for a nuclear first strike against the Soviet Union in case of any direct military confrontation with the Russians anywhere in the world. Thus, an all-out war could start from some small local war in which the United

Journal of Humanistic Psychology, Vol. 22, No. 4, Fall 1982, 9–20. Reprinted by permission of Sage Publications, Inc.

States and the Russians confront each other indirectly through military forces they sponsor.

There is no such thing as a limited nuclear war. President Reagan's incredible remark, twice repeated, about the possibility of a nuclear war limited to Europe, and Secretary Haig's plan to fire off a nuclear weapon in Europe simply to demonstrate our capability to the Russians, show both a profound disregard for human life and an ignorance of governmental psychology. Suppose a limited nuclear war begins. One side will be the loser. Can anyone believe that the loser would not then push the all-out nuclear button? It would be inevitable. So a limited war means an all-out war.

Another dreadful fact is that the military in both of the superpowers believe that a nuclear war can be won. George Bush, now our vice-president, when he was a candidate for the presidency was interviewed by a reporter on the subject of nuclear war. He indicated that he believed that a nuclear war was winnable. The reporter asked, "How do you win a nuclear exchange?" Bush: "You have a survivability of command in control, a survivability of industrial potential, protection of a percentage of your citizens, and you have a capability to inflict more damage on the opposition than they can inflict upon you. That's the way you can have a winner and the Soviets' planning is based on the ugly concept of a winner in a nuclear exchange." Reporter: "You mean like five percent would survive? Two percent?" Bush: "More than that. If everybody fired everything he had, you'd have more than that survive" (Los Angeles *Times*, January 4, 1980). Some experts believe that as many as fifteen percent might survive. But Bush is thinking incredible thoughts. My home city of San Diego has roughly a million inhabitants. Bush is saying that perhaps 850,000 of us would be killed, and only 150,000 would be left wandering about in deadly radioactive rubble. And he calls that winning!

Admiral Hyman Rickover, the father of nuclear submarines and an expert on nuclear warfare, was asked in the Senate hearing on January 28, 1982, what he thought of the prospects of nuclear war. His reply was essentially "I think we will destroy ourselves, and then perhaps a better, wiser species will emerge."

The Impact Now

What is the prospect of this incredible holocaust doing to us now? I believe that it is so horrendous that we often tend to trivialize it, or to deny its seriousness, or blot it completely out of our thinking. We refuse to grasp the *meaning* of its consequences. I believe that it is dynamics of this sort that help to account for the statements of Reagan, Haig, and Bush, and the horrifying course upon which they have set our nation and our military might.

The utmost of this socially suicidal mentality was achieved in a speech on March 1 by the advisor to the president, Edwin Meese. He referred to nuclear war as "something less than desirable"!! (*Time*, March 29, 1982, p. 20.)

This trivialization of the horror of nuclear war is shown in the popular video games of missiles and satellites falling on cities. I observed members of a family playing such a game. The skylines of cities were on the lower edge of the screen; missiles and even more powerful satellites kept falling from the top of the screen and the game was to try to stop them in midair and explode them. But often they did get through and a common remark was, "Oops, there goes your city!" We are making nuclear war thinkable by treating it as though it were just a game.

Within the young, who perhaps ponder more deeply about such things, it often produces a hopelessness. The National Urban League reports that among our young black people between the ages of fifteen and twenty-nine, suicide has become the number one cause of death. This sobering fact is attributed not only to the lack of opportunity, but to hopelessness about the future. Undoubtedly the possibility of a nuclear war plays a part in that hopelessness.

Last year my granddaughter, Frances Fuchs, taught in a training program for adolescents who had been rejected by their schools. These were obviously not ordinary young people. Yet what she found is significant. Early in the term she asked them to write some paragraphs describing what they envisioned for themselves in five to ten years. The majority of them saw themselves dead in a thermonuclear holocaust or living desperate lives in a harsh, polluted, overcrowded world (Fuchs, 1981). Here are a few quotes: "In five years I will either be dead or in the Army or playing lead guitar in a band. I do think the war will come before five years and that most of us will be dead." "I believe in five years if Reagan hasn't gotten us blown up that our natural resources will either disappear or they will be very difficult to get hold of. I really think that in five years I will be dead or really, really bad off." Or, from a young alcoholic, "I drink to get wasted. I drink whenever I feel like it and I enjoy the high I get. When I get drunk, it feels great. Nothing seems to matter." How many other young people see no more positive possibilities for their future than to get wasted?

So that's what the prospect of nuclear war is doing to some of our young people. It hangs as a black cloud over all of us, but the young are especially sensitive and aware and especially hopeless.

Are these young people too gloomy? What is the view of those scientists, physicists, and engineers who understand the technology of the situation? According to Capra many of them have two blind spots: (1) They are employed by the military-industrial complex to build nuclear weapons or by the nuclear power industry to build nuclear power plants; (2) they often see only a narrow, or fragmented view of their own task and have no conception of how it all fits together. Consequently, the only experts who can provide an unbiased and comprehensive assessment of the situation are those who are independent of nuclear development and, not surprisingly, they all tend to be in the antinuclear movement. Those who know the most are the most strongly opposed to the steps we are taking toward nuclear war, as the work and publications of the Union of Concerned Scientists clearly shows.

And what about military men who know the plans and strategies for nuclear war? The Center for Defense Information strongly opposes nuclear war, the senseless arms race, the escalating military budget. And who are its leaders? Two rear admirals of the Navy, and a major general of the Marines. They have all been deeply involved in planning nuclear war. Now retired, they are devoting full time to try to stop our self-destructive military policies. So it is clear: those who really know nuclear possibilities are most deeply committed to *stopping* the arms race, and stopping it *now*!

Prevention

What can we do to prevent the possibility of a nuclear war? Psychologists have made valuable proposals as to steps that might be taken. Perhaps the most exciting is Charles Osgood's plan for "Graduated and Reciprocated Initiatives in Tension Reduction" (GRIT).

Very briefly, he proposes that a nation can take unilateral action to reduce tension. President Kennedy was acting in accordance with Osgood's principle when on June 10, 1963, he declared that the United States would stop all nuclear testing in the atmosphere, and would not resume such tests unless another nation continued them. On June 15, Krushchev welcomed this step and ordered a halt in the production of Russian strategic bombers. On June 20, Russia, after long previous delay, agreed to the "hot line" between the two leaders. In July the stalled test-ban treaty was earnestly negotiated, and in August it was signed. Kennedy approved a large sale of wheat to the USSR. The sequence was halted by his assassination.

Put in more general terms, one nation, without reducing its capacity to wage war, takes a step toward reducing tension. This involves a small but manageable risk. Its intent is announced in advance. The opposing nation is invited to verify that the action has been taken, and invited to reciprocate. If it does reciprocate, a further step can be taken by the first nation. Gradually, tension is reduced. The Russians called the 1963 actions "the policy of mutual example." Although the "experiment" was so brief, the relationship between the two nations perceptibly improved.

Osgood's 1962 book, *An Alternative to War and Surrender*, should be carefully restudied by all of us, especially by those in government.

Dealing with Social Tensions

I want to discuss at greater length another pathway to prevention, which I can speak of from personal experience.

One example involving much bitter confrontation was the conference of the National Health Council several years ago. It is an organization made up of representatives of the American Medical Association, dental associations, nurses' organizations, health insurance companies, and health-oriented agencies. The council decided on this occasion that they, as "health providers," should invite to the conference a group of "health consumers" from the urban ghettos and the rural underprivileged. It was a courageous decision, but they only gradually realized the risk that was involved. The health consumers were selected by local groups. They were all poor, many black, some Chicano. As the time of the conference approached, the planners became uneasy and invited the staff of our center to act as facilitators of groups at the conference. Though they could pay no more than our expenses, we accepted.

When the conference opened, the hostility of the consumers was so thick it was palpable. The conference threatened to split wide open. The consumers announced they were going to withdraw. It was very fortunate that we were there, also fortunate that we were receiving no fee. We were able to tell them in a very heated session that we had come all the way across the country, for no fee, simply to be certain that everyone in the conference had a chance really to express his or her own views and feelings, and to be heard. This statement held the conference together, though a split was still a possibility. Twenty groups of 20 to 25 each were formed, each containing both providers and consumers, and each facilitated by one of our staff members. I remember well the group I facilitated. The bitterness of the group erupted in full force. Their anger at white professionals, at the lack of health services, at the lack of any voice in their own health care, was so strong that some of the professionals were frightened, while others were self-righteously angry in response. One black man, voicing his hatred of oppression, said that the Marines had trained him to kill and that if need be he would use that training against the people and institutions that were holding him down. The value of a facilitator who could truly understand and clarify the feelings expressed—even the very bitter emotions of two opponents—was most clearly demonstrated.

As the group sessions continued, there was a small, significant growth in mutual understanding. The white professionals really began to see their functioning as it appeared to the recipients. A ghetto member who hated health insurance companies realized that the insurance company executive in our group was not all bad and that they could communicate. A Chicana woman finally told tearfully how she felt totally scorned and uncared for by both blacks and whites.

During our sessions the existing conflicts, such as those between haves and have-nots, between blacks and whites, between professionals and recipients, between establishment and radicals, burst into the open, but these violent outpourings occurred in a climate in which each person was permitted to state his or her feelings without interruption, a climate in which the facilitators showed that their caring concern was for the dignity of each person and their primary purpose was to understand each expression and to foster open communication. In this atmosphere the issues became greatly clarified. What is perhaps equally important, persons emerged as separate, unique individuals, each with his or her own perception of those issues. The labels — black, white, provider, consumer, conservative, radical — began to disappear. Little by little, real interpersonal communication began.

A surprising development was that the consumers, though they had never known one another before, began to coalesce and take real leadership. A black woman with little formal education emerged as one of the strongest leaders, first in our group, and later in the conference as a whole. The consumers began to formulate resolutions. They were then told that it was the established policy of the council not to adopt resolutions, that it was only a forum. Nevertheless, they persisted. By majority vote, after a long and heated discussion, they took over the last meeting of the conference, dismissed the speakers with thanks, and presented their resolutions, most of which were passed. A final astonishing fact is that during the following year most of those resolutions were put into effect by the National Council.

This is a good example of what can be accomplished by experienced facilitators. By accepting hostile and divergent opinions — some of the hostility directed toward the facilitators themselves — the most irrational of the feelings are somewhat defused by being fully expressed and by feedback from group members. Little by little, understanding and acceptance of other points of view develops. Confidence grows, both in the individual and in the group. There is a more realistic consideration of the issues, with less overload of irrationality. The group moves toward innovative, responsible, and often revolutionary steps, steps that can now be taken in an atmosphere of realism. All of these things occurred in this particular conference.

I could tell of other experiences, such as the workshop at El Escorial in Spain where 170 people from 22 nations gathered. They ranged in politics from Marxists to conservative capitalists, from priests to atheists, from old to young. National and racial hostilities were clearly evident, especially hostility toward the "imperialistic policies" of the United States. Yet during this ten-day workshop, in the presence of a facilitative climate, members began gradually to hear each other, then slowly to understand and respect. The large group step by step became in every sense a harmonious community. Not a community whose views were all similar—most assuredly not—but a community where individuals with their diverse views and convictions came to be understood and where persons and their differences were prized and respected. Individuals felt empowered to take more risk in developing themselves, and in carrying through constructive social actions.

On the basis of these experiences I feel it is not too much to say that if feuding parties are willing to meet in the same room, and willing even to talk at each other, steps toward better understanding and more constructive actions are almost certain to ensue, if there are skilled facilitators present who can understand and accept the diverse, hostile, fearful attitudes that are expressed.

The International Level

You may feel this is all very well with conferences and encounter groups, but such a process could not possibly help with international issues where we are dealing with large political entities. In this connection I would like to call your attention to the Camp David experience. I have no way of knowing whether President Carter had any psychological advice, but the Camp David sessions had many of the qualities of an intensive group experience, such as I have described, and many of its outcomes were similar. In the first place, it was informal. There was no protocol, no standing on ceremony, no formal attire. The leaders especially, and their staff members to some extent, met simply as persons.

Second, there were many facilitative efforts. In one tense and angry meeting near the beginning, Carter simply listened to Sadat and Begin. Then at the conclusion of the meeting he summarized, much as a facilitator might have done, the issues that had been raised by each leader. The difference was that he was able to state and clarify these issues in a calm and understanding way where they had been expressed in highly emotional ways. On another occasion, when the hostility between Sadat and Begin ran too high, Carter acted as a facilitative intermediary, carrying messages back and forth until they were willing to meet again (Dayan, 1981).

Another important facet of the experience was that it was self-contained and private. There were no onlookers. No members of the media were admitted. Consequently, there was no advantage to putting up a façade for the world to see. It was also possible to make tentative and exploratory statements without being held to these views. They could simply talk together as persons.

Another similarity to the intensive group experience was the "pressure cooker" aspect. For twelve days these men were kept in constant contact with each other. To be in close communicative contact for a considerable period of time with someone with whom you violently disagree, together with a person who can act as a facilitator, almost inevitably leads to a better understanding and greater acceptance of the other. While President Carter was far from neutral, and sometimes more of a persuader than a facilitator, he did serve a very facilitative function.

There were two notable outcomes. First, these two world leaders, starting from very divergent points of view, were able to come to a major agreement on constructive next steps. The second outcome is astonishing. Begin and Sadat were almost violently hostile toward each other at the outset. At the end of the twelve days they felt sufficiently warm toward each other that they embraced on public television. Here is definite evidence that the same kind of process can work with world leaders as operates in workshop groups. To be sure there were deficiencies. There was insufficient inclusion of all staff members in the interchange. There appears to have been no recognition of and no preparation for the familiar "back home" problem, in which the participant finds that he has moved away from his own constituency toward a more conciliatory point of view. There were other deficiencies, but Camp David marks a new step in international negotiation. It affirms the potentialities of the intensive group experience. It is a model that should be utilized and improved.

Application to the Nuclear Situation

Does this process of communication and improved mutual understanding have any application to the international nuclear tension? I believe it does. I wish to look at the general psychological context and then at the more specific possibilities.

In the people there appears to be a will toward peace. In Europe millions are making known their desire to stop the deployment of nuclear missiles. This movement is making its strength felt. As I write this, news comes of the election in West Germany where the result is attributed to the antinuclear protest. The U.S. government is trying to discount it by saying that it is Communist inspired. But it acknowledges its power.

In the United States the millions are just beginning to move. A Gallup poll in June 1981 showed that seventy-two percent of the American public wanted the United States and the USSR to stop building nuclear weapons. There is great support for a bilateral nuclear weapons freeze, a proposal that both nations "halt the testing, production, and further deployment of all nuclear weapons . . . in a way that can be checked and verified by both sides."

And in Russia? Our information is scanty, but twenty million Russians died and an equal number were injured in World War II. The dread of war is even greater among the Russian people than in ours. Two Russian dissidents give us a current picture of the attitudes of their countrymen (Medvedev & Medvedev, 1982). According to these writers, the people live in great and understandable fear of the United States. They are especially fearful of an American nuclear first strike.

There is, then, every reason to believe that many millions of people in many countries desire peace. If that desire is strongly voiced by massive numbers, it can stop the two governments in their disastrous course. We have evidence of this in my country. It was public protest that eventually stopped the Vietnam war.

What is needed is a great popular uprising to bring a halt to the step-by-step escalation toward nuclear war. President Dwight Eisenhower, not a flaming radical, said it well many years ago.

> Some day the demand for disarmament by hundreds of millions will, I hope, become so universal and so insistent, that no man, no men, can withstand it. We have to mobilize the hundreds of millions; we have to make them understand the choice is theirs. We have to make the young people see to it, that they need not be the victims of the Third World War.

Those millions are beginning to move, to be heard.

The goal of this movement must be twofold: to stop the nuclear buildup and nuclear threats, and to substitute a process for making peace. The need for this positive program cannot be overstated.

The first step is to change the policy of the U.S. government. At the present time the top officials show not the slightest intention of wishing to have peace with Russia, or of wishing to understand the Russians, or of trying to work out a peaceful solution to our mutual problems. They make phony proposals knowing in advance that they cannot be accepted by Russia. They and their supporters are a perfect example of the pattern of which I spoke. "We are right and good. You are wrong and bad." This very accurately describes their attitude. Threat seems to be almost their only diplomatic tool. We excoriate Russia for its invasion of Afghanistan, and its part in the military dictatorship in Poland. We threaten to cut off any negotiations as a punishment for their actions. Deplorable as those actions are, we should view them with some humility in view of our own conduct in Vietnam, Chile, and El Salvador.

The present stance of the American government must be changed. We need to communicate with the Russian people. We need to try to understand their point of view. We need to help them understand our point of view. We need to dialogue with them at official and unofficial levels. This will not be easy to achieve. But in meetings of government officials, in professional conferences, in business contacts, and with Russian visitors we need to encourage dialogue. Experienced facilitators, where needed, can be drawn from other countries.

We need to bring pressure on the government of the United States to embark on a serious, vigorous program of communication with the USSR and the Russian people.

We pour billions into creating redundant nuclear weapons sufficient to destroy the planet many times over. We need to put some of that money and energy to work in pursuing, developing, expanding the communicative process that leads toward peaceful reconciliation. We have the models. We need to put them to work. With a minute fraction of the dollars we spend for war, we could, as we know from experience and research, make definitive progress toward peaceful interaction that would prevent the holocaust from overwhelming us.

We have very little time. This is a life-and-death issue for all of us. Can we stop the drift toward destruction? We all have a responsibility in answering this question. It is to carry out my personal share of this responsibility that I have spoken out so strongly. I intend to continue. I hope you will join me — and millions of others — in working for a stop to our terrible insanity — the trend toward nuclear war.

REFERENCES

Capra, F. *The Turning Point.* New York: Simon & Schuster, 1982.

Dayan, M. *Breakthrough: A Personal Account of the Egypt-Israel Negotiations.* New York: Knopf, 1981.

Fuchs, F. *The Guru or the Labor Market.* Unpublished manuscript, 1981.

Medvedev, R. A. & Medvedev, Z. A. A nuclear "Samizdat" on America's arms race. *The Nation,* 1982, 234, (2), 38–50.

Osgood, C. *An Alternative to War and Surrender.* Urbana, IL: University of Illinois Press, 1962.

32
The Rust Workshop

Introduction

I have recently returned from a most unusual experience, working as one of a group of staff members, facilitating an international workshop different from any in which I have participated before.

I want to write of it from my perspective. This means I will be speaking of it as a psychologist, interested in group process, intent on applying therapeutic principles to conflict situations. It might reasonably be approached from a political interface, or from the point of view of an observer interested in diverse personalities. I hope its story may be told from each of these vantage points. My account is personal and psychological.

General Description

In my opinion, a historic event took place in Rust, Austria, in the Seehotel, November 1–4, 1985. There were a number of elements that made it unique. First, it was a meeting of fifty participants who, although leading figures in government and in various fields of thought, were meeting as *persons*, not as roles—not as former presidents, ambassadors, senators, authors, or professors—simply as persons. Second, although they came from seventeen nations, they came together to focus on

---

AUTHOR'S NOTE: I have written this report, but the workshop it describes was brought into being by many individuals. Rodrigo Carazo, former president of Costa Rica, and Murray Silberman, his associate, both of the University for Peace, Costa Rica, were responsible for bringing together leading government officials from Central and Latin America. They were also helpful in inviting leaders from other countries. The administrative and facilitative staff, headed by Gay Swenson and myself, was drawn from the Center for Studies of the Person, La Jolla, California. They were the following: Dee Aker, Maria Bowen, Norman Chambers, Valerie Henderson, Marvalene Styles Hughes, Douglas Land, David Malcolm, Lawrence Solomon, Alberto Zucconi.

Journal of Humanistic Psychology, Vol. 26, No. 3, Summer 1986, 23–45. Reprinted by permission of Sage Publications, Inc.

one area of crisis: "The Central American Challenge." Third, this was not a media event, but a workshop held in a private retreat setting—a lovely small hotel on the border of Austria, with Hungary and the Eastern Bloc countries on the other side of the salty lake that separates them. Fourth, it was facilitated by a staff with long experience in dealing with diverse attitudes and antagonistic feelings. Fifth, although only four days long, it reached a point at which individuals listened to one another, actually *heard* one another, and began to build strong personal bonds where only suspicion and mistrust had existed before.

Let me try to state the results in a more personal way. The workshop had more significance, more impact, opened more lines of communication, brought together more divergent persons than we had any reasonable right to expect. It was a deeply satisfying positive experience. We learned that people of high status, political leaders, government officials, prominent shapers of public opinion are, in important ways, just like the folks we usually deal with—they desire more personal contact, deeper communication, more closeness, and more searching and intimate dialogue. These things happen *providing*—and that's a very important word—that we can create a climate that has elements of warmth, informality, sensitive understanding, a desire to hear, a genuine caring, a willingness to be ourselves—even awkwardly if necessary—and a skill in the facilitation of communication. Whether because of our experience or our skill or luck or Providence or whatever, we were somehow able to bring together enough of the subtle qualities of this kind of climate that extremely exciting events took place. But let me back up and give a few of the facts.

As stated, there were fifty participants in the workshop (although four could attend only one or two sessions). They were, indeed, a distinguished gathering. I have tried to divide them into crude categories. There were three ex-presidents of Central American countries, the current vice-president of Costa Rica, three from ministries of foreign affairs, seven ambassadors, seven legislators, four lesser or retired government officials; there were eight from academia, mostly professors; there were eight participants from institutes, foundations, and other organizations, several of them concerned with communication and cooperation;

there were five invited primarily because they were peace activists; there were two who were invited primarily because of books they had written (although many others had also written books); there were two officials from the bank that subsidized the gathering in Austria. Many other individuals had been invited who were unable to come or declined our invitations. The seventeen nations from which the participants came are the following: Costa Rica, Honduras, El Salvador, Nicaragua, Colombia, Venezuela, Mexico, Chile, Austria, the United States, West Germany, Sweden, India, Poland, Hungary, the Philippines, and Switzerland, and two Palestinians living in Jerusalem.

As to staff, there were nine facilitators from the Center for Studies of the Person—two for each of the four small groups that were formed, but active also in the general group—and me; there were three translators, all from Latin American countries, all experienced in working with us; there were six administrative staff who worked literally day and night to keep things moving smoothly, getting out materials in Spanish and English, and devoting themselves selflessly to making the conference work.

Sponsorship and Financing

The gathering was sponsored by the University for Peace (UP), Costa Rica, and the Center for Studies of the Person (CSP), La Jolla, California. The co-directors were Carl Rogers (CSP) and Rodrigo Carazo (UP), former president of Costa Rica and founder of the University for Peace.

In preparing for the workshop, Gay Swenson was the co-director of the team from CSP and was the responsible administrator of the project in La Jolla. Murray Silberman was actively engaged in the preparatory work in Costa Rica, working with Rodrigo Carazo.

The financing of the operation was complex. In mid-1984, Karl Vak, head of a large Viennese bank, offered to pay the expenses of the workshop at the Seehotel, and he more than kept his promise. That help, a $30,000 anonymous gift, and $25,000 from the Carnegie Corporation have been the largest gifts, but there have been many individual donors and two special benefits. We went ahead on faith, and the event has been held! Everyone will be reimbursed for expenses. And payments beyond that will be minimal. Payments or not, I believe all of us would agree that it has been eminently worthwhile.

Purposes

There were several major purposes:

1. To bring together high-level influential figures — especially policymakers and shapers of public opinion — who were involved in international relations, especially those affecting Central America.

2. To bring a staff who had had experience in creating a climate of psychological safety in which persons could meet freely as persons, not in their official capacities, the type of person-centered climate we have created in dealing with diverse and antagonistic groups in Belfast, South Africa, and other places.

3. To facilitate free expression of opinions, attitudes, and feelings — especially in regard to the critical Central American situation — in such a way as to increase mutual understanding, reduce tensions, and foster good communication.

4. To initiate a process out of which the group would develop more trusting relationships and would create initiatives and policies that would make peaceful interaction between nations more possible and more likely.

In brief, we wanted a gathering in which influential international figures could meet "off the record" and talk, argue, shout, embrace in a situation in which the staff made it safe to do so, until they could come to know one another deeply, come to trust one another more fully and work together for peaceful solutions.

During the four days, it appears that substantial progress was made in meeting each of these four goals. During the coming year the staff will be keeping in contact with the participants to determine the degree to which their actions and their policies have been affected. Only then can we assess more fully the usefulness of this gathering.

The Beginnings

Some of the apparent outcomes have already been described. By what process did these come about? As always in a person-centered workshop, it was not smooth; but gradually the group began to empower itself. Rather than generalize, I will attempt to highlight a few of the elements I observed.

By Thursday night, October 31, most of the participants had arrived and there was a brief reception with cocktails held before dinner. This was simply an informal mingling in order to begin to get acquainted. Many were suffering from jet lag and there was no attempt to hold a meeting that evening. The reception was followed by dinner, at which people sat in various informal groupings.

Friday morning, at 10:00 o'clock the workshop convened in a very comfortable room. I introduced Karl Vak as our host; he welcomed the group and spoke of the symbolic significance of our location — Rust being on the border between Austria and Hungary, which had maintained peaceful relations in spite of obstacles. I then called on Rodrigo Carazo, who welcomed the group and stressed the fact that peace is a matter of the will to peace. He particularly quoted the proverb: If one won't fight, two can't.

I thanked the various individuals and groups who had made the conference possible. I introduced the facilitative staff in pairs, mentioning that they would take part in the large group but would also, in these pairs, facilitate the small groups. I stressed that they had been selected because of their experience.

I then expressed some of my hopes for the workshop: that we could learn to listen to one another; that together we could create a climate of safety; that we could reach a greater degree of mutual understanding; that we could come to respect the other person and cherish our differences. I also stressed that this would be *our* conference, which we would create together.

I then mentioned the fact that, although we seemed to be the only people in the room, there were various unseen audiences: the people of our many countries and cultures; various church groups and friends who were hoping and praying for the success of this workshop; our children, grandchildren, and great-grandchildren, whose world we are helping to shape.

Following this, Rodrigo Carazo suggested we take a break, which we did for about half an hour. It gave us a chance to mill about and get acquainted with various participants. When we reassembled I simply said, "Now it is up to us."

After several brief remarks by participants, there was a sharp challenge by one of the U.S. citizens. He addressed a Nicaraguan member, asking, "Why do you restrict the freedoms of your people?" and going on to specify the various ways in which the government has recently imposed restrictions. A Nicaraguan participant, a government official, stated that he regretted that the issue of Central America had started with Nicaragua, but he hoped that the participants from the United States would go back home with more facts. He then recounted some of the ways in which the United States had intervened in Nicaragua. He gave a great deal of background as to how the United States had treated Central America as "banana republics," dealing with them only out of self-interest. Now the Reagan administration was trying to overthrow a legally established government in Nicaragua. A participant from Venezuela spoke up, saying that he wanted to invite dialogue without argument. Another participant from Venezuela referred to my remarks about our children and went on to speak about the fact that our educational systems speak of violence and war. That is the history that we know. The discussion was thus gently steered away from Nicaragua. I believe that the group felt unwilling to face such a direct confrontation at this time.

It is difficult to summarize what went on during the remainder of Friday morning. People gave "presentations," which were often somewhat relevant to what had been said before, but there was little or no direct dialogue. Sometimes the presentations were introduced by tagging them onto some remark made by a previous speaker, but then going off in quite a different direction. It seemed that there was some listening and the remarks were relevant to the general topic of Central America or to the issue of peace, but persons were not speaking to persons.

In the middle of the session, Leopold Gratz, the Austrian foreign minister, entered the room with news cameras flashing. We interrupted the session to introduce him and he made a brief welcoming talk and spoke to the issue of peace and cooperation.

When our time was up, I spoke again of the small groups. A question was raised as to how they had been constituted and I explained. Persons had been preassigned to each small group in such a way as to make each as representative as possible of the workshop as a whole. The proportion of men and women, the proportion of those from Central America, and so on had all been taken into account in making up the small groups. The explanation seemed satisfactory. I also mentioned that the format was not a rigid one and if they did not like it, it could be changed, but that for today we would meet in the small groups as assigned. A staff member raised the question whether anyone objected to the pictures that were taken when Leopold Gratz was present. There seemed to be no objection. It was announced that Friday evening I would give a talk, which would be followed by questions and dialogue, and that Saturday evening Rodrigo Carazo would give a talk, also to be followed by discussion. The meeting closed.

As I was not involved in the small groups, I will leave to others the presentation of what happened in them. It is my understanding that Friday afternoon the groups were rather intellectual in nature, resembling the Friday morning session.

In the evening I met with the group in a slightly more formal arrangement, as I was the speaker. I tried to tell them of my development from a young "diagnostic-prescriptive" clinical psychologist to one who had come to trust the great potential residing within the individual for self-understanding and self-direction. I endeavored to present the essential principles of a client-centered/person-centered approach and its developing application in education, management, and intercultural relationships. I stressed the trust that I felt in the individual, the group, and in this group. I spoke of this as an opportunity to see whether the principles that had operated in other situations could also be useful in international relationships, in building trust and improved communication. I spoke of my confidence in the group process and in the wisdom of the group. This means that I do not know precisely what the outcomes will be, or what goals will be achieved, but I can be sure that they will be constructive. I emphasized that it would be *our* group and this would be our process.

Saturday morning the talks and "presentations" continued, with little person-to-person dialogue. I learned later that some people were becoming quite impatient. In the afternoon the small groups showed more evidence of the beginning of dialogue. That evening Rodrigo Carazo told about the various aspects of the University for Peace. Later, in the lobby, the atmosphere began to shift. The Central American/Latin American group met together and continued talking far into the night. There was some shouting and arguing, but from the reports I heard the communication was very constructive. The remaining members of the workshop met in another group, also in the lobby. It seemed a division that was natural and appropriate at the time.

In Mid-Process

Sunday morning the air was electric. The mood was very different. The atmosphere in the general session was decidedly changed. There was recognition that there was hate, as well as pleasant feelings, involved. At different times several people expressed very bitter feelings against the United States; in one case, the person was surprised to discover how deep and strong his bitterness was. Two persons spoke of being torn between two cultures—Latin American and United States. Passionate speeches were made by the Nicaraguan and by others, but these were very different from presentations. Persons were talking to persons. A U.S. citizen spoke of how powerless she felt, and this feeling of powerlessness was echoed by others from different countries. There were arguments, with people differing sharply with one another. Some Latin Americans criticized the United States because its policies were always based on self-interest, not on interest in democracy or self-government, but simply on its own economic and political interests. Several made plain their strong desire for self-determination in Latin America, without intervention from any other country. Several times the issue of male dominance of the meeting—the whole issue of sexism—was raised very emotionally. It was pointed out that there were different polarities in the session: There was on the one hand the expression of personal concerns as compared to the discussion of political issues. Would the personal and political planes ever intersect? There was the issue of men and women. Was equal coexistence possible in such a session? There was the issue of those with psychological and therapeutic backgrounds over against those who came from entirely different disciplines. At one point a participant mentioned that group therapy was not necessary here and this brought a violent reaction from a therapist member of the group.

Trust and basic goodwill were slowly developing. One participant put it well when he said that the arguments made it clear to him that some people may be misguided, but that no one in the group was malevolent. In other words, the perceptions of reality were very, very different, but no one was speaking with evil intent.

The outstanding thing, however, was that people were listening to one another; they were responding to one another; there was real dialogue going on; the group process was clearly at work. Personally, as I rested after the morning session, I felt very relaxed and truly joyful. I knew now that whatever the conclusion of the workshop might be, it would be constructive. The process we had hoped to help initiate was under way. This was borne out by the reports that came from the small groups that afternoon.

The Heurigen: A Facilitating Event

The Heurigen is an old Austrian custom. It is a celebration at the time of harvesting the grapes. New wine is drunk, usually in large quantities, and food is made available. Eduard Schmiege and the hotel staff had planned for the workshop to be involved in this celebration on Sunday night. We walked a short distance to a nearby inn where there was a large room with long tables and benches. It was barely large enough to hold all the members of the workshop, and the noise was rather deafening. As people sat and talked and drank together, many significant conversations took place, many relationships were deepened and extended. As the evening extended far into the night and the early morning hours, there is no doubt that a great deal of closeness developed that might not otherwise have come about. An American and a Nicaraguan developed plans for peaceful coexistence between Nicaragua and the United States and vowed to present these plans to their governments. Two other participants from rival countries exchanged pictures of their children and made tentative plans for an exchange of children for a period of weeks or months. There is no doubt that some mistrust was dissolved in alcohol. This seemed valuable, even though temporary.

When I walked into the room at the inn, there was spontaneous and prolonged applause. I was personally touched by this but it had a broader and, to me, more significant meaning. We, the staff, had been relatively quiet until this morning when we had taken a modest part. Up until this morning there had simply been no differences of opinion to facilitate. I had felt that the importance of our function would probably have been missed by the participants. The applause meant to me that the presence and attitudes and words of the facilitative staff, even though subtle and not intrusive, had been appreciated by the participants. This was definitely heartening. I did not, however, remain at the Heurigen for more than half an hour. The noise was simply too great for me to be involved in conversation. I could not hear or be heard, but I realized that a great deal of important communication was going on.

I would not want it to seem that all the communication was positive. One U.S. citizen made hostile and threatening remarks to a woman who had specialized in knowledge of Central America and who had an understanding of the poverty, misery, and oppression in which the revolutions found their roots. According to reports, she was visibly upset by the verbal assault on her, and it is fascinating that one of the Nicaraguan men was the first to leap to her side and persuade her that she should not let her own self-esteem be damaged. "That is the enemy," he said, indicating that a judgmental rigidity was the real enemy of progress. That the man's hostile remarks were not simply due to the effect of too much wine was indicated the following day when he repeated much the same threatening words.

On balance, the facilitative effects of the Heurigen seemed positive. New friendships were formed, intense and significant communications took place, differences were aired, mistrusts were gradually cleared away. Undoubtedly, negative feelings were also aired and certainly not all of them were resolved, but by and large it proved to be an important and generally constructive occasion.

The Process Peaks: Monday Morning

The Monday morning session opened on an inauspicious note. A press conference had been planned by Karl Vak and others, to be held at the bank in Vienna at 6:00 p.m. on Monday. This would have meant cutting the afternoon session short, leaving by 4:30, but that seemed possible. Now we were told that the press conference could not possibly be held at 6:00 p.m. It must be held at 4:00 p.m. Consequently, we would have to leave at 2:30. At breakfast a list of those to attend the press conference was handed to me and I was told that they had already been invited. There was no woman on the list and I insisted that the Swedish member of parliament, a woman, be added.

This unfortunate change of the hour of the press conference was one of the few circumstances or events which, in my estimation, damaged the group process. When the change in time was announced, I at first said that I would not attend, that my first loyalty was to the whole group and its process. Karl Vak and the bank had done so much for us that it was difficult to refuse his request and I was persuaded to go. It meant, however, that ten people from the workshop were leaving at 2:30, thus effectively sabotaging any plans for a fourth meeting of the small groups or even any large group meeting during the afternoon.

The whole problem was briefly discussed in the opening moments of the general session. People wanted to know who would attend and what kind of plans could now be made. There was some apprehension in the group about what might be said at the press conference, whether it would break the confidentiality of the meeting. It was decided that there be a preliminary meeting of the group attending the press conference at two o'clock, to agree on confidentiality and on what would and would not be discussed. It was also agreed that there would only be informal groups in the afternoon and that a large group meeting would be held Monday evening. Then the substantive discussion was opened by a man from El Salvador, who was going to have to leave early and who presented some of the problems and disagreements that he had with other participants. He was disturbed about the possibility of military intervention from Nicaragua. He strongly favored the Contadora movement because it would avoid intervention from *any* other countries and would thus make external interference and intervention unnecessary. A woman spoke up to point out that the origins of the revolutions in the Central American countries existed quite regardless of external interventions. A Venezuelan pointed out that there had been no revolution in Central or Latin America that had been successful without foreign support. Revolution could not be maintained without external help. The discussion was somewhat disputatious and the man from Chile took the risk of shifting the topic. He reminded the group that in the Heurigen hearts were opened, no matter what political positions were held. He felt that there was love and togetherness that was also a part of the meetings, but that these more tender feelings were mostly expressed outside of the conference sessions. He felt sadness that the trust was not brought into these meetings.

Rodrigo Carazo spoke up with considerable passion:

> I want to insist on something very important. In my small group there has been total frankness in our approach to all the problems. There has been no diplomatic language. In the political area there has been clarity. We have even been rude at times and that has been hard for me to show. Men are a mixture of heart and reason. In our small group I gave up the idea that when we talk we lose. [Meaning that if one expresses real feelings someone else might conquer by oneupsmanship.] This morning that attitude of the small group is not clearly here. We are speaking in the language of hypotheses: suppose this, suppose that. I have found that sort of thinking works negatively so far as solutions are concerned. I am clear—excuse my arrogance—I want peace. I don't want the Contras or the Sandinistas to win. I want *peace*. I have no official position, no reason to keep quiet in regard to intervention on the part of either country. But last night, as L. said, there was the human will to search for alternatives *in* the realities of Central America. I beg from all of you here present, let us inform each other of alternatives in Central America. But let us not bring back our previous positions, our previous stance. Let's have enough humility to be spectators, to have them [the Central American countries] carry on.

Then a person from Nicaragua spoke:

> I am convinced that there *are* possibilities. Before coming here, I thought the same. But what got confirmed here is that it seems to be possible that a great power will listen to a small country, and *here* mistrust *has* been overcome. Even aside from economic and political problems, there is a *lot* of *mistrust*. I hope none of us will contribute to that mistrust. The possibility *really* exists to talk and solve the problems in Central America. [Spontaneous applause from the group.]

From this point on, a number of people expressed how much meaning the experience had had for them. An American said that he was uplifted by the process and felt sure that not all the love and caring had disappeared from the sessions. A man from the Philippines, who had expected to leave earlier, stayed, although he was due elsewhere, and said that he was going with the hope that Filipinos could profit by this kind of experience. There is here a meeting of hearts and minds. He said that it had been a very deep personal experience. A speaker from Mexico stressed two themes that had been important to him: The first, the stress on the right to determine one's own destiny, a country's right to determine its own form of government; second, he was impressed that in the climate that had been created, deeper understandings had been reached. A man from Costa Rica was impressed with the fact that in the Saturday night gatherings, the groups were really person-centered but they had facilitated themselves. I remarked that "I sit here, largely in silence, and surprising things happen. The understandings that have been reached could not have been predicted or expected. A facilitative climate has been created by all of us. I feel that we have reason to congratulate ourselves, but the real test will be later." A man with a Sufi background pointed out that here peace was no longer external, peace had become an *experience*. There have been new understandings, individual and collective.

A Palestinian said that he was jealous of the conference here. He requested that those who had brought about this conference should try to arrange a similar workshop involving the PLO and the Israelis.

A high government official from Central America said that he had had many doubts as to the success of the methods we were using. He thought that to work without an agenda was disorderly, and he was very dubious. But now he thinks that we were right. He feels the methods have succeeded. The result is higher than he expected. He was very impressed with the contacts that have been made between one of the Americans and one of the Nicaraguans. He is convinced that peace begins *inside* each of us. We must try to destroy the mistrust that separates us.

A woman from the West German Parliament said that she had learned a great deal here. She hoped to use it at home. She belongs to a peace party, but when she attends one of their meetings she thinks it is a war party. She has never attended a meeting like this one, in spite of the wishes of the members. She obviously hoped she could take this process home. She said that forty years after World War II, Germany is still an occupied country. She hopes they can become a nonaligned country. The Green Party wants to achieve unilateral and unconditional disarmament by their own government. She says the Green Party is the only party of radical pacifism: "We must be the first to *stop*!"

Rodrigo Carazo brought up the message that had been drafted, endorsing the Contadora process. He hoped that individual members would be willing to sign this message. (No statements are being issued by the workshop as an organization.) The message can then be sent to Luxembourg, where the Contadora group is meeting with the European Common Market, to see if they can reach political and economic accord.

An American spoke up to say that the essentially human aspect of the workshop should be uttered in a whisper. Peace is not out there but in here, inside of us. Destructive ego needs can be expressed even in peace activities and can spoil them. Our only hope is to face the great obstacles that are ahead of us. For example, he feels enormous hope in regard to the conversations he's had with a man from Nicaragua, but he realizes that a long painful process of work and talk is ahead. He regretted that more conservatives from the administration were not present. For him, this has been a marvelous experience.

At this point the Palestinian members presented lovely Israeli vases filled with flowers, one for Rodrigo Carazo and one for me. They asked that we pray that Arabs and Israelis might look in a mirror and discover that they are brothers.

The meeting closed with agreement to meet informally in the afternoon and a large group session in the evening.

The Press Conference

The meeting with the press was held in sumptuous quarters in a building that the bank has restored as a conference center. The members of the press were from Austrian and German newspapers. The international press, unfortunately, was not able to come because the notice had been too short.

There were eleven people present. Rodrigo Carazo and I were there as co-directors of the project. Karl Vak was there as representative of the bank. In addition, there were participants present from Costa Rica, Honduras, El Salvador, Nicaragua, Venezuela, Sweden, the United States, and Austria, represented by Dr. Vak. The Salvadoran, because of early departure time, was completing his statement when we arrived, and I do not know its content. The other ten participants all spoke of the workshop in favorable terms. Karl Vak, who had attended only the initial session on Friday and the most recent session on Monday morning, said that the two sessions were like night and day. The first was so full of tensions and in the second the spirit was truly fraternal. The participant from Sweden suggested that the UN Commission on Building of Trust, which meets every year in Stockholm, should utilize the same person-centered approach in their sessions, and she hoped that they would invite us to facilitate their work. One of the Americans and the Nicaraguan both spoke of the bonds they had developed during the workshop and the fact that they planned to meet again in Paris, to continue making plans that they would transmit to their governments.

It was a first opportunity to assess the outcomes of the conference, and the fact that all of those present felt that the workshop had been a useful experience was encouraging. The press reports corroborated this positive note. The workshop was called "an unusual political and psychological experiment." It was emphasized that the person-centered approach might be "the catalyst of a long-lasting peace process, and should also be applied to other politically explosive zones of the world."

The Final Session

The group met again on Monday evening, although a number of members had already left. There were three major elements to the session. Participants continued to express the positive meanings the workshop had had for them. I feel that insufficient effort was made to draw out any possible negative feelings. The second element was the presentation of the report mentioned by Rodrigo Carazo in the morning — a statement supporting the Contadora process, which people were urged to sign. A third element was the presentation of a declaration by John Vasconcellos strongly affirming the usefulness of the person-centered approach in the reduction of tension, both in this conference and possibly in other areas of international crisis as well. The meeting ended with many fond embraces and hopes of meeting in the future.

It seems clear that for most of the participants this had been a very meaningful and useful experience. We know of at least one person who felt very negatively about the workshop. I am sure there must be others. We are trying hard to collect all the data that would give the complete picture. But essentially, substantial progress was made in meeting the purposes that brought the workshop into being. Tensions were reduced. Lines of communication were opened. There was an experience of peace.

One Week Later

The real test of the workshop will be in the months that follow. Nevertheless, the meaning that it had for one participant is contained in a letter that was written eight days following the end of the workshop. Excerpts from the letter follow.

> Thank you for a very important experience! I think the result of those four days is amazing, changing hostility to trust. I do wish your method will be used in many peace efforts.

> For me personally your way of meeting me I think will change my life. My beloved grandfather used to tell me not to "apologize for being" and he used to like it when I stood up for inconvenient points of view. But that was long ago. Now, when you said "Don't apologize!" in that very earnest way, I felt accepted as I am.

> I used to think that there really was nothing I honestly would like to do. Now life seems full of bright prospects. I feel that I am all right the way I am and if people don't think so I don't really care. My emotions are close to my consciousness and I have warm feelings for most people, also those I used to dislike.

> Of course I realize this can be some sort of euphoria, but the calm happy feeling grows in me. I am reading your book and it gives me great joy!

> In the participants' questionnaire I answered "quite" on the question of how useful the workshop experience had been to me. Now, after a week, I would not hesitate to answer "extremely!"

Not all comments were favorable. Another participant, also writing some days after the conclusion of the workshop, was disappointed in the composition of the group. Not enough power was represented, particularly from the United States. The sessions also came in for criticism. There was "rarely a consistent thread to a discussion. . . . We were never clear whether to discuss substance or personal attitudes; either would have been fine, but . . ."

From the information available thus far, it appears that a large majority regarded it as a very positive experience, but some were dissatisfied.

Mistakes and Disappointments

Let me turn to some of the inadequacies we recognize. One of the difficulties in preparing for the workshop and that continued through the workshop was that there was inadequate communication and inadequate understanding between the co-sponsors. Distance made it very difficult to keep in close contact. The fact that we came from different cultures and different ways of thinking added to the deficiencies in our communication. I believe that we probably both underestimated the contribution that the other was making to the workshop.

Our translators, who served so brilliantly in very difficult situations, made us aware of the fact that because of cultural differences and differences in our respect for protocol, we often offended members of other cultures.

It is undoubtedly true that the facilitative staff did not mingle sufficiently with the other participants. This came out of a puzzling no-win situation. It was essential that the staff keep in solid communication so that our unity would help the unity of the group. It was also essential that we serve as a support group to one another in a new and challenging situation. This meant that we met early in the morning and also at the end of the day, after the small-group sessions. Consequently, our opportunities to mingle with the participants at breakfast and at dinner were limited. It is probable that, to many, we seemed aloof because of this. At the time, we could not see any way of remedying this deficiency.

A major disappointment was that the administrative branch

of the U.S. government was not represented in the workshop. We had worked very hard on this, particularly with the help of John Marks, and had been able to gain a number of acceptances — one sure and one possibility from the State Department, another significant government official, and several close advisers to the Reagan administration. We know that one official of the administration was highly enthusiastic about the workshop and eager to attend; yet only days before the workshop was to start, all U.S. administration officials and advisers canceled their acceptances without explanation. It made for a most unfortunate gap in the process of the workshop.

Reasons for Effectiveness

The workshop appears to have been even more effective than we had dared to hope. What are the reasons behind its apparent success? In my judgment, there are many such reasons, some of which we can take credit for; others were due entirely to circumstance or good fortune. I will comment briefly on a number of the elements that I see accounting for the results achieved.

1. The general idea behind the workshop was sound and appropriate. Initially, the aim was to reduce international tensions by inviting leaders influential in policymaking and opinion shaping in international affairs to meet in a workshop facilitated in a person-centered way. As this aim evolved and changed it became more specific and more complex. It was to focus on one area of tension, specifically Central America; to invite such significant figures, not only from the countries involved, but from other nations concerned about peace; to hold the gathering in a place with minimal distractions; to make it private, unofficial, "off the record," confidential; to utilize a facilitative staff experienced in the person-centered approach and in dealing with groups containing differing, antagonistic, or even hostile factions.

This whole pattern of aims appears to be an idea whose time has come, if we can judge by the intense and widespread interest it has generated.

2. A good theme was chosen for the workshop: "The Central American Challenge" points to a critical international situation, yet it is one in which persons are still willing to talk with one

another and which is not yet as frozen in rigidity as the East-West confrontation. We were fortunate that the University for Peace insisted on this theme. We had initially thought of a workshop without a theme, but clearly this would not have attracted suitable personnel.

The theme was unexpectedly valuable in facilitating the process. Because it focused the interactions, there was none of the quibbling about minor issues that often occurs in a workshop. Because the theme involved issues of life and death in Central American countries, the interactions were always serious in intent, and almost no extraneous matters were brought into the sessions. The theme kept us together, was a unifying influence.

3. We were fortunate in our co-sponsor. There is no doubt that President Carazo's worldwide contacts enabled him to bring together, in spite of many obstacles and one period of despair, a notable group of persons of high status from Central American, Latin American, and European countries.

It was the fact that this was a high-level group with influence on international policy and influence on shaping of national and world opinion that gave the workshop much of its significance. A similarly successful workshop composed of individuals from the same countries but made up of persons without special status would have had little later impact. This group, on the contrary, is likely to have a considerable impact in various quarters.

4. The approach to the workshop was not an experimental approach. It was something that had been tried again and again in very diverse groups and in groups containing hostile and antagonistic factions. Consequently, the staff knew in general what they might expect and were not panicked by any of the overintellectual or disorderly events at the beginning of the workshop. Experience, in other words, paid off.

5. It was an excellent facilitative staff. Because they had worked together, because they had dealt with sharp differences and anger and bitterness, they were not easily frightened. Their trust in the group and in the group process was very deep. This was an exceedingly difficult workshop, because so many of the people had no idea of the kind of group process that they themselves were helping to initiate. It was also difficult because many of the

participants were deeply distrustful of other participants or of the viewpoints they represented. The group was also sophisticated and accustomed to talking in public, so that, in many ways, they facilitated themselves. It could be said that this was not a demonstration of person-centered procedures; it was a demonstration of a person-centered way of being on the part of the staff that helped to create the climate. (In fact, some of the participants who are knowledgeable about group dynamics were quite disappointed that I and the staff did not "demonstrate" person-centered techniques.)

6. It was an excellent setting for such a workshop. It could not have been better. It was a real retreat, free of distractions, in a small village, yet the accommodations were very comfortable, the food was excellent, the service good, so that there was nothing to distract the participants from their meetings together.

Because the bank and the project helped with the expenses of all participants, they were essentially guests, not tuition-paying members. Perhaps this helps to account for the fact that there was almost no criticism of accommodations, meals, schedules, or staff—criticisms that often occur.

7. We chose what seemed to be just the right amount of structure. Whether this was good judgment or good fortune, it is hard to say. At any rate, the format of a large group in the mornings and preassigned small groups in the afternoon gave people a feeling of security. The sessions were further structured by having a theme. This common focus gave the group a unity it would not otherwise have had. The reason for thinking that this was just the right amount of structure is that there was none of the arguing or bickering about schedule, assignments, and format that so often accompanies a workshop. To our amazement, there was not even a discussion about smoking or non-smoking. Smokers simply went to the door of the room whenever they wished to "light up," without the matter ever having been discussed.

8. It appears to have been a wise choice that the media were completely excluded. This made it much easier for people to be themselves, both in the small groups and in the large.

9. To be faced by no set agenda must have been shocking to some of the participants. There is no doubt that it was regarded

as a strange procedure. Yet our past experience showed clearly that the group would gradually seek out its own personal and collective agendas. This view was justified by the experience at Rust. It was pleasant to have the wisdom of this choice confirmed by at least one important participant.

10. Many of the above elements entered into the fact that all of us—the facilitative staff, the administrative staff, the hotel staff, the participants—were successful in creating a climate in which there could be freedom of expression for both negative and positive feelings. The establishment of such a climate is an extremely subtle process. There is no doubt that the facilitative staff played a large part in this, and yet the staff was joined by many of the participants in bringing this climate into being. It is important to note that there was enough freedom that other modes of encouraging group process could be utilized. For example, there were those present who had used other procedures in reducing tension and negotiating conflict resolution. Eventually, these approaches were used, not in the sessions of the workshop, but in the informal gatherings outside the regular sessions.

11. One final element is our good fortune in being in Austria at the time of the Heurigen celebration. There is little doubt that this ancient custom helped to build closer ties. Our celebration of it came at exactly the proper moment in the dynamics of the workshop. It was one of the circumstances that helped to make Rust the memorable event that it was.

There is no conclusion to be drawn at this point. We have taken a first step. We have set a precedent. It is to be hoped that this will be followed by other person-to-person workshops, based on, and learning from, the gathering at Rust.

33
Inside the World of the
Soviet Professional

"You're too pushy. I don't like you!"
 "My wife and I quarrel a lot."
 "Your director grabbed some of the places away from us!"
 "You're lying!"
 "I think you [Carl] were bribed to say that!"
 "Nobody appreciates how hard it is to be a teacher."
 "I'm almost completely estranged from my son by my first marriage."
 "I don't know who I am, really."
 "I like a wife who is silent, who just gets my meals. I'm joking, of course."
 "You're just jealous of them!"
 "I think none of us is really saying how he feels."
These are statements selected from the early sessions of two intensive workshops. Where were these groups held — in California, Brazil, Italy? No, they were two groups of professionals — psychologists, educators, researchers — held in Moscow and Tbilisi, a city in the southern area of the Soviet Union.

How did all this come about? As is so often the case, there was a great deal of intensive and thoughtful preparation. Ruth Sanford knew that I wanted to meet with groups in the Soviet Union. She knew that Francis Macy, of the Association for Humanistic Psychology, spoke Russian, had many Russian contacts, and had arranged American/Soviet exchanges. After a fruitless search for him, they met by chance in Moscow while she was on tour there and they immediately began to lay plans for a venture by the three of us in the Soviet Union. Then came much effort

AUTHOR'S NOTE: This is a joint report of work carried on by Carl Rogers and Ruth Sanford. The account was largely written by Carl, but both of us [Carl and Ruth] contributed to it.

Journal of Humanistic Psychology, Vol. 27, No. 3, Summer 1987, 277–304. Reprinted by permission of Sage Publications, Inc.

by Macy, which eventuated in an invitation from the Ministry of Education, an invitation sponsored by Dr. Alexei Matyushkin, requesting Carl Rogers, Ruth Sanford, and Francis Macy to conduct seminars in Moscow and in Tbilisi—all expenses paid while on Soviet soil. This invitation was dated June 3, 1986, and the working dates were to be from the twenty-fifth of September to the fifteenth of October, 1986. Ruth and I had already sent a very careful statement of what we wished to do—primary emphasis on an intensive five- or six-day residential retreat workshop in each city, composed of no more than thirty selected individuals, with public meetings to accommodate all those who were interested. Topics were suggested both by the Institute of General and Pedagogical Psychology, of which Dr. Matyushkin is the director,* and by us. There was to be stress on humanistic education, on individualized instruction, on methods of fostering creativity. We could hardly believe that these last two topics were desired by Soviet officials, but they were.

The idea of a residential retreat workshop was totally foreign to the Soviets. We finally settled for four-day workshops in each city, nonresidential, but with everyone committed to come for all of the sessions of the four days.

The Public Meetings

Although our highest priority went to these intensive groups, some of the public meetings deserve attention. The first was arranged by Dr. Matyushkin in the auditorium of his institute, which held three hundred and fifty people. There was an overflow of some forty or fifty in another room. Ruth and I spoke together, in a way we have learned to utilize, swinging the conversation back and forth between us, all of it being translated into Russian by Dima and Irina, our faithful translators.

We explained the possibility of a demonstration therapy in-

---

*There is nothing in the United States which quite corresponds to the various institutes of the Soviet Union. They are scientific adjuncts to the university system and to the government. The word *science* has enormous importance in the Soviet Union. It is, however, differently understood than in the U.S. It is my impression that any rigorous scholarly work is "scientific." Certainly any development of theory is also scientific. Empirical research seems not to have as high a priority as it does in the United States, but it, too, is to some degree carried out by these institutes.

terview, and the crowd was pleased. During the short break Ruth selected a client from among the volunteers and I conducted the interview. It was not simple. The English-speaking client and I faced each other on stage, each with a microphone. Behind each one of us stood a translator, translating each statement into Russian. It all seems so artificial that it is hard to believe how intense and deep such an interview can be. The woman client talked of her difficulties with her husband, her seventeen-year-old son, and finally of her relationship to her mother. Though she is a grown woman, she still feels dependent on her mother, fearful of her, afraid to stand up to her. She does very well in most aspects of her life, but when she enters her home — where her mother lives — she is almost completely stifled and paralyzed. She is fearful she will explode. I endeavored to be an understanding companion to her, as she explored her relationships and her self. By the end of the interview she was at least considering expressing her feelings openly in that relationship.

There was much to discuss about the interview, and the audience clearly appreciated the opportunity. Questions were asked of me, of the client, and comments and interpretations were made. I had to protect the client from being the recipient of overzealous and "profound" interpretations.

The morning session lasted from 10 to 1, the afternoon session from 3 to 6, consisting mostly of response to questions, widely diverse in nature.

Another public meeting was held later at the University of Moscow, with about nine hundred in attendance, students and faculty. Again, a demonstration interview gave them a feeling for a client-centered/person-centered approach to therapy — an opportunity to experience, vicariously, the powerful impact of an empathic, acceptant listener. This time it was quite a difficult interview with a woman urgently asking for advice. She was sad that she no longer felt love for her eighteen-year-old daughter, and wanted a prescription. She was disappointed when her expectations were not met. It was only at the end of the discussion, as she was leaving the stage, that she said, "I think now I know what has been happening in me."

After the break, there was an opportunity for dialogue. We had asked only for oral questions, but people insisted on pushing forward written questions, until there was a mass of one hundred such questions, none of which could be answered in the meeting. It was indicative, however, of the intense interest. These questions were later translated and analyzed. They were well informed, serious, challenging, probing the theory and its limitations. They ranged from questions about unconditional positive regard, and meeting the personal needs of the therapist, to the role of religion in therapy.

All told, we met with almost two thousand people in Moscow in the public meetings and the workshop, though a number of these were "repeaters" attending more than one of the sessions.

What We Found

I will try to summarize some of the attitudes and situations which we found in both the public sessions and the intensive groups.

We found an enormous interest in humanistic psychology and in the client-centered/person-centered approach. There was a very widespread knowledge of my work. When I asked the audience at the university how many had read at least one article or chapter of mine, at least 85 percent of them raised their hands. When we were entertained by a woman professor in her home, it turned out that she had been teaching her classes in a student-centered fashion (with the usual difficulties), and her husband, a mathematician, had been fascinated by my article on empathy and had translated it into Russian, where it was included in a standard Russian textbook containing chapters by many eminent psychologists from various cultures.

We found in our audiences many sophisticated therapists and knowledgeable psychologists. There seemed to be relatively few educators, even though this was supposed to be the emphasis of our visit. The educators who were present seemed less vocal than the psychologists.

We found that in both Moscow and Tbilisi the papers we had sent on, months in advance, had been studied and discussed in special seminars held for that purpose. Many of the papers had been translated into Russian, and in Tbilisi were being translated into Georgian. We found that in Dr. Matyushkin's institute there was a strong interest in publishing my recent book, *Freedom to Learn for the 80's*, in Russian translation.

We found a great deal of personal openness in the large audiences and in the small. There was a willingness to voice skeptical and negative attitudes as well as supportive ones. Almost all of the questions and comments showed careful thought and a thorough background of knowledge. We found a great deal of personal warmth and hospitality. We received many gifts, many with inscriptions which clearly came from the heart.

We found some peculiarly Soviet habits and manners. For example, almost everything in the USSR is a *big deal*. Ordering a meal, arranging a meeting, deciding which car to take, everything is a matter for prolonged and heated discussion. Another discovery was that schedules and plans, which seem to be clear and definite, are very often changed at the last moment for reasons which seem quite unclear. Another is that from various hints and indirect statements, we realized that the politics of the Soviet hierarchical bureaucracies are even more complicated than the similar politics in the United States.

Probably the most important thing we found is that the professionals with whom we came in contact—and those were the people we came to know—were astonishingly similar to their counterparts in the U.S. in their problems, the issues which concern them, the hopes they have for the future, their personal aspirations.

What We Brought

Fran Macy brought a speaking knowledge of Russian, which was invaluable, an excellent ability to make contact, a knowledge of Soviet life and ways, and an ability to negotiate plans. Ruth and I brought a number of things. Perhaps the most important was that we brought a coherent theory of psychotherapy and of its application to education, management, and conflict resolution. We brought long experience in working together, with both large and small groups. In the large groups we were accustomed to making joint presentations and answering all types of questions and responding to comments. We also had experience in arranging for, conducting and commenting on demonstration therapeutic interviews.

In the small groups we brought experience as facilitators receptive to negative as well as positive feelings, whether directed toward organizations, individuals, or ourselves. We were accustomed to permitting the group to develop its own direction and flow, and gradually to empower itself. We brought a willingness to try to live a person-centered way of being in our relationship with each other, in our relationship to groups both large and small, and in our relationship to individuals from those groups. We brought a willingness to be separate persons, able to differ with each other and to supplement and support each other. We brought patience. Sometimes it seemed to me that this was the most valuable commodity we possessed: a willingness to wait through talk, silence, vituperation, ambiguity—a willingness to wait for the process to develop at its own pace.

We brought a willingness to express our own persistent feelings as our own, not as accusations or comments on others. At one point I expressed my feelings of shock at what participants were doing to each other. I will describe that later. On the last morning of one of the intensive groups, Ruth could contain her feelings no longer. She opened the session by saying that since the morning of the day before she had become increasingly aware that she was being almost completely ignored in the group. In the large public meeting she had felt accepted as a person in her own right, and privately in this group many of them had come to her. She was not asking for reassurance or sympathy and she didn't need verbal response, but she wanted it known that she had a brain, which she respected, as well as feelings, and that she resented having it ignored. Was it a cultural expectation that they looked to the man as the authority? The response was a long silence, followed by a very thoughtful and at times heated discussion of men-women relationships, the only one we had in the USSR.

Finally, we brought with us a willingness to adapt as much as possible to the expressed needs of our host institutions and personnel. There was, however, a limit to this willingness. We had to be stubbornly insistent to protect some time for rest and relaxation. Otherwise, our hosts would have filled every waking moment with scheduled work or proferred entertainment.

The Process in the Intensive Groups

We had asked to have no more than thirty in the intensive groups, because it was our experience that in a larger group it became difficult to develop the personal intensity and depth which is feasible in an intimate group. Before the first meeting of the Moscow intensive, Dr. Matyushkin came to us almost with tears in his eyes. It had been a terribly difficult selection process and he finally had it whittled down to forty, but did not see how he could cut it further. We finally agreed to the forty, and in a public meeting he read out the names of the forty who had been included. There were smiles of pleasure and murmurs of disappointment.

The next day, when we entered the room for the small group, we found at least forty-five people in the room. There were five of us (Fran, Ruth, myself, and our two interpreters), so fifty people really crowded the room badly. Then we learned that some of the people whose names were on the list were "standing outside the door" (a phrase which we were to hear over and over again that day), and that quite a number of those in the room had pushed their way in.

We settled down (I thought), and Ruth and I opened the first session with brief introductory comments. I particularly stressed that though we, Matyushkin, and others had been active in bringing the group together, it was now *our* group, not Carl and Ruth's group. Hopefully we would be able to integrate the cognitive and the experiential, the personal and the professional. Also I hoped we would be able to make it possible for people to empower themselves. I concluded by saying that the group would find and take its own direction.

We had wondered whether it would be easy for the group to express feelings in the first meeting. We need not have been concerned! Rarely, if ever, have I heard such personal vituperation, such vicious hostility directed personally toward present members of the group. There were accusations of unfair dealings. There was resentment of those who had pushed their way in. There was a feeling that some groups had been discriminated against. There was strong feeling that some should be thrown out, especially one man who had brought a melon as a peace offering, indicating that he knew he was not on the list but that he wanted to be in. There was a strong feeling that no one whose name had been read in public should be left out. There were solutions and countersolutions, attacks and counterattacks. Sometimes it rose to a crescendo of shouted accusations, suggestions, and questions.

Dr. Matyushkin, who had been responsible for the public list, had felt that his duties made it impossible for him to be a member of the group, so it was clearly up to the group to settle its own membership. Ruth indicated a strong desire that the group be small. I, in my soft-heartedness, felt that perhaps we could accommodate more than the forty we had agreed to take. Though nothing was said about this at the time, we learned later that this difference, this "antagonism" between the two facilitators, was the subject of much concern to the participants. Some felt we must have planned it that way in order to provoke further conflict in the group.

After hours of wrangling, one man said that he would give up his place in the group to permit someone else to be in. Two members whose names had been clearly spoken in public were admitted. Two women left. This, however, did not stop the bitterness, which continued for the full day.

So acrimonious and vocal was the dispute that Ruth and I rarely had much opportunity to respond. There was very little possible in the way of empathic understanding. Patience, acceptance, and an unwillingness to evaluate or to make decisions for the group—these were our primary contribution. I suggested a few moments of silence before we left for the day. We were told at the end of the day by an experienced professional that this wrangling would continue until we gave the cue to stop it and that it was essential that we give some signal that the bitterness was to cease. My own feeling was that when the group considered that night that there were four days in which they were to be together, and that they could spend all four days wrangling if they so desired, that they would change the flow of the sessions.

The second day started with a dramatic change in the climate. People had thought about it overnight. They did not like what they were doing to one another. They did not like to spend all their time on the membership of the group. Consequently, though occasionallly this issue would flare up briefly, the day was spent in much more personal sharing. There was a beginning of attempts really to listen to one another, though these were few. For the most part, when an individual expressed some personal problem, whether family problem or concern about self or, in one instance, negative feelings toward several members of the group, the responses came flooding in. They were almost invariably probing interrogations, dogmatic and judgmental interpretations, intellectual analyses, critical evaluations, or personal attacks. As mentioned in the preceding section, I became so appalled by the way in which these persons—mostly therapists—were dealing with one another in an apparent attempt to be helpful, that I finally exploded with my feelings. I said that when a person expresses something personal, he or she is exposed and vulnerable, and that it is a very risky experience. I felt that in such situations they were much more sensitive to attack than when they were buttoned up in their usual defenses. Yet it was just when individuals exposed themselves in this way that the group was most savage in its interpretations, probings, and negative judgments. I felt *horrified* by what was going on and said so. My outburst was greeted with a long silence, but later it was clear that it had had a powerful impact.

I believe it was during the second day that it became evident that many of their personal problems relate to the great frequency of divorce. In this educated and sophisticated group, it is similar to the United States. One woman spoke of the way in which she and her husband had gradually worked toward a better and seemingly more permanent relationship. She was definitely the exception. Nearly everyone else spoke of "When I left my first husband"; "I have a problem with my child by my second marriage"; "If I leave my second wife." There was talk of the insecurity and estrangement of children of previous partnerships; the difficulty of maintaining relationships with one's children when they are at a distance; the interference of ex-wives and ex-mothers-in-law—the whole gamut.

The one classroom teacher in the group (she was actually a principal as well as a teacher) stated that she would like to be interviewed by me in front of the group. We took chairs facing each other, but that was as far as the interview got. She hardly looked at me but she exploded to the group about how useless psychologists were when they came to her school. The teachers wanted advice but didn't get it or it was not useful. Besides, psychologists had no appreciation of what it was like to be a teacher. She told how they'd had the walls freshly painted in one of the rooms and then she came in to find that children were putting their hands or feet on the freshly painted walls to leave their own impression. She told of taking students on a field trip and two of them went off in the forest with a boy who lived in the forest, causing great furor for fear the students were lost. She poured out complaint after complaint, and yet through it all it became very evident that she loved children, that she was not too upset by these problems, that she was proud of the fact that her school was regarded by some outsiders as a "lunatic asylum" because she permitted so much freedom, and, in short, she showed herself as a most innovative and responsive educator, trying to create a climate of freedom for children. Yet when appreciation of her was voiced, she immediately turned it away. The whole situation was amusing because from time to time I tried to shut off the flow of the torrent and was completely unsuccessful. She was going to be heard and she was! There was also no doubt that people listened to her and that they did gain a clearer understanding of what it was like to be a teacher with gifted children, who have minds of their own, children of educated parents. (It turned out that she is the principal of the experimental school maintained by Matyushkin's Institute of Pedagogical Psychology.)

The Triads

By the morning of the third day, it seemed that the group might be ready for something different. We proposed an empathy experience and described what we meant. The group was puzzled but interested. We suggested that we have a demonstration of it in the middle of the group. The first person to volunteer said she would be the observer, but then someone volunteered to be the client and another volunteer reluctantly agreed to be the therapist. It had been proposed that the client talk about some problem which was of real concern, not role playing. This client told of really tragic estrangement between himself and his children. The "therapist" was not very helpful and yet the release was profound. When the roles were rotated and the observer became the client and the client became the therapist, people began to get the idea and seemed quite responsive to it. By that time it was time for the lunch break.

After lunch, when the triads were formed, the floodgates were really opened. (This was also true in the Tbilisi group, from which some of the examples will be drawn.) One man simply drowned the therapist and observer, both women younger than himself, in his bitterness and indignation and criticism of his daughter. He treated them somewhat as he has treated his daughter. They could not stop the flow. It seemed to them, and to him, that little had been accomplished in this outpouring, which lasted a long time.

Another man—one of the most clearly rational, logical, theoretical individuals in the group—became completely personal as he told of the distinctively different problems he was having with each of his two daughters. He seemed like a different person when he was talking on the personal level.

One woman poured out her feelings of early restriction by her parents. She went on for forty minutes, quite ignoring the fifteen-minute limit which had been set for all the interchanges.

In many cases, the therapists seemed quite unskilled and certainly totally unaccustomed to listening without evaluation. Their responses were full of advice, personal experiences of their own, interpretation of behavior—everything but the empathic listening which they were trying to practice. It was abundantly clear that being truly heard, without evaluation, is perhaps even more rare in the Soviet Union than in the United States. It was equally clear that people were hungry to be heard as they were, without judgment or interpretation. The experience in the triads seemed a very valuable and sobering lesson for all concerned, a recognition that though they had read about listening, talked about it, taught about it, they had actually never *done it*!

As the group proceeded, there were many deep issues that came to the fore. There was a discussion about death and dying and whether one could give permission to a person to die—whether that was ever appropriate. In Tbilisi the director of the institute openly discussed his administrative policies. He wants to be humanistic, but he feels he knows very little about how to do so. His colleagues and subordinates were very open with him. It seemed to be a good and developing relationship. Then there was, as I have hinted, much discussion of marital breakdown, sometimes regret over what had occurred and concern over what was happening with the children.

Changing Patterns

Some brief description of individuals may indicate the changes in some participants.

Marina, a psychologist who had spent much of her professional life as a loyal assistant to others, spoke with some exultation of what had happened to her in the triad and after. She felt that she had, for the first time in her life, been genuinely acceptant of herself as a person, separate and unique. On the final day of the group she told how she had met herself, and she flung open her arms as she greeted herself, "Hullo, Marina!" Her gesture indicated her new ability to fly on her own, clearly leaving the nest she had lived in for so many years.

The experience of Lena was both similar and different. Marina's process of change was attributed to the group and especially to her experience in the triad. Lena identified the source of her change as the way of being of one of the facilitators. The difference seems important because it is an aspect of creating a climate in a group which is easily overlooked. On the last day Lena said, with tears in her eyes, "It was not therapy that took place in the group. It was *being* with *you* these four days. I know now that life has meaning. *My* life has meaning." It was she who had said, the first day, "I feel hopeless. Nobody can help me, not even myself."

She is a professional woman in her early forties, functioning well in her work as a psychologist, apparently relating well to colleagues and her family. But she had been living with an inner despair, feeling that life should have more meaning than daily routine and meeting the expectations and needs of others, but, like others in the intensive group (especially women), could not find a way to realize even a small part of the fulfillment for which she longed—for some joy and purpose in living.

The man who had overflowed with bitterness about his adult daughter, spoke up in the last session. On the previous day his daughter had asked him to buy some things for her, but he had forgotten. "But this morning at breakfast I apologized for having forgotten, and this noon I did the shopping and took the things home to her. She thanked me and smiled at me—the first time in years." He felt this smile was a good omen for their relationship.

Julia had a strict father, a military officer who had devoted his life to "the Cause." He is getting old and is not very well and is writing feverishly to promote "the Cause," but feels he has not been as successful as he had hoped. He thinks that Julia's interest in psychology is utter nonsense and frequently berates her for this foolishness. This always ends in a big fight. This time she was telling him about the workshop and again he ridiculed it as the most stupid nonsense. She felt more independent and stood her ground without quarreling. She also realized that he was a disappointed old man, disappointed in himself for not having done more for "the Cause," and disappointed in her that she had gone off in a different direction. Suddenly she felt compassion for him and instead of leaving with bitter words, as had been her wont, she went around to the other side of the table and kissed him before leaving the house.

The director of an institute said that the day after the workshop he would begin to initiate new administrative policies. One was that he would make *proposals* to his staff, rather than giving *orders*.

A man of high status brought his wife to the final party. During the dinner he announced that he wanted his wife to know that he had been much affected by the discussion about men-women relationships, that he had not treated her as an equal, nor encouraged her career as she deserved, and that he wanted her to know that he was going to try to change this in the future.

In the very last hour of the workshop, one woman spoke of her experience. She said that on day one she had been very skeptical that anything could happen. People knew each other too well. There was mistrust. She knew she would never speak up in the group. On day two, she was so bored she decided she would leave, but somehow she remained. On day three, when there was the demonstration triad, she found to her surprise that she was completely involved in the client's feelings, really listening, though she was not in the triad herself. She was astonished by the intensity of her listening: nothing existed for her at the moment except the client's inner world. However when it came time for everyone to participate in a triad, she was very reluctant. (I had taken her by the arm and helped her find two other members with whom she could sit.) Then when it was her turn to be the client, she found that she poured out her feelings for more than forty minutes about her childhood, how she had been inhibited by her parents from crying, and many other feelings she had. By the end of that time she felt that she was able again, for the first time in years, to cry. "It was the most beautiful experience in my life," she said, speaking of her time in the triad. On day four, she felt that she had somehow become a new person, that she was freshly able to meet the world in her own unique way.

These are samples of the small, immediate, but significant and symbolic changes in behavior and attitude which we saw, even during the final days of the two workshops.

There was one person in each workshop who was a "holdout." In Moscow one man, who held an important position, made it very clear, by his words but especially by his posture, that he was definitely aloof from the process. Until the last session, he tended to sit with his arms folded, superior to, and rejecting of, what was going on. But in the last session he seemed genuinely to join the group, and in the later meeting with the Scientific Council, he made one of the most powerful statements, reporting the solid nature of the group process and its effects.

In Tbilisi one brilliant young man was vocal in his skepticism and his resistance throughout the four days. But in the final sessions he softened, and clearly wished to be a full member of the group. In his gifts to us, and in his personal statements after the workshop, it was evident that it had had a major impact on him.

In both of these instances, the element which brought about the change appeared to be the contacts that Ruth made with each of these men. In the breaks, and outside the sessions, she made it a point to talk with them in ways which showed respect for them as persons, and a willingness to accept their negative feelings about the group. This respect seemed to give them the permission they needed to become fully involved in the process.

Some General Observations

On the whole, it seemed to me that the participants were often rather insensitive to one another, yet there was one marked exception. When any participant spoke from the heart, or with a real visceral feeling, silence reigned and everyone listened intently. When a man spoke of the grief he felt in visiting his brother's grave at the cemetery, about how he asked himself, "Is this really *me* grieving, or am I simply playing the role of a good family member and *acting* as though I were grieving?" you could have heard a pin drop. On the other hand, when someone was advancing intellectual ideas about the group or telling why they were skeptical of the group process, or interpreting someone else's behavior, there was often whispering going on between pairs of individuals or small groups. It was only when something was spoken from the depths that there was this intensity of listening.

As Ruth studied the direct quotations she had jotted down during the sessions, she noted in her journal another feature of our sessions. "There is a certain 'lostness' that seems to run through the most deeply personal statements, particularly in Tbilisi. Was it a combination of strong family attachments, or a cultural trait? There was a general jocularity in Georgian social situations, but underneath a pervading sense that there should be more to life, a deep despair about ever finding it — a brooding quality. The theme was repeated again and again.

> 'I know how I want to be, but I feel helpless to change.'
> 'I want to get more from life, but I don't know how.'
> 'I am disappointed and in pain with my relationship with my daughter [repeated by others to include son, father, mother], but trying to change it seems impossible.'
> 'I feel nobody can help me, not even myself.'
> 'There is no use in talking about this. It can never change.'
> 'Nobody here can do anything to help me.'
> 'Is it fate? I can't choose, like you say, to change and grow.'
> 'I am pulled by fate. Do you think this is so?'

Of the eight quoted directly here, five told the group, during the third or fourth days, that they had gained some acquaintance with their desired selves, or that relationships had changed.

Although the Moscow and Tbilisi groups were quite different, the Tbilisi group starting out much more slowly, it was true in both groups that the contrast between the first and last days was dramatic. By the fourth day, there was a great deal of free expression; there was much more ability to listen to one another. A feeling of unity in the group was both experienced and verbalized.

The Parties

At the conclusion of both the Moscow and Tbilisi groups, at the end of the fourth day, with considerable secrecy and whispering, some astonishing events took place. Ruth and I were told to rest a while and there would be a little party or, in Tbilisi, we would have a little "Georgian therapy," which we understood to be wine. At the end of the waiting we were, in each case, ushered into a room utterly transformed. Tables had been set up; food was heaped on the tables; there were forty-five places set; there were toasts offered, gifts (often very personal in nature) presented, speeches made, embraces shared. It was an outpouring of goodwill and affection, not only toward us but toward each other. There were affectionate farewells all around. In both cities, some of the toasts had to do with the hope for peace, the hope for better understanding between our countries, the hope for continuing exchange.

As I thought about the experience of each of the intensive groups, it seemed to me that the issues raised were very similar to those that are raised in similar groups in the United States, in Brazil, in Mexico, in Japan, in Poland, in Hungary, in Italy, in the United Kingdom. It is astonishing how much there is in common. Certainly one of the elements found in every culture we have dealt with — and here I would especially include South Africa with the others — is the hunger for deeper and more personal communication and the desire to be accepted as a real person, problems and all, a unique individual with worth and significance.

There were certain topics which tended to be omitted by the two Soviet groups. One was that although tension between men and women was quite evident in behavior, in jokes, in various ways, it was never openly discussed except in Tbilisi where Ruth raised the issue in regard to herself.

Another issue that was never touched upon was politics in the narrow sense. There was never any open discussion of systems of government or anything of that sort. Only once in all our stay did a person say, when an American presented a personal problem, "Nothing like that could happen in the Soviet Union." However, she was immediately interrupted by another Russian woman who said, "That's not true. My situation is exactly like that."

As I have mentioned, though politics in a narrow sense was

not discussed, there was frequently expressed the keen desire for more dialogue, more understanding between our nations, a hope for peace, a hope that war could be avoided at all costs.

Two Days Later—Meeting with the Scientific Council

One of the immediate outcomes of the Moscow group was so surprisingly extravagant that it demands to be reported in some detail.

Dr. Matyushkin told us that he wanted to add to our schedule a meeting with the Scientific Council. This is a prestigious group—members of the Academy of Science and of other institutes—which serves as kind of a board of directors to his institute. They have great influence on the level of support for his work, so he was much involved. He wished us to report to them on "what you have achieved." I told him that any report we might give would be inevitably biased—that if he wished real evidence he should ask members of the intensive workshop for their evaluations, negative as well as positive, of their experience.

Dr. Matyushkin liked this suggestion. When he was invited to the final moments of the workshop, to be thanked for his efforts in bringing it about, he broached the idea. He said that if they could leave their work, they were all invited to attend this meeting, two days later, with the Scientific Council. (The meetings of the council are always open meetings.) They might speak of their experience if they wished.

When the time arrived, we could see that many members were present. It was an awesome audience. In the front row sat the members of this presidium of well-known scientists. In addition, the auditorium was filled to capacity—three hundred and fifty persons who wanted to hear about the workshop. Dr. Matyushkin opened the meeting by saying that he, Ruth, and I had all agreed that the best way of conducting this session was to ask participants concerning their experience. He asked that those willing to speak limit their statements to no more than five or ten minutes. If they wished to speak they should write out a slip of paper with their name and title. In no time, a small blizzard of white slips was being passed to the podium. *Thirty* members of the workshop wanted to speak! Dr. Matyushkin said that women had the same rights as men, that this corresponded to the manner of work in the intensive group, so he would call first on a man and then a woman. In all, nine members of the workshop spoke for a total time of an hour and a half, leaving twenty-one very frustrated members who wished they might have spoken. One by one the nine members came to the podium and spoke forcefully and eloquently, with no apologies and no hesitation. It was clear that they had empowered themselves and simply wanted to tell this august audience what the workshop had meant to them. Their statements were most impressive, covering both the personal and professional aspects of their experience.

A recorder was placed in front of Dima, our translator, so that most of the statements were captured. The material is so rich, it begs to be quoted in full, but of course that is impossible. Some statements can be quoted from the first few speakers. The first was a psychiatrist. He said that he came to the workshop as a psychotherapist. He had many fears about it. [He had been a very skeptical member of the group in the early sessions.] He had read about my work, but learned "much more than in reading books. This group allowed us to gain so much — a lot more than we had expected. This experience will stay with us forever." He went on, "Humanistic psychology: Was it a science? Was it a scientific approach, or not? Rogers's coming is of great importance for humanistic psychology and research." He added, in a very personal way, "I can't find the right words because a very large part of my self is still present in the atmosphere of that room, where we joined in our work."

The second speaker was a woman. "I have such strong reactions. I have been longing to share something. Yesterday I began my work with clients and I found I was starting to apply this approach. It was very important to me as a professional. I have learned that clients or friends don't want your advice, your interpretation. Before the workshop I was kind of a detective, trying to investigate, to find the underlying reason for this or that act. But then in the workshop *I* was the client and I learned it was very bad to be listened to by a detective. I hadn't really listened. I realized it meant a lot just to be listened to. I don't want to find some theoretical model. I just want to listen, to give my attention. I know this sounds commonplace, but I want you to realize what I've been feeling. I shouldn't treat others as objects on which we are going to try to impose our help. Formerly, I based my work on the idea that a person coming to me for help was guilty of something. When they feel guilty and we reinforce that guilt, it does not help.

"Working with a person yesterday, I tried to understand her pain, feeling her feelings. This was very helpful. She told me of beating her child. Formerly I would have been indignant, but this time I listened and understood. When she left she told me that it was the first time in her life that she felt understood. I have learned that it is important to stand in the other person's shoes. Before this I knew the theories. Now we have learned from the inside."

When Dr. Matyushkin called on the next person, a man, he said, "I'll call people by their first names, since that is common in humanistic psychology." Sasha, the next speaker, said, "This is just two days after the experience and I am still a participant. I am a psychologist, not a psychotherapist. I have known Rogers's theory but this was a process in which *we* were personally involved. I didn't realize how it applied. I want to give several impressions. First was the effectiveness of this approach. It was a kind of process in which we all learned. Second, this process was moving, without a motor. Nobody had to lead it or guide it. It was a self-evolving process. It was like the Chekov story where they were expectantly awaiting the piano player and the piano started playing itself. Third, I was impressed by the manner of Carl and Ruth. At first I felt they were passive. Then I realized it was the silence of understanding. Fourth, I want to mention the penetration of this process into my inner world. At first I was an observer, but then the approach disappeared altogether. I was not simply surrounded by this process, I was absorbed into it! It was a revelation to me. We started moving. I wasn't simply seeing people I had known for years, but their feelings. My fifth realization was my inability to control the flow of feelings, the flow of the process. My feelings tried to put on the clothes of my words. Sometimes people exploded; some even cried. It was a reconstruction of the system of perception. Finally, I want to remark on the high skill of Carl and Ruth, of their silences, their voices, their glances. It was always some response, and they were responded to. It was a great phenomenon, a great experience."

A professor said, "I want to speak as a scientist." He told of being impressed with the theory and principles underlying the person-centered approach. "These laws of human communication, discovered in America, were surprisingly functional in our situation." A bit later he made another point. "We are tempted to think that this is something that pertains only to Rogers, but this is not true. We, too, can concentrate for forty-five minutes, and can be effective in creating a therapeutic climate, recognizing negative feelings as well as positive." He emphasized that he was speaking of "our *clients — not* our *patients!*" He also said that he "would like to mention the great contribution of these two people to the increase of mutual understanding between our two countries. It is good to know that across the ocean there are human beings who have a warm feeling for us."

A woman spoke next. "It was useful to me personally. Now, how to bring it about? To let people be themselves? We have experienced a clear way. I have experienced great changes in myself. I have seen with my own eyes that it is possible, that people *can* be *real*. There is some psychological essence, an inner self, that constitutes the individual's personality." She added later, "People I had known for years were in the group, but only now, after the four days, do I feel I know them. We began with conflict — conflict that came from before we were in the group. Before this we had ignored each other, and our conflicts had *not* gone away."

A school psychologist "thought at first that Rogers was doing nothing, and people felt, 'Do something!' But I realize that this mode, not analyzing, not administering, is better." He added, "The workshop helped me to solve some serious problems I face as a practical psychologist, for example, the very common conflict between children and teachers. I love children, but I did not like teachers. Now I want to know teachers and work with them." He saw conflicts resolved in the group, and this "was real, not a game."

Another speaker: "After these four days Ruth, Fran, and Carl are with me and my family. This experience has changed my way of treating people. This is bringing theory into everyday life. It is not a technique; it is a way of being. It is not magical because it can be understood and repeated, by creating certain conditions which we called the climate. This approach had never been applied in our society before. It is new to us. Traditional experience was in our way of empathic listening. But then we began to lay aside evaluation and silences gave us an opportunity to concentrate on others' feelings. In silence we learned also from ourselves. As a therapist, I learned that a therapist is an expert only in learning to follow the client."

A woman was the final speaker. "It is difficult for me to speak, to share this great emotional experience. We had therapy. We worked not as professionals but as human beings. When you treat a person as a human being, not trying to interpret, he or she opens up. At first, you try to convince each other, evaluate each other. We shouted at each other! Then all of a sudden, people started looking at their problems. This experience will stay with us forever, to the end of our days. It is not just a method. It is a way of being."

Long-Range Outcomes

Obviously, at this date, we have no way of evaluating the long-range outcomes. However there are several channels by which we hope to get reports. Irina, Dr. Matyushkin's assistant, has promised to give us reports of any feedback she obtains from the Moscow intensive group. I am also particularly eager to get a further report of the demonstration client at the university, who seemed rather dissatisfied at the time. I suspect that she will have some changes in behavior as time goes by.

Francis Macy will be in both Moscow and Tbilisi a couple of weeks after the close of the workshops and hopefully will be able to supply further data. Clearly, the real impact of the intensive workshops will not be known for months, but we will endeavor to collect information, anecdotal though it may be.

Below the Surface

Small bits of conversation indicated that we were living in a highly controlled society. A person of some status said, "I would like very much to entertain you in my home, but I can't and unfortunately I can't give you any explanation." Another individual, in a private conversation: "I hate the system, but please be sure you don't repeat that to anyone here." Another: "Values keep changing all the time, with each new leadership. Parents don't know what to tell their children because the situation and the values change. We need something more stable to cling to. That may be the reason for the current interest in religion." Another: "Everyone knows that something is seriously wrong. Even the government officials know something is wrong. We don't know what will resolve this crisis." It should be emphasized that these remarks come from a very small number of the people we contacted. Since they fit the American stereotype of the Russian situation, it is probably easy to overestimate their importance.

On the other hand, we felt that participants felt very free to talk about their family life and problems, their personal and professional issues. We never detected any concern on the part of anyone that there might be informers in the group. It seemed that there is a great deal of freedom of expression, but this freedom of expression is within certain limits.

Comparison with Other Guests

We were told of the visits of various eminent psychologists to the Soviet Union in recent years. Their practice was to give one or two lectures and then leave. Gradually we realized the many striking differences between our visit and those of other psychologists.

In the first place we were, in every situation, testing a scientific psychological hypothesis, but testing it not in the laboratory but in life. Briefly, the hypothesis was that *if* certain conditions existed (all definable, even measurable), *then* a definable process would emerge, with characteristics which could be described. Furthermore, people could observe with their eyes and ears, and feel in their experience, the confirmation or disconfirmation of this hypothesis. It was a truly scientific experience in Soviet terms, and this was often mentioned in their reactions to the workshops.

Another fundamental difference was that the learning which took place as a result of our visit was experiential as well as cognitive. People experienced it in their hearts, in their viscera, as well as in their brain cells. Universities and institutes in this country as well as ours have been primarily devoted to intellectual learning. This was indeed a sharp difference.

As will have been evident from the account, we worked with

people, not simply talked to them. We spent time with them. Briefly stated, it may be said that we spent from two to six hours with large groups of from three hundred fifty to nine hundred. We spent twenty-four to thirty hours of intensive work with groups of forty-five and forty respectively. This time commitment was also something that marked our visit as different from previous visits.

We were willing to demonstrate our work. In one sense everything we did was an outgrowth of our basic hypothesis, and of our trust in the individual and the group. Especially was this true in the four-day intensives. There were also three interviews conducted in front of large audiences and two groups had opportunities to view another interview on a videocassette. The fact that we demonstrated our work was decidedly new to Soviet psychologists and was commented on in their reactions.

We were able to create a climate in which observable changes in attitudes and behavior took place within a four-day period. This seemed to be a total surprise to our Soviet colleagues. The concept that we could make a difference of more than a temporary sort during such a period of time seemed to be something they had never anticipated.

The fact that a man and a woman could work comfortably together, without competing, as separate and different individuals, was often commented on, and in this male-dominated society seemed to have a decided impact.

Concluding Remarks

We felt that we learned a great deal about the concerns of professional Soviet citizens. It was strikingly clear that their concerns differ very little from the concerns felt by a similar professional group in the United States. It was abundantly evident that the professional person in the Soviet Union has a warm feeling toward the United States, is interested in what we may contribute to them, is hungry for communication with Americans, eagerly devours any literature we can bring, professional or otherwise, and desires nothing so much as peace between our two nations. It is also evident that they wish to be recognized for their contributions to their fields.

It was important to us to learn that the psychological climate which produces certain predictable results in the U.S., Latin America, European countries, and South Africa, produces the same predictable results in the Soviet Union.

We learned a great deal about the enormously variable set of cultures which exist within the Union of Soviet Socialist Republics. We acquired a deep respect for the history of Russia, dating back to very early times. We recognized that in the Soviet citizen there is a much deeper fear of war than exists in the United States, a fear which is based on fairly recent memory. In the siege of Leningrad, for example, 900,000 citizens, military and civilian, died in the 900 days of the siege. Our guide to Leningrad, a most talented young woman, said that her mother was the sole survivor of any branch of her family. All the others had died or been killed in the siege. We have, in our history, nothing whatsoever to compare with this.

In the Future

We came away hoping that if there is a next trip to the Soviet Union, that it could include a wide diversity of high-level American citizens, with all shades of political opinion, to meet in an intensive group with an equally wide diversity of high-level Soviet citizens. It would be a privilege to help facilitate such an encounter. We could now select some Soviet facilitators to work with us if such a program were realized. It is a development devoutly to be wished for.

REFERENCES AND
BIBLIOGRAPHY
ACKNOWLEDGMENTS
INDEX

REFERENCES AND BIBLIOGRAPHY

The full bibliographic citation for each reading in this book is located on the first page of each reading.

References *within* each of the readings are included immediately after each reading, just as they originally appeared.

Finally, references to the Introduction and to the seven section introductions of this book are provided below. Also included here is bibliographic information on Carl Rogers's sixteen books and several other volumes on Rogers's life and work.

Coulson, W. R. and Rogers, C. R. (Eds.). *Man and the Science of Man.* Columbus, OH: Charles Merrill, 1968.

Evans, R. *Carl Rogers: The Man and His Ideas.* New York: E.P. Dutton, 1978.

Farson, R. *Journey Into Self.* 16mm film. La Jolla, CA: Western Behavioral Sciences Institute, 1968.

Heesacker, M., Heppner, P., and Rogers, M. E. Classics and Emerging Classics in Counseling Psychology. *Counseling Psychology*, Volume 29, No. 4, July 1982.

Kirschenbaum, H. *On Becoming Carl Rogers.* New York: Delacorte Press, 1979.

Kirschenbaum, H. and Henderson, V. (Eds.). *Carl Rogers: Dialogues.* Boston: Houghton Mifflin, 1989.

Rogers, C. R. *Measuring Personality Adjustment in Children Nine to Thirteen Years of Age.* New York: Teachers College, 1931.

Rogers, C. R. *The Clinical Treatment of the Problem Child.* Boston: Houghton Mifflin, 1939.

Rogers, C. R. *Counseling and Psychotherapy: New Concepts in Practice.* Boston: Houghton Mifflin, 1942.

Rogers, C. R. *Counseling with Returned Servicemen.* Washington, DC: United Services Organization, 1945.

Rogers, C. R. *Client-Centered Therapy: Its Current Practice, Implications and Theory.* Boston: Houghton Mifflin, 1951.

Rogers, C. R. *On Becoming a Person.* Boston: Houghton Mifflin, 1961.

Rogers, C. R. Client-centered therapy, Film No. 1. In E. Shostrom (Ed.), *Three Approaches to Psychotherapy.* Three 16mm color motion pictures. Orange, CA: Psychological Films, Inc., 1965.

Rogers, C. R. *Freedom to Learn: A View of What Education Might Become.* Columbus, OH: Charles Merrill, 1969.

Rogers, C. R. *Carl Rogers on Encounter Groups.* New York: Harper and Row, 1970.

Rogers, C. R. *Becoming Partners: Marriage and Its Alternatives.* New York: Delacorte Press, 1972.

Rogers, C. R. *Carl Rogers on Personal Power: Inner Strength and Its Revolutionary Impact.* New York: Delacorte Press, 1977.

Rogers, C. R. *A Way of Being.* Boston: Houghton Mifflin, 1980.

Rogers, C. R. *Freedom to Learn in the 80s.* Columbus, OH: Charles Merrill, 1983.

Rogers, C. R. and Dymond, R. (Eds.). *Psychotherapy and Personality Change.* Chicago: University Press, 1954.

Rogers, C. R., Gendlin, E. T., Kiesler, D. J., and Truax, C. B. (Eds.). *The Therapeutic Relationship and Its Impact: A Study of Psychotherapy with Schizophrenics.* Madison: University of Wisconsin Press, 1967.

Rogers, C. R. and Skinner, B. F. Some issues concerning the control of human behavior. *Science,* Volume 124, No. 3231, November 1956, 1057–1066.

Rogers, C. R. and Stevens, B. *Person To Person: The Problem of Being Human.* Lafayette, CA: Real People Press, 1968.

Smith, D. Trends in Counseling and Psychology. *American Psychologist,* Volume 37, No. 7, July 1982.

ACKNOWLEDGMENTS

The editors are grateful for permission to reprint the following articles by Carl Rogers:

"This is Me" from *On Becoming a Person*. Copyright © 1961 by Houghton Mifflin Company. Used with permission.

"My Own Marriage" from *Becoming Partners: Marriage and Its Alternatives*. Copyright © 1972 by Carl R. Rogers.

"Growing Old: Or Older and Growing" from *A Way of Being*. Copyright © 1980 by Houghton Mifflin Company. Used with permission.

"On Reaching 85" from *Person-Centered Review*, vol. 2, no. 2, May 1987. Copyright © 1987 by Sage Publications, Inc. Reprinted by permission of Sage Publications, Inc.

"A Newer Psychotherapy" from *Counseling and Psychotherapy*. Copyright 1942 by Carl R. Rogers.

"Characteristics of Directive and Nondirective Viewpoints" from *Counseling and Psychotherapy*. Copyright 1942 by Carl R. Rogers.

"The Case of Herbert Bryan" from *Counseling and Psychotherapy*. Copyright 1942 by Carl Rogers.

"The Characteristics of a Helping Relationship" from *Personnel and Guidance Journal*, vol. 37. Copyright © 1958 by the American Association for Counseling and Development.

"Reflection of Feelings" from *Person-Centered Review*, vol. 1, no. 4, November 1986. Copyright © 1986 by Sage Publications, Inc. Reprinted by permission of Sage Publications, Inc.

"Comment on Shlien's Article 'A Counter-theory of Transference'" from *Person-Centered Review*, vol. 2, no. 2, May 1987. Copyright © 1987 by Sage Publications, Inc. Reprinted by permission of Sage Publications, Inc.

"A Client-centered/Person-centered Approach to Therapy" from *Psy-

chotherapist's Casebook: Theory and Technique in Practice. Copyright © 1986 by Jossey-Bass Inc. I. L. Kutash and A. Wolf, editors. Used by permission.

"Ellen West—And Loneliness" from *Review of Existential Psychology and Psychotherapy*, 1961.

"Toward a Modern Approach to Values: The Valuing Process in the Mature Person" from *Journal of Abnormal and Social Psychology*, vol. 68, no. 3. Copyright © 1964 by the American Psychological Association. Reprinted by permission of the publisher and author.

"Shall We Get Married?" from *Becoming Partners: Marriage and Its Alternatives.* Copyright © 1972 by Carl R. Rogers.

"What I Learned from Two Research Studies" Copyright © 1986 by Carl R. Rogers. Previously unpublished.

"The Use of Electrically Recorded Interviews in Improving Psycho-therapeutic Techniques" from *American Journal of Orthopsychiatry* vol. 12. Copyright 1942 by the American Orthopsychiatric Association, Inc. Reprinted with permission from the *American Journal of Orthopsychiatry.*

"The Necessary and Sufficient Conditions of Therapeutic Personality Change" from *Journal of Consulting Psychology*, vol. 21. 1957.

"A Theory of Therapy, Personality, and Interpersonal Relationships, As Developed in the Client-Centered Framework" from *Psychology: A Study of Science*, Vol. III. Copyright © 1959 by McGraw-Hill. S. Koch, editor.

"Some Thoughts Regarding the Current Presuppositions of the Behavioral Sciences" from *Man and the Science of Man.* Copyright © 1968 W. R. Coulson and Carl R. Rogers.

"Toward a More Human Science of the Person" from *Journal of Humanistic Psychology*, vol. 25, no. 4. Copyright © 1985 by Sage Publications, Inc. Reprinted by permission of Sage Publications, Inc.

"Personal Thoughts on Teaching and Learning" from *Merrill-Palmer Quarterly*, vol. 3, Summer 1957. Reprinted by permission of the Wayne State University Press.

"The Interpersonal Relationship in the Facilitation of Learning" from *Humanizing Education.* Copyright © 1967 by the Association for Supervision and Curriculum Development.

"The Politics of Education" from *Journal of Humanistic Education*, vol. 1, no. 1, 1977. Reprinted by permission of the Association for Humanistic Education.

"Can I Be a Facilitative Person in a Group?" from *Carl Rogers on Encounter Groups.* Copyright © 1970 by Harper & Row.

"Some New Challenges to the Helping Professions" from *American Psychologist*, vol. 28, no. 5. Copyright © 1973 by the American Psychological Association. Reprinted by permission of the publisher.

Index